Housing Finance
and Public Policy

Housing Finance and Public Policy

Cases and Supplementary Readings

Michael A. Stegman

VAN NOSTRAND REINHOLD COMPANY
New York

332.6324
581h

Teachers interested in obtaining an instructor's manual free of charge
may do so by writing: Academic Sales—Architecture,
Van Nostrand Reinhold Company, 115 Fifth Avenue, New York, New York 10003.

Copyright © 1986 by Van Nostrand Reinhold Company Inc.
Library of Congress Catalog Card Number 85-13408
ISBN 0-442-28035-1

Printed in the United States of America
Designed by Rose Delia Vasquez

Van Nostrand Reinhold Company Inc.
115 Fifth Avenue
New York, New York 10003

Van Nostrand Reinhold Company Limited
Molly Millars Lane
Wokingham, Berkshire RG11 2PY, England

Van Nostrand Reinhold
480 La Trobe Street
Melbourne, Victoria 3000, Australia

Macmillan of Canada
Division of Canada Publishing Corporation
164 Commander Boulevard
Agincourt, Ontario M1S 3C7, Canada

16 15 14 13 12 11 10 9 8 7 6 5 4 3 2 1

Library of Congress Cataloging in Publication Data

Stegman, Michael A.
    Housing finance and public policy.

Includes index.
    1. Housing—United States—Finance—Case studies.
    2. Housing policy—United States—Case studies.
    I. Title.
    HD7293.Z9S74   1986   332.63'24'0973   85-13408
    ISBN 0-442-28035-1

Contents

PART TWO: READINGS IN FINANCE AND INVESTMENT ANALYSIS

Preface

I have written the cases and selected the supplementary readings contained in this book with four objectives in mind. First, the book is intended to help city planning, public policy, business administration, and other students interested in real estate, architecture, and development to acquire the technical skills needed to analyze private housing investment decisions, public financing programs, and government housing policies. My aim is to sensitize business and real estate students to public aspects of private investment and development decisions and to improve planners' analytical skills to enable them to evaluate the financial implications of their housing and development-related responsibilities. It has been said that a good case is the vehicle by which a chunk of reality is brought into the classroom. In that spirit, this book provides students with nine distinct realities to consider, each requiring the application of techniques of real estate investment analysis as an aid to private or public decision making.

By placing students in the simulated decision-making role of a private investor, a public regulator of rents, a project syndicator, or a designer of housing programs, the cases help achieve the second objective of this book: to demonstrate the strengths and limitations of the tools of investment analysis. Optimal housing decisions are not always a matter of maximizing profits, nor are social objectives always furthered when measures of investment returns are ignored by the public sector.

The third objective of the book is to illustrate how the use of the formal tools of real estate investment analysis can be expanded into the sphere of low-income housing problems that are traditionally viewed as nonmarket in character, such as the design of housing assistance programs and self-help efforts to recover abandoned housing.

The fourth and final objective of the casebook is to use techniques of real estate investment analysis, which are typically applied to project-specific data and individual investor circumstances, to evaluate national housing programs and policies that have societal implications.

The book is organized into two parts. Part one consists of nine original cases that are divided into five chapters.

Chapter 1 concerns individual investor strategies. In the case presented, a university professor and his wife, fed up with an ever-increasing federal-income-tax burden that resulted from inflation-induced "bracket creep," consider investing in real estate to reduce their tax liability. They have three investment alternatives: buying one or more limited partnership interests in

a large syndicate that invests in low-rise apartment complexes in the Sunbelt; construction and fee-simple ownership of a fourplex that would be
rented to qualifying lower-income families; or construction and fee-simple
ownership of a luxury rental fourplex. The case emphasizes the importance
of tax considerations in real estate investment, the effects of future market
conditions on investment returns, and the use of sensitivity analysis in making real estate decisions.

Chapter 2 discusses two cases in public/private financing partnerships. In
the first, the director of rehabilitation services in a small Midwestern city
must design a new rehabilitation program for multifamily housing. The city's
only prior experience with rehabilitation has been in the ownership sector,
where income-eligible families have been given grants. The new program
must deal with income-producing properties and with absentee landlords
who view their properties as investments. Public subsidies must be sufficient
to encourage rental property owners to make publicly desired improvements
without providing them with windfall gains. The case emphasizes important
differences between owner-occupied and rental housing-rehabilitation programs and between before- and after-tax returns. It also deals with various
subsidy mechanisms, including deferred-payment loans, and introduces students to the historic-preservation tax credit.

In the second case, public/private housing ventures are focusing with
increasing frequency on ways to adapt vacant, obsolete public structures to
economically viable, productive uses. The R. M. Wilson case examines the
process through which a vacant school in Rocky Mount, North Carolina,
was converted into a fifty-unit apartment building for lower-income elderly
tenants. The narrative reviews the original plans of the Rocky Mount Housing Authority to finance and develop the project plans, which were thwarted
by soaring interest rates in the tax-exempt market. David Weil, a private
investor experienced in subsidized housing development, and the private
planning and real estate consulting firm of Anderson Benton Holmes are
called in to redevelop the school property as a privately owned project
under a long-term lease from the housing authority. The case reviews the
formation of R. M. Wilson Associates, the limited partnership formed to
own the property, and takes the student through the financing and syndication process, including pricing partnership interests.

Chapter 3 concerns two aspects of regulating private market activities.
The first discusses the legalization of loft living in New York City. Illegal
loft conversion involves the renting of unimproved space in underused industrial or commercial buildings to tenants for residential purposes. These
"commercial" transactions have been conducted largely outside the framework of existing city housing codes and the laws governing residential rents
and evictions.

After much political wrangling, the city developed standards for loft conversions and created a loft enforcement unit in the Office of the Mayor to
deter new illegal conversions and monitor the legalization of existing ones.
A very significant difference between the city's new loft laws and the city's

other rent laws is that the loft law provides for the direct pass-through to residential tenants of both the owner's capital and of financing costs of bringing the lofts up to minimum housing standards (thereby legalizing them). As the loft board's director of operations, Bill Bernstein's job is to draft a set of regulations that will implement the pass-through provisions of the law. Bernstein knows that the regulations are likely to attract the attention of housing officials across the country who have resisted pressures by landlords to consider financing charges and mortgage costs in determining the periodic rent increases they will permit owners to levy under their respective rent-control programs.

As an exercise in regulation writing, the case presents the student with the deceptively simple-sounding assignment to implement legislative intent. The problem is that a one-time rent increase to include landlord interest costs requires that these costs be known and certain, which is no longer possible in the world of variable-rate financing. Also, at today's high interest rates, regulations that pass through to tenants the full costs of their landlords' improvement loans could raise their rents to unaffordable levels. If that happens, a law designed to protect tenants' rights will lead to their displacement.

The second involves rent regulation. As a member of the New York City Rent Guidelines Board, Karen Eisenstadt must decide how much to permit owners of New York City's one million rent-stabilized apartments to charge on new leases. Separate rent orders must be approved for one-, two-, and three-year leases, and the guidelines board also must determine two other issues: whether landlords should be permitted to levy a separate vacancy rent increase upon a turnover in occupancy; and how much that increase may be. Eisenstadt has a summary of previous rent orders at her disposal, as well as data on recent changes in rents and operating costs for stabilized apartments, on changes in the ratio of operating costs to total rents, and on related housing market issues. The case immerses the student in the real-world complexities of rent regulation, the use of incomplete market and operating data in policy decisions, and the difficulties of determining the effects of rent regulations on private investment decisions.

Chapter 4 examines two cases in nonmarket investment decision making. The first describes the efforts of a group of low-income tenants to rehabilitate and eventually convert an abandoned tenement building to a tenant-owned cooperative using sweat equity (self-help labor) and a low-interest city loan. The case involves the analysis of alternative financing arrangements on monthly carrying costs, including a graduated-payment loan that would shift the burden of the mortgage payment into the future. The question of the feasibility of self-help rehabilitation efforts under various conditions is raised. Another issue considered here is whether the outright donation of landlord-abandoned buildings with moderate rehabilitation grants might be more cost-effective than very complex programs that rely on a combination of sweat equity and long-term, subsidized government loans.

The second examines the special problem of *in rem* housing. An apartment building at 504 Norfolk Street is one of New York City's more than four thousand *in rem* dwellings—partially occupied multifamily buildings that have been abandoned by their owners and foreclosed on by the city for back taxes. The Lower East Side neighborhood in which it is located is quite deteriorated, but the area around 504 Norfolk is beginning to show some private reinvestment activity. The possibilities for the property are the same in many ways as those for large portions of the city's entire *in rem* housing stock. As a senior staff member of the city's Department of Housing Preservation and Development, Greg Farris must develop a property-disposition strategy for the building. His analysis involves three options: to keep 504 Norfolk in city ownership until the private market has recovered and then auction the building to the highest bidder; to sell 504 Norfolk at today's market price to a private investor who wants to develop the property into cooperative apartments for upwardly mobile households; or to train the building's tenants in self-management, then sell the building to them at a subsidized price of $250 per dwelling unit. Resolution of the case requires Farris to sort out conflicting city housing goals, such as increasing home-ownership opportunities for lower-income families, returning city-owned buildings to the private market and city tax rolls, and encouraging neighborhood revitalization and private reinvestment without displacement.

Chapter 5 describes two national housing policy issues. The first compares the tax positions of rentals, condominiums, and cooperatives. The federal tax system subsidizes equity investors in rental housing and share-owners in housing cooperatives and owners of condominiums in different ways. The case involves an analysis of the indirect federal-tax subsidies to these forms of housing tenure as a basis for learning more about federal tax expenditures for housing and how they influence private investment decisions.

The second involves multifamily housing production during a recession. Which of the countercyclical multifamily production stimulus programs proposed by the General Accounting Office will have the desired effect of increasing rental housing construction at the least possible government cost? The case involves an assessment of program options that range from a tax credit to equity investors to deferred-payment second-mortgage loans. Students must have a thorough knowledge of the field of multifamily housing investment, good grounding in government programs, and an ability to use investment analysis as a basis for making sound judgments about the broader potential economic impacts of alternative programs.

All cases can be resolved by the student without reference to outside readings. Each case consists of a narrative statement of the problem to be resolved, the identity and objectives of the decision maker, and the constraints under which he or she is operating. The data needed to resolve the cases are contained in the narratives and in exhibits that are integral parts of the cases. Supplements (when present) contain additional qualitative or

contextual materials pertaining to the case; the supplements should, however, be considered integral parts of the cases.

Part two of the book contains previously published articles on real estate
finance and investment analysis that are intended to provide students with
the technical backgrounds needed to resolve the cases.

The readings are divided into three chapters, the first of which consists
of two entries on fundamentals of real estate finance. The initial article
by Wendt and Cerf on the development of the compound-interest tables
introduces students to the concept of the time value of money and to the
mathematics of discounting, rate-of-return analysis, and the development of
loan-amortization schedules. I believe this work to be among the best introductions to the foundations of real estate investment analysis in print. The
second piece is a compound-interest problem set, which should be used in
conjunction with the Wendt and Cerf article. I designed the problems to
take students on a "guided tour" of the compound-interest tables. Individual problems deal with compounding and discounting money flows and net
sales proceeds in future years, developing loan-amortization schedules, and
determining unpaid loan balances over the mortgage period. Other problems
deal with quantitative assessments of the value of various provisions of the
federal tax code that are designed to attract equity capital into the real estate
sector, including those dealing with accelerated depreciation and the conversion of ordinary income to capital gains. Students should complete the
problem set before tackling the cases, since the more complex cases require
some facility with the methods used to solve the problems. For those with
little background in real estate investment it would be useful to read Nolan
and Smith's article in chapter 8 before tackling the problem set. Although
their paper deals primarily with syndication, they do an excellent job of
introducing the reader to the language of finance and tax considerations in
real estate investment, which one must understand in order to complete the
problem set.

The second chapter in part two contains three readings on more sophisticated aspects of real estate investment analysis. Roddewig and Shlaes begin
with an introduction to market feasibility and the components of a feasibility
analysis; this is followed by Page's report on the criteria used by major
classes of investors to evaluate real estate investment alternatives. The
article describes a wide variety of before- and after-tax measures of profitability used by the real estate industry, including income capitalization, net
and gross income multipliers, the equity dividend rate, and various discounted cash flow methods of analysis, such as the internal rate of return.

The chapter concludes with an article by Martin on important shortcomings of the internal rate of return (IRR) as a measure of project worth. He
focuses on two elements in the IRR equation, the reinvestment rate (which
is the rate of interest that cash flows generated by a particular investment
are assumed to earn from being invested in other profitable endeavors) and
the contribution of net sales proceeds to the overall internal rate of return.

He illustrates how sensitive the IRR is to assumptions about resale price and how a project can simultaneously produce a very attractive IRR and an unappealingly low rate of after-tax cash earnings.

The final chapter contains six essays on real estate syndication. It begins with an article by Williford on the tax treatment of partnerships, the ownership form used in real estate syndications. Three introductions to syndication follow. Nolan and Smith's primer on syndicating housing-rehabilitation projects for lower- and moderate-income families covers such basic topics as the formation of limited partnerships, how to estimate the equity-raising potential of a housing project, and the pricing of syndication shares. Next, Howell analyzes the syndication potential of low-rent public housing projects to determine whether the selective sale of this scarce community housing resource represents a potential solution to the financial difficulties facing local public housing authorities across the country. Next, Stanger takes us step by step through the syndication process for a market rate property, illustrating how the new owner must restructure a transaction for resale to limited partners and where the sources of profit lie in an unsubsidized syndication.

The chapter and book conclude with an article by Smith on resyndication, which is a change in the ownership of a previously syndicated property and the packaging and sale of new limited partnership interests. Certain provisions of the 1984 Tax Reform Act having to do with the tax treatment of deferred interest on mortgages taken back by the seller may discourage transactions such as those discussed here; but Smith's article on how resyndication has been used to regenerate financially distressed federally subsidized rental projects is an informative treatise on how changes in tax laws create and dissolve market value.

Acknowledgments

As with any major undertaking, the efforts of many people were necessary to make this book possible. Several generations of graduate students of city and regional planning served, knowingly and unknowingly, as guinea pigs for the problem sets and cases contained herein. The ways they interpreted the narratives, picked up on cues intended to direct their thinking, and used or failed to find exhibits and data helpful to them, and the feedback they gave me, have considerably strengthened the final case presentations.

The individual contributions of two former students and one current deserve special mention. As my research assistant, Susan Hyman devoted many hours to "running the numbers" for early drafts of several cases. She made sure that the cases could, in fact, be resolved and that the narratives were clear in their policy intent. Ann Hafrey, who entered the planning program at the University of North Carolina having had prior professional experience as an editor, applied her considerable editorial skills to early drafts of the cases. Although she graduated before the project was completed, I wish to acknowledge her early assistance. I would also like to acknowledge the efforts of Chris Kentopp, a first-year graduate student and my current research assistant, who helped me refine the two cases dealing with city-owned housing in New York City.

Several colleagues helped me by providing case materials. Bill Bernstein, executive director of the New York City Loft Board, supported my efforts to write a case based on a consulting assignment I completed for him on financing loft improvements. His comments on an early draft of the loft case have improved the final version. Karen Eisenstadt, a distinguished graduate of the University of North Carolina planning program and member of the New York City Rent Guidelines Board, helped me to write the rent regulation case. She sat through a lunchtime interview, gave me data, and reviewed a draft of the case. Her editorial comments, which have been incorporated into the final version of the case, are greatly appreciated and her continued friendship highly valued. David Weil and Bill Benton, who with their associates turned an abandoned school into senior citizen housing, have made possible the R. M. Wilson case. They gave me a prospectus and other financial information on the project and reviewed an early draft of the case. Their generous assistance is gratefully acknowledged.

Dennis Eisen kindly granted me permission to create a case out of a consulting assignment he completed for the National Association of Housing Cooperatives, which had asked him to determine whether housing cooperatives or rental housing were favored more by the federal tax laws. Dennis reviewed a draft of the tax expenditure case, making several helpful suggestions.

My good friend Chuck Laven, from whom I have learned much about sweat equity and other community-based efforts to improve poor peoples' housing, wrote early drafts of two cases contained in this book. The Columbus Avenue case is based on an early experience Chuck had as executive director of the Urban Homesteading Assistance Board in New York City. The multifamily rehabilitation case is a generalized version of a problem situation he encountered as a rehabilitation consultant to communities who wanted to shift their rehabilitation emphasis from owner-occupied to rental housing. I acknowledge his creative efforts and thank him for letting me build upon those early drafts.

I also wish to acknowledge the less tangible contribution of an anonymous reviewer who was retained by another publisher to review the proposal for this book. The reviewer thought the casebook emphasized public-sector activities too heavily to be attractive to instructors of housing finance in business schools and real estate programs. His suggestion that the book be purged of the regulatory cases because the "rent control sector is likely to be quite distasteful to business types" convinced me of the correctness of my initial instincts to broaden the cases to include issues of public concern.

Scott Verner assumed the final editing chores in his characteristic professional manner. His meticulous copyediting of the nine cases in this book has improved their clarity, readability, and technical precision. Academic and professional literature would be far more accessible to their intended audiences if those of us who produce it shared his penchant for ridding the world of jargon and verbiage.

Finally, I would like to acknowledge the tireless efforts of my administrative assistant, Bertina Baldwin, who typed what must have seemed like an endless stream of drafts of the cases. Though short in length, the case narratives required enough revisions to improve their clarity and precision to result in a typing burden equal to that of a much longer manuscript. Her patience and understanding of the need for "just one more draft" are gratefully appreciated.

While the casebook could not have been written without the assistance of many individuals, I, of course, take full responsibility for all errors and lack of clarity that remain in the cases.

PART ONE

Cases in Housing Finance and Public Policy

1 Individual Investor Strategies

The High- or Low-Income Fourplex

Dennis Albright was fit to be tied. He had just picked up his 1983 federal income tax return from his accountant and discovered that he was being taxed as if he were a millionaire. With a combined adjusted gross income of around $75,000, Albright and his wife were close to the 50 percent marginal tax bracket. Their total tax bill for 1983, including federal, state, and local taxes, exceeded $25,000 for an average effective rate of 33 percent (table 1-1).

Like so many other middle-income American families with two wage earners, the Albrights had become victims of "bracket creep," in which inflationary increases in nominal income push the taxpayer into ever-higher marginal tax brackets even though real income may not be rising at all. Ironically, Albright's tax exposure was probably greater than that of wealthier people. Unlike the rich, who are conscious of the true extent of their

Table 1-1. 1984 Federal Personal Income Tax Tables: Married Taxpayer Filing Joint Return

Base Income	Base Tax	Percent on Excess
0	0	0
$3,400	0	11%
5,500	$231	12
7,600	483	14
11,900	1,085	16
16,000	1,741	18
20,200	2,497	22
24,600	3,465	25
29,900	4,790	28
35,200	6,274	33
45,800	9,772	38
60,000	15,168	42
85,600	25,920	45
109,400	36,630	49
162,400	62,600	50

wealth and take great pains to minimize their tax liabilities, Albright never felt rich enough to engage in formal tax planning. Nor did he find the concept of tax shelters very appealing, thinking of them as loopholes used by the wealthy to avoid paying their fair share of income taxes. As a consequence, nearly all of his and his wife's income, including the interest on the $80,000 they had invested in moneymarket funds, was considered taxable. As he drove home from his accountant's office, Albright decided he had had enough. He would no longer bear more of the nation's tax burden than was absolutely necessary.

A colleague of Albright referred him to Carter Fortney, an investment counselor who had a sizable clientele among the practicing physicians at a local medical school. The Albrights met one evening with Fortney, president of Consolidated Tax Planning, Inc. (CTP), and discussed their financial affairs in great detail, including their long-term earning potential, their children's educational needs, and their retirement objectives. They also reviewed the small portfolio of stocks and bonds they had accumulated. Much to their surprise, the Albrights discovered that, despite their relative youth, the value of their combined estate, including the face value of their respective life insurance policies and the equity in their home, totaled nearly a half-million dollars.

Over the next several weeks, Fortney helped the Albrights build a retirement program around a series of tax-deferred annuity programs (TDAs), including individual retirement accounts (IRAs) that could be used to shelter some of Mr. Albright's independent consulting income. With the assistance of an attorney to whom Fortney referred them, the Albrights created an education trust to shelter part of the interest from investments that were targeted to pay their children's college tuition. On the advice of their attorney, they also had their wills redrawn to minimize the tax consequences their deaths would have on their estate. Finally, Fortney recommended that his new clients invest some of their available savings in oil and gas and in real estate ventures.

According to Fortney, the oil and gas deal would provide immediate tax relief because the tax benefits available to investors under current law were substantial, with a tax write-off of more than two dollars for each equity dollar invested in the year of investment. A $10,000 investment in 1982 could shelter $25,000 of what would otherwise be taxable income. The tax shelter benefits of the oil and gas deal would be largely short-term, however, and a successful project could begin to generate taxable income relatively quickly. Therefore, Fortney recommended that the oil and gas project be supplemented with a real estate investment, which would combine tax shelter with strong possibilities for capital appreciation over a longer period. Of the many real estate ventures the Albrights discussed with Fortney over the next few weeks, the most attractive and affordable were the following:

· A limited partnership interest in a real estate fund (Century Properties Fund XVII) that invests in new and recently constructed low-rise apart-

ment complexes, mostly on the West Coast and in other rapidly growing Sunbelt communities in the Southwest;
· Fee-simple ownership of a new luxury fourplex that would be built for Albright by a construction company affiliated with CTP. The fourplex would be located in a rapidly growing neighborhood in the northern section of Raleigh, North Carolina's capital city;
· Fee-simple ownership of a new fourplex, which also would be built by CTP's affiliate, but this one located in a predominantly black, lower-income neighborhood in southeast Raleigh.

Each of the investments had different equity requirements. Limited partnership interests in Century Fund XVII were available in $10,000 units. The high-income fourplex required an equity investment of above $50,000, more than 8 percent higher than the cash needed for the lower-income property.

Although investment returns on multifamily property syndications had been uneven over the years, the general partner of Fund XVII had an exceptional track record. One of his recently liquidated partnerships showed an after-tax simple return of 23 percent per year to the 50 percent tax bracket investor over a twelve-year investment period (table 1-2; supplement 1-1).

Despite the attractive potential returns from Fund XVII, Fortney seemed to favor the fourplex options for Albright. The current economic climate made it difficult to build large apartment complexes for middle- and upper-middle-income families. Even though Fortney was convinced that from economic and demographic standpoints, the long-term prospects for conventional rental housing investments were positive, he was less optimistic about

Table 1-2. Century Properties Fund 71

The following chart shows the total benefits to an investor in CPF 71, a prior affiliated partnership that recently completed the sale of its properties.

Analysis of Total After-Tax Benefits to a 50% Tax Bracket Investor [1]
(Per $10,000 Original Investment)

	Cash Distributions	Tax Deferral (Ordinary Income Tax Payable)	(Capital Gains Tax Payable)	Total Benefits
Benefits as of December 31, 1981				
From Operations				
Cash Benefits	$ 8,868	—	—	—
Tax Benefits	—	$1,164	—	—
From Property Sales				
Cash Benefits	13,960	—	—	—
Tax Liabilities	—	—	—	—
Totals Benefits Through December 31, 1981	22,828	1,164	$(4,046)	$19,946

Table 1-2. Century Properties Fund 71 (continued)

	Cash Distributions	Tax Deferral (Ordinary Income Tax Payable)	(Capital Gains Tax Payable)	Total Benefits
Anticipated Future Benefits [2,4]				
From Property Sales (per Sales Agreements)	20,129	—	(3,806)	—
From Operations [3]	1,366	(350)	—	—
Anticipated Total Benefits [4]	21,495	(350)	(3,806)	17,339
Grand Total [4]	$44,323	$ 814	$(7,852)	$37,285

Return of Capital: 100%
Return **on** Capital: 272.9%
   Life of Fund: ÷ 12 Years

   22.7%/Year simple rate of return **after** taxes. [4]

1. Amounts shown are simple averages.

2. In the event that purchasers default, or elect to prepay any of the notes, distributions and tax consequences would be altered materially.

3. The partnership has elected to establish a portion of the estimated interest income on the notes outstanding in an interest-bearing reserve account to allow for debt service payments on the underlying mortgages of partnership properties, to which the partnership assumes a secondary position. In addition, a reserve is being set up to offset the balloon payment in the amount of $200,000 due on the second note taken back from the sale of Cielo Grande Mobile Home Park. If unused, these reserves will be disbursed upon maturity of the notes.

4. The note received from the sale of Cielo Grande Mobile Home Park may be extended from August 1, 1983 to February 6, 1985, if on August 7, 1983, satisfactory refinancing of the property has not been arranged. If the maturity date on the promissory note is extended to February 6, 1985, "anticipated future benefits" would be as follows: cash distributions would increase by $678, tax deferral would decrease by $339 and capital gains tax payable would be unchanged. Total benefits would increase by $339. In addition, the simple rate of return for the fund would decrease to 21.2%.

The properties described above are properties that were acquired by Century Properties Fund 71. Prospective investors should be aware that the investment objectives of Fund 71, and the tax considerations and general economic conditions applicable to Fund 71, differ in certain significant respects from the investment objectives of Fund XVII, and the tax considerations and general economic conditions applicable to Fund XVII. Accordingly, prospective investors must not assume that they will experience returns, if any, comparable to the returns experienced by investors in Fund 71. For further information on all prior public limited partnerships sponsored by Fox & Carskadon Financial Corporation, prospective investors are urged to read the track record section of the Fund XVII Prospectus.

Source: Sales of Properties by Other Fox Partnerships, Fox & Carskadon Securities Corp., San Mateo, California, March 1982.

the short term, even in the Sunbelt. In his judgment, the economics of small rental housing construction and operation were more favorable over the short term and would continue to look very good over the longer term as well, especially if the fourplex units could eventually be sold to individual buyers as condominiums. The fourplex investments combined attractive tax-shelter features with strong capital growth possibilities, and Albright would not have to share the capital gains with any partners because he would own the property outright.

Fortney explained to Albright how Consolidated Tax Planning had arranged with a local builder to develop duplex, triplex, and fourplex properties exclusively for the company's clients. Since beginning the local real estate phase of the business some twenty-two months before, CTP had built nearly 140 apartments in forty-five buildings, each of which was rented during construction and has been fully occupied since. CTP would not begin construction until a client decided to invest and put up the cash to acquire one of the several improved lots that CTP had purchased. Still, although each building essentially was constructed to order, total development costs tended to be somewhat below the market average. For the low-rent project, that was because a standard design was used and the apartments averaged only about 750 square feet for a two-bedroom unit. More modest development economies in the high-rent fourplex arose largely from the fact that CTP would forego much of the builder/developer markup because it could capture many other fees through its various investment counseling, brokerage, and tax-planning services. Those fees were in addition to the fees earned by CTP's property management subsidiary, which, at the investor-owner's request, would assume complete management responsibilities for the properties, including the screening and selection of tenants, rent collection, maintenance, repairs, and yard work.

The total development cost of the low-rent fourplex would be $109,000, including $16,000 for the improved lot (table 1-3). Construction financing was available for $75,000 at a 15 percent interest rate. Despite the difficult mortgage market, CTP had a commitment from a local mortgage company for FHA-insured, fixed-rate permanent financing at a 12 percent interest rate (plus a .5 percent mortgage insurance premium) for thirty years (plus three discount points). Because the fourplex was not to be owner-occupied, the maximum FHA loan that could be secured was for $81,150. Including all front-end costs, an investor must contribute nearly $27,700 to complete the deal.

Fortney's pro forma analysis projected constant gross rents of $300 a month over the holding period. He explained to Albright that while rents in southeast Raleigh had been increasing at a slower rate than the overall cost of living for the past few years, property values had been climbing at about 8 percent annually (table 1-4). Albright noted that the analysis made no allowances for maintenance and repairs, which Fortney's management firm would take care of when needed and would charge against collected rents. Like rents, taxes and insurance costs were projected to remain constant over the holding period. Management costs of 6 percent of gross collections were included in the cash-flow statement, although a vacancy allowance was not. "My management firm has a waiting list a mile long," Fortney said. "Don't worry, we never have any trouble keeping our apartments occupied since we are the only ones building new apartments in neighborhoods that moderate-income people can afford to live in. In fact," he continued, "if you don't mind the hassle of dealing with low-income families

Table 1-3. Development Cost of a Low-Rent Fourplex: Raleigh, North Carolina, 1983

Building Costs		$84,000
Construction Financing Cost		3,713
Interest 6 months @ 15% on $75,000	2,813	
Loan origination fee (1%)	750	
Attorney fee	150	
Prepaid Items		920
Hazard insurance (15 months)	311	
Real estate taxes (6 months)	568	
FHA mortgage insurance premium (1 month)	41	
Closing Costs		4,194
Permanent loan origination fee[1]	812	
Discount points on permanent loan (3.0%)	2,435	
Land survey	150	
Credit report	75	
Appraisal fee (to FHA)	150	
Title insurance	162	
Recording fee	10	
Attorney fee	400	
Improved Cost of Land		16,000
Total		$108,827

1. Permanent loan: FHA-insured 30-year fixed rate mortgage of $81,150 at 12.5% (including a .5% mortgage insurance premium).

and the federal bureaucracy, we can make the fourplex an even more attractive real estate investment.''

He explained to Albright that because his rents would not exceed the maximum Section 8 fair market rent for an existing two-bedroom apartment in Raleigh, Albright would be able to rent the fourplex to low-income tenants holding Section 8 certificates. Those families would be referred to Albright by the local public housing authority. According to Fortney, by charging rents no higher than the Section 8 maximum, Albright would be able to take advantage of the more favorable federal income tax provisions for low-income housing, including an immediate write-off of construction period interest and taxes and more generous depreciation allowances over his expected holding period.

The high-rent fourplex would cost $143,000, including $25,000 for the improved land (table 1-5). Higher land prices accounted for about 25 percent of the increased development cost of this fourplex, whereas 75 percent of the difference stemmed from actual construction. Although the high-rent fourplex, like its low-rent counterpart, also contained two-bedroom units, each high-rent apartment was more than 100 square feet larger. In contrast to the low-rent apartments, each of which contained a single window air-

Table 1-4. Selected Housing Market Data for Raleigh, North Carolina, 1970 and 1980

	Raleigh		Low-income Neighborhood		High-income Neighborhood	
	1970	1980	1970	1980	1970	1980
Number of year-round housing						
units	38,412	57,866	1,622	1,210	1,195	1,978
Built before 1940	9,247	7,194	835	3,332	31	28
Built since 1970	—	18,650	—	168	—	1,072
Number of owner-occupied units	18,494	26,670	338	212	607	934
Median number of rooms, all units	5.0	5.0	4.1	4.1	5.4	4.0
Number of units lacking complete						
plumbing	739	476	100	23	1	14
Number of overcrowded units	2,390	1,662	416	137	13	34
Number of units vacant for rent	1,138	1,731	51	10	79	110
Median gross rent	$104	$255	$68	$129	$175	$340
Median value for owned units	$19,700	$54,400	$10,800	$22,100	$30,400	$78,100
Number of black households	6,987	12,955	1,554	1,112	1	277
Median income:						
Families[1]	$10,085	N.A.[2]	$4,496	N.A.	$13,747	N.A.
Households	N.A.	$17,022	N.A.	$8,085	N.A.	$22,180
Percentage of households below						
poverty level	10.4%	12.2%	41.9%	30.0%	3.0%	5.5%

1. *Families* include people related by blood or marriage who occupy a single housing unit, whereas *households* include all persons, regardless of relationship, occupying a single housing unit. In 1980, the Bureau of the Census began to report income for households rather than for families.

2. Data not available.

conditioning unit in the kitchen, the high-rent apartments were centrally air conditioned. Construction materials in the high-rent fourplex were generally better, and more attention was paid to construction detail and exterior site treatment. Another difference was that the low-rent fourplexes were sparsely landscaped and had gravel driveways and parking areas, but the high-rent properties were well landscaped and had asphalt drives and parking lots.

The construction and permanent financing arrangements for the high-rent fourplex paralleled those for the low-rent property. On the operating side, the pro forma analysis projected constant gross rents of $350 a month, although Fortney seemed confident that rents could be raised to $375 a month within two years. Unlike properties in southeast Raleigh, he claimed, values in the north of town had been climbing by more than 12 percent a year. To be conservative, however, Fortney's pro forma analysis assumed a 9 percent annual rate of appreciation. As in the case of the low-rent fourplex, Fortney's analysis made no allowance for either vacancies or repairs, because "demand was so strong and the structures would be covered by a ten-year builder's warranty, and the building systems and appliances would be warranted for a shorter period by their respective manufacturers."

It was now up to the Albrights to decide which of the three investment

Table 1-5. Development Cost of High-Income Fourplex, Raleigh, North Carolina

Building Cost		$107,626
Construction Financing Cost		4,867
Interest 6 months at 15% on $98,250	3,684	
Loan origination fee	983	
Attorney fee	200	
Prepaid Items		1,250
Hazard insurance (15 months)	446	
Real estate taxes (6 months)	750	
FHA mortgage insurance premium (1 month)	54	
Closing Costs		4,861
Permanent loan origination fee[1]	910	
Discount points on permanent loan (3.0%)	2,729	
Land survey	100	
Credit report	75	
Appraisal fee (to FHA)	250	
Title insurance	182	
Recording fee	15	
Attorney fee	600	
Improved Cost of Land		25,000
Total		$143,404

1. Permanent loan: FHA-insured 30-year fixed rate mortgage of $90,950 at 12.5% (including a .5% mortgage insurance premium).

alternatives was best for them. One or more limited partnership interests in Century Fund XVII properties seemed hard to beat. They would not have to worry about the day-to-day operations of the apartment complexes; the risk was lessened because Fund XVII would own a large number of properties in many different housing markets; and projected after-tax returns seemed very competitive (although Albright was not sure that the internal rate of return he was using to assess the profitability of the fourplexes was consistent with the after-tax simple return measure described for the limited partnership interests in table 1-2). On the other hand, both fourplex investments also had good potential. The Albrights liked the idea of individual ownership and not having to share capital gains with any partners. Even though each of the fourplex options would concentrate investment risks in a single property, they felt good about the Raleigh housing market and the strong competitive position either of the fourplexes would hold in its neighborhood.

Nevertheless, many issues still remained unresolved in the Albrights' minds, not the least of which was that both fourplexes required high equity investments relative to the amount of capital they could borrow to finance them. Moreover, even if the high-rent property were to outperform the low-rent fourplex, would that justify a cash investment in excess of $50,000? The same equity could buy the low-rent fourplex plus two limited partnership interests in Fund XVII.

In terms of the low-rent fourplex, Albright wondered about the tax implications of mixing subsidized and unsubsidized tenants. He also wondered whether he would be able to qualify for the added tax benefits if he merely rented his apartments at rents no higher than the Section 8 limits, or whether he actually had to establish a formal relationship with the local housing authority and rent to Section 8 program participants in order to qualify. If the latter, what would be the tax consequences of replacing a Section 8 tenant with a non–Section 8 tenant? Would earlier accelerated depreciation benefits be recaptured? Moreover, he wondered whether he could count on any significant amount of appreciation if the property were used for subsidized housing. Those and many other questions and concerns swirled around inside Albright's head. His confusion, if nothing else, was leading him toward Fund XVII. But the idea of owning their own apartment building, small as it might be, still appealed to the Albrights.

SUPPLEMENT 1-1.

Questions and Answers about Century Properties Fund XVII

· *Who is Fox Partners?* Fox Partners is the general partner of Century Properties Fund XVII, of which Fox & Carskadon Financial Corporation ("Fox"), Century Partners, and Fox Partners '82 are general partners. Fox is a privately owned real estate investment company with headquarters in the San Francisco Bay area. It is one of the largest and oldest companies specializing in real estate limited partnership programs in the United States.
· *What experience does the general partner have in real estate syndications?* Since 1969, Fox & Carskadon Financial Corporation and its affiliates have participated in over fifty real estate limited partnerships with approximately 56,000 separate investments. These partnerships have purchased over 22,000 apartment units, over 3.3 million square feet of commercial, industrial and office space, over 4.4 million square feet of shopping center space, over 8,000 mobile home pads and five hotels with over 1,300 rooms; all located in over eighty cities, primarily throughout the western and southern United States. Total original cost of these properties, including all cash and mortgages, is approximately one billion dollars.
· *How does one become a limited partner in Century Properties Fund XVII?* Qualified investors who can meet certain suitability standards may invest through qualified securities dealers. A check payable to Century Properties Fund XVII trust account for the full purchase price of the interest being subscribed must be accompanied by a completed and signed instrument of purchase, which is contained in the prospectus. The minimum investment is $5,000 (five units at

*From "Questions and Answers about Century Properties Fund XVII," Fox & Carskadon Securities, San Mateo, California, March 1982.

$1,000 per unit) ($2,000 minimum investment for IRA or Keogh Plan accounts in most states). After the initial investment, additional investments in $1,000 increments may be made anytime until the offering is fully subscribed or closed to further investment.

· *As an investor in Century Properties Fund XVII, what will I own?* An investor will own a limited partnership interest in a real estate limited partnership. As a limited partner, an investor does not own a direct interest in real property; however, when the partnership purchases real property the investor, in effect, has an indirect and proportionate interest in each property owned by the partnership.

· *What reporting information will I receive as a limited partner in Century Properties Fund XVII?* In addition to the documents evidencing ownership, information regarding the progress of the investment will be mailed quarterly and an annual report with pertinent financial information will be issued each year. Moreover, tax information will be prepared and mailed to each investor within seventy-five days of the close of the calendar year. Finally, each limited partner will receive from the general partner, shortly after investment, a binder in which to store the information for handy reference.

· *What types of properties have prior Fox & Carskadon partnerships acquired?* Prior partnerships sponsored by Fox have acquired only conventional income-producing properties. The emphasis by such partnerships has been on multifamily residential properties, shopping centers, office and industrial properties. The properties acquired have been new or existing. Prior partnerships sponsored by Fox have not acquired private homes, nursing or retirement homes, low-income/subsidized housing projects or any other specialized type of properties. Fund XVII intends to invest primarily in existing multifamily residential properties.

· *What forms of depreciation are used?* Depreciation, for financial statement purposes, will be computed on the straight line method. For income tax purposes the partnership will use the "accelerated cost recovery system," or such methods of depreciation on a property-by-property basis as are considered appropriate by the general partner, including such accelerated methods as may be available.

· *How long will it take for me to get my money back?* Cash, if available, will be distributed to investors in Century Properties Fund XVII in a variety of ways, from a variety of sources and at varying times throughout the life of the partnership. First, cash distributions may result from the successful operation of the properties which would produce positive cash flows after expenses, debt service and reserves. This cash distribution from operations is contemplated to be distributed quarterly. Second, cash distributions may result from the refinancing of properties or the sale of properties within a five to eight year period of ownership. These distributions could result from the net cash proceeds of such refinancings or sales, and from payments received on any notes which may be taken back by the partnership as consideration for the sale of properties. Properties may be refinanced or sold earlier or later than currently anticipated if determined to be in the best interest of the partnership.

· *What evidence of ownership will I receive if I become a limited partner of Century Properties Fund XVII?* Investors will receive from the general partner a Certificate of Limited Partnership as evidence of ownership of units.

· *Will investments in Century Properties Fund XVII be assessable?* No. Investments are nonassessable. Investors will not be asked by the general partner to invest additional capital after their original investment.

· *May I sell or transfer my partnership interest in Century Properties Fund XVII?* No market for limited partnership units exists, nor is one expected to develop. Investors may not be able to liquidate their investment in the event of an emergency or for any other reason. The sale of limited partnership units by a limited partnership unit holder may result in substantial adverse federal income tax consequences. Investment units are transferable with the general partner's written permission and in compliance with certain state regulatory requirements. Upon request, brokers may assist an investor desiring to transfer his or her units.

· *How does a limited partner know that properties have been bought at fair prices?* Of the many properties the general partner's acquisition staff examines, those which are selected for acquisition represent the general partner's assessment of the very best in terms of value, revenue-producing potential and equity appreciation. Affiliates of the general partner maintain a large fulltime professional staff to conduct all the many tasks associated with such a critical selection with the most modern management tools available to aid their evaluations. In addition, every property acquired must be appraised by an independent appraiser, who is a member of a nationally recognized society of appraisers, at a value equal to or exceeding the purchase price paid to the seller including all acquisition fees. Please note: appraised values are opinions and, as such, may not represent the realizable value of the properties.

· *What are the advantages of leverage?* Leverage involves the use of borrowed money to magnify any increase in property value to a larger increase on the actual cash invested. For example, if you are a homeowner and have a mortgage on your house, you are using leverage.

To illustrate, assume that an $80,000 home should increase in value by $4,000 each year, which is a 5 percent per year increase in the property value. However, if the house was acquired using a $40,000 loan and $40,000 of equity the $4,000 increase in property value each year is a 10 percent per year increase on the cash you invested ($4,000 of increase in value divided by the $40,000 original equity). The use of leverage does contain certain risk factors in that a decrease in property value will reflect a larger decrease in cash invested.

· *What are some of the risk factors and conflicts of interest of an investment in Century Properties Fund XVII?* Investment in the partnership is subject to various risk factors. In addition, there are certain conflicts of interest arising out of the partnership's relationship with the general partner and affiliates of the general partner.

2 Public/Private Financing Partnerships

Multifamily Housing Rehabilitation: Tax Considerations Cannot Be Ignored

Fred Atwater, director of Housing Rehabilitation Services (HRS) in a small Midwestern city with a population of about 130,000, wondered how he would implement the new multifamily housing rehabilitation program the Community Development director had unveiled with such fanfare at last night's public hearing on the CD budget. City officials had a good deal of experience—not all of it positive—with single-family housing rehabilitation. Although the single-family home rehabilitation program had been popular over the last six years, it had cost a lot—between $15,000 and $20,000 per dwelling. The program seemed to have stabilized the two older moderate-income neighborhoods, located just east of the central business district, where most of the rehabilitation had been concentrated. Yet the single-family home program had not always worked as smoothly as it might have seemed to the casual observer. When Atwater had been brought in to run the program two years before, he had found the files in disarray, important loan documents missing, and some of the payments records not up to date. After straightening out the files and implementing a consumer-oriented loan servicing system, Atwater had been able to reduce late payments significantly. The seriously delinquent loans were much harder to work out because many of them should never have been granted in the first place. The high rate of defaults on loans was as much a result of poor underwriting by the HRS staff as of poor collection procedures.

Knowing that and recognizing the added importance of sound underwriting in a program for multifamily rental housing rehabilitation, Atwater arranged to enroll his staff in an intensive training program in real estate investment analysis, loan underwriting for income-producing properties, and neighborhood and housing market analysis. All of these skills would be needed if the staff were to design and implement a cost-effective rental rehabilitation program that would produce rents affordable to moderate-income families.

* This case is based on a draft case prepared by Charles Laven.

14

Over the past five years, the city had invested annually about two million dollars of its Community Development Block Grant entitlement funds in the single-family housing improvement program. But the city's entitlement was being reduced because of cutbacks in federal funding. The high cost of the single-family home rehabilitation program and the threat to progress apparently posed by distressed multifamily buildings in the target neighborhoods made the rehabilitation of rental housing a timely addition to the city's program.

One of the two target single-family neighborhoods was in a historic district where many of the properties were eligible for the National Register of Historic Places. Atwater believed that this would be a good area to begin the multifamily rental program because of the program's ability to attract private investment and the importance of supporting the millions of dollars the city had invested already in helping to rehabilitate owner-occupied housing in the area. The relatively few small multifamily buildings in the district were strategically located—for example, on key intersections—so the effects of their deterioration spilled over onto more than one block. A quick survey of the neighborhood confirmed that the condition of the single-family houses improved with distance from these apartment buildings, which had obsolete heating, plumbing, and electrical systems, general undermaintenance, and high vacancy rates. The neighborhood was in an early stage of decline, but the rental market remained reasonably strong because of its proximity to downtown office and shopping facilities and the high demand for affordable housing. Rents, which averaged $270 a month for a two-bedroom apartment in a modest but standard building, had been rising at the approximate city-wide rate of 6 percent a year and could be afforded by families with incomes of as little as 80 percent of the city median income.

THE FOSTER PROPERTY

One of the first multifamily properties Atwater's staff had selected for rehabilitation was in the heart of the historic district. The outlook for the building after rehabilitation was good, although nearly all its eighteen apartments were vacant. The building was structurally sound, not all major systems needed replacing, and, because it was almost empty, rehabilitation could be accomplished more efficiently, at less cost, and without disrupting the lives of many families. More important, Ed Foster, the new owner, was an industrial engineer who was knowledgeable about construction techniques and wanted to do the rehabilitation correctly. His wife, Nancy, was employed as a nurse; together, they had an annual income of about $60,000 a year. The Fosters had purchased 1514 Cumberland for $30,000 in cash and a loan assumption of $29,000, which had six more years to run and carried payments of about $5,800 a year. Atwater thought the Fosters were the kind of committed young property owners the neighborhood needed if it was to bounce back and he vowed to do everything within reason to help make the rehabilitation of 1514 Cumberland feasible.

THE LOAN PACKAGE

According to the HRS staff's report on the Foster property, the total rehabilitation cost would be about $11,500 per unit. The staff concluded that the city would have to come up with more than $110,000 to make the numbers work; the balance ($97,000) would be paid by the Fosters from a combination of a private mortgage loan and their own funds. The city's participation would include a fifteen-year direct loan of $82,000 at 5 percent interest and a deferred-payment loan (DPL) of $32,000 (table 2-1). The DPL would be non-interest-bearing and nonamortizing; the full mortgage amount would become due at the time of sale or upon refinancing of the property. To facilitate private financing of a portion of the rehabilitation, the city would subordinate its interest in its municipal loans to the conventional loan, thus ensuring the private lender of a second lien on the property.

Atwater was pleased with his staff's work. The amount of public financing committed to the job seemed fair, was well within the program guidelines, and was certainly much less per unit than the city had been investing in its single-family home rehabilitation program.

With the financing almost complete, the Fosters began having second thoughts. Although they were considering moving into one of the apartments in their building in order to save money and to become a part of the neighborhood, they still worried about the lack of cash flow the property

Table 2-1. Development Cost and Operating Data for 1514 Cumberland Road

ACQUISITION COST

Equity	$30,000
Outstanding balance of original $80,000, 6 percent 30-year loan	29,000
Total	$59,000
Estimated rehabilitation costs	$207,000
Financed by:	
15 percent, 15-year private second mortgage	$93,000
City loan at 5 percent, 15 years	82,000
Interest-free deferred-payment city loan	32,000

OPERATING STATEMENT

Gross income	$58,320
Less: Vacancy (7 percent)	4,082
Effective gross income	$54,238
Less:	
Real estate taxes	1,700
Maintenance and operating	21,600
Net operating income	$30,938
Less:	
Assumed loan	$5,756
Private second mortgage	15,620
City loan	7,781
Before-tax cash flow	$1,781
Gross return on initial equity	5.9%

would generate, which would amount to a return of less than 6 percent on their initial equity. They knew they could be earning much more than that in a risk-free certificate of deposit or in moneymarket funds and they appealed to the city to increase the amount of the deferred-payment loan. While the HRS staff was sympathetic to their plight, Atwater was less so. He knew whatever he did on his first multifamily building would set a precedent, and he did not want to become known as someone who would ''give away the store.'' Besides, the CD director had announced to the press that, unlike the single-family home program, the multifamily housing rehabilitation program would minimize public contributions and maximize private investment in the multifamily housing stock so that the city would be able to stretch its limited CD dollars farther than ever before. Atwater was under orders to keep the city's financial participation just high enough to make rehabilitation feasible and to ensure rents that moderate-income families could afford.

Atwater had little experience in rehabilitating multifamily buildings, but knew more about income-producing properties than his staff did. He realized that the Fosters were concerned about their pretax investment returns and that Congress provided significant tax incentives to encourage investments in income-producing property in general and particularly in renovation of low-income housing and historic properties (supplements 2-1 and 2-2). He was sure that these inducements could make an important difference in the profitability of the Cumberland Road property. With the help of a local lender, he prepared a revised pro forma operating statement that took into consideration various tax benefits available to the property owners. With the results of these analyses in hand, Atwater directed his staff to come up with a revised financing plan that would address the Fosters' principal concern while minimizing the city's long-term costs.

SUPPLEMENT 2-1.

The Impact of Current Federal Tax Law on Historic Preservation

Present provisions of the Internal Revenue code substantially influence preservation and reuse of historic properties. Some impacts are direct and obvious, such as the code's treatment of investment in the rehabilitation of historic properties versus new construction. Others, such as estate tax–generated pressures that may induce the subdivision of historic properties, are more subtle, but are nonetheless potentially significant. As a whole, federal tax law plays a major role in determining whether many of the nation's historic structures will continue to serve useful, contemporary functions in society or, indeed, will survive at all in the face of competing demands for building sites.

*Advisory Council on Historic Preservation, "The Impact of Current Federal Tax Law on Historic Preservation," in *Federal Tax Law and Historic Preservation: Report to the President and the Congress,* 1983, U.S. Government Printing Office, Washington, D.C.

The impact of the tax system is critical, because it has long been recognized that direct federal outlays can ensure the preservation of only a minute percentage of the nation's historic resources. Even at the peak level of funding in 1979, the National Historic Preservation Fund contributed only $27 million to promote restoration or rehabilitation of about 1,760 historic properties. By comparison, there are currently over 197,000 individual properties included in the National Register of Historic Places, the basic inventory of the nation's historic resources worthy of preservation. The framers of the National Historic Preservation Act anticipated this circumstance. The purposes and policies of that Act continually assert the primary role of private individuals and organizations in ensuring the continued preservation and use of historic properties.

Accordingly, policymakers concerned with stimulating private sector investment in historic preservation have sought methods of federal assistance other than direct grants. Early review of the federal tax system revealed that there were no tax incentives in the code specifically targeted to encourage preservation, and, moreover, that certain provisions strongly discriminated against reuse of historic buildings in favor of modern replacements. A proposal to redress this imbalance, removing the negative biases and adding some modest incentives, originated in 1971 and eventually became law in the Tax Reform Act of 1976. These revisions focused on amending amortization and depreciation rules to encourage rehabilitation, rather than replacement, of historic structures. The provisions required the Secretary of the Interior to certify properties as historically significant and their rehabilitation as compatible with their historic character in order to qualify. Other provisions eliminated incentives that encouraged demolition of historic buildings and allowed charitable contribution deductions for donation of preservation easements. With the exception of the easement provisions, the tax incentives and disincentives extended only to income-producing properties.

These tax law revisions, augmented in 1978 by a 10 percent investment tax credit for rehabilitation, produced the desired effect. Despite uncertainties stemming from ambiguities in the tax laws and an absence of comprehensive implementing regulations, certified rehabilitations approached $140 million for fiscal years 1977 and 1978, climbed to $300 million the following year, and reached almost $350 million in fiscal year 1980. Over the four-year period, nearly 2,300 privately initiated rehabilitation projects were certified for the tax incentives. By comparison, federal historic preservation grant funds totaled $76.4 million for that period, benefiting approximately 3,600 historic properties. Similarly, although precise figures are not available, it would appear that the easement provisions enacted in 1976 and made permanent in 1980 have encouraged owners of historic properties to donate preservation easements to nonprofit organizations.

The Economic Recovery Tax Act of 1981 (ERTA) made sweeping changes to tax treatment of investment in real estate development. The Accelerated Cost Recovery System (ACRS) superseded the depreciation system, simplifying and enhancing the deduction that compensates a taxpayer for deterioration and obsolescence of business property. A three-tiered investment tax credit (ITC) system was introduced to stimulate investment in the rehabilitation of older structures, including but not limited to historic buildings. This authorized tax credits equivalent to 15 percent of the investment in qualified rehabilitation expenses for thirty-year-old commercial buildings and 20 percent for those forty years old. It also authorized a 25 percent tax credit for historic buildings, provided the Secretary of the Interior certified both the significance and the rehabilitation. ERTA modified the demolition disincentives, retaining only the provision denying a deduction for demolition cost and losses. The ERTA changes took effect for the most part on January 1, 1982. Further technical revisions occurred during 1982, but the basic incentive/disincentive structure remained unchanged. Today the impacts of federal tax law include those flowing from this refined scheme of encouragement and deterrence. However, there are also a number of unanticipated ways the tax laws influence preservation. To assess current federal tax law as it affects historic properties, it is useful to examine separately those provisions designed to encourage preservation directly and those of general applicability that unintentionally affect preservation.

CURRENT FEDERAL TAX PROVISIONS DIRECTLY AFFECTING HISTORIC PRESERVATION

CREDIT FOR REHABILITATION EXPENDITURES

A taxpayer who renovates a historic building may qualify for a tax credit equal to 25 percent of the rehabilitation expenditure, provided five tests are met:

- The property must be used subsequently for income-producing purposes, which includes residential rental use.
- The property must be a "certified historic structure," as determined by the Secretary of the Interior. A property individually listed in the National Register of Historic Places automatically meets this test; a building within a historic district either listed in the National Register or established under an Interior-certified state or local statute may also be eligible if the Secretary of the Interior certifies the building as being of historic significance to the district.
- The Secretary of the Interior must certify that the work is consistent with the historic character of the property or the district.
- The rehabilitation must be "substantial"; i.e., it must cost more than $5,000 or the adjusted basis of the building, whichever is greater.
- At least 75 percent of the existing external walls must remain in place as external walls.

The credit is computed from qualified rehabilitation expenditures, which do not include costs of acquisition nor costs attributable to enlargements or new construction.

The 25 percent credit for certified historic structures exists as part of a tiered system of rehabilitation credits. The code also allows a 15 percent credit for the rehabilitation of commercial buildings at least thirty years old and a 20 percent credit for those at least forty years old. The rehabilitation credit for these classes of properties is available if the buildings are income producing and meet the "substantial rehabilitation" and "75 percent of walls" tests. There are no mandatory reviews or certifications regarding historic significance or quality of renovation work, nor are the 15 or 20 percent credits available for buildings used for residential rentals. One other distinction between the historic and nonhistoric building credits is the adjustment to basis required when a credit is taken. For certified historic structures, basis must be reduced by one-half the value of the credit claimed; for all other properties, the reduction is the full value. This affects the amount of the annual depreciation deduction and adds to the differential between historic and nonhistoric building rehabilitation credits.

DEMOLITION DISINCENTIVES

While the code normally permits a deduction for costs associated with demolition of an income-producing property except when the property is acquired expressly for razing, a special rule covers certified historic structures. The cost of demolition and any loss occasioned by razing a historic building that had an adjusted basis greater than zero must be charged to the capital account of the land on which the structure stood. This means that the taxpayer is denied immediate benefit of an income tax deduction, receiving a tax reduction only when the property is sold, since the increase in adjusted basis reduces the capital gain. The provision applies to all certified historic structures and includes properties within registered historic districts, unless they have been individually "decertified" by the Secretary of the Interior.

DONATION OF PRESERVATION EASEMENTS

The code allows a taxpayer to take a charitable contribution deduction for the value of an easement or certain other real estate interests given to protect historic properties. A preservation easement is a private agreement between the landowner and a holding organization obligating the owner and successors to preserve significant historic features of the property. Other contributions qualifying taxpayers for the deduction are remainder interests, i.e., donating a property while retaining the right to use it during the donor's lifetime, and entire interests wherein the donor retains qualified rights to subsurface minerals. The code requires the easement or interest to be granted in perpetuity "exclusively for conservation purposes." This latter standard includes preservation of certified historic structures and historically important land areas. Unlike the rehabilitation credits, the charitable contribution deduction extends to easements and interests in any historic property, whether income producing or not, although different rules apply to each type.

GENERAL TAX PROVISIONS AFFECTING HISTORIC PRESERVATION

While the preceding discussion has focused on those tax provisions specifically designed to affect preservation activity, there are other code provisions of general applicability with inadvertent impact on historic preservation. While the contract research identified several of these areas, the council has determined that only estate and gift taxes deserve consideration in this report.

ESTATE AND GIFT TAXES

Recent changes in the estate and gift tax rates and coverage leaves somewhat in question the status of a longstanding preservation concern. It has been recognized that the requirement to value the property of a decedent at fair market or "highest and best use" has compelled the sale of large historic estates for development. Even though a historic property has traditionally been used as a residence or farm and the heirs wish to keep it that way, valuation based on development potential may result in a tax bill that can be satisfied only by sale for development.

Another aspect of the impact of estate tax provisions on historic properties is the requirement that estate taxes be paid within nine months of the date of death. When the estate's principal asset is a historic property, a forced sale may result in order to pay the tax bill.

Recent changes to the code grant special treatment for family-owned farms and businesses in order to avoid the hardships generated by both of these estate tax impacts. Special use valuation allows a property to be valued at current use, rather than highest and best, as long as certain requirements are met as to the continuation of the existing use. Likewise, the code permits a five-year deferral of estate tax payments when a family farm or business constitutes more than 35 percent of a decedent's estate. Historic properties that qualify under the code as family farms or businesses are entitled to the benefits of these provisions. The council's investigation of the impact of federal tax laws on historic preservation has revealed a number of strengths and weaknesses in the basic statutory framework. Recognizing that its legislative charge is to make recommendations to further the purposes of the National Historic Preservation Act through the federal tax laws, the council has reached the following conclusions and makes the accompanying recommendations for consideration by the President and the Congress.

INVESTMENT TAX CREDITS FOR REHABILITATION OF CERTIFIED HISTORIC STRUCTURES

The council finds that the 25 percent investment tax credit for certified rehabilitation of certified historic structures has been an effective tax incentive for stimulating private investment in the preservation of significant historic buildings.

After ERTA, private investment in the rehabilitation of historic properties accelerated dramatically. The dollar value of projects submitted for Interior certification in fiscal year 1981, $738 million, was over twice that of the preceding year. Recent figures compiled by the Department of the Interior indicate that the new 25 percent ITC, which went into effect on January 1, 1982, is stimulating preservation investment even more. Interior reports that during the first half of fiscal year 1983, 1,355 projects representing $793 million of investment were certified as eligible to qualify for the credits. This is a 75 percent increase in certifications over the same period in the preceding fiscal year, a particularly noteworthy achievement in light of the depressed state of the construction industry during that time.

Since the initial incentives became law in late 1976, Interior reports that 92 percent of all applicants have obtained certification. This has resulted in a projected investment by mid-1983 of $3.45 billion of private capital in nearly 6,300 certified historic rehabilitation projects. By comparison, grants from the National Historic Preservation Fund for the preservation and restoration of historic properties came to only $82.3 million over the same period. Significantly, developers reported in a survey that nearly one out of two historic rehabilitation projects would not have been undertaken in the absence of existing federal tax incentives.

Evidence indicates that the tax incentives are being used on relatively small projects. In 1982, the average project was $441,250; 44 percent were under $100,000. The research revealed that the primary users of the tax incentives have had a yearly gross business income of less than $100,000 and typically complete no more than one project a year.

The council believes that the basic approach of the 25 percent ITC for certified rehabilitations of certified historic structures is effective as an incentive to stimulate private investment in historic preservation.

Because developers often perceive older buildings to be at a market disadvantage, many historic buildings would have continued to deteriorate and become lost to future generations. However, significant amounts of private capital are now being attracted into the rehabilitation of historic structures. Developers who renovate historic buildings find the 25 percent ITC the most attractive encouragement for rehabilitation. Indeed, 48 percent of all certified historic rehabilitations have occurred since enactment of ERTA.

Also significant are the uses to which these rehabilitated buildings are put. Interior reports for fiscal year 1982 that over 46 percent of the projects were for housing, 23 percent for mixed commercial-residential use, 17 percent for office space, 8 percent for solely commercial use, and 3 percent for hotels. From passage of the initial incentives through fiscal year 1982, over 19,800 new housing units were created by certified historic rehabilitations. Half of these were for low- and moderate-income families.

Equally important is the careful control over the renovation of these buildings by the mandatory certification process administered by Interior with the active participation of State Historic Preservation Officers. Ill-conceived or poorly executed rehabilitation often destroys the significant features of historic buildings, resulting in as much of a loss to the nation's heritage as outright demolition. The council believes that the additional demands on a developer to produce a quality rehabilitation justify the increment in the 25 percent ITC over those credits available for nonhistoric buildings. From a preservation perspective, it is essential that the federal government ensure that its considerable assistance to private investors through these tax incentives be limited to those projects in which renovation is undertaken in a manner compatible with the historic character of the property. The certification process as it is currently constituted achieves this.

The council is cognizant of the revenue loss occasioned by the use of the 25 percent ITC. Latest Office of Management and Budget estimates indicate the revenue loss from historic preservation tax credits to be $270 million for fiscal year 1983. By comparison, the revenue loss estimate for the 15 percent and 20 percent credits for noncertified rehabilitations over the same period was $335 million, about 24 percent greater.

However, other factors must be considered when assessing the impact of the 25 percent ITC on contemporary society. The council has also considered the positive impacts of historic preservation on job production in labor-intensive renovation; energy conservation through reuse of existing structures that represent a substantial energy investment; and secondary effects of recycled historic buildings on neighborhood conservation and stability, downtown revitalization, tourism, reduction of new demands on infrastructure and city services, and increases in local government tax bases. (These issues were considered in two 1979 Advisory Council on Historic Preservation studies: *Assessing the Energy Conservation Benefits of Historic Preservation: Methods and Examples* and *The Contribution of Historic Preservation to Urban Revitalization.*) Although these benefits are difficult to quantify, they cannot be ignored in any assessment of the overall effect of these tax incentives.

Eligibility criteria for the 25 percent investment tax credit should be reviewed to differentiate better between rehabilitation projects that are desirable from a historic preservation standpoint and thus merit federal subsidies from those projects that are not.

While the council believes the general tax incentive for rehabilitation of historic buildings works well, the investigation has revealed certain areas in need of adjustment to ensure that the intended purposes of the incentives are fully met. Two areas of concern have been identified over the course of the contract research.

Objective tests determine the eligibility of a project to ensure that the benefits of the 25 percent credit do not extend to projects other than those originally intended by the Congress. The current eligibility criteria set rigid limitations both on the amount of historic building fabric that must remain after rehabilitation and on the level of investment in the project. There are substantial rehabilitation projects involving highly significant historic structures that have been denied the credit because they have not met the eligibility criteria, while other projects either less substantial or involving less significant structures have qualified. Furthermore, the arbitrarily assigned limits have presented administrative problems and caused biases in the application of the credit provisions that were never intended when the law was passed. The tests could be improved to have the eligibility criteria include alternative objective tests more closely related to the goals of the National Historic Preservation Act. Improvement in the eligibility criteria could be achieved without expanding eligibility or increasing the cost of the federal subsidies. This should be considered in two areas: the "75 percent of walls" test and the "substantial rehabilitation" test, which users have identified as presenting significant problems.

Alternative objective tests to the current "75 percent of walls" test should be considered for determining if a project is primarily new construction.

The current requirement that 75 percent of existing external walls be retained in place as external walls was established to provide an objective test to distinguish between rehabilitation and new construction. However, the test as currently articulated may deny the credit to projects that are actually rehabilitation rather than new construction and that otherwise satisfy Interior certification requirements.

Each of the elements of the test has its negative impact. The "retained in place" requirement has proved troublesome when a wall must be reconstructed because it has deteriorated, fails to meet seismic code requirements, or requires rebuilding for some other legitimate reason. Such treatment may be acceptable to the Secretary of the Interior for a certified rehabilitation consistent with the historic character of the structure, but at the same time fail to meet the requirement that 75 percent of existing external walls be retained in place. Retention as "external walls" is also problematic, as the addition of a required stair tower or other external changes can result in a retained existing "external" wall becoming "internal." Restoring a historic building may quite properly result in the removal of later additions that are incompatible with the historic character of the original building but which, because they include "existing" and "external" walls, fall within the 75 percent retention requirement. Application of the test to urban mid-block buildings designed with one significant external wall, the facade, can inhibit adaptation of such structures to a viable contemporary use by removal of nonsignificant walls. Finally, complex wall configurations of older buildings, involving parapets, towers, arcades, and the like, can make computation of the existing external walls quite difficult and arbitrary.

The objective of distinguishing between new construction and rehabilitation could be achieved with a more flexible test applicable to historic projects. A different articulation of requirements to retain a substantial amount of historically significant fabric would improve this eligibility criterion for the tax credit. Alternative tests based on objective criteria should be considered.

Alternative objective tests to the current "substantial rehabilitation" test should be considered that would minimize geographical biases and ensure that otherwise certifiable rehabilitations which significantly extend the useful life of a certified historic structure qualify for the 25 percent credit.

Another test required for projects to qualify is the "substantially rehabilitated" requirement. This limits the 25 percent credit to those cases in which rehabilitation expenditures in a 24-month period exceed the greater of $5,000 or the adjusted basis of the building. The purpose of this provision is to substitute an objective test for the prior subjective eligibility criteria which required that the rehabilitation materially extend the useful life of the building, significantly enhance its usefulness, improve its condition, or enhance its historic value.

One effect of the substantial rehabilitation test has been to discriminate against buildings whose market value—and, accordingly, purchase price and a new owner's adjusted basis—are quite high. This has created an unintended geographic bias in the application of the 25 percent ITC. Research shows that the 25 percent ITC is used significantly less in cities in which strong real estate markets have kept values of commercial buildings high. In New York City only thirteen applications were submitted for the 25 percent credit in 1982. By comparison, thirty-eight projects were submitted from Albany. The comparative value of these rehabilitations also demonstrates the geographic bias. The average New York City project was $3.26 million, while the Albany average was $183,000. As noted, the national average in 1982 was $441,250.

The substantial rehabilitation test also excludes those investments that may have considerable public benefit in terms of historic preservation but fail the test because of high adjusted bases. The level of investment required to qualify when a developer purchases a highly valued building has no particular relation to the cost of rehabilitation necessary to "significantly extend the useful life of the building." Indeed, in some cases developers may incur unnecessary expenses just to meet the test.

It would be desirable to develop alternative objective tests that would be consistent with the original Congressional intent that the credit be available only for a major renovation effort that adds to the useful life of a historic building. Further analysis of alternative objective tests is necessary to determine the appropriate modification of the current eligibility criteria to improve the targeting of this incentive without expanding eligibility or increasing the cost of the program.

The code should ensure an adequate margin in actual incentives for certified historic rehabilitations as compared to noncertified rehabilitations.

The final area of concern with the current ITC structure is the differential between the 25 percent credit for certified rehabilitation of historic properties and the credits for thirty- and forty-year-old buildings. The incentive value of the rehabilitation credit depends on the rate of credit and the extent to which the developer can take the depreciation deductions on the value of the property subsidized by the credit. A recent change in the requirement that the depreciable basis of a historic building be adjusted by one-half of the 25 percent ITC has reduced the margin between the two categories of credits.

The justification for the higher incentive level for certified historic rehabilitation rests primarily on the fact that a property owner who undertakes renovation of a historic building in a manner that preserves and enhances its significant features will spend more than if the renovation were to disregard those features. The framers of the tax incentive program also recognized that the requirement of a review process for certifying historic significance and proposed work adds costs and an element of uncertainty to the historic rehabilitation project. The survey of users and nonusers confirms this. If the perceived benefits are insufficient to outweigh the anticipated costs, a property owner may choose to forego the certification process and take the lesser but uncontrolled tax credit route.

Elimination of the current requirement that the basis of a certified historic structure be reduced by one-half the value of the credit would increase the depreciation deductions for such properties and increase the margin of the incentive. Because nonhistoric rehabilitations require reduction in basis by the full amount of the credit, this change would enhance the certified historic rehabilitation incentive.

Modification of the credit rates for historic and nonhistoric rehabilitations is another effective way to increase the margin. While the council does not believe that the existing incentive provided by the 25 percent credit level should be raised, adjustment of the 20 percent and 15 percent credits for rehabilitation of forty- and thirty-year-old buildings to improve the differential needs further study. This would discourage the avoidance of the certification process, reinforcing the original intent of Congress that historic buildings receive tax benefits only when the rehabilitation is consistent with their historic character. Augmenting the margin in this manner has the additional advantage of reducing revenue losses. However, this study only evaluated the historic preservation credit and has not assessed the purposes or cost-effectiveness of the other rehabilitation credits. The council notes that the rehabilitation of nonhistoric buildings, which include many that undoubtedly will be found eligible for the National Register with the passage of time, is an important national policy. Adjustments to the relative rates of credit should not have the inadvertent effect of diminishing the attractiveness of rehabilitation in comparison to new construction.

THE DEMOLITION DISINCENTIVE

The effectiveness of the existing tax disincentive for demolishing historic buildings is difficult to establish.

The current demolition disincentive requires the owner of a demolished certified historic structure to add otherwise deductible demolition costs and losses to the capital account for the land upon which the structure stood. The impact of the disincentive on individual decisions to demolish historic buildings appears negligible, quite possibly from a lack of awareness.

The majority of both users and nonusers of the preservation incentives surveyed during the study were unaware of the demolition disincentive, indicating a significant enforcement problem. Of those who were aware, only a small percentage saw the provision as having any impact on redevelopment decisions. Those acknowledging a major role for the demolition disincentive accounted for less than 4 percent of the total survey population. While no figures are available on actual application of the provision, it is apparent that its deterrent effect to date has been minimal.

Interior reports additional concerns over the impact of the disincentive on the national historic preservation program. In 1980, the National Historic Preservation Act was amended to require that owners of properties nominated to the National Register of Historic Places be given the opportunity to object to listing. One factor leading to this provision was the existence of demolition disincentives in the Internal Revenue code. While the disincentives have been scaled back, Interior has nevertheless noted a concern of property owners over these negative aspects of Register listing. This impact on the National Register program needs additional evaluation.

Because of these questions, the council believes that further analysis of the effectiveness of the demolition disincentive is warranted.

DONATION OF PRESERVATION EASEMENTS

Current tax provisions that allow a deduction for the value of preservation easements are effective in encouraging donations of easements to protect historic properties.

Like the rehabilitation incentives, the charitable contribution deduction for gifts of preservation easements has proved effective in meeting the purposes of the incentive.

While comprehensive figures on the number of preservation easements in the United States are not available, a survey of forty of the approximately 175 easement-holding organizations identified by Interior is instructive. Only 14 percent of the easements held were obtained before the 1976 changes to the Internal Revenue code. Indeed, more than half of the holding organizations surveyed did not even begin accepting easements until 1977. Exploring the rationale of donors, nearly equal percentages (45 and 46 percent, respectively) listed either tax savings or desire to preserve the historic aspects of the property as their prime motivation. However, 88 percent reported that tax savings played some role in their decisions, and 55 percent claimed they would not have donated the easements without the existing tax incentives.

Another important effect of this provision, unanticipated at the time of its enactment, has been its use in conjunction with rehabilitation projects using the 25 percent ITC. The study found that 20 percent of all projects using this credit also employed the donation of a preservation easement. The developer receives an increased tax benefit in return for a legally binding commitment to the long-term preservation of the historic building. While this results in greater tax expenditure, the public benefits from the assurance that the structure will not be lost after its next cycle of economically useful life expires. Most properties (51 percent) that used both the 25 percent credit and the easement donation provision were not subject to any other regulation or legal control that would ensure their continued preservation.

Review of this provision reveals no need for legislative action to better carry out the purposes of the National Historic Preservation Act, as improvement of the incentive does not appear warranted.

ESTATE AND GIFT TAXES

Further study is necessary to determine whether the impact of federal estate tax provisions governing valuation of properties and payment requirements on historic properties warrants modification of the code.

The research examined the longstanding concern of the preservation community over the impact of fair market or highest and best use valuation on historic properties passing at death. This concern is based on tax-generated pressures to sell a historic property to realize the market value in order to pay federal estate taxes. A related issue is the requirement to pay estate taxes within nine months of death, which is perceived by some to impose pressure for the sale and possible redevelopment of a historic property.

Offsetting these potential effects are the recent revisions of the estate tax rates and credits to substantially lessen the scope and impact of federal estate taxes. While a model currently exists in treatment of family farms and closely held businesses for alternate valuation based on current use and deferral of estate tax payments, the council believes further assessment of the actual impact of the revised estate tax laws is necessary before action is taken. The contract research found insufficient evidence of these effects to be conclusive. Besides the availability of the family farm and business provisions for qualifying historic properties, the council notes that the charitable deduction for conservation easements may permit the owner of a historic property to limit the highest and best use of the property to a use consistent with the preservation of its historic character. The council believes that further study is desirable for the use of alternate valuations and payment systems when combined with the grant of a perpetual easement.

NEED FOR FURTHER STUDY

While the council's legislative charge for conducting this study was broad, the resources available were quite limited. A careful screening process therefore focused the investigation on issues and areas having the greatest impact on historic preservation. The council recognized certain areas, such as the desirability of tax incentives to encourage the preservation of archaeological resources, as worthy of attention but of a lower priority, which excluded them from consideration in this study. Further investigation of these areas would be valuable.

SUPPLEMENT 2-2.

Rental Rehabilitation: A Practitioner's View
Jerry L. Doctrow

The recently enacted Rental Rehabilitation Program gives local housing officials a great deal of responsibility for designing and implementing the new program. The challenge facing practitioners is to design rental rehabilitation programs that meet local housing needs, satisfy federal accountability guidelines, and make quick use of available funds so managers demonstrate the need for continued and even expanded funding.

To minimize the amount of rental rehabilitation funds needed to induce property owners to undertake rehabilitation, a local government must interest enough landlords in the program to create a competitive environment. By using effective marketing techniques, carefully designing project subsidies, and using streamlined application and selection procedures, local officials can make the program attractive to a broad range of landlords.

MARKETING

Experience in the rental rehabilitation demonstration program indicates that mass mailings, public meetings, and news articles—which typify most local marketing efforts—are ineffective in attracting landlords to a public financing program with limited subsidies. Personal contact with individual landlords is required to explain this type of program adequately and to answer specific questions. However, personal contact is extremely time-consuming. It is therefore essential to identify landlords who are likely to be receptive to the program before beginning solicitation.

A key first step in identifying receptive landlords is to identify areas in which the program should be economically viable. According to federal precepts, a neighborhood in very poor condition will not be able to generate sufficient investor interest to make the rental rehabilitation program work, and a neighborhood with a great deal of investor interest will not be able to provide long-term housing for low- and moderate-income tenants under the program, which prohibits rent controls.

In Baltimore, the agency will rely heavily on planners, program managers (community organizers), the housing authority staff, and housing inspection personnel to identify priority neighborhoods for the program. The agency also will discuss the program with industry groups, neighborhood organizations, and public interest groups.

*From Jerry L. Doctrow, "Rental Rehabilitation: A Practitioner's View," *Journal of Housing*, May/June 1984. Reprinted with permission of the *Journal of Housing*.

Input from these outside sources will be used along with staff recommendations in neighborhood selection and program design. This approach will allow the department to be sensitive to a wide range of issues in selecting target areas and to coordinate the program with other public and private development activities within the city.

After identifying target areas, managers will use information from the Housing Inspection Division of the Baltimore Department of Housing and Community Development to identify landlords who might be good prospects for the program. Three years ago, the city enacted an ordinance requiring owners of rental property to register the properties and to appoint local agents empowered to receive housing violation and other legal notices.

This has cut through the maze of corporate and out-of-town ownership to provide a reliable and accessible record of property ownership. To identify investors who are likely to be receptive to the program, managers can correlate rental registration data indicating the location and extent of a landlord's holdings and with data on vacant units, neighborhood rent levels, property sales activity, housing violation records, and subjective judgments by housing inspection and Section 8 staffs on a landlord's level of sophistication and management ability.

The agency is particularly interested in owners of only a few properties because a recent study indicated that small landlords are the most likely candidates to abandon their properties. To better understand the problems faced by small landlords, officials intend to survey owners of ten or fewer units. This survey will indicate factors that separate successful and unsuccessful landlords, as indicated by their housing code violation records; assess the technical assistance needs of small landlords; and pinpoint those interested in our program.

By studying information available from these sources, the department will identify particular landlords with properties in substandard condition and make some judgments about an individual landlord's financial and managerial abilities before approaching him or her with information on the program. This research will enable the department to begin personal contacts that should generate a great deal of investor interest in the rehabilitation program.

While not all communities may have the benefits of a rental property registration system and an extensive data base, by working with planners, members of the housing authority staff, and members of the local real estate industry, every community can systematically identify a pool of potential rehabilitation program applicants. Experience indicates that market research will be essential to create a competitive environment for local rental rehabilitation programs. This research should be reviewed by local housing officials as the first step in program implementation.

SUBSIDY DESIGN

The Office of Urban Rehabilitation within the Department of Housing and Urban Development encourages use of deferred loans as project subsidies because they are the most cost-effective means of leveraging private dollars for rehabilitation. Deferred loans postpone repayment of any principal and interest due until sale or refinancing of a property. Because no monthly payment is required with a deferred loan, all of the net cash flow available for debt service from a rental project can be used to underwrite private borrowing, creating maximum leverage.

In Baltimore, the agency has used deferred loans on many other different types of rental housing projects. However, for the rental rehabilitation program, a loan that requires payment of a small amount of interest monthly and a balloon payment of principal after ten years or upon sale or refinancing of the property will be used. Here is how this would operate on a hypothetical property:

Assume that a five-unit property with $10,000 of rehabilitation costs per unit has a total rehabilitation budget of $50,000 and a rental rehabilitation subsidy of $25,000. The city would provide this subsidy in the form of a 6 percent interest-only loan, deferring all but 1 percent of the interest ($21 per month). At the end of ten years, or upon sale or refinancing, the original $25,000 in principal and unpaid interest of $12,500 would become due. At that time, the city would have the option to extend the loan, if the property still serves low- and moderate-income families, or to recapture its rental rehabilitation funds for use in other properties.

Because it requires a monthly payment, Baltimore's approach to a rental rehabilitation subsidy reduces the amount of rehabilitation work that can be privately financed below the amount that could be financed using a deferred loan (by about $1,500 to $2,000 in this example). The city accepts this reduced level of private financing because a monthly payment program provides a cost-effective means of monitoring landlord performance.

Baltimore's rental rehabilitation loans will be placed with a private servicing agent. The payment of periodic interest, however small, will ensure continuing contact between the loan servicer and the landlord. Monthly statements will provide a system for distributing questionnaires on tenant incomes and rent levels, and slow payment or nonpayment of interest will indicate a landlord with a problem that warrants the city's attention.

The servicing agent will contact property owners who do not pay their loan interest in a timely manner and will physically inspect properties that become delinquent. A private law firm with specialists in real estate law will be employed to develop loan documents; handle loan accelerations, foreclosures, and other legal actions necessary to obtain loan repayment; or enforce program requirements, such as keeping a property available for rent.

The program requires landlords receiving assistance to keep properties available for rent for ten years, but separates tenant and building subsidies. As a result of the separation of subsidies, a local government will need to establish a monitoring program separate from Section 8 in order to enforce the requirements of the program.

Local officials should consider ways to monitor rental rehabilitation units at the same time they design project subsidies.

SELECTION

Application and selection procedures for a rental rehabilitation program are of critical importance. Slow, cumbersome procedures discourage applications, reduce competition from landlords for program funds, and result in higher administrative costs. Yet ineffective screening can result in poor project selection. This dilemma is inherent in any rehabilitation program. These issues are more complicated, however, in the rental rehabilitation program than in a program aimed at owner-occupied properties.

In Baltimore, the department has developed and adopted a UDAG-like application and project selection process for rental properties. This process enables the department to review rental projects thoroughly and promptly before committing public funds. The selection process begins with a preliminary application from a landlord.

The application is intended to be self-explanatory, and must be submitted before any serious consideration can be given to funding a project. Preliminary applications must be accompanied by a nonrefundable fee and a strict review schedule is observed. All applications received during a given month are reviewed and acted upon within thirty days from the end of each month. The agency reviews applications in groups, which encourages qualitative judgments, rather than "yes" or "no" decisions.

Preliminary applications are reviewed by a panel comprised of a planner, program manager (community organizer), housing inspection supervisor, representative of the housing authority, member of the department's development staff, and financial and construction personnel from its rehabilitation staff. Panel members obtain relevant information on the projects in their areas of specialization for each review session while the rehabilitation services staff prepares and presents a construction and financial feasibility study on each of the proposed projects.

Once a project receives preliminary approval, a great deal of responsibility is placed on the landlord for securing final construction proposals and any private financing or equity funds committed in the preliminary application. When an investor satisfies the conditions of the preliminary commitment, his or her rental project is reviewed once again by the staff and presented to a loan committee for final approval. The loan committee includes representatives from the Department of Housing and Community Development, the Urban Services Agency, the mayor's office, and the city treasurer and budget offices.

The department will not establish formal financing arrangements with a private lending institution for the rental rehabilitation program. Rather, it will provide subsidy commitments directly to the investor, who can shop for financing. If an investor needs assistance in obtaining financing, the department will be able to refer projects on a case-by-case basis to several institutions with which it works on a regular basis.

These application and selection procedures are extremely useful. They allow prompt decisions and save staff time by minimizing the effort spent reviewing infeasible projects. The preliminary review process involves a wide range of actors in the project selection, providing for a thorough review and helping to ensure a good working relationship that will speed project completion. It also allows for development of a pipeline of projects to take advantage of funding opportunities when they appear.

The R. M. Wilson School: From Classrooms to Housing for the Elderly

At the age of forty-three, David Weil already had experience in several businesses, including petroleum distribution, fertilizer manufacturing, broadcasting, and real estate. Although they did not concentrate their real estate interests exclusively in subsidized housing, Weil and his associates, Bill Benton and DeWayne Anderson of the private consulting firm Anderson Benton Holmes (ABH), had successfully developed several low-income housing projects in North Carolina. Preferring the challenge and aesthetic dimensions of rehabilitation to new construction; recognizing the contribution that the conversion of older, underused buildings can make to the revitalization of central business districts; and recognizing the accessibility to needed services that central locations provide to older people, Weil had concentrated his recent real estate activities on converting old hotels into housing for senior citizens. In 1976, together with several associates, he acquired and converted the Goldsboro Hotel in Goldsboro, North Carolina, into eighty-five apartments that were now receiving assistance under HUD's Section 8 rental program. In 1978 he converted and rehabilitated the Sir Walter Hotel in downtown Raleigh, North Carolina, into 140 Section 8 apartments for low- and moderate-income elderly people. And, in 1980, he completed a third conversion and renovation: the Cape Fear Hotel in central Wilmington, North Carolina, now houses elderly people in a ninety-one-unit Section 8 project.

Because of their superior track record, Weil and ABH were retained by the City of Rocky Mount, North Carolina, to assist in the conversion of an abandoned high school into a fifty-unit housing project for the elderly. Negotiations for the sale of the R. M. Wilson School property from the city to the Rocky Mount Housing Authority were well under way when Weil and Benton determined that the tax-exempt interest rates, at which the housing authority could borrow to finance the rehabilitation, were too high to make a straight housing authority–owned Section 8 project feasible. HUD-approved fair market rents for the Rocky Mount area were too low to support the estimated 9 percent, thirty-year borrowing cost. Alternative financing plans were needed that would have to include private participation to raise the necessary capital to make the project work. Although they had not considered the possibility before, Weil and Benton now began viewing the project from the perspective of potential equity investors.

To start the financial restructuring process, Anderson and Benton proposed that the housing authority notify HUD of the change in project plans and request that the fifty-unit Section 8 allocation originally assigned to the

* The author gratefully acknowledges the assistance of David Weil and Bill Benton in the preparation of this article.

housing authority for the R. M. Wilson project be reassigned to Anderson Benton Holmes. The Section 8 subsidies would be reassigned if the housing authority, HUD, and ABH could achieve mutual agreement on a new financing plan. While in all likelihood the Section 8 allocation eventually would be reassigned permanently to an individual investor-owner (or to a limited partnership if the project were to be syndicated), a temporary assignment to ABH would make it possible for the firm to apply for a Federal Housing Administration (FHA) mortgage commitment for the project.

As soon as HUD confirmed the conditional assignment of the subsidy to ABH, Benton applied for FHA mortgage insurance. He knew the project would qualify for a mortgage amount of either the capitalized value of 90 percent of project net operating income or 90 percent of replacement cost, whichever was less. The capitalization rate that FHA would use to determine the mortgage limit was the applicable mortgage constant that would be based on a 7.5 percent, forty-year loan. (Maximum mortgage amount equals lesser of .90 [net operating income] divided by .078972, or 90 percent of replacement cost.) This was the subsidized interest rate available to sponsors of selected Section 8 and other special purpose government-assisted housing projects.

Benton culled the necessary data about operating income and development costs from previously completed market feasibility studies and final building specifications produced by the housing authority's architect. As he ran through the numbers for the first time, it became abundantly clear that the project would not be able to support outright purchase of the school property from the city. With the full cooperation of local officials and the

Table 3-1. Rent and Operating Data for R. M. Wilson Apartments

41 1 br, LR-DR, K, bath	$325/month
9 2 br, LR-DR, K, bath	$375/month
Anticipated occupancy rate	95%
ADMINISTRATIVE COSTS	
Advertising	$18
Other	$79
OPERATING COSTS	
Elevator	$34
Utilities	$647
Garbage removal	$12
Payroll	$100
Lease payments to housing authority	.24
MAINTENANCE COSTS	
Maintenance and repairs	$354
Exterminating	$6
Insurance	$30
Real estate taxes	$179

* All operating costs represent dollars per unit per year.

housing authority, a deal was struck under which the R. M. Wilson School would be conveyed by the city to the housing authority, which would, in turn, lease it to the private entity that would sponsor the housing project. The net lease would be for seventy-five years at a rental of a dollar a month.

Each of the forty-one one-bedroom units would rent for $325 a month, including utilities, while each of the nine two-bedroom units would have a gross rent of $375 a month (table 3-1). All apartments would include kitchenettes with refrigerators, electric ovens, and ranges, full baths, carpeting in all living areas and bedrooms, drapes, and an emergency call system. The project would be air conditioned and would have two passenger elevators. Development costs were based on rehabilitation costs of $23.87 per square foot for nearly 51,000 square feet of gross floor area (table 3-2).

To estimate the maximum mortgage amount based on net operating income, Benton first completed Section E of FHA form 2013 (table 3-3; supplement 3-1). He computed the maximum mortgage limitation, using a mortgage constant for a 7.5 percent, forty-year loan. Then he proceeded to work down the development cost side of form 2013 (Section G), using data from table 3-2 and FHA fee schedules noted on form 2013 (lines 56, 57, and 58). Before proceeding very far, Benton learned that a mortgage based on 90 percent of replacement cost would greatly exceed one based on 90 percent of capitalized net operating income. He therefore revised downward the carrying charges and financing section of form 2013 to reflect the lower fees associated with the smaller mortgage.

The developer of the R. M. Wilson project would be entitled to a Builder Sponsor Profit Risk Allowance (BSPRA) equal to 10 percent of total development cost (line 68, table 3-3), which directly reduces required equity contributions. But because the permanent loan would be for less than 90 percent of replacement cost and the GNMA discount on the permanent loan

Table 3-2. Estimated Development Costs, R. M. Wilson Apartments

Gross floor area	50,931 square feet
Rehabilitation costs	$23.87 per square foot
General requirements	3.7% of rehabilitation costs
Architect's fees: design and supervision	4.8% of rehabilitation costs
Builder's overhead	2% of rehabilitation costs
Construction interest	13% over 13-month construction period
Bond premium	$16,000
Construction loan financing fee	2% of construction loan
GNMA commitment fee for permanent loan	2% of permanent mortgage loan
Insurance during construction	$1,500
Real estate taxes during construction	$258
Legal/organizational/title and recording fees	$8,500
GNMA discount upon purchase of permanent loan (nonmortgageable)	2.25% of permanent mortgage
75-year ground lease for land and building (one-time payment to City of Rocky Mount)	$10,000

Note: Builder's profit is included in BSPRA (line 68 of Form 2013).

Table 3-3. FHA Form 2013

E. ESTIMATE OF ANNUAL EXPENSE:

ADMINISTRATIVE—
- 1. Advertising .... $
- 2. Management ....
- 3. Other ....
- 4. TOTAL ADMINISTRATIVE .... $

OPERATING—
- 5. Elevator Main. Exp. .... $
- 6. Fuel (Heating and Domestic Hot Water) ....
- 7. Lighting & Misc. Power ....
- 8. Water ....
- 9. Gas ....
- 10. Garb. & Trash Removal ....
- 11. Payroll ....
- 12. Other ....
- 13. TOTAL OPERATING .... $

MAINTENANCE—
- 14. Decorating .... $
- 15. Repairs ....
- 16. Exterminating ....
- 17. Insurance ....
- 18. Ground Expense ....
- 19. Other ....
- 20. TOTAL MAINTENANCE .... $
- 21. Replacement Reserve (.0060 × total for structures Line 41) ....
- 22. TOTAL EXPENSE .... $

TAXES—
- 23. Real Estate: Est. Assessed Val. $ @ $ per $1000—
- 24. Personal Prop. Est. Assessed Val. $ @ $ per $1000—
- 25. Empl. Payroll Tax ....
- 26. Empl. Social Security ....
- 27. Other ....
- 28. TOTAL TAXES .... $
- 29. TOTAL EXPENSE & TAXES .... $

G. ESTIMATED REPLACEMENT COST:

- 36a. Unusual Land Improvements . $
- 36b. Other Land Improvements ...
- 36c. Total Land Improvements .... $

STRUCTURES—
- 37. Main Buildings .... $
- 38. Accessory Buildings ....
- 39. Garage ....
- 40. All other Buildings ....
- 41. TOTAL STRUCTURES .... $
- 42. General Requirements .... $

FEES—
- 43. Builder's Gen. Overhead @ % .... $
- 44. Builder's Profit @ %
- 45. Arch. Fee—Design @ %
- 46. Arch. Fee—Supvr. @ %
- 47. Bond Premium
- 48. Other Fees
- 49. TOTAL FEES .... $
- 50. TOT. for all Imprmts. (Lines 36c, 41, 42, & 49) .... $
- 51. Cost Per Gross Sq. Ft.
- 52. Estimated Construction Time .... Months

CARRYING CHARGES & FINANCING—
- 53. Int. Mos. @ % on $ .... $
- 54. Taxes
- 55. Insurance
- 56. FHA Mtg. Ins. Pre. (0.5%)
- 57. FHA Exam. Fee (0.3%)
- 58. FHA Inspec. Fee (0.5%)
- 59. Financing Fee (%)
- 60. AMPO (%)
- 61. FNMA Fee (%)
- 62. Title & Recording
- 63. TOTAL CARRYING CHGS. & FINANCING .... $

LEGAL AND ORGANIZATION—
- 64. Legal .... $

F. INCOME COMPUTATIONS:

30. Estimated Project Gross Income .... $ _____
31. Occupancy (Entire Project) Percentage .... _____ %
32. Effective Gross Income (Line 30 × 31) .... $ _____
33. Total Project Expenses (Line 29) .... $ _____
34. Net Income to Project (Line 32 – Line 33) .... $ _____
35. Expense Ratio (Line 29 ÷ Line 32) .... _____ %

•65. Organization .... $ _____
66. TOTAL LEGAL AND ORGANIZATION .... $ _____
•67. Consultant Fee .... $ _____
68. Builder and Sponsor Profit & Risk .... $ _____
69. TOTAL EST. DEVELOPMENT COST (*Excl. of Land or Off-site Cost*) (*Line 50 + 63 + 66 + 67 + 68*) .... $ _____
70. LAND (Est. Market Price of Site) _____ sq. ft. @ $ _____ per sq. ft. .... $ _____
71. TOTAL ESTIMATED **REPLACEMENT COST OF PROJECT** (*Add 69 + 70*) .... $ _____

H. TOTAL REQUIREMENTS FOR SETTLEMENT:

Source of Cash to meet Requirements:	Amount
	$
	$
	$
	$
	$
	$
TOTAL	$

72. DEVELOPMENT COSTS (Line 69) .... $ _____
73. LAND INDEBTEDNESS (or Cash required for land acquisition) .... $ _____
74. SUBTOTAL (Line 72 + 73) .... $ _____
75. Mortgage Amount .... $ _____
76. Fees Paid by Other Than Cash .... $ _____
77. Line 75 + Line 76 .... $ _____
78. CASH INVESTMENT REQUIRED (Line 74 – 77) .... $ _____
79. INITIAL OPERATING DEFICIT .... $ _____
80. ANTICIPATED DISCOUNT .... $ _____
81. Working Cap. (2% of Mtge. Amount) .... $ _____
82. ADD Off-site Construction Costs .... $ _____
83. TOTAL ESTIMATED CASH REQUIREMENT (Lines 78 + 79 + 80 + 81 + 82) .... $ _____

I. ATTACHMENTS: (Required Exhibits)

1.	Location Map
2.	Evidence of Site Control (Option or Purchase) and Legal Description of Property
3.	Form 2010 Equal Employment Opportunity Certification
4.	Form 3433 Eligibility as Non-Profit Corporation
5.	Evidence of Last Arms-Length Transaction Price
6.	Sketch Plan of Site
7.	Personal Financial & Credit Statement of Sponsors
8.	Form 2530 Previous Participation Certification
9.•	Architectural Exhibits—Preliminary
10.•	Architectural Exhibits—Final
11.•	Survey
12.•	Evidence of Architect E & O Insurance Coverage
13.•	Copy of Owner-Architect Agreement

and the working capital requirements would not be mortgageable (table 3-2, section H), Benton determined that a substantial equity investment would still be necessary to make the project work. Weil and ABH now had to determine the best way of raising the equity. Should the project be developed as a joint private owner/housing authority–managed project, with Weil and ABH as co-investors, or should it be syndicated through a limited partnership, with the two of them serving as general partners?

One major factor tipped the scale in favor of syndication. The project required an equity investment exceeding $300,000, which was quite large for a relatively small apartment development. Although Weil and Benton could come up with the necessary cash, the available tax shelter from the project, especially in the early years, would be greater than they could use profitably. That was because the portion of total project costs that could be allocated to substantial rehabilitation on a low-income housing project could be depreciated over a sixty-month period on a straight-line rate (pursuant to Section 167(k) of the Internal Revenue Code).

Once they had settled on the syndication option, Weil and Benton had to select a syndicator to work with. They had to choose carefully because they knew that, in many respects, the syndicator is at least as important as the developer in enabling a project to achieve its maximum potential. The syndicator's job has two components: structuring the deal, including pricing and selling limited partnership interests in a project; and representing the interests of equity investors throughout the life of the limited partnership. Structuring involves "negotiating a good investment with fair allocations of benefits, risks and protections. The structuring function is completed before the investor is ever admitted, and the investor has a chance to review the syndicator's work before he commits his equity."[1] Investor representation involves "following the investment throughout its life, turning the projections and documents into reality, and working to make the investment as good as it can be. The investor representative role begins when the investors are admitted as limited partners and continues until the property is sold and its final tax return filed (Smith, p. 83). After much consideration, Weil and ABH selected as their syndicator Interstate Securities Corporation (ISC), a firm based in Charlotte, North Carolina.

Like most small assisted housing projects, R. M. Wilson Apartments would be syndicated through private placement. This meant R. M. Wilson Associates, the limited partnership that would own the project, would not have to be registered with the Securities and Exchange Commission as long as it followed several rules:

· no public advertising or active solicitation of buyers is made
· the number of total offerees and total purchasers is small (the current federal standard is thirty-five purchasers who buy less than $150,000 each)

---

1. David A. Smith, *Subsidized Housing As a Tax Shelter* (Fair Haven, NJ: Robert A. Stanger and Co., 1983), p. 83.

- All investors can be shown to be rich and smart. Wealth is measured in comparison with the size of the investment contemplated. Knowledge is measured either by the investor's prior experience with investments of the type offered or by reliance on competent advisers who have prior experience
- The prospectus contains all the information investors need to make an informed decision, especially including a discussion of all the risks
- The offering conforms with various procedures designed to prevent tampering with an investor before he has all the facts
- State securities laws are also complied with (Smith, pp. 37–38)

Pricing limited partnership interests is a complicated process. The price an investor will pay for a limited partnership interest will vary with the size of the project and the share of operating profits and losses, cash distributions, and residual value to which ownership entitles him. Price also will vary with the size and timing of tax-shelter benefits, the property's income-earning potential, and opportunities for capital appreciation at the end of the subsidy period. Moreover, the pay-in schedule can affect the price and marketability of limited partnership units. If the full price of the unit can be paid in several installments that are due at one-year to eighteen-month intervals, that will lessen the investor's immediate cash burden. More important, it also will permit him to make most of his installments with tax-sheltered dollars that, in the absence of his partnership interest, would be paid to the federal government in taxes. The investor frequently will pay a premium for this added benefit.

Before evaluating the potential tax shelter and other benefits from the project, Weil and Benton capitalized the partnership with an initial cash contribution of $1,500 and, with ISC, determined that the partnership would allocate 99 percent of all net profits, losses, and cash flow from operations to the limited partners and the remaining 1 percent to the general partner. Upon sale of the leasehold interest, or a refinancing of partnership assets, net profit would be allocated 50 percent to the limited partners and 50 percent to the general partners and net losses would be allocated in proportion to capital contributions. Also, ISC determined that the partnership would be divided into thirty limited partnership units, each unit having a 3.3 percent share of aggregate limited partner benefits. Having made these two key decisions, ISC now had to estimate the amount of equity that would have to be raised from the sale of project benefits to make R. M. Wilson Apartments a reality.

The first step in this process required the development of a sources and uses of funds statement, detailing the amount of money required to meet all development, financing, and syndication costs and the sources from which the funds would be raised (see table 3-4 for blank form).[2] Data for this

---

2. For purposes of clarifying the nature of the syndication process, the steps involved in structuring a deal are described here in different order than they actually occur in practice. Rather than beginning with the

Table 3-4. Estimated Sources and Uses of Project Funds, R. M. Wilson Associates

Sources of funds

Gross proceeds from sale of limited partnership units $_____

Less: Organization fees and syndication costs

Organization fees payable to general partners   _____
Legal and accounting fees payable to general partners   _____
Sales and management fee payable to Interstate Securities Corporation   _____
Promotion fee payable to general partners   _____
Legal, accounting, and other expenses of syndication   _____

Total organization fees and $_____
   syndication costs   _____

Equals: Net proceeds from sale of partnership units $_____
Net proceeds from sale of limited partnership units (above) $_____

Plus: General partners capital contribution $_____
First mortgage loan   _____

Equals: Total funds available $_____

Use of funds

Total for all improvements (line 50, FHA 2013) $_____
Construction management/overrun fee payable to general partners
   (table 3-5)   _____
Lease acquisition fee payable to City of Rocky Mount (table 3-2)   _____
Leasehold fee payable to general partners (table 3-5)   _____
   Subtotal (I) $_____

Permanent Loan Costs
GNMA discount on permanent loan (table 3-2)   _____
FHA mortgage insurance premium, examination and inspection fees
   (lines 56–58, FHA 2013)   _____
FNMA/GNMA committee fee (line 61, FHA 2013)   _____
Financing fee payable to general partners (table 3-5)   _____
Legal/organizational, title and recording (lines 62, 64, 65, FHA 2013)   _____
   Subtotal (II) $_____

Expenses to be deducted currently as incurred:
Taxes and insurance during rehabilitation (lines 54, 55, FHA 2013)   _____
Rehabilitation loan interest (line 53, FHA 2013)   _____
Interest on bridge loan (table 3-5)   _____
   Subtotal (III) $_____

Working Capital (line 81, FHA 2013) $_____

Total Use of Funds (Sum of I, II, III, IV) $_____

**Table 3-5. Syndication Costs and Fees Payable to the
General Partners, R. M. Wilson Associates**

Organization fee payable to general partners	$30,000
Legal and accounting fees payable to general partners for organizing partnership	16,500
Sales and management fees payable to Interstate Securities Corporation (ISC)	70,000
Legal, accounting, and other expenses associated with syndication	9,500
Promotion fee payable to general partners	5,800
Financing fee payable to general partners	12,090
Construction management–cost overrun fee payable to general partners	116,000
Leasehold fee payable to general partners	7,500
Interest on short-term (bridge) loans to partnership	40,600
Total fees paid to general partners	$307,990

statement were derived from the FHA form 2013, which itemizes development and mortgage-related financing requirements; from table 3-5, which lists payments to the general partners and other syndication costs; and from supplement 3-2, which presents additional details on the syndication. In lieu of a 10 percent Builder Sponsor Profit and Risk Allowance (BSPRA) that FHA allows as a mortgageable item, the sources and uses fund statement contained several fees payable to the general partners (Weil and Benton) that substituted for and, depending on how well the construction process would go, might exceed the value of a BSPRA by a substantial amount. Certain fees payable to the general partners were direct reimbursements for out-of-pocket expenses, such as legal and accounting fees, and some were for services rendered to the partnership, such as the financing fee for arranging the permanent mortgage loan. The largest fee, for managing the construction process, if it did not have to be spent in its entirety, would be an important determinant of how profitable the project would be for the general partners. In order to increase the marketability of the limited partnership units, however, ISC obtained the general partners' agreement to commit all of the funds that might be necessary to meet construction cost overruns and other contingencies during the construction period up to the full amount of their construction management fee. How much of the $116,000 fee Weil and Benton ultimately would be able to retain would depend largely on how well they managed the development process.

Table 3-5 also contains a list of syndication costs that are entered on the sources and uses of funds statement. These costs are of two kinds: legal and

development of sources and uses of funds statement and proceeding to a pro forma analysis of project operations, generally, the syndicator will begin structuring a deal by estimating the tax shelter potential of a project. This enables him to approximate the gross profit margin available to the general partners in the form of various fees and payments for services rendered to the limited partnership that will own the project. Since it is not possible for the uninitiated student to work backwards from a pro forma analysis of the tax shelter potential of the R. M. Wilson apartments to a full specification of general partner fees, I have reversed the order of presentation. In this case, the syndication process begins with completion of the sources and use of funds statement and analysis of the tax aspects of the project to confirm the project's syndication viability.

**Table 3-6. Preliminary Pricing of Limited Partnership
Interests, R. M. Wilson Associates**

Total funds available (from table 3-4)	$_____
Less proceeds from first mortgage loan (table 3-4)	_____
Less capital contributed by general partners (table 3-4)	_____
Plus sum of organization fees and syndication costs (table 3-4)	_____
Equals gross syndication proceeds	_____
Divided by 30 equals price of one limited partnership unit	$_____

accounting, and sales commissions and management fees for marketing and selling the limited partnership units; and estimated interest costs on short-term loans the partnership would have to take out to compensate for the fact that the limited partners will contribute their equity over time. The size of the bridge loan would be roughly equal to the difference between total fund requirements, the general partners' initial capital contribution, the sum of the first mortgage loan, and the aggregate amount of the limited partners' payments on their first equity installment. The $40,600 estimated interest cost in table 3-5 reflects an expected interest rate of 14 percent on a short-term loan of about $217,500.

Since the gross proceeds from the sale of limited partnership units would have to cover the difference between total funds requirements and the sum of the general partners' capital contribution and proceeds from the first mortgage loan, ISC now knew for how much each of the thirty limited partnership units would have to be sold to raise the required equity (table 3-6).[3]

Now that aggregate gross syndication requirements and the price of individual partnership units had been determined, it was necessary to run some pro forma operating analyses to determine whether the tax-shelter benefits and anticipated cash distributions to the limited partners would be sufficiently attractive to encourage private investors to commit the required funds. The ten-year projections of income and cash flow from operations showed negative taxable incomes during the construction period and the first five years of project operations (complete tables 3-7, 3-8, and 3-9 while consulting supplement 3-2 for details) and positive taxable incomes thereafter. This desirable earnings pattern resulted from the very large depreciation deductions that would be available to the partnership during its first five years in service under the sixty-month low-income rehabilitation provisions of the federal tax code. Positive taxable income in the later years resulted from the fact that there was no remaining depreciation allowance to deduct against net rental income after 1985. Cash flow from operations was modest throughout the ten-year holding period.

3. Although it is difficult to generalize, an operable rule of thumb in the syndication industry is that a good low-income substantial rehabilitation project should command $1 of equity for every $2–$2.20 of negative taxable income it provides to an investor in the 50-percent bracket. The more desirable the project and the better the developer's and syndicator's track record, the lower the ratio of tax losses to equity dollars and the higher the price a limited partnership unit will command.

Table 3-7. Cost Amortization Schedule, R. M. Wilson Associates

	Total	1980	1981	1982	1983	1984	1985	1986	1987	1988	1989	1990
Rehabilitation loan interest and taxes during construction												
Rehabilitation loan financing fees (Note J)												
Permanent loan fees (Note J)												
Organization expenses (Notes F and K)												
Lease acquisition fees (Note O)											$	$
Total amortized costs	$	$	$	$	$	$	$	$	$	$	$	$

Note: Consult supplement 3-2 before completing this statement.

Table 3-8. Statement of Before-Tax Cash Flow from Operations, R. M. Wilson Associates

	1980	1981	1982	1983	1984	1985	1986	1987	1988	1989	1990
Gross income (Note C)											
Less: Vacancy factor (Note D)											
Equals: Effective rental income											
Less: Apartment management fees (Note P)											
Operating expenses (Note E)											
Equals: Net operating income											
Less: Debt service											
Rehabilitation loan interest and taxes during construction											
Rehabilitation loan financing fees											
Permanent loan fees											
Organization expenses											
Lease acquisition fees											
Equals: Before-tax cash flow											
Less: Partnership management (Note F)											
Equals: Before-tax cash flow available for distribution to partnership											

Table 3-9. Statement of Income or (Loss), R. M. Wilson Associates

	1980	1981	1982	1983	1984	1985	1986	1987	1988	1989	1990
Net operating income	——	——	——	——	——	——	——	——	——	——	——
Less: Interest expenses on permanent loan	——	——	——	——	——	——	——	——	——	——	——
Depreciation of rehabilitation costs (Note M)	——	——	——	——	——	——	——	——	——	——	——
Amortization of capitalized costs (table 3-7)	——	——	——	——	——	——	——	——	——	——	——
Equals: Taxable income	$——	$——	$——	$——	$——	$——	$——	$——	$——	$——	$——
Multiplied by: Limited partner's marginal tax rate	——	——	——	——	——	——	——	——	——	——	——
Equals: Tax liability or (savings)	——	——	——	——	——	——	——	——	——	——	——
Plus: Before-tax cash flow available for distribution	——	——	——	——	——	——	——	——	——	——	——
Equals: After-tax cash flow	——	——	——	——	——	——	——	——	——	——	——
Distribution											
General partners (1%)	——	——	——	——	——	——	——	——	——	——	——
Limited partners (99%)	——	——	——	——	——	——	——	——	——	——	——
Per limited partner	——	——	——	——	——	——	——	——	——	——	——

Table 3-10. Projection of Return on Investment for One Limited Partnership Unit, R. M. Wilson Associates

Tax bracket: 46%
Distribution:
  Cash flow: 99%
  Profits (losses): 99%
Percentage ownership per unit: 3.3%

	Investor Contribution	Annual After-Tax Cash Flow (from table 3-9)	Cumulative Benefit
1980	_____	_____	_____
1981	_____	_____	_____
1982	_____	_____	_____
1983	_____	_____	_____
1984	_____	_____	_____
1985	_____	_____	_____
1986	_____	_____	_____
1987	_____	_____	_____
1988	_____	_____	_____
1989	_____	_____	_____
1990	_____	_____	_____

The 11-year, after-tax internal rate of return on investment is
_____.

Note: The internal rate of return on investment is the computed annual discount rate at
   which the present value of the stream of total annual benefits is equal to the present value
   of the stream of total equity contributions.

A way to test the potential market appeal of this syndication is to run a ten-year rate of return analysis for a single limited partnership unit (using as a guide the blank form in table 3-10). Before doing so, however, it is necessary to derive the pro rata tax losses or gains and cash distributions from the project that would accrue to a single limited partnership unit. (These can be derived from table 3-9.) As part of the analysis, it is also necessary to decide the amount and timing of the three installment payments the investor must make (which will amount to the full price of a partnership unit, as calculated in table 3-6).[4]

Once that is done, one can derive an annual rate of return to the limited partner assuming no sale or refinancing of the project over the ten-year period of operations. If the estimated yields are competitive, ISC can proceed to complete the necessary paperwork to bring R. M. Wilson Associates to life. If, however, the estimated investment returns to the limited partners are much lower than anticipated, the syndication might not be viable and the project might have to be reconsidered, repackaged, or abandoned.

4. The difference between gross syndication proceeds and the bridge loan taken out by the partnership is equal to the aggregate first year's payment by the thirty limited partners. Subsequent limited partners' installments must pay off the bridge loan.

SUPPLEMENT 3-1.

Preparing FHA Form 2013: Computing the Maximum Allowable Mortgage

The attached FHA form 2013 has been filled out for an actual FHA-insured multifamily housing project. The computations begin with an approximation of the total cost of structures and land improvements and proceed down the form by adding appropriate fees, financing charges, and other costs.

COMPLETING FHA FORM 2013, BEGINNING WITH ESTIMATES OF TOTAL STRUCTURES AND LAND IMPROVEMENT COSTS (LINE 41)

1. Start with total structure and land improvements (line 41):

    $2,645,306   (line 41)
    +   79,359   General Requirements 3% (line 42)

2. Next, compute fees, based on sum of lines 41 and 42:

Builder's overhead 2%	$54,493 (line 43)
Architect's design fee 3%	81,740 (line 45)
Architect's supervision fee 1%	27,247 (line 46)
Bond premium	18,000 (line 47)
Other fees	0 (line 48)
	$181,480 (line 49)

3. Total for all improvements = sum of lines 41, 42, and 49:

    $2,645,306 + 79,359 + 181,480 = $2,906,145 (line 50)

4. Compute carrying charges and financing fees:

Knowns		Unknowns (Compute in percentages)			
Taxes	$8,000 (line 54)	Interest	5.25%	$\frac{(.07 \times 1.5)}{2}$	line 53
Insurance	$12,000 (line 55)				
Title/Rec.	$12,000 (line 62)	MIP	.50		(line 56)
Legal/Org.	$19,500 (lines 64, 65)	Ex. Fee	.30		(line 57)
Total	$51,500	Insp. Fee	.50		(line 58)
		Fin. Fee	2.00		(line 59)
		FNMA/GNMA	1.75		(line 61)
		Sum	10.30%		

5. Adjust unknowns for BSPRA:*

$$10.30 \times .99 = 10.197$$
$$100 - 10.197 = \underline{89.803}$$

6. Next, add up the following:

Total for all improvements (line 50)	$2,906,145
Sum of known charges	51,500
Subtotal	$2,957,645

7. Adjust subtotal for BSPRA:

$$\$2,957,645 \times 1.1 = \$3,253,410$$
$$\text{Add land} \quad \underline{224,000}$$
$$\text{Subtotal} \quad \$3,477,410$$

8. Finally, blow up cost to take account of unknown carrying charges:

$$\frac{\$3,477,410}{.89803} = \$3,872,265$$

Estimated replacement cost = $3,872,265

Mortgage @ 90% of replacement cost = $3,485,039

9. Now, go back and fill in unknowns:

Interest (.525)	$182,964
MIP (.5)	17,425
Exam Fee (.3)	10,455
Inspection Fee (.5)	17,425
Financing Fee (2)	69,700
GNMA Fee (1.75)	60,988

$$\text{BSPRA} = \frac{\$3,872,265 - \$224,000}{11} = \$331,660$$

ALGEBRA FOR ILLUSTRATING THAT BSPRA EQUALS REPLACEMENT COST LESS LAND DIVIDED BY 11

$$H = \text{Hard Costs}$$
$$L = \text{Land Cost}$$

---

* Builder Sponsor Profit Risk Allowance (BSPRA) represents developer's fee for packaging and building the project. The amount of the BSPRA is 10 percent of all hard costs, excluding land, and can be computed as Replacement Cost less land, divided by 11. When BSPRA is charged, there can be no builder profit entered on line 44.

$$H + L + BSPRA = \text{Replacement Cost}$$
$$H + BSPRA = \text{Replacement Cost} - L$$
$$BSPRA = .1H$$
$$H + .1H = \text{Replacement Cost} - L$$
$$1.1H = \text{Replacement Cost} - L$$

$$H = \frac{\text{Replacement Cost} - L}{1.1}$$

$$BSPRA = (.1)\frac{(\text{Replacement Cost} - L)}{1.1}$$

$$BSPRA = \frac{\text{Replacement Cost} - L}{11}$$

SUPPLEMENT 3-2.

R. M. Wilson Associates: Notes to Financial Projections and Assumptions

A. General

The partnership was organized as a North Carolina Limited Partnership. The partnership has agreed with the Housing Authority of the City of Rocky Mount, North Carolina, to lease the real property formerly known as the R. M. Wilson School for a term of seventy-five (75) years at a monthly rental of one dollar. The real property is to be rehabilitated and converted to fifty low- and moderate-income apartments.

The accompanying projections are prepared on the basis that the proposed offering will be completed by October 1, 1980. For accounting and income-tax purposes, the projected loss for 1980 will be allocated to limited partners from the date they become partners. Accordingly, if the offering is completed after October 1, 1980, the loss allocated to the limited partners will be reduced.

B. Accounting Method

The accrual method of accounting will be used for accounting and income-tax reporting purposes.

C. Gross Income

Rental income from apartments is projected for four months in 1981 at the initial rental rates approved by the Federal Housing Administration (table 3-1). The rents include the amount of the subsidy to be received under the Section 8 program.

The Section 8 program provides for automatic annual cost increases and in certain cases HUD may approve additional requested rent increases. For purposes of the pro forma analysis and projections, assume that rents will increase at the rate of 5.5 percent per year. If HUD-approved rent increases average less than 5.5 percent per annum, cash flow available for distribution to the partners may be less than shown in the accompanying projections.

D. Vacancy Allowance

For purposes of the accompanying projections, the general partners have projected a vacancy allowance of 5 percent of gross income.

E. Operating Expenses

Projected operating expenses for the first full year of operations (1982) are set forth in table 3-1. For purposes of the projections, assume that operating expenses will increase at the rate of 4 percent per year beginning in 1983. Operating expenses for 1981, when the project will be only partially occupied, should be estimated at 40 percent of the amount shown in table 3-1.

Cash flow available for distribution to the partners may be increased or decreased from that shown in the projections for years beginning in 1983 if operating expenses, including the assumed inflationary factor, are different from that projected. However, see Note C as to possible HUD approval of rent increases. Also, as explained in Note F, the partnership management fee is contingent upon adequate net cash flow.

F. General Partners' Fees

The general partners will receive a fee of 6 percent of effective gross income for management of the partnership. This partnership management fee is contingent upon net cash flow available for payment in each calendar year. The amounts for this fee may be more or less than shown in the projections if actual gross income is more or less than the projected amounts. The fee may also be decreased by a deficiency in net cash flow available for payment in any calendar year.

The following fees will be paid to the general partners from proceeds of the offering or projected short-term borrowing:

Partnership organization fee (Note K)	$30,000
Promotion fee for promotion of the sale of limited partner units (Note L)	5,800
Financing fee in connection with first mortgage commitment (Note J)	12,090
Construction management–overrun fee (Note M)	116,000
Leasehold fee	7,500
Total	$171,390

The construction management–overrun fee is being paid to the general partners for their agreement to pay (up to the total amount of the fee) any amount by which construction period costs in the aggregate exceed the projected construction period costs as set forth in the estimated sources and uses of project funds (table 3-4). In addition, the general partners have agreed to fund from this fee any costs disallowed for funding by HUD/FHA which result in the first mortgage loan being less than that reflected in form FHA 2013, to the extent such loan deficiency is not offset by savings in construction period costs.

G. First Mortgage Loan

The partnership has obtained a loan commitment from Highland Mortgage Company of Raleigh, North Carolina, in the amount of the lesser of 90 percent of replacement cost or the capitalized value of 90 percent of net operating income (where the capitalization rate is the applicable mortgage constant). The commitment is for construction, interest, and fees as approved by HUD/FHA. In connection with making the loan, Highland Mortgage Company has obtained a commitment from the Government National Mortgage Association (GNMA) to purchase the loan upon financial certification and endorsement by HUD/FHA.

The loan bears an interest rate of 13 percent until final endorsement by HUD/FHA and 7½ percent thereafter. Monthly installments are payable beginning on or about September 1981, to amortize the loan over forty (40) years at 7½ percent interest. The partnership will pay a 2-point financing fee to Highland Mortgage Company for the construction loan and has paid a 2-point GNMA commitment fee. A 2¼ point discount will be paid by the partnership upon purchase of the loan by GNMA. A fee of $12,090 is payable to the general partners upon final endorsement by FHA for their services in connection with obtaining the financing.

The loan will be insured by HUD/FHA and will be secured by a first mortgage deed of trust on the partnership's leasehold estate in the land, building, improvements, furnishings, fixtures, and an assignment of rents, profits, and income. The loan is without recourse to the partnership.

H. Short- and Intermediate-Term Bridge Loans

Based upon the projected sources and uses of funds, as shown in table 3-4, the partnership must borrow money on an interim basis during 1981 and 1982 to complete the project and pay necessary fees and interest. The general partners have agreed to arrange and guarantee all interim loans. It is intended that the interim loans will be repaid from capital contributions received in 1983 from the limited partners.

The general partners have not obtained firm commitments for the interim loans, but, based upon past experience and the financial resources of the general partners, the general partners are of the opinion that such loans will be available. The financial projections include interest payable on the projected bridge loans at an estimated 14 percent per annum. Therefore, the pro forma statement should reflect this interest cost allocated over the period 1980–1982.

I. FHA Replacement Reserves and Future Capital Replacements

The agreement with HUD/FHA requires monthly deposits placed in an escrow account to be used for approved replacements of property and equipment. For purposes of the accompanying projections, it is assumed that the annual required deposits are left in the escrow account to accumulate interest for ten years and that at the end of each ten-year period the entire balance is used for replacements.

The amount spent for replacements each ten years is depreciated over a ten-year life using the double declining balance method.

J. Loan Fees and Costs

All loan fees and costs are deferred in the accompanying projections and capitalized as rehabilitation costs or over the loan amortization period. These fees and costs are summarized as follows:

1. Amortized as Rehabilitation Costs (Note N)
Financing fee paid to Highland Mortgage Company (line 59, FHA form 2013)
FHA mortgage insurance premium (line 56, FHA form 2013)
GNMA commitment fee (line 61, FHA form 3013)
2. Amortized over Loan Amortization Period (40 years)
Discount (points) to be paid upon purchase of loan by GNMA (line 80, FHA form 2013)

E. ESTIMATE OF ANNUAL EXPENSE:

ADMINISTRATIVE—
- 1. Advertising .... $ _____
- 2. Management ....
- 3. Other ....
- 4.   TOTAL ADMINISTRATIVE .... $ 30,000

OPERATING—
- 5. Elevator Main. Exp. .... $ _____
- 6. Fuel (Heating and Domestic Hot Water) ....
- 7. Lighting & Misc. Power ....
- 8. Water ....
- 9. Gas ....
- 10. Garb. & Trash Removal ....
- 11. Payroll ....
- 12. Other ....
- 13.   TOTAL OPERATING .... $ 96,000

MAINTENANCE—
- 14. Decorating .... $ _____
- 15. Repairs ....
- 16. Exterminating ....
- 17. Insurance ....
- 18. Ground Expense ....
- 19. Other ....
- 20.   TOTAL MAINTENANCE .... $ 219,919
- 21. Replacement Reserve (.0060 × total for structures Line 41)
- 22.   TOTAL EXPENSE .... $ 345,919

TAXES—
- 23. Real Estate: Est. Assessed Val. $ _____ @ $ _____ per $1000—
- 24. Personal Prop. Est. Assessed Val. $ _____ @ _____ per $1000—
- 25. Empl. Payroll Tax ....
- 26. Empl. Social Security ....
- 27. Other ....
- 28.   TOTAL TAXES .... $ 38,500
- 29. TOTAL EXPENSE & TAXES .... $ 384,419

G. ESTIMATED REPLACEMENT COST:

- 36a. Unusual Land Improvements .. $ _____
- 36b. Other Land Improvements .... $ _____
- 36c. Total Land Improvements .... $ _____

STRUCTURES—
- 37. Main Buildings .... $ _____
- 38. Accessory Buildings ....
- 39. Garage ....
- 40. All other Buildings ....
- 41.   TOTAL STRUCTURES .... $ 2,645,306
- 42. General Requirements .... $ 79,359

FEES—
- 43. Builder's Gen. Overhead @ 2 % .... $ 54,483
- 44. Builder's Profit @ __ %
- 45. Arch. Fee—Design @ 3 % 81,740
- 46. Arch. Fee—Supvr. @ 1 % 27,247
- 47. Bond Premium 18,000
- 48. Other Fees ....
- 49.   TOTAL FEES .... $ 181,480
- 50. TOT. for all Imprmts. (Lines 36c, 41, 42, & 49) .... $ 2,906,145
- 51. Cost Per Gross Sq. Ft.
- 52. Estimated Construction Time .... 18 Months

CARRYING CHARGES & FINANCING—
- 53. Int. 18 Mos. @ 7 % on $ 102,962 .... $ 162,962
- 54. Taxes 8,000
- 55. Insurance 12,000
- 56. FHA Mtg. Ins. Pre. (0.5%) 17,425
- 57. FHA Exam. Fee (0.3%) 10,455
- 58. FHA Inspec. Fee (0.5%) 17,425
- 59. Financing Fee (%) 69,700
- 60. AMPO (%) .... N.A.
- 61. FNMA Fee (%) 60,988
- 62. Title & Recording 12,000
- 63.   TOTAL CARRYING CHGS. & FINANCING .... $ 390,955
- 64. LEGAL AND ORGANIZATION
  - Legal .... $ 11,500

F. INCOME COMPUTATIONS:

30. Estimated Project Gross Income	$	709,915
31. Occupancy (Entire Project) Percentage		95 %
32. Effective Gross Income (Line 30 × 31)	$	674,419
33. Total Project Expenses (Line 29)	$	384,419
34. Net Income to Project (Line 32 – Line 33)	$	290,000
35. Expense Ratio (Line 29 ÷ Line 32)	$	43 %

H. TOTAL REQUIREMENTS FOR SETTLEMENT:

72. DEVELOPMENT COSTS (Line 69)	$	3,648,260
73. LAND INDEBTEDNESS (or Cash required for land acquisition)		224,000
74. SUBTOTAL (Line 72 + 73)	$	3,872,260
75. Mortgage Amount ... $ 3,485,034		
76. Fees Paid by Other Than Cash ... $ 331,660		
77. Line 75 + Line 76	$	3,816,694
78. CASH INVESTMENT REQUIRED (Line 74 – 77)	$	55,566
79. INITIAL OPERATING DEFICIT	$	—
80. ANTICIPATED DISCOUNT		34,950
81. Working Cap. (2% of Mtge. Amount)		69,700
82. ADD Off-site Construction Costs		100,000
83. TOTAL ESTIMATED CASH REQUIREMENT (Lines 78 + 79 + 80 + 81 + 82)	$	260,116

I. ATTACHMENTS: (Required Exhibits)

1.	Location Map
2.	Evidence of Site Control (Option or Purchase) and Legal Description of Property
3.	Form 2010 Equal Employment Opportunity Certification
4.	Form 3433 Eligibility as Non-Profit Corporation
5.	Evidence of Last Arms-Length Transaction Price
6.	Sketch Plan of Site

Organization _8,000_

•65. TOTAL LEGAL AND ORGANIZATION	$	19,000
66. Consultant Fee		N.A.
•67. Builder and Sponsor Profit & Risk	$	331,660
68. TOTAL EST. DEVELOPMENT COST (Excl. of Land or Off-site Cost) (Line 50 + 63 + 66 + 67 + 68)	$	3,648,260
70. LAND (Est. Market Price of Site) _____ per sq. ft. @ $ _____	$	224,000
71. TOTAL ESTIMATED REPLACEMENT COST OF PROJECT (Add 69 + 70)	$	3,872,260

Source of Cash to meet Requirements:	Amount
HARD COSTS	$ 3,540,600
LESS MORTGAGE (90%)	$ 3,485,034
CASH NEEDED	$ 55,566
	$
	$
TOTAL	$

7.	Personal Financial & Credit Statement of Sponsors
8.	Form 2530 Previous Participation Certification
9. •	Architectural Exhibits—Preliminary
10. •	Architectural Exhibits—Final
11. •	Survey
12. •	Evidence of Architect E & O Insurance Coverage
13. •	Copy of Owner-Architect Agreement

FHA examination and inspection fees (lines 57 and 58, FHA form 2013)
Financing fee payable to general partners (table 3-5)
Legal fees and miscellaneous (lines 62 and 66, FHA form 2013)

K. Organization Costs
   The costs of organizing the Partnership will be capitalized and amortized over sixty months as required by the Internal Revenue Code. These costs are as follows:

Fee to General Partners for services in organizing the partnership (table 3-5)
Legal and accounting fees payable to general partners (table 3-5)

L. Syndication Costs
   Costs applicable to promotion and sale of partnership units are not deductible for federal income tax purposes. These costs are capitalized and recognized as a loss by the partners upon dissolution or termination of the partnership or sale of their partnership interest. The following are included as syndication costs:

Sales and management fee to Interstate Securities Corporation (table 3-5)
Accounting and other expenses (table 3-5)
Promotion fee to general partners (table 3-5)

M. Rehabilitation Costs
   The estimated costs to be capitalized as rehabilitation costs are summarized as follows:

Total structures (lines 41 and 42, FHA form 2013)
Total fees (line 49, FHA form 2013)
Construction loan costs and commitment fees (lines 56, 59, and 61, FHA form 2013)
Insurance (line 55, FHA form 2013)
Construction management–overrun fee to general partners (table 3-5)

   Under Section 167(k) of the Internal Revenue Code, rehabilitation costs allocable to apartment units that qualify as low- or moderate-income housing may be depreciated over a sixty-month period. The general partners intend to amortize all rehabilitation costs over a sixty-month period beginning September 1, 1981.

N. Letters of Credit
   In compliance with FHA requirements, the partnership will be contingently liable to a bank on letters of credit to be issued to Highland Mortgage Company, as follows:

For payment of GNMA points upon purchase of the permanent loan by GNMA
For FHA working capital requirements

O. Lease Acquisition
   The partnership will pay a fee of $10,000 to the city of Rocky Mount for services rendered with regard to the acquisition of the lease. The partnership intends to capitalize this amount and amortize it over the seventy-five-year term of the lease.

P. Apartment Management

The project will be managed by the Housing Authority pursuant to a management agreement with the partnership. The management agreement will provide for a fee of 5 percent of effective rental income to be paid the Housing Authority for its management services.

Q. Gain Upon a Sale or Exchange of the Property or Partnership Termination and Recapture of Accelerated Depreciation

The Partnership will realize a gain for tax purposes upon a sale (including a foreclosure) of the property to the extent the outstanding debt plus cash proceeds exceed the adjusted basis (original cost less depreciation taken) of the property. Since rehabilitation costs will be depreciated over 60 months, this could result in a substantial gain to the partnership, which will be taxable to the individual partners. This would also be the case if an individual partner sells or exchanges his partnership interest. Termination of the partnership without a prior sale may also be treated as a sale or exchange of a partnership interest.

Under the Internal Revenue Code, any gain realized during a period of 100 months (eight years, four months) from the date the project is first placed in service would be taxable to the partners as ordinary income to the extent depreciation under Section 167(k) previously taken exceeds depreciation computed on a straight-line method. The amount that would be ordinary income under this computation is reduced 1 percent per month for a holding period in excess of 100 months. After a holding period of 200 months (sixteen years, eight months) the ordinary income amount is reduced to zero. Any gain not taxed as ordinary income would be a capital gain to the partnership under present federal income-tax laws.

Each partner must report his share of partnership capital gain on his individual tax return and it must be combined with all other capital gains or losses. If the partner reports a net long-term capital gain, he will normally take a capital gain deduction (presently 60 percent of the net long-term gains).

3 Regulating Private Market Activities

The Lofty Ideal of Artists' Housing: Legalizing Loft Living in New York City

Bill Bernstein thought he had seen it all as director of research in New York City's Office of Rent Control. He was sure that no more complex system of rent regulation existed anywhere in the country, and probably in the civilized world, than in New York City. Regulations governing rent increases in New York City varied by building size and age; by whether they received any form of city real estate tax abatements or exemptions when they were built or subsequently rehabilitated; by turnover rates; by the cost of operations; and by whether there were elderly or handicapped people in occupancy. Having participated in the development of countless sets of implementing regulations while he was with the Office of Rent Control, Bernstein was confident he could handle his new responsibilities as director of operations for the city's newest rent regulating agency, the New York City Loft Board.

Instituted by the state legislature in June 1982 to oversee the legalization of residential loft units in old factories, warehouses, or office buildings, the Loft Board's major responsibilities were as follows:

· to determine which buildings or units were covered by the new loft law;
· to set interim rent increases for them;
· to determine how much of the landlord's costs in legalizing the building would be passed on to tenants as rent surcharges;
· to assist the Rent Guidelines Board in setting annual rent guidelines for lofts once legalization was under way and tenants had received new residential leases;
· to set minimum "housing" service and maintenance standards for lofts until they became class-A multiple dwellings;
· to resolve landlord-tenant controversies over fair market values of tenants' improvements; and
· to hear landlords' claims for exemptions from the law on financial or structural grounds, such as hardship exemptions.

* The author gratefully acknowledges the assistance of William Bernstein in the preparation of this paper.

The board, whose nine members are appointed by the mayor, included an impartial chairman, one representative of loft owners whose tenants were engaged in manufacturing and commercial activities, one representative of the real estate industry, and one representative of loft residential tenants. The other five members representing the public were the commissioner of the Department of Buildings, serving *ex officio,* and four others who were neither professionally nor personally involved with loft issues. The loft law was the centerpiece of the city's comprehensive policy to deal with illegal loft conversions, which involved the renting of unimproved space in under-used industrial or commercial buildings to tenants for residential purposes. For years, commercial transactions had been conducted largely outside the framework of existing city housing codes, zoning codes, and laws governing residential rents and evictions. What the *New York Times* has called "the last of the city's housing frontiers," which the Loft Board now was trying to tame, opened up in the late 1960s.

Artists and craftsmen seeking large, inexpensive spaces where they could live and work moved into loft buildings that legally could be occupied only for commercial or manufacturing use. The new tenants often had to provide their own appliances, fixtures and amenities. Landlords accepted the illegal tenants to fill space in aging buildings that no longer suited most modern manufacturing businesses.[1]

The pressure on the city to bring some degree of law and order to the loft frontier resulted from the increasing demand for housing in Manhattan. When the housing demand began to affect the loft market, it threatened to price marginal industrial tenants and the original loft pioneers out of their units (supplement 4-1). Having organized to fight mounting rent increases and to protect their investments in their furnishings and fixtures, the early loft tenants took their case to the courts, which tended to agree with them that their buildings were de facto multiple dwellings and that loft residents should have the same rights as other residential tenants in New York City (supplement 4-2). These decisions had the effect of clouding the rights of owners to collect rents, because their loft units failed to meet the city's minimum housing standards for health and safety that applied to all multiple dwellings. After much political wrangling, the city developed a loft policy designed to balance the legitimate but conflicting needs of industrial and residential uses for loft space. The policy contained several elements, including certain zoning map amendments that reflected actual residential conversions since 1961, minimum standards for loft conversions, provisions for relocation assistance to displaced industrial firms, the elimination of tax incentives for loft conversions in certain Manhattan neighborhoods, and the creation of a loft enforcement unit in the Office of the Mayor to deter new illegal conversions.

The framework for legalizing lofts in New York City was spelled out in Article 7-C of the New York State Multiple Dwelling Law (supplement

1. New York Times, November 18, 1983.

4-3). Article 7-C recognized the residential status of dwellers in illegal lofts in designated areas of New York City, thereby bringing them within the protection of the city's housing laws, including those governing rent increases and minimum housing standards. By granting tenants legal status, the law also clarified the right of owners of illegal lofts (which the law calls *interim multiple dwellings,* or IMDs) to charge and collect rents from their residential tenants, which the courts had prevented many of them from doing.

Bernstein knew from experience that the loft law would be at least as complicated and pose even greater regulatory challenges than any of the city's other rent control measures. For one matter, the loft law gave the Loft Board jurisdiction over a class of housing that had no previous legal status. The board estimated that there were somewhere between 7,500 and 10,000 illegal lofts in IMDs, but it did not know for sure. All owners of IMDs were required to register with the Loft Board as the first step toward legalization, and those who did so had their authority to collect rent affirmed and were awarded interim rent increases as incentives to register their buildings. But it was clear from the low number of loft owners who responded to this incentive that not all of them could have registered.

Second, because they often installed fixtures and improvements in their units at their own cost, tenants argued that they had an equitable interest in their units; that they were co-owners of their lofts. Their personal investments in their units, and the certain knowledge that the loft law would end up increasing their housing costs even as it secured additional rights for them, made for an informed and active tenancy. Indeed, the cost factor was partly responsible for undermining some tenant support for the loft law: loft dwellers in Brooklyn, whose units were in less demand than those in Manhattan, were much less enthusiastic about Article 7-C's potential benefits than were their Manhattan counterparts (supplement 4-4). While the law recognized the co-investment feature of lofts by providing for a one-time landlord purchase of fixtures and furnishings when the tenant vacated the site, landlords and tenants were miles apart on how the fixtures should be valued. Whereas owners, predictably, favored a replacement cost less depreciation approach, tenants demanded prices based on the value of the long-term occupancy rights of their lofts as residential units.

Another major difference between the loft law and the city's other rent laws was that Article 7-C provided for the direct pass-through to residential tenants of the owner's capital and financing costs of bringing the lofts up to minimum housing standards (that is, legalizing them).

The loft law stated that an owner could apply to the Loft Board for a rent surcharge based on the costs of bringing the units into compliance with the city's multiple dwelling laws. After determining an owner's cost to be "necessarily and reasonably incurred, including financing, in obtaining compliance . . ." the rent adjustment needed for legalization could be computed in either of two ways:

. . . by dividing the amount of the cash cost of such improvements exclusive of interest and service charges over a ten-year period of amortization, or . . . by dividing the amount of the cash cost of such improvements exclusive of interest and service charges over a 15-year period of amortization, plus the actual annual mortgage debt service attributable to interest and service charges in each year of indebtedness . . . provided that the maximum amount of interest charged includable in rent shall reflect an annual amortization factor of one-fifteenth of the outstanding principal balance [Section 286(5)(i) and (ii)].

Bernstein knew that the pass-through provision of the law, especially the part dealing with financing charges, would be particularly difficult to implement and would likely attract the attention of city housing officials in New York and elsewhere who, thus far, had resisted pressures by landlords to consider financing charges and mortgage costs in determining the periodic rent increases they would permit owners to levy. He also was aware that if loft owners were unable to recover their costs from higher rents, they also would be unable to obtain mortgages to finance the necessary improvements to their units, and the whole legalization effort would probably fail.

Because of the critical importance of the law, Bernstein wanted to make sure that the Loft Board members, few of whom were experienced in real estate finance and each of whom viewed legalization from a different perspective, were well versed with the many technical issues raised by legalization before he drafted any implementing regulations for the Loft Board to consider.

The key issues he needed to determine include the following:

· the potential effects of legalization on existing residential tenants in terms of rent;
· how legalization costs should be allocated among existing tenants;
· how the provisions of Section 285(ii) of Article 7-C regarding the pass-through of financing charges should be modified through amendments or administrative regulation to deal with variable-rate loans and mortgages with balloon payments; and
· whether any additional interest costs resulting from refinancing existing loans that might be required by lenders as a condition for extending new loans to finance legalization should be passed through to tenants.

Since the Loft Board's initial consideration of legalization was just two weeks away and Bernstein had other, more immediate, deadlines to meet, he knew his overview memo to the board on critical issues in financing the legalization of residential lofts might not be as complete or detailed as he would like it to be. Moreover, time pressures demanded that he make some simplifying assumptions, the two most important being that legalization costs would average $15,000 per residential unit, including dwelling-specific and building-wide improvements, and that if fixed-term loans were available

Table 4-1. Cash-Flow Statement for Typical Residential Loft Building, New York City, 1983 (For Building Without Long-term Vacant Space)

	All Buildings	Landlord Pays Heat	Tenant Pays Heat
Gross rent	$31,190	$31,904	$29,050
Less: Residential vacancy (5 percent)	1,559	1,595	1,453
Effective gross income	$29,631	$30,309	$27,597
Less: Operating and maintenance	23,265	25,712	18,080
Net operating income	$ 6,366	$ 4,597	$ 9,517
	(20.4%)	(14.4%)	(32.8%)

Notes

1. Average building size is 15,035 square feet available for all uses. Residential use averages 68% of building area; commercial use, 31%; and industrial use, 1%.

2. The average loft building contains 6.1 residential units averaging 1,761 square feet each.

3. Average residential rent per square foot is $3.06; for lofts in which the landlord provides heat, it is $3.13, and where the tenant provides heat, rent is $2.85.

4. Tenant pays for own heat in 31.5 percent of all loft buildings; landlord pays for heat in 68.5 percent of all buildings.

5. Average operating and maintenance costs in buildings without vacant space are $3,814 per unit; $2,964 when tenant pays for heat, and $4,215 when landlord pays. These costs include legal expenses, which average $244 for buildings with no vacant space.

Sources: "The Economics of Loft Housing," prepared for the New York City Loft Board by Urban Systems Research and Engineering, June 1, 1983, pp. 3–5; and "Supplemental Analysis of Expenditures Patterns in Residential Lofts," also by USR&E, June 21, 1983.

to loft owners, these would be at a 13 percent interest rate for fifteen years. And although the Loft Board had little hard data on how profitable illegal lofts were, a recent field survey by one of its consultants provided some current information on rent levels and operating and maintenance costs for lofts that had been registered by June 1983 (table 4-1). With this information and the above assumptions, he started to work on his memo.

SUPPLEMENT 4-1.

The Legal Lowdown on Converting Loft Buildings
Andrew O. Shapiro

During March, some Manhattan loft dwellers had an unexpected visitor: a housing inspector from the Department of Buildings. He was ringing bells and climbing stairs at the start of what may well turn out to be the department's largest concerted hunt for illegally converted lofts. The inspector's marching orders, which he is pursuing on a full-time basis, result from a survey of Manhattan loft living completed in September 1977 by the Department of City Planning. According to the survey, 936 out of 1,023 converted loft buildings south of 59th Street contain illegal residences. Some loft dwellers who blithely settled into these 936 targeted buildings may, before the year is out, be confronted with a disagreeable choice: either carry out major upgrading or carry out the furniture and vacate.

There are good reasons for taking the trouble to convert a loft building in compliance with the law. One, you can't be evicted for being an illegal resident. Two, following the rules could save your life in case of fire. Three, you may get a sizable break on your real-estate taxes.

When a building is legally converted, it receives a certificate of occupancy (C of O) for residence from the Department of Buildings. (The illegal residences in the survey all lacked the necessary C of O.) This C of O is an official stamp of approval, certifying that the building is sufficiently safe and sound for human beings, not machines, to spend the night.

To determine whether a loft building can qualify for a C of O, you need to answer two questions: (1) Does the zoning law permit residential living in the building? (2) How much upgrading will be required, and what kind of improvements will be permitted in order to bring the building within health and safety standards imposed by the building codes?

ZONING

Generally speaking, all parts of New York City are zoned into one of three categories: residential ("R" zones), commercial ("C" zones), or manufacturing ("M" zones). Residential use of a loft building is permissible in any "R" zone and in all but certain "C" zones. (Areas zoned as C7, for example, are restricted to commercial recreational uses.)

Residential housing is not usually allowed in "M" zones. But in lower Manhattan, amendments to the zoning law have created special loft-living districts within certain "M" zones.

The best known of these "M" zones are SoHo (south of Houston Street) and NoHo (north of Houston Street). Industrial-loft space in both areas can be converted into joint living-working quarters for artists. Residential lofts for nonartists are not permitted, except for certain inhabitants of NoHo who resided there prior to April 27, 1976.

To qualify for conversion, loft buildings must have a lot coverage under 5,000 square feet. Buildings with frontage along Broadway must have a lot coverage of under 3,600 square feet. The minimum size for artists' lofts in SoHo and NoHo is 1,200 square feet. If the floors in the building have less than this minimum area, conversion is still authorized, provided there is no more than one loft per floor.

Normally, the ground floor and second floor in SoHo and NoHo loft buildings are restricted to commercial and industrial use. However, the City Planning Commission can grant a special permit, allowing artists' lofts below the third floor (for example, in the case of an artist working in a heavy or bulky medium which is not easily transported to upper floors).

Just south of SoHo lies the old Washington Market area, now known as "Tri-BeCa" (triangle below Canal Street). Zoning amendments adopted in 1976 make TriBeCa the first "M" zone where conversion can take place for general residential purposes as well as for artists' quarters. The minimum floor area for a general residential TriBeCa loft is determined by a sliding scale, which is based on how much light and ventilation the windows provide. Artists' lofts, as in SoHo and NoHo, have a minimum area of 1,200 square feet. In no event can the number of lofts in a building average out to more than one per every 1,000 square feet of dwelling space.

TriBeCa buildings containing fifteen or more converted lofts must be equipped with rooftop recreational areas covering at least 30 percent of the roof. As in SoHo and NoHo, the first two floors of TriBeCa loft buildings are reserved for commercial or industrial uses, but these restrictions can be modified by either the commissioner of buildings or the City Planning Commission.

Most loft buildings in the city are located in "C" zones where conversion is permitted, or "M" zones, where it is not (except for SoHo, NoHo, and TriBeCa). In certain "R" zones, notably the West Village, loft buildings still exist, and conversion there is legal. Even in zones where conversion is generally prohibited, exceptions can occasionally be made. The Board of Standards and Appeals has the power to grant zoning variances, which are exceptions to the zoning law designed to avoid undue hardship. Securing a variance can be a drawn-out procedure, however, with no guarantee of success. Professional assistance from a lawyer or architect is essential, and the fees may run as high as $10,000.

Assuming zoning poses no obstacle to conversion, the next question is what steps must be taken to bring an industrial loft into compliance with residential-living standards. Since the building codes are incredibly complex and subject to considerable interpretation, there is no pat list of dos and don'ts. Each conversion presents a unique set of problems, and regulations that apply in one case may not apply to another. Nevertheless, some general guidelines may be offered, covering such major concerns as fire egress, light and ventilation, and room subdivision.

FIRE EXITS

Every converted loft building must have adequate exits in case of fire. Ordinarily, two means of fire egress must be accessible from each loft. Exactly what means of egress will suffice depends on whether the building is fireproof (basically constructed with steel and concrete floors) or nonfireproof (construction with wood floors). In a fireproof building, there must usually be two interior stairways, both accessible from a common hallway that can be entered directly from the loft. The means of egress in a nonfireproof building can consist of one interior stairway accessible from a common hallway and one exterior fire escape directly accessible from the loft.

In many loft buildings a serious problem can be created when one floor is subdivided into two lofts. Subdivision may cut off one loft's access to the fire escape, leaving it with only one means of egress. A common misconception among loft dwellers is that a doorway connecting the two lofts is a legally acceptable—even legally mandated—means of access to the fire escape. Such a door is illegal, and a violation will be issued if the door is discovered. The legal solution to a cut-off fire escape can be expensive: for example, constructing a special passageway through the obstructing loft, installing a sprinkler system, or adding another interior stairway.

The rules governing fire egress also affect another common feature found in many lofts: sleeping platforms or "mezzanines" erected above the main floor space. Elevated platforms are legal for sleeping, provided there is headroom of seven feet. (Actually, there must be a seven-foot clearance below as well as above the platform.) The platform must be equipped with a stairway (at least two feet six inches wide) that terminates no more than twenty feet from an exit door or fire escape. All portions of the platform must be within 50 feet of the exit door or fire escape. Smoke detectors may be required in every sleeping area, whether it is a platform or a regular bedroom.

LIGHT AND VENTILATION

Every converted loft must have adequate light and ventilation. In general, the window area must be equal to at least 10 percent of the floor area of the room that it serves (a 5 percent ratio is permissible in some circumstances), and 50 percent of the window area must be openable. For example, a loft space of 500 square feet requires 50 square feet of window area, of which 25 square feet is openable.

Certain floor areas may be excluded when calculating the total area served by any given windows: for example, foyers, bathrooms, enclosed storage areas, and kitchenettes (under 59 square feet and served by mechanical ventilation).

More important, certain windows cannot be included in the calculation of window area. So-called lot-line windows are the most common example. They are windows in any wall built on the boundary with an adjoining vacant lot. Lot-line windows may become obstructed if a building is erected or enlarged on the adjoining lot. No matter how much sunshine you may see pouring through a lot-line window, remember, the law sees only a solid brick wall. Conceivably, lot-line windows can be legalized if the adjoining landowners grant a light-and-air easement, agreeing not to erect any obstruction.

The layout of a loft can be vitally affected by the window-to-floor ratio. Picture a loft space 100 feet deep with legal windows at the front and back ends only. The total window area may more than adequately serve the entire loft space, but if the space is subdivided improperly, part of the loft may be deprived of adequate light and ventilation. For example, a row of bedrooms, twenty feet deep, built along one end of the loft will leave 80 percent of the floor area to be served by only 50 percent of the window area. While the window-to-floor ratio may be more than ample in the bedrooms, it will probably fall short elsewhere.

A well-thought-out plan can take maximum advantage of the existing window-to-floor ratio. For example, using low partitions (three to four feet) or open shelves, which suggest spaces, allows all available windows to service the entire floor area.

DESIGNING A KITCHEN

Many loft dwellers like to have open kitchens—that is, kitchens not walled off from the rest of the loft. There is no rule against open kitchens. They can, however, cause problems when a loft consists of one undivided space containing the kitchen: The entire loft may be deemed a kitchen. While there are many things you can do legally in a kitchen—eat, sit, type, sculpt, even play a piano—sleeping is not one.

There are architectural solutions to this legal dilemma. You can separate the kitchen sufficiently to create a discrete room without necessarily losing the desired effect of an open kitchen. If the kitchen area is less than 59 square feet and has mechanical ventilation, you might separate the kitchen by installing waist-high counters and mounting a two-foot drop arch on the ceiling. The drop-arch enclosure will trap gases for the ventilator exhaust fan. In effect, you will have created a self-contained but still open kitchenette; the loft space outside the kitchenette can then be used for sleeping.

If the kitchen area is greater than 59 square feet, you have a full kitchen, which requires natural ventilation through a legal window (not a lot-line window). Once again, you may be able to employ a drop arch, this time to unite the kitchen area with a nearby window.

To successfully convert a loft building, you will need the services of an architect and probably those of an attorney. Hiring an architect (or engineer) who is experienced in loft conversions is particularly important. He must file the plans for your conversion with the Department of Buildings. He may frequently have to interpret the building code and argue fine points in order to overcome objections raised by building inspectors.

The successful conclusion of a legal conversion effort is issuance of a certificate of occupancy. As long as your building continues to meet the standards essential for issuance of the C of O, you will not have to fear the building inspector's knock at your door. Your C of O will also have important financial consequences. For one thing, when the mortgage comes due on a converted loft building, many banks now require a C of O for refinancing.

TAX BREAKS

Perhaps the best financial incentive for securing a C of O is the tax break you get under the city's J-51 program (named for a section of the Administrative Code). J-51 tax relief is the pot of gold at the end of the loft-conversion rainbow, and it is available only to buildings with a C of O.

A building qualifying for J-51 benefits gets both an exemption from paying certain local real-estate taxes and an abatement, or reduction, of local taxes that are not wiped out by the exemption. Any increase in the assessed valuation of the building that results from the conversion is exempt from all local taxes for twelve years. Say a loft building had a preconversion assessed valuation of $70,000. The conversion results in a new assessed valuation of $280,000. The building would be exempt from local taxes on the $210,000 increase in assessment for a period of twelve years.

Not only is the owner exempt from these higher taxes, but also his normal taxes on the lower assessment can be abated—in some cases to zero. J-51 allows taxes to be abated annually by as much as 8.33 percent of the reasonable cost of the conversion. Sometimes this abatement may actually exceed whatever tax is due. If so, the owner pays no local taxes and furthermore earns a "carry-over" for the excess abatement. This carry-over is a credit in later years, when the exemption does not reduce taxes to zero.

A J-51 abatement can last anywhere from 10¾ to 20 years. Generally speaking, the total amount of the abatement cannot exceed 90 percent of the reasonable cost of the conversion.

To apply for J-51 tax benefits, write: J-51 Program, Department of Housing Preservation and Development, 100 Gold Street, New York City 10038.

SUPPLEMENT 4-2.
New York Artists Have Lofty Ideals About Low Rents

Robert Guenther

NEW YORK—Being an artist here requires more than inspiration, genius and creativity. Some people say it requires lofts.

And not just any old lofts, either, but lofts where the rent isn't so high. Without such places, these people warn, New York's reign as a world cultural center may end.

* From Robert Guenther, "New York Artists Have Lofty Ideals About Low Rents," *Wall Street Journal,* January 28, 1982. Reprinted by permission.

Many people who hold this view are in the art world—for example, Guillermo de Osma, the director of the Latin American office for art dealer Sotheby Parke Bernet Inc. "New York is a city that doesn't produce anything—just culture," Mr. de Osma says. "It's a point of reference world-wide. But if we don't protect the artist's environment, he will move elsewhere."

Many of those who don't fully sympathize with the artist are landlords. Most loft owners agree that painters, sculptors, photographers and the like contribute to the city's vitality, but they don't see why they should subsidize them. "Nobody is willing to face economic realities," says loft owner Helen Mills. "Costs aren't what they were in 1970. My $175,000 mortgage came due recently, and I'm now paying two percentage points over prime instead of 9 percent."

Two points over prime comes to almost 18 percent these days. Now, 18 percent may not be an artistic statement, but it sure draws a lot of oohs and ahs from those who grasp its true inner meaning.

TWO ADVERSARIES

On the issue of artist-tenants vs. landlords, few people are further apart than Mario Pikus and Eliahu Lipkis. Mr. Pikus, 37, is an Argentine-born painter and sculptor. Mr. Lipkis, 62, is an Israeli immigrant who owns a number of loft buildings, including the one where Mr. Pikus lives in lower Manhattan.

For more than four years now, Mr. Pikus hasn't paid a cent of rent for his 3,700-square-foot loft. He and nine other tenants of Lipkis' loft building are on a rent strike that Mr. Pikus started. Mr. Lipkis says the back rent now totals more than $150,000. He has waged a long court battle, but the dispute doesn't get resolved. Any time a ruling is handed down, it has been appealed by Mr. Lipkis or Mr. Pikus, both stubborn, volatile men.

The two don't even agree on what the issue is. Mr. Pikus says he went on strike because Mr. Lipkis didn't intend to renew his lease; Mr. Lipkis says he offered Mr. Pikus, who was paying $500 a month rent, a two-year lease with $25-a-month annual increases. The real issue, Mr. Lipkis says, is the strikers' desire for a free ride. He says they simply want to get away without paying any rent. (The money has been paid into an escrow account under court order.)

UNUSUAL ASPECTS

Besides having dragged on for four years, the dispute has a number of other unusual aspects: In the building where Mr. Pikus lives, some strikers sublet part or all of their lofts to friends while refusing to pay Mr. Lipkis rent; some tenants of that building who are paying rent suspect that rent strikers have pried locks off the front door, smashed a mailbox and painted graffiti in the hallway to drive nonstriking "scab" tenants away; and Mr. Lipkis once wielded a pair of scissors as he chased Mr. Pikus down the street. Mr. Lipkis explains that he happened to be carrying the scissors because he had just cut down a rent-strike banner.

But for all its peculiarities, the dispute is more representative than rare, in that it involves lofts that are legally manufacturing space—and illegal as residences. City officials have said that, like most such lofts, they are unsafe as residences until they are improved to meet such things as fire and plumbing codes.

And the dispute is only one of many—so many, landlords say, that owners are suffering financially. Tenants say that only 5 percent of them or less are on strike, but even that is a sizable amount: The city estimates that 15,000 people live illegally in commercial lofts in Manhattan; tenants put the number at 50,000, landlords at 10,000.

The current "mess," as everyone involved refers to it, has its roots in the migration of small manufacturing firms from Manhattan. Between 1965 and 1978, manufacturing jobs in Manhattan dropped by 37 percent, according to the city. That meant there was a lot of vacant space in loft buildings, usually aging four- and five-story structures that were built for light industry. As a result, the prices of these buildings plummeted.

Thomas Berger, a Hungarian refugee who runs a vending-machine company, and other small-business men saw opportunities in these seemingly obsolete buildings. "You could buy a building for $65,000 with $15,000 down," says Mr. Berger, who now owns three of them. "We had faith in this city when all of the big guys were trying to sell and get out."

Renting the space was a problem. "Instead of getting manufacturers answering our ads," Norma Wiener says, "we had photographers and artists who wanted to work and live in the lofts. We saw the handwriting on the wall. We had to rent to artists." Mrs. Wiener owns several loft buildings.

When erected, the lofts weren't envisioned as places to live. They had no bathrooms, kitchens or interior walls. But artists liked all that space. In exchange for the artists' making the space livable—although still not legally so—landlords charged them, say, $400 a month instead of $1,000. Making the lofts legally residential would have been costly—$30,000 to $40,000 a loft, according to one estimate.

Carl Weisbrod, the director of the city's loft enforcement office, acknowledges that the city initially winked at the illegal residences, because it seemed in everyone's interest.

THE CHIC INVASION

Then professionals and well-to-do non-artists decided that lofts in such neighborhoods as SoHo, Tribeca and Chelsea were chic. The pioneering tenants, economically forced to move elsewhere, often to other lofts, nevertheless reaped some gain: They were able to charge the new tenants "fixture fees" for the kitchen and bath facilities they had put in, frequently charging far more than true value.

But the higher rents paid by the invaders—leading in some cases to conversion of illegal loft buildings into legal ones—raised artists' fears that all loft rents would rise beyond their ability to pay. In response to these fears, Mayor Edward Koch's administration is seeking state creation of a city loft board empowered to regulate the rent increases. At the same time, however, it has announced a crackdown on illegal lofts. Fearing that they will be locked into low rents and forced to bring the lofts up to legal status, many landlords have refused to give long leases or else have raised the rent. That sparked many of the rent strikes.

"It's a paradox," says Mr. Pikus, the anti-Lipkis striker. "This is an artists' neighborhood, and the artists are being pushed out. What we demand is the right to stay here. This city is the center of the arts. Tourists don't come here to see landlords. Artists speak through their work, and you need your own world to do it. We're tired of improving neighborhoods and then being sent to new 'reservations.' I have a legal and moral right to live here."

USING THE SYSTEM

Even outside the ranks of landlords, sympathy for the rent strikers isn't universal. One city official says: "For many of these people, this business about being struggling artists is a life choice. They're middle-class, well-educated, and they know how to use the system. It isn't like they're from Bedford-Stuyvesant and can't find a job."

Loft owners say that tenants have been aided by sympathetic lower-court judges in Manhattan. Tenants, on the other hand, criticize higher-court rulings against them. The city's Mr. Weisbrod agrees that the situation is intolerable. "This is the kind of issue that government traditionally has tried to avoid," he says. "It's an issue where you don't make friends, just enemies."

Such fights take their toll on everyone involved. Mordecai Lipkis, son of the landlord, says, "They've made us hate the whole thing." Mr. Pikus says, "It disturbs your life emotionally and psychologically."

In fact, much of Mr. Pikus's art has centered on the court system and landlord-tenant relationships. Along one wall of his loft hangs a huge canvas called "Tribeca." It shows pallid tenants being evicted by city marshals bearing shields and halberds. In other works, judges who have ruled in favor of Mr. Pikus are lionized while those who have ruled against him are depicted unflatteringly.

Mr. Pikus fantasizes about establishing a separate enclave for artists, "Loftonia." After all, he says, the original loft dwellers are the misfits of New York, and New York attracts the misfits of the country.

SUPPLEMENT 4-3.

LOFTS—LEGALIZATION OF INTERIM MULTIPLE DWELLINGS
CHAPTER 349
Approved June 21, 1982, effective as provided in section 3

AN ACT to amend the multiple dwelling law, in relation to legalization of de facto multiple dwellings in cities of over one million

The People of the State of New York, represented in Senate and Assembly, do enact as follows:

Section 1. The multiple dwelling law is amended by adding a new article seven-C to read as follows:

ARTICLE 7-C
LEGALIZATION OF INTERIM MULTIPLE DWELLINGS
Section 280. Legislative findings.
281. Definition of "interim multiple dwelling."
282. Establishment of special loft unit.
283. Occupancy permitted.
284. Owner obligations.
285. Owner protection.
286. Tenant protection.
287. Alternative compliance.

280. Legislative findings. The legislature hereby finds and declares that a serious public emergency exists in the housing of a considerable number of persons in cities having a population of over one million, which emergency has been created by the increasing number of conversions of commercial and manufacturing loft buildings to residential use without compliance with applicable building codes and laws and

* Article 7-C, Legalization of Interim Multiple Dwellings, Chapter 349 of the New York State Multiple Dwelling Law, June 21, 1982.

without compliance with local laws regarding minimum housing maintenance standards; that many such buildings do not conform to minimum standards for health, safety and fire protection; that housing maintenance services essential to maintain health, safety and fire protection are not being provided in many such buildings; that as a consequence of the acute shortage of housing as found and declared in the emergency tenant protection act of nineteen seventy-four the tenants in such buildings would suffer great hardship if forced to relocate; that as a result of the uncertain status of the tenancy in question the courts have been increasingly burdened with disputes between landlords and tenants regarding their respective rights and obligations under the existing circumstances; that some courts have declared such buildings "de facto" multiple dwellings; that illegal and unregulated residential conversions undermine the integrity of the local zoning resolution and threaten loss of jobs and industry; that the intervention of the state and local governments is necessary to effectuate legislation, consistent with the local zoning resolution of the present illegal living arrangements in such "de facto" multiple dwellings, and to establish a system whereby residential rentals can be reasonably adjusted so that residential tenants can assist in paying the cost of such legalization without being forced to relocate; that in order to prevent uncertainty, hardship, and dislocation, the provisions of this article are necessary and designed to protect the public health, safety and general welfare.

281. Definition of "interim multiple dwelling." 1. Except as provided in subdivision two of this section, the term "interim multiple dwelling" means any building or structure or portion thereof located in a city of more than one million persons which (i) at any time was occupied for manufacturing, commercial, or warehouse purposes; and (ii) lacks a certificate of compliance or occupancy pursuant to section three hundred one of this chapter; and (iii) on December first, nineteen hundred eighty-one was occupied for residential purposes since April first, nineteen hundred eighty as the residence or home of any three or more families living independently of one another.

1. Notwithstanding the definition set forth in subdivision one of this section, the term "interim multiple dwelling" includes only (i) buildings, structures or portions thereof located in a geographical area in which the local zoning resolution permits residential use as of right, or by minor modification or administrative certification of a local planning agency, (ii) buildings or structures which are not owned by a municipality, (iii) buildings, structures or portions thereof within an area designated by the local zoning resolution as a study area for possible rezoning to permit residential use, or (iv) buildings, structures or portions thereof which may be converted to residential use pursuant to a special permit granted by a local planning agency. In the case of classes of buildings specified by paragraphs (iii) and (iv) of this subdivision and those buildings specified by paragraph (i) of this subdivision which require a minor modification or administrative certification, however, the provisions of subdivision one of section two hundred eighty-four of this article regarding compliance with this chapter shall not be applicable, but the other provisions of this article shall be applicable. Upon rezoning of any such study area or the granting of any such special permit, minor modification or administrative certification to permit residential use of any such building or portion thereof, subdivision one of section two hundred eighty-four of this article shall be applicable, with the timing of compliance requirements set forth in such section commencing to run upon the effective date of such rezoning or permit approval. If such rezoning does not permit residential use

of the building or a portion thereof, or if a special permit, minor modification or administrative certification is denied, such building shall be exempt from this article.

3. In addition to the residents of an interim multiple dwelling, residential occupants in units first occupied after April first, nineteen hundred eighty and prior to April first, nineteen hundred eighty-one shall be qualified for protection pursuant to this article, provided that the building or any portion thereof otherwise qualifies as an interim multiple dwelling, and the tenants are eligible under the local zoning resolution for such occupancy. A reduction in the number of occupied residential units in a building after December first, nineteen hundred eighty-one shall not eliminate the protections of this article for any remaining residential occupants qualified for such protections. Non-residential space in a building as of the effective date of the act which added this article shall be offered for residential use only after the obtaining of a residential certificate of occupancy for such space, and such space shall be exempt from this article, even if a portion of such building may be an interim multiple dwelling.

282. Establishment of special loft unit. In order to resolve complaints of owners of interim multiple dwellings and of residential occupants of such buildings qualified for the protection of this article, and to act upon hardship applications made pursuant to this article, a special loft unit referred to herein as the "loft board" shall be established which shall consist of from four to nine members representative of the public, the real estate industry, loft residential tenants, and loft manufacturing interests, and a chairperson, all to be appointed by the mayor of the municipality and to serve such terms as he may designate. The compensation of the members of the loft board shall be fixed by the mayor. The members of the loft board shall not be considered employees of the state or the municipality, provided, however, that state or municipal employees or officers may be named to the loft board. The mayor shall establish the loft board within ninety days of the effective date of the act which added this article. The loft board shall have such office and staff as shall be necessary to carry out functions conferred upon it and may request and receive assistance from any state or municipal agency or department. The loft board shall have the following duties: (a) the determination of interim multiple dwelling status and other issues of coverage pursuant to this article; (b) the resolution of all hardship appeals brought under this article; (c) the determination of any claim for rent adjustment under this article by an owner or tenant; (d) the issuance, after a public hearing, and the enforcement of rules and regulations governing minimum housing maintenance standards in interim multiple dwellings (subject to the provisions of this chapter and any local building code), rent adjustments prior to legalization, compliance with this article and the hearing of complaints and applications made to it pursuant to this article; and (e) determination of controversies arising over the fair market value of a residential tenant's fixtures or reasonable moving expenses. The violation of any rule or regulation promulgated by the loft board shall be punishable by a civil penalty determined by the loft board not to exceed one thousand dollars which may be recovered by the municipality by a proceeding in any court of competent jurisdiction. The loft board may charge and collect reasonable fees in the execution of its responsibilities. The loft board may administer oaths, take affidavits, hear testimony, and take proof under oath at public or private hearings.

283. Occupancy permitted. Notwithstanding any other provision of this chapter or any other law, code, rule or regulation, occupancy for residential purposes of residential units covered by this article is permitted, if such occupancy is in compli-

ance with this article. Nothing contained herein shall be construed to limit local authorities from issuing vacate orders for hazardous conditions, if appropriate.

284. Owner obligations. 1. (i) The owner of an interim multiple dwelling (A) shall file an alteration application within nine months from the effective date of the act which added this article, and (B) shall take all reasonable and necessary action to obtain an approved alteration permit within twelve months from such effective date, and (C) shall achieve compliance with the standards of safety and fire protection set forth in article seven-B of this chapter for the residential portions of the building within eighteen months from obtaining such alteration permit or eighteen months from such effective date, whichever is later, and (D) shall take all reasonable and necessary action to obtain a certificate of occupancy as a class A multiple dwelling for the residential portions of the building or structure within thirty-six months from such effective date. The loft board may, upon good cause shown, and upon proof of compliance with the standards of safety and fire protection set forth in article seven-B of this chapter, twice extend the time of compliance with the requirement to obtain a residential certificate of occupancy for periods not to exceed twelve months each.

(ii) If there is a finding by the loft board that an owner has failed to satisfy any requirement specified in paragraph (i) of this subdivision, such owner shall be subject to all penalties set forth in article eight of this chapter.

(iii) In addition to the penalties provided in article eight of this chapter, if there is a finding by the loft board that an owner has failed to satisfy any requirement specified in paragraph (i) of this subdivision, a court may order specific performance to enforce the provisions of this article upon the application of three occupants of separate residential units qualified for the protection of this article, or upon the application of the municipality.

(iv) If, as a consequence of an owner's unlawful failure to comply with the provisions of paragraph (i) of this subdivision any residential occupant qualified for protection pursuant to this article is required to vacate his unit as a result of a municipal vacate order, such occupant may recover from the owner the fair market value of any improvements made by such tenant, and reasonable moving costs. Any vacate order issued as to such unit by a local government shall be deemed an order to the owner to correct the non-compliant conditions, subject to the provisions of this article. Furthermore, when such correction has been made such occupant shall have the right to re-occupy his unit, and shall be entitled to all applicable tenant protections of this article.

(v) The occupants of a building shall, upon appropriate notice regarding the timing and scope of the work required, afford the owner reasonable access to their units so that the work necessary for compliance with this article can be carried out. Failure to comply with an order of the loft board regarding access shall be grounds for eviction of a tenant.

2. Every owner of an interim multiple dwelling, every lessee of a whole building part of which is an interim multiple dwelling, and every agent or other person having control of such a dwelling, shall, within sixty days of the effective date of the act which added this article, file with the loft board or any other authority designated by the mayor a notice in conformity with all provisions of section three hundred twenty-five of this chapter and with rules and regulations to be promulgated by the loft board.

285. Owner protection. 1. Notwithstanding the provisions of section three hundred two or three hundred twenty-five of this chapter, the owner of an interim multiple dwelling may recover rent payable from residential occupants qualified for

the protection of this article on or after April first, nineteen hundred eighty, and maintain an action or proceeding for possession of such premises for non-payment of rent, provided that he is in compliance with this article.

2. Notwithstanding any other provision of this article, an owner may apply to the loft board for exemption of a building or portion thereof from this article on the basis that compliance with this article in obtaining a legal residential certificate of occupancy would cause an unjustifiable hardship either because: (i) it would cause an unreasonably adverse impact on a non-residential conforming use tenant within the building or, (ii) the cost of compliance renders legal residential conversion infeasible. Residential and other tenants shall be given not less than sixty days notice in advance of the hearing date for such application. If the loft board approves such application, the building or portion thereof shall be exempt from this article, and may be converted to non-residential conforming uses, provided, however, that the owner shall, as a condition of approval of such application, agree to file an irrevocable recorded covenant in form satisfactory to the loft board enforceable for fifteen years by the municipality, that the building will not be re-converted to residential uses during such time. The standard for granting such hardship application for a building or portion thereof shall be as follows: (a) the loft board shall only grant the minimum relief necessary to relieve any alleged hardship with the understanding if compliance is reasonably possible it should be achieved even if it requires alteration of units, relocation of tenants to vacant space within the building, re-design of space or application for a non-use-related variance, special permit, minor modification or administrative certification; (b) self-created hardship shall not be allowed; (c) the test for cost infeasibility shall be that of a reasonable return on the owner's investment not maximum return on investment; (d) the test for unreasonably adverse impact on a non-residential conforming use tenant shall be whether residential conversion would necessitate displacement. Such hardship applications shall be submitted to the loft board within nine months of the establishment of the loft board, but shall not be considered, absent a waiver by the loft board, unless the owner has also filed an alteration application. In determination of any such hardship application, the loft board may demand such information as it deems necessary. In approving any such hardship application, the loft board may fix reasonable terms and conditions for the vacating of residential occupancy.

286. Tenant protection. 1. It shall not be a ground for an action or proceeding to recover possession of a unit occupied by a residential occupant qualified for the protection of this article that the occupancy of the unit is illegal or in violation of provisions of the tenant's lease or rental agreement because a residential certificate of occupancy has not been issued for the building, or because residential occupancy is not permitted by the lease or rental agreement.

2. Prior to compliance with safety and fire protection standards of article seven-B of this chapter, residential occupants qualified for protection pursuant to this article shall be entitled to continued occupancy, and shall pay the same rent, including escalations, specified in their lease or rental agreement to the extent to which such lease or rental agreement remains in effect or, in the absence of a lease or rental agreement, the same rent most recently paid and accepted by the owner; if there is no lease or other rental agreement in effect, rent adjustments prior to article seven-B compliance shall be in conformity with guidelines to be set by the loft board for such residential occupants within six months from the effective date of this article.

3. Upon or after compliance with the safety and fire protection standards of article

seven-B of this chapter, an owner may apply to the loft board for an adjustment of rent based upon the cost of such compliance. Upon approval by the loft board of such compliance, the loft board shall set the initial legal regulated rent, and each residential occupant qualified for protection pursuant to this article shall be offered a residential lease subject to the provisions regarding evictions and regulation of rent set forth in the emergency tenant protection act of nineteen seventy-four, except to the extent the provisions of this article are inconsistent with such act. At such time, the owners of such buildings shall join a real estate industry stabilization association in accordance with such act.

4. The initial legal regulated rent established by the loft board shall be equal to (i) the rent in effect, including escalations, as of the date of application for adjustment ("base rent"), plus, (ii) the maximum annual amount of any increase allocable to compliance as provided herein; and (iii) the percentage increase then applicable to one, two or three year leases, as elected by the tenant, as established by the local rent guidelines board, and applied to the base rent, provided, however, such percentage increases may be adjusted downward by the loft board if prior increases based on loft board guidelines cover part of the same time period to be covered by the rent guidelines board adjustments.

5. An owner may apply to the loft board for rent adjustments once based upon the cost of compliance with article seven-B of this chapter and once based upon the obtaining of a residential certificate of occupancy. If the initial legal regulated rent has been set based only upon article seven-B compliance, a further adjustment may be obtained upon the obtaining of a residential certificate of occupancy. Upon receipt of such records as the loft board shall require, the loft board shall determine the costs necessarily and reasonably incurred, including financing, in obtaining compliance with this article pursuant to a schedule of reasonable costs to be promulgated by it. The adjustment in maximum rents for compliance with this article shall be determined either (i) by dividing the amount of the cash cost of such improvements exclusive of interest and service charges over a ten year period of amortization, or (ii) by dividing the amount of the cash cost of such improvements exclusive of interest and service charges over a fifteen year period of amortization, plus the actual annual mortgage debt service attributable to interest and service charges in each year of indebtedness to an institutional lender, or other lender approved by the loft board, incurred by the owner to pay the cash cost of the improvements, provided that the maximum amount of interest charged includable in rent shall reflect an annual amortization factor of one-fifteenth of the outstanding principal balance. Rental adjustments to each residential unit shall be determined on a basis approved by the loft board. An owner may elect that the loft board shall deem the total cost of compliance with this article to be the amounts certified by the local department of housing preservation and development of such municipality in any certificate of eligibility issued in connection with an application for tax exemption or tax abatement to the extent such certificate reflects categories of costs approved by the loft board as reasonable and necessary for such compliance. Rental adjustments attributable to the cost of compliance with this article shall not become part of the base rent for purposes of calculating rents adjusted pursuant to rent guidelines board increases.

6. Notwithstanding any provision of law to the contrary, a residential tenant qualified for protection pursuant to this chapter may sell any improvements to the unit made or purchased by him to an incoming tenant provided, however, that the tenant shall first offer the improvements to the owner for an amount equal to their

fair market value. Upon purchase of such improvements by the owner, any unit subject to rent regulation solely by reason of this article and not receiving any benefits of real estate tax exemption or tax abatement, shall be exempted from the provisions of this article requiring rent regulation if such building had fewer than six residential units as of the effective date of the act which added this article, or rented at market value subject to subsequent rent regulation if such building had six or more residential units at such time. The loft board shall establish rules and regulations regarding such sale of improvements which shall include provisions that such right to sell improvements may be exercised only once for each unit subject to this article, and that the opportunity for decontrol or market rentals shall not be available to an owner found guilty by the loft board of harassment of tenants.

7. The local rent guidelines board shall annually establish guidelines for rent adjustments for the category of buildings covered by this article in accordance with the standards established pursuant to the emergency tenant protection act of nineteen seventy-four. The local rent guidelines board shall consider the necessity of a separate category for such buildings, and a separately determined guideline for rent adjustments for those units in which heat is not required to be provided by the owner, and may establish such separate category and guideline. The loft board shall annually commission a study by an independent consultant to assist the rent guidelines board in determining the economics of loft housing.

8. Cooperative and condominium units occupied by owners or tenant-shareholders shall not be subject to rent regulation pursuant to this article.

9. No eviction plan for conversion to cooperative or condominium ownership for a building which is, or a portion of which is an interim multiple dwelling shall be submitted for filing to the department of law pursuant to the general business law until a residential certificate of occupancy is obtained as required by this article, and the residential occupants qualified for protection pursuant to this article are offered one, two or three year leases, as elected by such persons, in accordance with the provisions for establishment of initial legal regulated rent contained herein. Non-eviction plans for such buildings may be submitted for filing only if the sponsor remains responsible for compliance with article seven-B and for all work in common areas required to obtain a residential certificate of occupancy. Cooperative conversion shall be fully in accordance with section three hundred fifty-two-eeee of the general business law, the requirements of the code of the local real estate industry stabilization association, and with the rules and regulations promulgated by the attorney general.

10. The functions of the local conciliation and appeals board of such municipality regarding owners and tenants subject to rent regulation pursuant to this article shall be carried out by the loft board until such time as provided otherwise by local law.

11. Residential occupants qualified for protection pursuant to this article shall be afforded the protections available to residential tenants pursuant to the real property law and the real property actions and proceedings law.

12. No waiver of rights pursuant to this article by a residential occupant qualified for protection pursuant to this article made prior to the effective date of the act which added this article shall be accorded any force or effect; however, subsequent to the effective date an owner and a residential occupant may agree to the purchase by the owner of such person's rights in a unit.

13. The applicability of the emergency tenant protection act of nineteen seventy-four to buildings occupied by residential tenants qualified for protection pursuant to this article shall be subject to a declaration of emergency by the local legislative

body. In the event such act expires prior to the expiration of this article, tenants in interim multiple dwellings shall be included in coverage of the rent stabilization law of nineteen hundred sixty-nine of the city of New York.

287. Alternative compliance. In any case in which a local building code or this chapter provides an alternative means of meeting the fire and safety standards of article seven-B of this chapter, an owner of an interim multiple dwelling may, to the extent permitted by such local code or this chapter, elect to comply with the standards of such code or this chapter rather than with article seven-B. Such an election shall not affect an owner's obligations to meet the deadlines for compliance set forth in this article, and in such cases references herein to article 7-B shall be deemed to include any such local building code or the applicable provisions of this chapter.

2. Separability. If any clause, sentence, paragraph, section or part of this act shall be adjudged by any court of competent jurisdiction to be invalid, such judgment shall not affect, impair or invalidate the remainder hereof, but shall be confined in its operation to the clause, sentence, paragraph, section or part thereof directly involved in the controversy in which such judgment shall have been rendered.

3. Effective date and termination. This act shall take effect immediately. The provisions of this act and all regulations, orders and requirements thereunder shall terminate ten years from the effective date, except in their applicability to buildings with six or more residential tenants as of the effective date in which case termination shall occur twelve years from the effective date.

SUPPLEMENT 4-4.

The Low-Profile Blues

Most of Brooklyn's loft tenants have moved into raw space since 1978. Most have longer leases and lower rents than their Manhattan counterparts. Relatively few have encountered the rent gouging, harassment and forced co-oping that are familiar across the river. So why do we need a law—especially one that will eventually increase our rents in return for building improvements many of us would gladly do without?

Most of us don't . . . yet. But the going rate for raw space has doubled since 1980. Those tenants whose long initial leases have expired are facing rent increases of 100 percent or more. And the real estate sharks are trying to make Fulton Ferry and Williamsburg the next "hot" loft neighborhoods.

BLT [Brooklyn Loft Tenants] was started in the belief that the sorry history of SoHo, TriBeCa, and Chelsea would repeat itself here, unless tenants acted to forestall it. That means working with community planning boards and neighborhood groups, taking an interest in zoning changes and variances, and sharing information among ourselves.

It also means abandoning the old "low profile" attitude—the belief that if we stayed quiet and didn't draw the city's attention to ourselves, everything would stay as quiet and cheap as it was in SoHo in 1967, or TriBeCa in 1972, or Chelsea in 1977.

If you still believe that, we have a great deal for you on a bridge. . . .

Ugly Fact #1: The city can find "illegal" loft tenants any time it wants to: through residential listings in the reverse telephone directory, through routine building in-

* From the *Brooklyn Loft Tenants Newsletter,* October 1982, p. 4. Reprinted by permission.

spectors' reports, through Con Ed and Brooklyn Union Gas, and through simply driving the streets after business hours.

Ugly Fact #2: Far more tenants have lost their lofts because of their landlords than because of the city. That same nice fellow who gave you two months rent-free to clean out the junk, and couldn't quite believe his luck in finding a tenant for a floor that had been empty for years, can turn very nasty when it occurs to him that there are people who will pay twice as much, or when a developer makes a jackpot offer.

Ugly Fact #3: Brooklyn has perhaps 2,000 loft tenants compared to Manhattan's 30,000 or more. It would have been nice to get a loft law tailored to our special circumstances or a loft enforcement policy that ignored us entirely but neither was ever in the cards. What looks good to a TriBeCa tenant with no lease and an expensive court case doesn't look so good from here, but we have to live with it. And since we have to live with it, it makes more sense to organize and have some influence on how the law is implemented than to keep our heads in the sand . . .

We believe that even with the many shortcomings of the new loft law and enforcement policy, they offer a better long-term prospect of staying in our lofts than we would have had otherwise. And we believe that the more you know about the alternatives, the more you'll agree.

Rent Regulation: Cast Your Vote as a Member of the Rent Guidelines Board

Not being very tall, Karen Eisenstadt had a hard time seeing over the policemen lined up in front of her and the other members of the New York City Rent Guidelines Board (RGB). Although the board members did not seem to be in immediate danger of physical harm, tenant demonstrations were threatening to get out of control as the board held its annual meeting to decide how much to allow landlords to raise their rents in the coming year. As often happened at these meetings, the auditorium was both packed and segregated: tenants on one side, landlords on the other, and a mixed group of independents, including the press, sitting in the center section. The meeting had some of the flavor of a political convention, with slogan-bearing placards, orchestrated "spontaneous" marches down the aisles, and chants —the most memorable one this year being the tenants' rendition, "open your books, you dirty crooks."

It seemed crazy to Eisenstadt that the decision about how much apartment rents could be increased in New York City was made every year in such a chaotic environment. As she and the others waited for the demonstrations to subside, she reflected on her reasons for wanting to serve on the board. The din at the meeting contrasted sharply with her more genteel work environment at the Morgan Guaranty Trust, where she made loans to state and local governments. She had accepted appointment to the board in June 1981, however, because she had missed being closely involved in setting public policy. After all, she had been involved in housing finance since 1970, first with the New York City RAND Institute, where she helped develop the maximum base rent system that was later incorporated into the city's rent control law, and later with the city's Office of Management and Budget, where she served as the chief of the Housing Task Force and then as deputy assistant budget director for finance, until she joined Morgan in 1979. While at the Office of Management and Budget, one of her principal concerns was restructuring financially troubled middle-income housing projects that had been financed by the city under the state's Mitchell Lama program.

She thought serving on the Rent Guidelines Board would be a good way to get back into public policy. Though she knew it would be thankless service because, as she said, "even if you do the best job possible, you never feel you accomplish much because there are so many inequities in the system," she understood how important the board's work actually was. Composed of nine members appointed by the mayor (two of whom represented tenants, two landlord representatives, and five, including Karen, who

* The author gratefully acknowledges the assistance of Karen Eisenstadt.

** Although the data used are drawn from the 1982 deliberations of the New York Rent Guidelines Board, the issues and discussion represent a composite of several years' considerations.

Table 5-1. Selected Data for Rental Apartments in
New York City: 1975, 1978, and 1981

	1975	1978	1981	Percentage Change 1975–81
Total rental units	2,056,005	1,988,712	1,976,044	− 0.6
Renter-occupied units	1,999,037	1,930,030	1,933,887	+ 0.2
Vacant for rent	56,968	58,682	42,157	− 28.2
Vacancy rate	2.8%	3.0%	2.1%	—
Median gross rent	$171	$210	$265	+ 26.2
Median income of all renters	$8,395	$8,979	$11,001	+ 22.5
Median gross	—	—	—	—
Rent as percent of income	24.7%	28.3%	28.0%	− 1.0
Percent of renters	—	—	—	—
With rent income	—	—	—	—
Ratios of .40 or more	25.2	31.6	30.5	− 3.5

Source: Michael A. Stegman, *The Dynamics of Rental Housing in New York City*, New Brunswick, NJ: Rutgers
University, 1982.

represented the public), the board's main duty was to set a ceiling on the increases for new and renewal one-, two-, and three-year leases for rent-stabilized apartments. (State legislation adopted in 1983 eliminated the requirement that landlords offer tenants the option of a three-year lease.) The board's guidelines apply to almost all New York City buildings built after 1947 that have six or more apartments. In addition, when older apartments regulated by rent-control guidelines are vacated, most of those apartments become rent stabilized.* Almost a million apartments were now covered. Table 5-1 summarizes the rent and vacancy status of the city's rent-stabilized inventory; tables 5-6 through 5-14 contain a variety of other data that depict the heterogeneity of the stock. The latter attribute, coupled with the diversity of New York's population, was what made the Rent Guidelines Board's task so difficult. No single rent guideline could possibly be equitable to all interested parties.

In setting its rent guidelines, the law required the board to consider, among other factors:

· the economic condition of the residential real estate industry in the designated area, including such factors as the prevailing and projected (1) real estate taxes and sewer and water rates, (2) gross operating maintenance

* Because rent control was initially enacted to prevent speculation and profiteering in New York City and other urban housing markets with large wartime defense industries, allowable rent increases were then infrequent, modest, and unrelated to the increases in the cost of living over time. The intent of the stabilization system is to regulate rather than rigidly control rents and to balance the interests of landlords and tenants in a tight housing market. Stabilization is designed to permit property owners to earn reasonable returns on their equity investments—the original rent control program was not. Under current law, a vacated rent-controlled apartment in a building containing six or more units becomes subject to rent stabilization. Upon a change in occupancy, a previously controlled apartment in a building with fewer than six units becomes decontrolled. In March 1984, 15 percent of New York City's rental housing was still under rent control, 64 percent was rent stabilized, and 21 percent was decontrolled or never regulated.

costs, including insurance rates, cost of fuel, and labor costs, (3) costs and availability of financing (including effective rates of interest), and (4) overall supply of housing accommodations and overall vacancy rates;
· relevant data from the current and projected cost-of-living indexes for the area; and
· such other data as might be pertinent.

Because this was the second rent-setting meeting she had participated in, Eisenstadt was quite comfortable with the part of the guidelines process that concerned how much rents should be increased to compensate landlords for inflationary increases in operating and maintenance costs. Contrary to popular conception, this component of the rent guidelines was determined objectively. This year she could concentrate more on the subjective elements of the process—what the RGB defined as *qualitative factors,* such as whether and how landlords should be compensated for other kinds of cost increases, such as rising interest rates and eroding equity values caused by sustained periods of rent regulation. These and the issues of maintaining housing quality and assuring affordable rents to the city's lower- and moderate-income families were at the heart of the guidelines process.

Today's meeting was the last in a series of public hearings and meetings —by law, the board could not hold private meetings—at which relevant data were presented and all members of the public could express their views, which were diverse and impassioned. As the demonstrations subsided and some degree of order was restored to the proceedings, the board summarized the method that would be used to determine the basic guideline for rent increases. One-year leases would compensate landlords for increases in operating and maintenance (O&M) costs that had occurred over the previous year. Longer leases would compensate for projected changes in costs. This method consisted of three steps.

First, a survey was carried out to determine changes in the prices of goods and services that make up landlords' operating budgets. The field survey, carried out by an independent contractor hired by the Rent Guidelines Board (and supervised by the board so it would have confidence in the results), collected price information on nine classes of O&M costs, including fuel and utilities, labor, taxes, and insurance (table 5-2). The price data were converted into percentage changes from the previous year. Each of the nine relative price changes was then multiplied by the percentage that particular item represented of total average O&M costs. The nine weighted changes in relative prices were then summed to determine the change in the operating cost index for rent-stabilized apartments for the current year. Thus, for example, as the staff explained, labor costs rose 8.3 percent between 1981 and 1982, but since labor costs represent just 11.7 percent of total O&M costs, this particular price increase caused only a 1 percent increase in the O&M price index (0.083 multiplied by 0.117). Also, because of the international oil glut, heating fuel prices, uncharacteristically, fell 8.3 percent between 1981 and 1982. Because fuel represented nearly 35 percent of total

Table 5-2. Percentage Changes in Components of Price Index of
Operating Costs for All Buildings, 1981–1982

	1981 Weights	multiplied by	1981–82 Percentage Change	equals	1981–82 Weighted Percentage Change
Taxes, fees, permits	18.4		12.8		2.4
Labor costs	11.7		8.3		1.0
Fuel	34.6		−8.2		−2.8
Utilities	9.0		−2.0		−0.2
Contractor services	10.9		11.1		1.2
Administrative costs	7.8		10.8		0.8
Insurance	3.9		4.6		0.2
Parts and supplies	1.9		7.1		0.1
Replacements	2.0		6.8		0.1
All items	100.0				2.8

Source: 1981 weights and 1981–82 percentage changes are from USR&E, *1982 Price Index of Operating Costs for Rent Stabilized Apartment Houses in New York City*, Table 2-1, p. 8.

O&M costs, the decline in the price of heating oil caused the O&M price index to fall by 2.8 percent (−0.083 multiplied by 0.346). Taken together, the changes in the nine components of the price index of operating costs produced an average increase in O&M prices for the 1981–82 period of just 2.8 percent. This important piece of information became the foundation of the new rent guideline. Because the Rent Guidelines Board had jurisdiction over newer buildings as well as older apartments that used to be rent controlled, changes in the operating costs index are computed separately for buildings built before and after 1947. (See table 5-15 for the differences in the price index for newer and older buildings.)

The second step in determining the basic rent guideline required the board's staff to forecast increases in operating and maintenance prices for two years into the future. These estimates were necessary because the law required landlords to offer, at the tenants' discretion, one-, two-, or three-year leases: the board had to issue separate rent guidelines for each lease term. "In making its forecasts, the board relied on expert assessments of likely price trends for the most important categories, taxes, labor costs, and fuel and utilities. For other categories, the board combined the history of increases in each category with judgments about general economic conditions to make specific projections."[1] The board projected an average increase in O&M costs of 5.8 percent for 1982–83 and another 5.6 percent for 1983–84 (table 5-3).

The third step in determining an increase in the basic rent guideline was to adjust the increase in the operating cost index to reflect the fact that O&M costs do not represent quite all of landlords' total costs. In fact, in 1981, the staff estimated, O&M costs consumed 71 percent of gross rent

1. "Rent Guidelines Board Order No. 14," *City Record*, August 31, 1982, p. 5.

Table 5-3. Annual Percentage Changes in Components of Index of Operating Costs

	Actual O&M Increase 1981–82	Projected O&M Increase 1982–83	Projected O&M Increase 1983–84
Taxes, fees, and permits	12.8%	2.0%	2.0%
Labor costs	8.3	7.5	6.5
Fuel	−8.3	5.0	5.0
Utilities	−2.0	5.0	5.0
Contractor services	11.1	10.0	9.1
Administrative costs	10.8	10.3	10.2
Insurance	4.6	7.7	7.7
Parts and supplies	7.1	4.7	1.8
Replacements	6.8	6.3	5.0
All items, pre- and post-1947 buildings	2.8	5.8	5.6
Index, with 1980–81 as base of 100	102.8	108.6	114.2

(the ratio of O&M costs to rent) for the average rent-stabilized apartment in New York City. The remaining 29 percent of gross rent (the ratio of capital costs to rent) could be used for capital cost items, including debt service and profit, if any. The adjustment procedure followed by the RGB staff involved multiplying the updated O&M price index by the current O&M rent ratio to derive a revised, updated ratio, and then adding to this the capital cost/rent ratio. This procedure was repeated separately for one-, two-, and three-year leases as follows (data on O&M Price Index from table 5-3).

Lease Term	O&M:Rent Ratio	multiplied by	Updated O&M Price Index	plus	Capital Cost: Rent Ratio	equals	New Rent Equivalent
1 year	71		1.028	73	29		102.0
2 years	73		1.058	77	29		106.2
3 years	77		1.056	82	29		110.6

To derive increases in base rent guidelines for the longer leases, the two- and three-year rent equivalents must be averaged:

$$\text{two-year leases} \left(\frac{102 + 106.2}{2} \right) = 104.1$$

$$\text{three-year leases} \left(\frac{102 + 106.2 + 110.6}{3} \right) = 106.3$$

Rounding off these averages produces increases in base rent guidelines of 2 percent for one-year leases, 4 percent for two-year leases, and 6 percent for three-year leases.

As she reflected on the multiyear renewal guidelines, Eisenstadt recalled the property owners' complaints that the board consistently underestimated price inflation with the result that tenants with two- and three-year leases paid lower rents than they should. The board's own records confirmed that claim. Of the twelve projections of operating and maintenance cost increases the Rent Guidelines Board had made since 1978, it underprojected actual increases seven times by a total of 40.5 percentage points and overprojected five times by a total of 22.7 percentage points, a net shortfall of 17.8 percentage points.[2] Because the board never made up for these defects by intentionally overestimating future price increases, rents would now have to increase by more than 20 percent to close the gap between stabilized rents needed to maintain operating income at its 1971 level, adjusted for inflation (Rent Stabilization Association, p. 13).

Eisenstadt also recognized that the basic rent guideline did not distinguish between large- and small-scale owners, although the latter frequently had to pay higher unit costs for many items, such as fuel, repairs, maintenance contracts, and insurance. Nor did the guideline recognize the plight of the owners of low-rent apartments, to whom a 4 or 5 percent rent increase translated into too few dollars to improve operating conditions. Perhaps even more important, if the final guideline enacted by the board did not explicitly consider a financing factor, rising O&M burdens would make it impossible for many landlords to meet the higher mortgage costs that refinancing had made necessary.

The staff found that 84 percent of all stabilized units were in buildings with mortgages and more than half of the mortgages were balloon or other types of partially amortizing loans. Interest rates for multifamily mortgage loans in New York City for 1980–82, when available, were above 14 percent, as shown in tables 5-4 and 5-5, and more than $1.5 billion in balloon loans on rent-stabilized buildings would be due between 1982 and 1984. A study funded by a landlord organization found that the average interest rate on existing mortgages that were refinanced in 1982 was 8.66 percent, while the average rate on the new loans was 15.65 percent. The average monthly payment for debt service in the 1982 refinancing was $87.42 per unit, an increase of $31.23 per unit over the previous debt service.

After the staff presentation was completed, the board members offered the following ten motions for consideration.

Motions offered by tenant representatives:
1. No rent increases for the coming year.

2. "Submission to the Rent Guidelines Board by the Rent Stabilization Association of New York City, Inc., Relative to Order No. 16," June 4, 1984, p. 18.

Table 5-4. Interest Rates on FHA Multifamily Mortgages

Date	Interest Rate (%)
April 1967	6.0
April 1968	6.75
April 1969	7.5
April 1970	8.5
April 1971	7.0
April 1972	7.0
April 1973	7.0
April 1974	8.55
April 1975	8.5
April 1976	9.0
April 1977	9.0
April 1978	9.0
April 1979	9.5
April 1980	10.0
April 1981	14.5
April 1982	16.5

Note: These were the rates in effect during April of each year. The rate fluctuates
and the April figure does not hold for the entire year.

**Table 5-5. Telephone Survey of Major
New York City Savings Banks**

**INTEREST RATES AND TERMS ON NEW MULTIFAMILY
MORTGAGE LOANS IN 1980, 1981, AND 1982; RATES
AND TERMS ON REFINANCING MULTIFAMILY
MORTGAGE LOANS IN 1982**

Bank A		Rate	Points	Terms
New mortgages	1980	13%	One	5–10 years
	1981	No new loans have been made		
	1982	since 1980.		
Refinancing	1982	Mortgages are not being rolled over at this time. Outstanding loans are called in as they come due.		
Bank B				
New mortgages	1980	12%	One	10 years
	1981	15%	One	3 years
	1982	No new loans made in 1982.		
Refinancing	1982	18%	Two	2 years
		Payment of principal required in some cases.		
Bank C				
New mortgages	1980	14–14½%	Two	3–5 years
	1981	16½%	Two+	3 years
	1982	17½%	One+	3–5 years
Refinancing	1982	16–17%	One-half	1 year
		Payment of principal required in some cases.		

Bank D

New mortgages	1980	12–14½%	One–Three	5–10 years
	1981	No new loans have been made		
	1982	since 1981.		
Refinancing	1982	16½%	Two	3 years

Bank E

New mortgages	1980	No new loans have been made		
	1981	since October 1979.		
	1982			
Refinancing	1982	16%	One	Negotiable

Rollovers on a case-by-case basis.
Equity participation is required.

Source: "Rent Guidelines Board, Explanatory Statement Rent Order No. 14," *City Record*, August 31, 1982, p. 12.

2. Increases at rates of 2, 4, and 6 percent for one-, two-, and three-year lease terms, respectively.

Motions offered by landlord representatives:
3. Across-the-board increases of 12, 22, and 30 percent for one-, two-, and three-year leases, with no add-on refinancing guideline.
4. Same as number 3 above, plus a 15 percent vacancy lease allowance to be paid only by new tenants.
5. A special add-on refinancing guideline that would pass to tenants the full increase in interest costs caused by refinancing existing balloon mortgages. The refinancing guideline would be approved on a case-by-case basis. (See supplement 5-1 for proposed mortgage pass-along application.)
6. Same as number 5 above, but the refinancing guideline would limit the additional rent increase to 5 percent of total rent, including the increase due to the basic rent guideline, in any twelve-month period.
7. A flat rate increase of $31.23 per month per unit to compensate owners for higher interest costs due to refinancing. The figure represents the average cost difference between old and new mortgages for rent-stabilized buildings whose landlords refinanced balloon mortgages between 1980 and 1982. The flat rate increase would be in addition to the basic guideline increase adopted by the board and would be approved only for those buildings whose landlord refinanced loans during 1980–82.

Motions offered by public members:
8. Increases of 4, 7, and 10 percent for one-, two-, and three-year leases with no special refinancing guideline or vacancy lease allowance for new tenants.
9. Same as number 8 above, but with the addition of a 15 percent vacancy allowance to compensate owners for various costs not reflected in the O&M price index, including higher interest rates and deterioration in their equity positions over the years.

10. Same as number 8 above, but with a special add-on guideline that would give owners of lower-rent units (those renting for under $200) an additional increase. The increase would be based on the length of time passed since the last vacancy. If the last vacancy occurred two years ago or since, the add-on increase would be 5 percent; if the last vacancy was between two and four years ago, it would be 10 percent; and if it was at least five years ago, the increase would be 15 percent.

As she contemplated the different motions, Eisenstadt tried to sort out various cases that had been presented. She was concerned about poor people who were unable to meet their present housing costs. She recalled the staff's report that, despite rent regulations, one in four renters had poverty-level incomes and that nearly half of all tenants in New York City now paid at least 30 percent of their incomes for rent and utilities. She was struck by the fact that between 1968 and 1981, the highest growth rate in relative housing costs in New York was among households for whom rent consumed at least 40 percent of their income. In 1981, three out of every ten renters fell into that category, an 83 percent increase since 1968. At the same time, many renters who could afford to pay more were being protected by rent regulation.

Eisenstadt also recognized the needs of owners. Rent regulation stifled their return on capital, especially compared to what they could realize if left to market forces in New York City, where housing is in tight supply. According to the board's data, the proportion of total rent revenues that landlords allocated to operating and maintenance costs in rent-stabilized buildings had increased from 55 percent to 71 percent between 1972 and 1982, leaving just twenty-nine cents of every rent dollar available now for payment of capital costs (including debt service) and for profits. That amount represented a decline of sixteen cents per rental dollar, or more than 35 percent in just ten years, and did not take into account inflation, higher interest rates, and higher returns available on other, frequently less risky investments. Moreover, inadequate returns would lead owners to defer maintenance or, possibly, abandon buildings, a tragedy for the housing stock.

There was no question in Eisenstadt's mind that refinancing was an important issue. The question was whether refinancing should be handled through a separate rent guideline that would be added to the basic guideline due to rising O&M costs and be granted only to those owners who actually refinanced their mortgages during the past year, or whether it should be folded into the basic guideline and be granted to all owners. If refinancing costs were to be treated separately, should the board be concerned with what owners had done with the capital they obtained from the loans that were now coming due? Should an owner who took out a balloon mortgage seven years ago to pay for a vacation trip, for example, be compensated today by his tenants? Or should refinancing rent increases be approved only in those cases in which the loan coming due was needed to acquire, im-

Table 5-6. Net Rental Vacancy Rates by Year Structure Built, New York City, 1981*

Year Structure Built	Available Vacancies	Net Vacancy Rate
Post-1947	11,930	1.63%
1978–1981	902	4.42
1970–1977	1,779	1.30
1960–1969	3,222	1.30
1947–1959	6,027	1.84
Pre-1947	29,353	2.41
Not Reported	873	3.39
Total	42,156	2.13

* Source for tables 5-6 through 5-14 is Michael A. Stegman, *The Dynamics of Rental Housing in New York City*, Center for Urban Policy Research, Rutgers University, 1982.

Table 5-7. Distribution of Rental Housing by Gross Rent, New York City, 1981

Gross Rent	Number of Apartments	Percentage
Less than $200	437,219	25.5
$200–299	643,610	37.6
$300–399	360,248	21.0
$400–499	135,100	7.9
$500 or more	137,765	8.0
Total Reported	1,713,942	100.0

Table 5-8. Classification of Occupied Rent-Stabilized Apartments in New York City, 1981

	Percentage Distribution	
	Pre-1947	Post-1947
Old-law tenement	18.3	0.6
New-law tenement	58.3	1.5
Multiple built after 1929	15.0	92.1
Apartment hotel built pre-1929	1.0	—
One- or two-family houses converted to apartments	6.0	5.6
Other	1.4	0.2
Total Multiunit Buildings	100.0	100.0

Table 5-9. Number of Units in Rent-Stabilized Apartments by Structure Type, New York City, 1981

	Percentage Distribution		
	Old-Law Tenement	New-Law Tenement	Multiple Built after 1929
1–5	14.5	5.9	1.5
6–9	23.2	10.8	1.7
10–19	29.2	9.2	2.4
20–49	29.2	44.3	15.8
50–99	3.1	23.2	26.4
100 or more	0.8	6.6	52.2
Median number of units	13.1	35.8	106.9

Table 5-10. Gross Rent:Income Ratios by Income of Household, All Renter Households, New York City, 1981

	Percentage with 25% or Higher Gross Rent:Income Ratio
	1981
Less than $4,000	91.6
$4,000–5,999	92.5
$6,000–6,499	90.8
$6,500–9,999	80.8
$10,000–12,499	65.7
$12,500–19,999	32.7
$20,000–24,999	16.6
$25,000–34,999	9.5
$35,000 or more	9.4
Total households	56.6

Table 5-11. Median Gross Rent:Income Ratio, All Renter Households, New York City, Selected Years

	1950	1960	1965	1968	1970	1975	1978	1981
Median gross rent:income ratio	18.9%	18.7%	20.4%	21.0%	20.0%	24.7%	28.3%	28.0%

Table 5-12. **Percentage of Households with Rent:Income Ratios over Specified Levels, New York City, Selected Years**

Percentage of Households with Rent:Income Ratio over Specified Levels

Gross Rent: Income Ratio	*1950*	*1960*	*1965*	*1968*	*1970*	*1975*	*1978*	*1981*
25% or more	NA	NA	34.9	37.2	35.5	49.1	57.1	56.6
30% or more	25.0	24.0	25.3	27.4	NA	38.1	46.3	45.6
35% or more	NA	19.0	18.7	21.2	23.2	30.8	38.0	37.1
40% or more	NA	NA	14.5	16.7	NA	25.2	31.6	30.5

Table 5-13. **Income by Structure Classification, All Renter-Occupied Units, New York City, 1981**

Percent Distribution

	Total	*Less than* *$6,500*	*$6,500–* *12,499*	*$12,500–* *24,999*	*$25,000* *or More*
Multiunit buildings	100.0	32.1	26.6	25.3	16.0
Old-law tenement	100.0	37.2	30.2	22.2	10.4
New-law tenement	100.0	38.4	28.5	22.9	10.2
Post-1929 multiple	100.0	27.0	23.8	26.9	22.3
One- or two-family house converted to apartment	100.0	25.8	27.8	32.1	14.3
One- or two-family house	100.0	23.4	25.5	32.3	18.8

Table 5-14. **Median Monthly Gross Rent, by Selected Control Status and Number of Rooms in Unit, for Selected Control Categories, New York City, 1981**

Rooms	*Occupied Units*	*Controlled*	*Stabilized* *Pre-1947*	*Stabilized* *Post-1947*
1 room	$244	$184	$252	$313
2 rooms	249	188	249	334
3 rooms	254	206	249	348
4 rooms	265	222	268	390
5 rooms	288	222	299	458
6 or more rooms	340	273	357	391
All renters	265	213	262	368

**Table 5-15. Application of Price Index of Operating Costs to
Pre- and Post-1947 Buildings**

While prices of operating and maintenance items used in both newer and older buildings are the same, their relative weights in the price index are different. Most notably, labor costs account for just 9% of total O&M costs in pre-1947 buildings, but nearly 17% in post-1947 buildings, which are more likely to have resident superintendents. Conversely, fuel costs account for nearly 41% of O&M costs in older buldings and for just 23% in newer ones. Thus, whereas the average increase in O&M costs for all buildings was 2.8%, staff estimated that costs rose an average of just 1.8% in older buildings and by 4.9% in newer ones.

Pre-1947 Buildings

Items	1981 Weights	multiplied by	1981–82 Percentage Change	equals	1981–1982 Weighted Percentage Change
Taxes, fees, permits	13.9		12.8		1.8
Labor costs	9.2		8.3		.8
Fuel	40.7		−7.9		−3.2
Utilities	8.3		−2.0		− .2
Contractor services	10.9		11.1		1.2
Administrative costs	8.6		10.8		.9
Insurance	4.3		4.6		.2
Parts and supplies	1.8		7.1		.1
Replacements	2.5		6.8		.2
Percentage change in O&M price index					1.8

Post-1947 Buildings

Items	1981 Weights	multiplied by	1981–82 Percentage Change	equals	1981–1982 Weighted Percentage Change
Taxes, fees, permits	27.3		12.8		3.5
Labor costs	16.6		8.3		1.4
Fuel	22.6		−8.8		−2.0
Utilities	10.4		−2.0		− .2
Contractor services	10.9		11.1		1.2
Administrative costs	6.2		10.8		0.7
Insurance	3.0		4.6		0.1
Parts and supplies	2.0		7.1		0.1
Replacements	0.9		6.8		0.1
Percent change in O&M price index					4.9

Sources: 1981–82 percentage changes are from *1982 Price Index of Operating Costs for Rent Stabilized Apartment Houses in New York City,* Table 2-15, p. 35. The 1981 weights are reported in Table 2-16, p. 36, and were derived from "The Explanatory Statement & Findings for RGB Order 13," Table IV, *The City Record,* August 6, 1981.

prove, or maintain the building? Eisenstadt now had to decide which motion to vote for, or, if necessary, how to draft a compromise that would gain support from a majority of the board.

SUPPLEMENT 5-1.

Proposed Mortgage Pass-Along Application

Deliver or mail this certificate to: New York State Division of Housing and Community Renewal, 2 World Trade Center, New York, New York 10047, together with affidavit of mailing or delivery of a copy of this certificate to each rent-stabilized tenant in building.

Certificate for Mortgage Interest Pass-Along for Actual Refinancing between January 1, 1980 and September 30, 1985.

1. Amount of mortgage(s) prior to refinancing $_____
2. Annual mortgage interest cost prior to refinancing
   (___% per annum, interest rate) $_____
3. Date of refinancing and name(s) of mortgagee(s)
   date: _____ mortgagee: _____
4. New annual mortgage interest cost after refinancing
   (___% per annum, interest rate)* $_____
5. Increased annual interest cost of refinancing
   (difference between items 2 and 4) $_____
6. Amount of annual rent roll on date of refinancing $_____
7. Mortgage interest pass-along adjustment percentage
   (item 5 divided by item 6)** $_____

I hereby affirm the truth of the foregoing, under penalty of perjury.

                                                          _____
                                                                  (Owner)
                                                          Address of building:_____

                                                          _____

                                                          _____
                                                          RSA#:_____

Sworn before me this _____ day of
_____, 19____.

_____
(Notary Public)

---

* The maximum annual interest rate and corresponding annual interest cost for the purpose of this certificate shall be deemed, in the case of a mortgage by a noninstitutional lender, not to exceed two percent (2%) above the average yield on long-term United States Treasury Bonds.

** The mortgage interest pass-along adjustment percentage shall be applied to increase by such percentage the lease rent of each existing and future stabilized tenancy commencing with the later of (a) the first month after the date of filing this certificate with the New York State Division of Housing and Community Renewal or (b) October 1, 1984, and monthly thereafter until the owner has recovered the increased annual interest cost of refinancing (item 5), provided, however, that the pass-along adjustment percentage (item 7) on any lease shall not exceed five percent (5%) during any twelve (12) month lease term.

4 Nonmarket Investment Decision Making

An Exercise in Sweat Equity or Futility: 991–993 Columbus Avenue

The Urban Homesteading Assistance Board (U-HAB), a nonprofit organization that provides technical assistance to community groups doing self-help rehabilitation in New York City, was approached in 1976 by Nelson Martinez, who wanted to buy, renovate, and convert two vacant, city-owned tenement buildings at 991 and 993 Columbus Avenue into cooperatives. The buildings, located directly above Manhattan Valley (a neighborhood that was fast losing its lower-income character through gentrification), were in one of the last truly low-income residential neighborhoods left on the West Side of Manhattan.

On the surface, at least, the sweat equity homesteading concept Martinez sought help in implementing was quite simple. Martinez and his small group of neighbors lived in a seriously deteriorated apartment building, a few doors down from 991, that was receiving few repairs and services from its absentee owner. The group would jointly purchase the two old buildings, which the city had taken for back taxes, and rehabilitate them into fifteen apartments that the new resident families would own and manage cooperatively. The rehabilitation and carrying costs could be kept relatively low because the buildings were still structurally sound and the homesteaders would do some of the work themselves (supplements 6-1 and 6-2). Rehabilitation of the buildings would be divided into three stages, two involving contributed labor, or sweat equity, by the homesteading families and one performed by a general contractor. The contractor would perform all work on the electrical and mechanical systems and all the major structural work, such as putting on a new roof and replacing burned-out beams. The homesteaders would gut the buildings and do much of the skilled and semi-skilled finishing—installing the sheetrock, finishing floors, and painting the apartments. The homesteaders' contributed labor would save about 20 percent of development costs, estimated when the project was first conceived.

The homesteaders' sweat equity notwithstanding, U-HAB realized, the

* Based on a draft case by Charles Laven.

amount of rehabilitation needed and the minimum debt service that would result from using the city's participation loan program as the principal financing vehicle would, when combined with the low incomes of the home-steaders, produce unaffordably high monthly carrying charges. (Under the participation loan program, the city contributes a portion of the permanent financing at a 1 percent interest rate for twenty years that, when combined with a private market rate loan, produces a "blended" interest rate on the total loan that will fall between 6 percent and 9 percent, depending on the market interest rate and the ratio of private to public funds. The participation loan program is funded from the city's Community Development Block Grant allocation.)

Since the participation loan program was unworkable in this situation, U-HAB petitioned the city to provide the homesteaders a direct, 1 percent interest, 25-year mortgage for the full development cost. Because U-HAB's request was contrary to the city's policy of leveraging its development funds with as much private capital as possible, eighteen months passed before the city took any formal action on the homesteaders' loan application.

Finally, in July 1978, U-HAB's and the homesteaders' effort showed the first signs of success, as the city's Department of Housing Preservation and Development (HPD) issued a letter of commitment to provide Martinez and his group with a permanent 1 percent mortgage loan in the amount of $377,000. Debt service on the loan, when combined with estimated operating costs of about $1,250 per apartment per year, would create monthly carrying charges of around $200 a month, an affordable amount for households whose incomes averaged $8,500 a year.

In the fall of 1978, the homesteaders obtained from a local foundation a seed money loan that enabled them to begin interior demolition. The seed money would be repaid out of the first draw-down from the construction loan the homesteaders secured from a commercial lender. Work on the buildings finally started, but the project was threatened once again. The original contractor, who had committed to do the rehabilitation at prices that were by then nearly two years old, pulled out. Building conditions had deteriorated since the project began, and construction costs had increased significantly. U-HAB worked with the homesteaders to secure new contractor estimates, but all the bids were rejected by HPD as too high. By the spring of 1979, it was clear that the amount of direct financing needed for the two buildings was more than HPD was either willing or able to invest, and all work on the buildings ceased. Clearly, a new project concept was needed.

The Urban Homesteading Assistance Board came up with yet another scheme, this one based on the federally funded Section 8 Substantial Rehabilitation program, administered locally by HPD. This program provided assistance to tenants to reduce their monthly housing costs to no more than 25 percent of their income (later increased by Congress to 30 percent). Maximum rents for new substantially rehabilitated apartments in the program were set at $488 a month for a two-bedroom unit in New York City, increasing at around 4 percent per year. With higher rents and deeper tenant subsidies, it would be possible to support the higher rehabilitation costs, now estimated at around $785,000 (nearly twice their original level), if HPD would still provide 1 percent financing for a sizable portion of the required mortgage loan.

U-HAB sought supplemental financing for the homesteaders from the newly instituted National Consumer Cooperative Bank (NCCB) and received a commitment for $291,000 at a 12 percent interest rate for 25 years. To make the project feasible, the city would have to provide the difference between the NCCB loan and total project needs (excluding the sweat equity) —in this case, more than $427,000. Not surprisingly, the city rejected this request as too costly but did not recapture the Section 8 subsidies it had agreed to commit to the project. The board members at U-HAB knew, however, that it was only a matter of time before the Section 8 subsidies would be recaptured if acceptable financing arrangements could not be made.

By September 1980, no construction had begun at 991–993 Columbus Avenue. In desperation, U-HAB tried to repackage the financing in what turned out to be a still more complicated fashion. The new plan would take advantage of the National Consumer Cooperative Bank's so-called soft loan window (authorized under Title II of its legislation, which was designed to assist lower-income cooperatives of all kinds). The new plan consisted of a market rate loan for $121,500 at 14 percent interest for twenty-five years, and a Title II graduated payment mortgage for $209,440, with a twenty-year amortization period. The interest on the graduated payment mortgage would start at 4 percent and increase 2 percentage points per year until a rate of 14 percent was reached in the sixth year of the term. Only interest on the original principal would be paid for the first five years; the loan would be amortized fully on a level payment basis during years six through twenty. The balance of the project funding would come from HPD in the form of a $100,000 grant and a 1 percent direct loan for twenty-five years. Total project development costs were still about $785,000, and operating and maintenance costs, excluding taxes, were now projected to average around $1,450 per unit, and to increase by 5 percent a year. Taxes were projected to be 15 percent of gross rents.

This three-part financing plan required that the positive cash flow in the early years of the project be invested at good yields to repay the growing mortgage in the later years. (Complete table 6-1 to test financial feasibility of this option.) Between the complicated financing arrangements and the deep subsidy payments from Section 8 needed to prop up the project, 991–993 Columbus Avenue had moved a long way from its original concept of sweat equity homesteading. The Urban Homesteading Assistance Board wondered whether the project had strayed so far from the homesteaders' simple goals that it was no longer worth fighting for. Charyl Edmonds, a U-HAB employee who had been involved in the project since its inception, thought back to the earlier financing possibilities that had been turned down

Table 6-1. 991–993 Columbus Avenue: Cash Flow from Operations—The Financing Option

	Year									
	1	2	3	4	5	6	7	8	9	10
Gross rent										
Less: Vacancies										
Equals: Effective rental income										
Less: Operating and maintenance expenses and real estate taxes										
Equals: Net operating income										
Less: Debt service:										
private loan										
city loan										
co-op bank loan										
Equals: Net cash flow										
Plus: Interest on net cash flow										
Equals: Cash reserves										

by the city as too costly.[1] "There must be a better way," she mused. "It would probably be cheaper if the city gave the buildings to the homesteaders along with $15,000 per apartment to do moderate rehabilitation and capitalize a modest replacement reserve fund which would protect the families from unaffordable cost increases due to major building system failures over the foreseeable future." (Complete table 6-2 to determine cost and feasibility of this option.) While the quality of rehabilitation under this alternative would be lower than that associated with Section 8, Edmonds was confident the homesteaders would willingly accept less quality for a greater degree of ownership and control over their living environment.

SUPPLEMENT 6-1.
Rehabilitating Sweat Equity
Bernard Cohen

Sweat equity, an ambitious attempt to save seriously deteriorated buildings in the poorest neighborhoods by using voluntary labor to keep costs low, is being battered by economic forces that experts say will probably make the housing too expensive for low-income people unless the program is modified soon.

Inflation, astronomical fuel prices and high interest rates have dealt a severe blow to an innovative program that is relatively unprotected by subsidy and geared for an income group that is already at the limit of what it can afford to spend on housing, many housing specialists agree.

The rehabilitation and operation of housing are so much more expensive today than anyone imagined even three years ago, thanks to 13 percent inflation and 90 cents a gallon oil, that architects of sweat equity are facing tough questions about whether the cost savings from contributed labor and other measures are sufficient to keep the housing affordable for low-income people. Terms such as "borderline feasibility" are becoming common.

Even at today's prices, sweat equity urban homesteading produces high-quality rehabilitated housing at remarkably low cost, compared with other programs. But there is growing agreement in housing circles that unless a deeper subsidy is incorporated, combined perhaps with lowering the sights of the construction effort, sweat equity as it operates in New York City will either go out of business or be forced to serve a moderate- to middle-income population.

"We are getting blown out of the water by costs," said Charles Laven, director of the Urban Homesteading Assistance Board, adding that privately owned and government-assisted housing everywhere is suffering from the same economic woes, a conclusion widely borne out by studies and statistics.

He and numerous other housing experts interviewed by *City Limits* reaffirmed their confidence in the concept of sweat equity and said there were many ways to

---

1. Cost to the city is the difference between the present value of the revenue received by the city (that is, loan repayments at 1 percent interest) and the present value of the cost to the city of raising the initial loan principal, using an 8 percent borrowing and discount rate and a twenty-five-year term.

* From Bernard Cohen, "Rehabilitating Sweat Equity—Part I," in *City Limits*, February 1980. Reprinted with the permission of *City Limits*, 424 West 33rd Street, New York, New York.

Table 6-2. 991–993 Columbus Avenue: Cash Flow from Operations—The Give-away Option

	Year									
	1	2	3	4	5	6	7	8	9	10
Gross rent										
Less: Vacancies										
Equals: Effective rental income										
Less: Operating and maintenance expenses and real estate taxes										
Equals: Net operating income										
Less: Cash rehabilitation costs*										
Deposit into replacement reserve										
Plus: Earnings on replacement reserve										
Equals: Net cash flow										

* The sum of initial rehabilitation costs and deposit into replacement reserve must equal $225,000 ($15,000 per unit).

keep the housing within the means of lower-income people. Some of the cost-cutting tools are already being tried out in other cities. "I really do believe in the design of the program," Laven said. "It's the right set of goals."

Sweat equity has been a creative response to two of the most scarring problems of the inner city: housing abandonment and unemployment. For many years, New York City has been losing housing through abandonment at the rate of about 15,000 to 20,000 units per year. The most recent job statistics show that unemployment here is about 9 percent of the general population and more than 11 percent for blacks and Hispanics.

As it is generally defined, sweat equity involves community-based housing development that uses primarily untrained or newly trained labor for the construction and emphasizes user participation in and control of the project. Neighborhood residents form an organization, buy an abandoned building, obtain a below-market interest rate (1 percent to 3 percent) loan and rehabilitate the structure. Their sweat, or labor, reduces development and operating costs and serves as their "equity" investment in the building. For example, homesteaders in the three buildings sponsored by the Banana Kelly Community Improvement Association in the South Bronx are required to put in 600 hours of free labor and take turns guarding the buildings at night. In the early 1970s, homesteaders received little or no income during construction. That hardship was later eased with job training funds through CETA (Comprehensive Employment and Training Act program).

Homesteading of multifamily buildings has evolved into a complex, sometimes unwieldy process involving the participation of at least two government agencies, a private lender, a community organization and a host of support personnel. Attempts to generalize about the success of sweat equity are difficult. Latest figures show fifty buildings totalling 583 units either completed or at some earlier phase of the rehabilitation program. Since sweat equity was never institutionalized, however, buildings were all packaged differently, and each has its own history. Most of the buildings have gotten high marks from housing specialists for the quality of the construction. In addition, the program has provided jobs and training and stimulated the direct involvement of local organizations and individuals in rebuilding their neighborhoods.

But many of the sweat equity buildings have suffered serious economic problems. Relatively few buildings are current with their mortgage payments, and some are far behind. Others have defaulted on their taxes. And all of the buildings are having a hard time making ends meet. Many are having to think about raising rents.

"Honest questions have been raised about the ability of the projects, once rehabilitated, to sustain themselves," says an unpublished study of sweat equity buildings by Professor Robert Kolodny of the School of Architecture and Planning at Columbia University. A survey by Kolodny of seven buildings found that not one was current with its mortgage payments. The best performer had met only two-thirds of its payments during twenty-one months of operation. The worst had made only one payment in a similar period.

Although it is now paying regularly, 519 East 11th Street, a Lower East Side tenement famous for the first inner-city application of solar collectors and windmill energy, is twenty-five months in arrears on its mortgage. Other buildings, such as 251 East 119th St. in East Harlem, have defaulted on taxes.

"We're feeling the pinch everyone is feeling," said Luqman Abdush-Shahid, a member of the Mosque of Islamic Brotherhood, Inc., sponsor of the sweat equity rehabilitation of two buildings in Harlem that are up to date with their payments. "Everything has gone up, and basically our incomes are fixed. We find ourselves tightening a belt that has already been squeezed." Despite savings from ongoing maintenance by the tenants and cooperative buying, rents will soon have to be increased, he added.

The mushrooming cost combined with the complexity of the process and the relative inexperience of all of the parties with this kind of program has led to a visible erosion of support for sweat equity. Chemical Bank, by far the most active private lending institution for sweat equity buildings, is thinking very seriously about dropping out. The U.S. Department of Housing and Urban Development, whose agreement to provide up to $4 million in mortgages for the buildings greatly accelerated the rate of sweat equity rehabilitation, is now talking in much more cautious terms about a modest program for the immediate future.

And a spokeswoman for the Department of Housing Preservation and Development said the city's sweat equity program is at a "standstill" because of the current cost problems.

"Most sweat equity has been marginally supported by the powers that be as an interesting fringe activity," Laven said. "The reason it got started was because the numbers worked well and because we were clever at putting together a wide variety of funding and support. Now, people can start backing away and have other than political reasons."

The reasons for the dramatic increase in the sweat equity pricetag fall into three clusters: inflation that has sent costs soaring while incomes were increasing only marginally; problems coordinating separate government and private funding pieces; and the inexperience of all the parties to a complicated, new program.

COSTS

Four years ago, the cost of materials alone for sweat equity rehabilitation was estimated at $10,000 per unit. That figure has risen to $17,000 per unit today and is expected to be closer to $20,000 for buildings scheduled for construction later this year, according to UHAB. A composite index of 100 different types of construction materials, compiled by the U.S. Labor Department, shows an overall price increase of 44 percent between 1975 and 1979. Lumber rose 70 percent in price and concrete was up 43 percent over the four years.

The cost of borrowing has also shot way up, mainly because of the ways the federal government uses the housing sector to curb inflation. Although the long-term mortgages have generally been subsidized at 3 percent or 1 percent (an exception is the city's Municipal Loan Program, which has a floating interest rate), the construction has been financed at much higher interest rates of between 10 percent and 17 percent. Except where it has applied a cap, Chemical Bank ties construction interest to 1½ percent above the prime rate, the amount banks charge their most credit-worthy customers. A look at what has happened to the prime tells the story. In 1976, the prime rate hovered around 6¾ to 7 percent. In May, 1977, it was still at 6½ percent. By January, 1978, it had risen to 8 percent. Twelve months later it was at 11¾ percent, and on November 16, 1979, the prime rate hit 15¾ percent, the highest in U.S. history.

Those buildings with long-term mortgages financed by the old Municipal Loan program, such as 251 East 119th St., have suffered financially as the interest rate has risen from 4 or 5 percent to 8½ percent.

When you add in the purchase price, architect and legal fees, the standard contingency fund and other costs, the total development pricetag, according to current UHAB figures, is about $22,000 per unit, nearly 50 percent higher than was estimated in 1976 and 9 percent above projections of two years ago. For buildings that go into construction this year, the total development cost is expected to be in the $22,000 to $25,000 per unit range.

Finally, there is the cost of maintaining and operating buildings. Here is where the leap in oil prices from above 45 cents a gallon in 1977 to 94 cents a gallon today has taken such a toll. For example, 519 East 11th Street estimates consumption of 7,400 gallons of No. 2 fuel oil per year. In June, 1977, when the cost was 46 cents per gallon, the total fuel bill would have come to $3,404 or $261 per unit. Seven months ago, when the building's current operating budget was planned, oil was projected at 76 cents per gallon for a total fuel bill of $5,624 or $432.60 per unit. At today's price of 94 cents per gallon, annual consumption would cost the building $6,956 or each apartment $535. Further price hikes that could increase the price of oil to one dollar per gallon are expected.

The simplest way to measure the impact of costs on sweat equity housing is to look at how rents have risen to keep pace. In 1973, when homesteading of multifamily buildings was really getting under way in New York City, rents of $23 to $25 per room were envisioned. By 1976, rents were up to $38 per room. The following year they rose to between $40 and $42. Today, it costs at least $50 per room to operate one of these buildings and pay off a rehab mortgage. That figure is already shaky and is expected to jump to as much as $60 per room for buildings that go into construction this year.

Incomes, meanwhile, have stagnated in comparison. From 1973 to 1977, rents went up 9.6 percent per year nationally while incomes rose only 5.6 percent, according to a 1979 report by the U.S. Comptroller General entitled "Rental Housing: A National Problem That Needs Immediate Attention." New York City reported in 1979 that for the first time in recent history, more than half (57 percent) of all tenants were paying more than 25 percent of their gross incomes for rent.

Interviews with representatives of six homesteading organizations plus many others familiar with the housing program revealed a general belief that residents need annual incomes of $11,000 to $15,000 to support sweat equity housing, a sizable cut above the $6,000 to $8,000 income group for whom the program was originally designed. In contrast, the median income for the Lower East Side, according to the 1970 census, was less than $5,000 per year.

"I wish it was a low-income program," said Eulogio Cedeno, director of the

URBAN HOMESTEADING DEVELOPMENT COST,
OPERATING COST AND MONTHLY
CARRYING CHARGE*

Materials	$119,000
Soft costs	22,098
Contingency allowance	14,109
Total mortgage amount	155,207
Development cost/unit	22,172
Maintenance and operation	9,060/year
Monthly carrying charge	49.10/room

* Seven-unit building completed in 1979.
Courtesy Urban Homesteading Assistance Board

Renigades Housing Movement in East Harlem, one of the earliest sponsors of sweat equity projects in New York City. "There should be a subsidy," he went on. "If the city is interested in saving neighborhoods and providing housing for poor people, this is what has to be done." As it is, "We are just holding the fort is what we are doing here," he added.

At today's costs, the 3 percent sweat equity loan program "is not for low-income people," said Herman Hewitt, a housing specialist with the Adopt-a-Building organization. "It's more for moderate-income people, those who are upwardly mobile and want to stay in the neighborhood and live in decent housing."

OTHER FACTORS

A great many other factors have contributed to the escalation of costs. Most played delaying roles. Timing is critical in construction, and delays are very expensive. Since sweat equity is a relatively new program for multifamily buildings, all partners—government, banks and homesteading organizations—have learned on the job. All did things to slow the process.

A major delaying force has been the inability of the partners to coordinate the various elements of the rehabilitation package. Chronic processing snafus left sponsoring organizations with no money to buy materials, idling their workers and throwing the construction off schedule. In many cases, CETA funds ran out, cutting off a crucial source of labor and forcing homesteaders to finish off the work themselves or hire outside contractors. Loan closing delays lasting months were also common.

Part of the problem can be laid to the inexperience of community sponsors and the shortage of technical assistance. Weak administration, bookkeeping, and accounting—critical backups for the rehab effort—hurts. And the construction work itself was bound to take longer when done by unskilled or newly trained CETA workers and homesteaders. Low pay, high turnover, and, in some cases, poor work habits, did not help either.

At the same time, community organizations were confronted with delays in getting vouchers and budget modifications approved, leading to chronic cash-flow problems. One group leader said it took two or three months to get approval for a burner that cost $2,000 more but better met the needs of the building. Another said he could not accept delivery of cabinets because of a delay in being able to draw down the money to pay for them. "You take this one time and multiply it out and it really has hurt us a lot," he said.

The organizations were also saddled with formidable bureaucratic requirements, especially under CETA, which was never designed for housing jobs and has never worked very well in this program. There are some today who advocate scrapping CETA altogether.

In addition, some contracts did not contain enough funds to pay the real cost of materials or competitive wages for construction workers. The effect was to reduce the pool of qualified talent interested in signing on and, perhaps, the commitment of some individuals to the projects. To stay within the budget, groups routinely had to scavenge for materials. "Society has to keep pace with changing conditions," said Imam K. Ahmad Tawfig, leader of the Mosque of Islamic Brotherhood, Inc. "You can't expect people to build in 1980 at 1970 prices."

Moreover, homesteaders moved into many of the buildings before the end of construction. Failure to finish off the jobs deprived them of the sizable property tax benefits to which they would have been entitled.

And in old buildings, there is always the unforeseen. In one, the rehabilitation was set back when a wall caved in. The staircase in another building collapsed. Demolition of a building next door to a third sweat equity building inflicted additional structural problems.

As a result, many sweat equity buildings took longer to complete and cost more than was originally projected, and some are in danger of not finishing at all under the current program.

The two buildings rehabilitated by the Mosque of Islamic Brotherhood, 55 St. Nicholas Ave. and 132 West 113th St., finished six months late at 10 percent over its approximately $300,000 budget. Residents moved in during the summer of 1978, but because of a few incomplete items such as storm windows (not in the original work specifications, according to the Mosque) and window gates, the loan was not closed out until January, 1979. The organization attributes the $30,000 overrun to inflation and delays that prolonged the construction loan on which they were paying 13 percent interest.

The original timetable for 310 East 4th St., a sixteen-unit building on the Lower East Side, called for completion by September, 1979. Today, the building is about two-thirds finished. It will take an extension of the CETA contract to do the rest. A nearby building, 518 East 11th St., was scheduled to be 85 percent complete by June, 1979. Today it is about 30 percent complete. Hewitt said Adopt-a-Building is committed to finishing both.

What all of this says to many is that eight- to ten-month construction timetables are unrealistic. Two years may be more like it. "No sweat equity group with CETA funds can complete a building at more than 8 percent a month," said Ted Ferguson of Chemical Bank. "Historically, we've found it's more like 5 or 6 percent."

The cost problems, while worrisome, are far from insurmountable, advocates of sweat equity believe. There are alternatives. While most of them involve a larger direct or indirect commitment of public funds, the subsidies are still modest and nowhere close to the amount calculated for the Section 8 program.

SUPPLEMENT 6-2.

Community Group Profit-Sharing

Susan Baldwin

For the first time in the history of Section 8 deals between community groups and private developers, neighborhood organizations are being guaranteed a multimillion dollar piece of the action, but they're not cheering. That's because the city stepped in to set the rules.

The city's Department of Housing Preservation and Development has circulated new regulations to the developers involved in fifty subsidized housing projects in the city's ten Section 8 Neighborhood Strategy Area (NSA) neighborhoods, which require them to give the community sponsor a minimum of 2.75 percent of the project mortgage for five years. At the same time, HPD is telling the group that it must spend 80 percent of its allotment on HPD-approved physical improvements to the neighborhood. A ceiling of 20 percent has been set for staffing community offices.

---

* From Susan Baldwin, "Community Group Profit Sharing," in *City Limits,* January 1981. Reprinted with the permission of *City Limits,* 424 West 33rd Street, New York, New York.

Dollar estimates of the community groups' share of the total NSA profits or "syndication of equity" range from $5 to $6 million.

The syndication or sale of the tax shelter is the grease that turns the wheels and is what makes subsidized housing so attractive to investors, developers, and banks. Syndication involves selling the "paper losses" of the ownership interest in a housing project to individuals in high tax brackets (persons taxed at anywhere from 50 to 70 percent of their total worth), who invest in the project and, in turn, are able to claim tax deductions connected to the project's depreciation, taxes, and interest. Under the Internal Revenue Code, the tax benefits from the rapid, five-year depreciation are equivalent for these high-income earners to a non-taxable capital gain.

The profits from this syndication are reduced by the costs involved (lawyers', brokers', accountants' fees), which frequently run as high as 25 percent of the investment. What remains after these costs are subtracted—the net proceeds—are further reduced by deducting cost overruns, the builder's fee, developer's cost to close the mortgage, or any additional site acquisition costs. The sum left after all these deductions is the tax shelter amount that the developer and community group split.

These new regulations have set off a furor in the ranks of the more sophisticated community groups because, they contend, their partnership arrangements with developers are their own private business and should not be scrutinized by the city.

Many argue they have worked out far more lucrative deals with the developers and are fearful that HPD's interference can only lead to weakening these relationships.

"All I can see these regulations do is cause a lot of resentment," said Doug Moritz, head of Los Sures, a community organization in the Williamsburg area of Brooklyn. "Certainly, that's my reaction to them . . . It's appalling for HPD to think it can tell us what to do. If you're going to monitor performance, both [the developer and the community group] should be monitored. Not just one."

Asking, "Who's kidding whom?" he added, "Where are they going to get the staff to do this monitoring? They can't take care of the programs they already have. This is a joke."

ANOTHER PERSPECTIVE

Coming from another perspective are a group of irate smaller developers and their attorneys who charge that the guaranteed 2.75 percent mortgage payment is too much. Many of them negotiated agreements of 1 percent or less (.5 percent) months ago and are not pleased with the city's change in policy.

"HPD has the total unmitigated gall to set itself up in the Section 8 housing business," charged Kevin Sullivan, attorney for developer John Skelly. "Here you have a program that has been working well for fifteen years. It has been very successful, so now they want to start playing around and do social planning." Sullivan and Skelly are both former city housing officials.

According to Sullivan, Skelly and several of his clients had negotiated for the 1 percent share and would find it difficult to pay out three times as much less than a year later. "When we mentioned this change to our general contractor," Sullivan reported, "he first threatened to back out of the job and then he said, 'Marvelous. That comes out of your part.' "

Why is the city taking on this role of policing community groups' intended use of their portion of the profits or syndication? Deputy Housing Commissioner Charles Reiss, of HDP's Office of Development, said, "The answer is simply this. We are talking about a significant amount of money and we want to standardize how it is used and where it goes . . . At the birth of these syndication guidelines was Bradley Plaza.''

Construction of Bradley Plaza, the 400-unit, $20 million low-income Section 8 complex planned for the Brownsville section in Brooklyn, has been stymied for more than a year while the city's Department of Investigation has been looking into the possibility that a conflict of interest existed between the community board and a community group—Brownsville Community Council. Certain members of the Community Board #16's Housing Committee and leaders in the BCC, the project's sponsor, were alleged to be the same individuals. According to Douglas Shafer, of the *People's Voice,* a Brooklyn community monthly that first broke the story, the group was to receive a syndicated fee of some $400,000 from the developer—Starrett —''not to do what a sponsor should do, such as criticize the atrocious architectural plan or help in tenant selection.''

STRUCTURED REGULATIONS

Reiss said the impetus for setting up the structured regulations was also prompted by New York City's receiving a lion's share of almost 25 percent of the national Section 8 allotment, constituting a 5,000-unit bonus under the NSA program. In his estimation, the money which derives from the housing rehabilitation and construction work in these Section 8 projects is public funding and should be plowed back into the physical improvement of neighborhoods.

Under the regulations, participating community groups are being told that eligible activities for 80 percent of the syndication funds include making small grants or loans to small homeowners and businesses, providing seed money for other rehabilitation work, sealing up buildings, painting benches, building parks, and planting trees. On the other hand, the city will only allow groups to spend 20 percent on administrative costs which include salaries, office supplies, additional staff, and tenant organizing and counseling. ''We think this is asinine to limit groups in this way,'' said Betty Terrell, executive director of the Association of Neighborhood Housing Developers. ''If you put money into an organizer you *are* preserving the community.''

''I think it's unfair to limit the administrative portion to 20 percent,'' said Richard Brown, director of the Crown Heights Progress Council, a newly formed Brooklyn community organization.

''Those of us who are new and trying to get stronger in the neighborhood so we can help more people need this money to strengthen our offices . . . What good does it do to make these brick and mortar improvements if there is no group around to protect them? And, besides, there are plenty of other places to get money for trees.''

How, then, is HPD going to make sure that each community group receives the minimum required share of the permanent mortgage—2.75 percent—and, in turn, uses its share in accordance with the 80-20 percent guidelines?

''We'll watch them [the groups] and if need be, intercede in their cash flow. We'll put it [the money] in escrow if we have to,'' asserted Reiss. He also said that he did not expect any developer to renege on the 2.75 percent amount, adding, ''There is no legal enforcement mechanism, but if they make a commitment to us, sign it, and then break it, we are going to have second thoughts about working with them again.''

Some community groups who are serving as co-venturers with the developers are threatening not to comply with HPD's regulations. They have negotiated deals that will net them more than 2.75 percent of the permanent mortgage—some say upward to 10 percent—and agree that the city should not tell them how to spend their money.

"We always plow the money back into the neighborhood. That's why we're still around. We never pocket any for ourselves," said Galen Kirkland, of the West Harlem Community Organization. "What gives HPD the authority to tell us what to do now?" Serving as community sponsor for 182 units of new construction in West Harlem, WHCO, according to Kirkland, will receive "a large amount, a very good deal," in the partnership worked out with Harlem Urban Development Corporation and the developer—Laub and Mars Construction Company.

CO-VENTURERS

Acting as co-developer with Harbro Development Corporation, Sunset Park Renewal Committee in Brooklyn will rehabilitate 459 units and will share in a $19 million mortgage on a 60 percent (Harbro)—40 percent (Sunset Park) basis of the 10 percent equity on which the tax shelter is sold. Also in Brooklyn, Flatbush Development Corporation will act as sponsor of a 117-unit rehabilitation and will receive a 50 percent share of the tax shelter after pre-construction, management, and relocation costs are deducted.

Manhattan Valley Development Corporation on Manhattan's Upper West Side will serve as managing general partner in its two NSA projects, totaling 259 units and costing some $10 million. "If they take out the builder's risk (Builder/Sponsor Profit Risk Allowance or development fee), we will share fifty-fifty with the one developer, Graphic Systems," said Leah Schneider, MVDC's planning director. "If not, the arrangement is sixty-forty." In the arrangement with Gardel, the minority developer and contractor for the second project, MVDC will receive a third of the tax shelter profits, Gardel, two-thirds. In each case, another neighborhood group— United Welfare League—will serve as the sponsor designated by MVDC. In the case of MVDC and Sunset Park, the responsibility for managing the buildings after the rehabilitation is completed will be assumed by the two groups.

"MAIDEN VOYAGE"

James L. Robinson, an architect who has embarked on a "maiden voyage" as a developer in Upper Manhattan's Hamilton Heights, plans to comply with HPD's regulations, asserting, "I know a lot of developers are complaining, but we want to get something done. We want and need the project . . . After all, 100 percent of zero is still zero."

Robinson's project consists of two phases—the first one, rehabilitation on West 155th Street and the second, new construction around the corner on Amsterdam Avenue—and will provide 151 units of low-income housing for a total of $9.4 million.

One of the major complaints raised about HPD's plans for carrying out the NSA Section 8 program and, for that matter, any future Section 8 or subsidized low-income program, is that it does not have the capacity to screen developers and community groups. Constant questions about prospective participants range from "Does he have a track record?", "Are they a paper organization?", to "Were they involved in the Municipal Loan Scandal?"

According to Reiss and Sheldon Gartenstein, project manager for the Crown Heights and Hamilton Heights NSAs, the local community board in each area must certify in writing the proposed community sponsor, and, if the city has reason to believe a group is bogus, it reserves the right to step in and set up an escrow account. The local borough president as well as HPD's Neighborhood Preservation offices are also supposed to help in this screening and monitoring process. If, for some reason, the community board refuses to approve the proposed community sponsor's application and HPD cannot find evidence supporting this decision, the agency may overrule the board and reinstate this application.

One group in Brooklyn's Crown Heights—the Real Estate Education Society of Brooklyn—has been questioned as to its authenticity and level of activity and, according to Mike Rechner, of the local NPP office, "They were inactive until fairly recently but now have become reorganized because of the availability of NSA funds." He also said that the group has recently submitted a list of suitable neighborhood improvements to the city.

Edward Corbett, president of the group, was reached at his real estate and insurance business and confirmed that his organization was slated to be the community sponsor for a half-dozen projects with Brooklyn developer Jacob Frankel and his sons-in-law, Chaim A. Wachsman and Moishe Beilush. He did note, however, that he had not talked to them recently. Asked about his organization's share of the mortgage, he added, "I know HPD says we're supposed to get a certain percentage, but I don't have the figures in front of me . . . We're mainly concerned in teaching people not to destroy properties and turn them into slums. So often, things are fixed up, only to become a dump again."

FIGURE QUADRUPLED

A check of agreements, signed in November 1979, showed that Corbett's group agreed to accept percentages of the mortgage ranging from .7 percent to 1.1 percent for amounts as small as $6,000 and as large as $50,000 to be received over a five-year period. But, under the 2.75 percent mortgage allocation, the .7 percent figure would be almost quadrupled, leaving one to wonder if there are serious plans to change this agreement.

In the case of all but one of the Real Estate Society's projects, the land is privately, not city owned, and for this reason, the developer does not need to go to HPD to close his deals. Rather, he can go directly to the area office of the U.S. Department of Housing and Urban Development. "They've threatened to do this, but so far we are not aware it has happened," said Assistant Housing Commissioner Manuel Mirabal. "Just one thing is sure. We will know when it happens." Frankel could not be reached for comment.

Commenting on the history that led to the city's decision to set the community share at 2.75 percent, Stephen Grathwohl, who was the main packager of this proposal at HPD before becoming a consultant/developer, said, "We implemented it because so many of the groups were getting more sophisticated and not accounting for where their money went . . . It will be difficult to monitor this application because the figures did change so many times . . . I can understand why developers are complaining, particularly if they're using private land because probably they are paying $1,500 to $2,000 a unit to buy it, and HUD only allows for $500 a unit. Obviously, part of their profit is being eaten up." But, he also noted that their complaints were not justified if they were using city-owned property because HUD covers the full $500-per-unit reimbursement in its mortgage.

Grathwohl is hopeful that the city's submission in mid-December for Section 8 rehabilitation of city-owned properties will be a better indicator of how many developers are willing to share a larger percentage of the mortgage with the community.

HPD is in charge of making these selections and in this case is requiring a 3.25 percent mortgage payment to the groups—a figure that some developers claim will drive the "smaller and more honest" participants out of the competition.

Asked about the threat of developers' going directly to HUD to close a project, Grathwohl said, "I guess HPD could threaten to take away the units, but HUD would have to concur, and I don't think HUD would like to lose those units. The philosophy is to build more . . . But, even if they [developers] were to go to HUD and close and were successful, I think they would have a real tough time being a developer next year."

No one knows what next year will be like under the Reagan regime. Some wonder if the low- and moderate-income housing programs as they now exist will be dismantled or consolidated with ones that are more favorable to the middle class.

"Anything could be better than what we got in our very unequal battle with someone who calls himself a not-for-profit developer," said Elizabeth Colon, chairwoman of the Coalition Housing Development, Inc. on Manhattan's Lower East Side. "We settled on a fixed amount—$75,000 in regular installments over a three-year period. We were supposed to get almost $250,000," for the 250-unit $14 million project . . . "To date, we have only received about $35,000. We help the developer and he doesn't pay us. All he says is, 'Sue me.' . . . He uses HUD money to pay his lawyer and other fees, but HUD does nothing to hold him accountable to his contract with us."

According to William Hubbard, head of the Center for Housing Partnerships, which is developing the project, increased costs in the construction of the project have whittled his earnings down to almost nothing. Only recently, said Hubbard, has HUD been willing to accept an increase in the mortgage amount to cover those overruns and he expects shortly to be able to pay the community group in full what the agreement calls for.

Asked about HPD's restrictive regulations, Colon concluded, "Look at our situation, and the answer is obvious. Anything is better than this. At least we would get something for the community. The project could not have been done without our help. It brings to the fore one touchy question: How can a project be closed without giving the community co-sponsor what was promised? Isn't that what is meant by a partnership?"

The Special Problem of In Rem Housing

As a recently hired member of the Division of Alternative Management Programs (DAMP), a part of the New York City government agency that administers all tenant and community initiatives involving tax-foreclosed (in rem) housing, Greg Farris was directed to develop a financially feasible and politically defensible plan to transfer ownership of the old-law tenement at 504 Norfolk Street from public to private ownership (supplement 7-1).

Although he had worked with the neighborhood organizations on low-income housing problems on the West Coast before moving east, Farris knew little about New York's tenement market or the recent history and controversy surrounding the city's fast foreclosure law and efforts to involve low-income tenants in public decisions about the future of their housing and neighborhoods. Before tackling the specifics of his Norfolk Street assignment, Farris did some background reading on these and other issues related to the city's in rem housing initiatives. Much to his surprise, he learned that the tenement, which was the first form of multifamily housing in New York, was still an important feature of the city's housing stock. The typical nineteenth-century tenement consisted of a "25-by-25-foot front house, four or five stories high, with dark interior stairs, having two lines of rooms on each floor with dark bedrooms in the center, and a 25-by-25-foot rear house at the end of the lot, leaving a 25-foot-square interior court." [1] Buildings with more interior light and air, fireproof shafts and stairwells, individual water closets, and less lot coverage were built later and are known as new-law buildings after the Tenement House Act of 1901, which rendered the less livable old-law tenement obsolete.

Farris discovered that although no new-law tenements were built after 1929, when the current multiple dwelling code was adopted, together with old-law tenements, they still provided almost 750,000 apartments—nearly 40 percent of the rental stock in New York City. And, since tenements were concentrated in some of the city's oldest, poorest, and most distressed neighborhoods, where neglect and abandonment were frequent, it stood to reason that eight out of ten buildings taken by the city for back taxes were tenements.

Local Law 45, New York City's "fast-foreclosure" law, was enacted in January 1977. Besides discouraging tax delinquency, the law was intended to preserve low-rent housing by preventing further deterioration of properties likely to be abandoned by their owners. By reducing from three years to one year the minimum duration of tax delinquency permissible before the city could foreclose, Local Law 45 made it possible for the city to obtain title to and assume effective control over marginally productive residential real estate before abandonment. Properties acquired under Local Law 45 were referred to as in rem, or city-owned. Between 1978 and 1982, the city

---

1. Anthony Jackson. A Place Called Home (Cambridge), MIT Press, 1976, p. 17.

carried out seven separate sets of *in rem* proceedings—two each in Manhattan and Staten Island and one in each of the other boroughs. Excluding redemptions by landlords who eventually paid their back taxes with a penalty, these property transfers had brought more than 16,500 residential buildings into city ownership.

From his own experiences elsewhere, Farris knew that housing abandonment was not unique to New York City. Indeed, he came across a 1978 General Accounting Office study that reported 113 of the 149 cities responding to its survey had a problem with abandonment.[2] Even back then, according to the study, many cities had initiated, as New York had, "creative and innovative approaches to adapting surplus or abandoned real estate to new uses consistent with the changing needs of their population."[3] What struck Farris as unique about New York's city-owned housing problem and efforts to deal with it, however, was that many of its buildings were occupied, even though they had been permanently abandoned by their owners.

Farris quickly learned that although it was not explicit city policy to own and manage abandoned stock permanently, local housing officials knew that the economics of marginal rental housing made private ownership of these properties unlikely in the short term without some form of subsidy. They recognized that, distressed as it was, the city-owned stock was the only housing option for thousands of poor families in New York. This was why the city had embarked on an ambitious set of initiatives, including management and rehabilitation programs that involved tenant and community-based organizations, and had begun to sell properties to nonprofit housing companies and other private owners. In most cases, the lower rents of the apartments in these properties were retained through heavy subsidization.

Just by walking through some of the city's most distressed neighborhoods, Farris could tell that not all of New York's *in rem* stock was occupied or even habitable. Many thousands of apartments in New York had been abandoned by tenants and landlords long before the city began foreclosure actions under the new law. He learned that in the past few years the city had demolished more than 1,600 vacant uninhabitable buildings. This figure included some of the nearly 1,200 *in rem* structures from which tenants had been relocated into more structurally sound city-owned buildings slated for repair, rehabilitation, and eventual sale. Despite these demolitions, more than 4,000 city-owned apartment buildings remained vacant, besides almost 4,000 occupied buildings. The annual rent roll of the more than 33,000 households in those buildings should have been around $52 million in fiscal 1981, but the city had managed to collect only $39 million. (The rent collection averaged less than 50 percent of rents billed before 1981.) These gross receipts—nearly $100 million since 1978—had been more than offset by

2. *Housing Abandonment: A National Problem Needing New Approaches,* U.S. General Accounting Office Report CED-78-126, August 10, 1978, p. i.
3. U.S. Dept. of Housing and Urban Development, *Adaptive Reuse Handbook, Executive Summary,* June 1980, p. 2.

program expenses of more than $342 million in the same period. HPD's budget indicated that nearly three-quarters of the costs of operating the *in rem* program had come from federal Community Development grants. (Program costs include major capital improvements, weatherproofing and rehabilitation of structually adequate and occupied buildings, emergency repairs to buildings awaiting rehabilitation and disposition, emergency fuel deliveries, management contracts with tenant groups and community sponsors, and program administration.)

Including sales and other transfers of ownership, about 1,600 *in rem* buildings containing 17,000 units had been returned to the private sector since 1977. Farris came across a 1981 HPD report on *in rem* programs, which claimed that the full range of management and disposition programs required to handle the huge city-owned inventory were now in place and that 1981 would be remembered as "the year that the city, working with tenants, community groups and private firms, turned the *in rem* problem into the *in rem* resource."[4]

The newspaper files Farris reviewed indicated that a number of community-based organizations working with tenants in city-owned buildings disagreed with this view. They alleged that most of the property transfers that had occurred thus far involved landlord redemptions and auctions to private investors (who had no commitment to long-term residents) rather than sales to tenants. These organizations accused the city of postponing further foreclosures in flagrant disregard of Local Law 45 (supplement 7-2). City officials had acknowledged that while there were more than 35,000 properties against which they could begin proceedings at any time, they were reluctant to do so for financial reasons. A November 1980 newspaper article quoted Nathan Leventhal, deputy mayor for operations, that the city had "deliberately sought to cut back on the number of properties it obtains from tax actions because it costs so much to take care of the houses . . . [and] the federal government, which provides most of the money for the occupied properties, is unhappy about the huge inventory and has demanded that it be reduced."[5] In this same newspaper article, both Leventhal and Deputy Housing Commissioner William Eimicke, who ran the *in rem* program, criticized the community groups who were pressing for speedier foreclosure, claiming that those very groups "have not been willing to purchase houses and run them for the tenants."

While the city's top housing officials downplayed the significance of the relationship between *in rem* sales and the pace of future foreclosure actions, many community groups perceived that link as a signal of a troubling change in New York policy. The community groups could not agree to any policy that would link the rate of property intake with sales volume, if for no other reason than that they believed tenant management of city-owned housing,

---

4. *The In Rem Housing Program,* Third Annual Report, N.Y. Department of Housing Preservation and Development, Oct. 1981, p. i.

5. Ron Howell, "City Is Deadbeat, Slows Foreclosings," *The Daily News,* Nov. 19, 1980.

even without an eventual sale to the occupants, was far more cost-effective than was city management.

Farris understood that community housing sponsors also rejected the notion that the low volume of sales was their responsibility. The sponsors argued that the rate of sales to tenants would be substantially higher if the city were to establish and abide by a set of realistic rehabilitation standards up to which all buildings would be brought before sale. Until now, Farris learned, rehabilitation standards and the number of major building systems to be replaced before sale had been dealt with on a building-by-building basis through negotiation between the building sponsor and the city. Tenant purchasers were well aware that the responsibility for emergency repairs and for correcting failures of major building systems remained the city's as long as the city owned the property, but that those responsibilities would be transferred when the title changed hands. Since most occupied *in rem* buildings were old and needed more rehabilitation than the city was willing or able to pay for, and tenants were too poor to finance much renovation after buying their apartments, he understood why the controversy over sales would not be resolved until the standards for rehabilitation had been established.

An equally contentious and more politically explosive element in the debate concerned the price at which city-owned buildings would be sold to tenants. In one respect, Farris thought the matter of price should not still have been up for discussion, let alone intense debate: he found in the files a copy of a March 1979 resolution of the New York City Board of Estimate concerning the sale of city-owned property to nonprofit housing organizations in neighborhoods eligible for Community Development funds. That resolution, and subsequent elaborations to it acted upon in February 1980, provided for "city-wide guidelines to set the price of each dwelling unit generally at $250." [6] The Commissioner of Housing was given the discretion to determine exceptions to these guidelines. City records showed that since February 1980 the Board of Estimates had approved plans to sell 193 apartment buildings to residents, all for $250 per unit. According to some community groups, however, "the discretionary loophole has grown big enough to accommodate buildings in several Manhattan neighborhoods . . . where real estate values have swelled." [7] The city had begun to demand market prices for *in rem* buildings in these "rising" market areas, and many would-be tenant purchasers could not afford those prices.

Whereas the current showdown on price was focused on twelve low-rent tenements in Clinton (a neighborhood in Manhattan's increasingly expensive West Side), Farris sensed that city officials' fear of the political repercussions from possible windfall profits to residents of those buildings had begun to distort the original aims of the sales program—namely, to return

6. Michael A. Stegman, "A Preliminary Analysis of DAMP Program Sales" prepared for the Fund for the City of New York, October 12, 1981 (mimeo, p. 9).

7. "Sales Prices for Clinton Buildings is Still a Secret," *City Limits*, August-September 1982, p. 10.

city-owned buildings to the private sector (and tax rolls) while securing low-cost housing (supplement 7-3). A good example of the increasingly unpredictable sales policy was reflected in a recent notice to tenant organizations that managed their buildings as a prelude to eventual purchase under contract with the city. In lieu of the $250 price specified in the Board of Estimate's March 1979 resolution, the letter from the Department of Housing Preservation and Development (HPD) stated:

If you have successfully completed the management period, which will be determined by HPD, we will initiate discussions with you to purchase the building. While we cannot give your group an option to purchase your buliding at this time or confirm what the sales price will be, we will give you first consideration to purchase the building at a fair market price to be determined by HPD. This is not a commitment as to sale price of the building, the method by which the sale price will be determined or how the sale will be processed. . . . You will be given the opportunity to purchase your building . . . at the price determined, but if you fail to meet the price determined, HPD may sell the building to some other purchaser.

Farris knew that the more cynical neighborhood activists would read this letter as a warning to tenants that after a year or more of giving the management and maintenance of their buildings their best efforts, they could expect to have their buildings sold out from under them. That was likely to happen if the property was located in an area where private market activity was increasing.

Although the city's unwillingness to confirm the $250 price under all circumstances and in all neighborhoods was difficult for community sponsors to accept, they were particularly disturbed by the mayor's compromise plan for Clinton and other rising market areas. Under the compromise, which was accepted by the city's Board of Estimate on a split vote in late 1982, the city agreed to sell city-owned apartments to tenants for $250 per unit with the condition that the city receive 40 percent of the profit from subsequent resales. Although tenant groups were smarting over their defeat, local officials, too, had become more and more sensitive to the criticism that the entire *in rem* program, not just the sales aspect of it, was costly and ineffective.

Finally, Farris read a recent analysis of the program published by the landlord- and developer-supported Citizens Housing and Planning Council, which concluded that unless "the city's approach to the problem of landlord abandonment and management of its huge tax-foreclosed inventory is drastically changed, operation of these properties by the city threatens to be a permanent, costly, and highly inefficient public housing program likely to require an annual expenditure level of no less than $100 million for the balance of the decade or longer."[8] The alternative strategy proposed by the council called for greater emphasis on finding measures to keep properties

8. *In Rem: Recommendations for Reform,* Citizens Housing and Planning Council of New York, Sept. 1981, p. 2.

from being abandoned, modifying rent regulations to enable landlords to generate enough income to afford adequate maintenance, and returning to large auctions and bulk sales of *in rem* properties to private investors in order to get the city out of the real estate business.

Having pored through the files and gained an appreciation of the inherent tensions in the *in rem* program between those who wanted to return the properties to private ownership and tax-paying status as rapidly as possible and those who valued long-term tenant interests over market and financial considerations, Farris now had a better understanding of why his Norfolk Street assignment had been defined in terms of both financial and political feasibility. Even without these major policy considerations, Farris considered this a particularly challenging assignment for several reasons: (1) 504 Norfolk Street was in relatively good condition; (2) it was strategically located in the middle of a block on which the city owned one-third of the buildings (down from 50 percent the previous year, thanks mainly to landlord redemptions); and (3) it had a dedicated group of long-time tenants who had remained throughout a succession of owners. Because of these factors, the alternatives for disposing of the property should have been broad. Farris thought the future of this building could set the tone for the rest of the street and maybe even for the surrounding area.

Although the assignment had few formal restrictions on it, Farris's boss had warned him to keep two points in mind: that the mayor was committed to returning *in rem* property to the tax rolls and that he was increasingly sensitive to criticism of the city's practice of selling this stock for $250 per apartment. Thanks to this not-so-subtle reminder, Farris conceded that one option to which he would have to give serious consideration was keeping 504 Norfolk Street in city ownership until the strength of the hoped-for private marked revival on the Lower East Side could be more accurately assessed.

Since it is impossible to project a likely sales price for the property several years into the future, Farris decided that the most appropriate way to judge the wisdom of this "wait and see" option was to estimate the probable costs of keeping the building in central management for that time, using total holding costs as an estimate of the minimum price the city would have to get for 504 Norfolk in order to make, say, a five-year wait worthwhile. In this way, Farris would get a better sense of the magnitude of the market revival that would be needed to justify an extended period of continued city ownership.

Farris felt reasonably comfortable with the conceptual soundness of his approach, but he recognized that the projection would be difficult to carry out because the data on program costs were incomplete. He could do nothing to remedy the information shortage, but knew that he could lessen its impact by carefully spelling out all of his cost assumptions. His first assumption was that gross rents in the twelve-unit building would not be likely to rise by much more than $20 or $30 above their current level of $200 per month over the five-year holding period. At these higher levels, Farris believed, the building would produce no higher or lower percentage of rent collections than the rest of the *in rem* stock managed by the city (60 percent) and would continue to have an occupancy rate between 70 and 80 percent.

Additional assumptions upon which Farris based his assessment of the "wait and see" alternative include the following:

· basic services to the building, including heating fuel and electricity, average $90 a unit per month and would increase 10 percent a year;
· the city would have to invest $2,000 per unit in emergency repairs over the next five years to keep the property at current occupancy and rent collection levels;
· no real estate taxes would be paid during the period of city ownership, but, once sold, the building would owe taxes equal to around 15 percent of gross rents;
· administrative costs of operating the central management program are around one dollar per building daily.

With these assumptions in hand, Farris was able to estimate the cumulative value of the costs of continuing city ownership of 504 Norfolk Street for an additional five years. *Cumulative value,* the sum of each year's holding cost plus 8 percent interest, compounded annually, represents the price that the city would have to obtain for the property five years from now just to recover its holding costs over the period (complete table 7-1). The interest factor represents the opportunity cost to the city of tying up its funds in the Norfolk Street building.

Although Farris expected strong opposition from tenants to this next option, he felt compelled to investigate the potential benefits to the city of selling 504 Norfolk Street to the highest bidder immediately, rather than waiting for the market to rebound. Despite a personal conviction that all *in rem* buildings should remain as low- or moderate-rent housing, Farris real-

Table 7-1. Net Cost of Keeping Norfolk Street in City Ownership

	Year					
	1	*2*	*3*	*4*	*5*	*Total*
Gross rent	___	___	___	___	___	___
Less vacancy/collection losses	___	___	___	___	___	___
Effective rental income	___	___	___	___	___	___
Less operating/maintenance	___	___	___	___	___	___
Emergency repairs	___	___	___	___	___	___
Program administration	___	___	___	___	___	___
Net cash flow	___	___	___	___	___	___
Less real estate taxes foregone	___	___	___	___	___	___
Net holding costs	___	___	___	___	___	___
Future value of holding costs*	___	___	___	___	___	___

* Use an 8 percent interest rate to derive future value of holding costs over five years.

ized that the city could not afford to keep all of these buildings indefinitely, nor could it sell them all at bargain prices. The fact that 504 Norfolk was in good condition and in an area where landlord redemptions had multiplied in the past year suggested that a private investor might want the property now.

Farris could not judge the long-term market potential of Norfolk Street, but he had collected data on rents in the thirty-odd buildings on the Lower East Side that had undergone some renovation in the past year and had attracted more affluent tenants than were usually found in *in rem* housing. Not all of these properties were fully occupied, nor had they been operated at "revitalized" rents long enough to establish the strength of the demand for them. Nonetheless, the asking rent for the average two-bedroom unit in these buildings was $385 per month.

When rehabilitated, 504 Norfolk Street would contain twelve two-bedroom apartments with 800 square feet of living area. Because the building was in sound condition, it could be rehabilitated for about $200,000 (approximately $24 per square foot), which was very modest for rehabilitation in New York City. Financing for up to 75 percent of acquisition cost, including necessary renovation expenses, was available through the participation loan program at HPD. Under the program, a private lender financed part of the total cost at market interest rates and the city paid for the rest out of community development funds at 1 percent interest. For 504 Norfolk Street, up to half of the financed portion of the building cost was available at 1 percent, and the other half at 16.5 percent. The term of this blended interest rate loan would be twenty-five years.

Farris decided that this option should not be mentioned until he had a good estimate of how much the city could expect to sell the building for in the future and how much it would save by selling now rather than later. His decision to remain silent stemmed from the certainty of tenant and community opposition to any sale of this property for market-rate apartments. The savings in operating and holding costs could be estimated fairly easily, but a good price estimate would be much harder to derive. Farris estimated the likely sales price of 504 Norfolk in stages. First, he computed net operating income for the renovated building, assuming real estate taxes at 15 percent of gross rents and O&M costs at $110 a month, to reflect the greater service demands of higher-income tenants. This is the maximum revenue the new owner would have available to pay debt service and receive a positive cash flow return. Since market value can be approximated by capitalizing net operating income, the second step in the valuation process involved the development of an appropriate capitalization rate. (Where v = value, i = net operating income, and r = capitalization rate, $v = i/r$.)

The capitalization rate, which here is a gross return on total investment, had to be computed in two steps because part of the investment would be financed with borrowed funds and part with an investor's personal funds. Since mortgage lenders and equity investors had different return requirements and would finance different proportions of the building cost, Farris had to compute a weighted capitalization rate to estimate the current market

Table 7-2. Estimating the Current Market Value of 504 Norfolk Street

I. Estimating Net Operating Income

	Gross rents	$_____
Less:	Vacancy	_____
Equals:	Effective rental income	$_____
Less:	Operating and maintenance	_____
	Real estate taxes	_____
Equals:	Net operating income	$_____

II. Computing a Weighted Capitalization Rate

	.75 × mortgage constant	
	(based on 8.75 percent 25-year loan)	_____
Plus:	.25 × investor's required before-tax	
	rate of return	_____
Equals:	Weighted capitalization rate	_____

III. Estimating Market Value

$$\text{Market Value} = \frac{\text{Net operating income} \quad \$_____}{\text{Weighted capitalization rate} \quad _____} = \$_____$$

IV. Net Cash to the City from Sale

	Market value	$_____
Less:	Estimated rehabilitation cost	− $_____
Equals:	Net cash from sale (investor equity)	= $_____

value of 504 Norfolk. Farris computed the capitalization rate assuming that 75 percent of the purchase price (including rehabilitation) would be financed with a participation loan having a blended interest rate of 8.75 percent and that a prudent investor would demand a 20 percent return on the quarter of the costs that would be paid for in cash (table 7-2).

Farris determined market value, or the maximum price an investor would be willing to pay for 504 Norfolk under the stated assumptions, by dividing net operating income by the weighted capitalization rate he had just computed. He was quick to realize, however, that the cash the city would receive for the building was not equal to its capitalized value. Two hundred thousand dollars of the building's value would have to be allocated to rehabilitation cost. The difference between estimated market value and these costs is the amount the city would obtain by selling the building under current market conditions (table 7-2). Of course, the results of this analysis would change if the city's share of the participation loan were reduced below 50 percent of total costs or if the interest rate on the city's share of the loan were raised above 1 percent.

Using the estimated market value, Farris was able to estimate a depreciable base for 504 Norfolk and run some analyses of after-tax cash flow and rates of return. (Equity is equal to the difference between estimated market value and participation loan proceeds. Farris assumed a depreciable base equal to 85 percent of market value.) He began by assuming that the building would have a stable value over a ten-year holding period and then varied his assumptions about future value. With the results of this analysis in hand, Farris felt confident that his opinions of a likely sales price for 504 Norfolk would hold up in agency discussions about the future of the building.

Farris's preference was to build on the tenant organization's efforts to save 504 Norfolk. This plan would combine two years of tenant management, some city-supported rehabilitation, and the sale of apartments for $250 each to a nonprofit housing company to be formed by residents. He was convinced that it made sense to bring 504 Norfolk Street into one of the city's alternative management programs. The condition of the property testified to the tenants' dedication and skill despite the noticeable decline in maintenance expenditures by the owners over the past six years. A period of city-sponsored self-management would hone tenants' abilities further and prepare them to assume the responsibilities of ownership in two years. Moreover, experience showed that tenant-managed buildings tended to have higher levels of occupancy and rent collections than did buildings that remain in central management.

Farris's tenant-oriented disposition plan was prepared based on the following assumptions:

· the self-management phase would last two years, after which the twelve-unit building would be sold to residents for $250 per unit;
· during this period, occupancy levels would rise to 95 percent, rent collections would increase to 90 percent, and rent levels would be raised to "take-out" levels (those necessary to operate a building on a financially sound footing);
· during this time, the city would invest $5,000 per dwelling for immediate repairs. After sale, the city would pay for another $10,000 of rehabilitation for each unit, as needed, at 5 percent interest over thirty years. This latter debt would have to be amortized by the buyers as part of their monthly carrying charges;
· post-rehabilitation property taxes would average 15 percent of gross rents; and
· rents would be set at 30 percent of tenants' gross income and all net cash flow would be placed in a replacement reserve.

Despite his personal conviction that this option was the one to pursue, Farris realized that the plan would not prove workable over the long run unless household incomes were high enough to meet all of the costs of owning and operating the building. Casual discussion with those tenants remaining in 504 Norfolk had indicated that incomes there ranged between $8,000 and $10,000 a year and probably averaged somewhat higher than the incomes of tenants of city-owned stock as a whole. With this additional information it should be possible to determine whether tenant ownership was financially feasible and, if not, how much more assistance families would need in order to own their homes.

He prepared his analysis and proposal for 504 Norfolk knowing that well-informed advocates of the various disposition alternatives he had investigated would be attending the meeting the Assistant Commissioner had called to discuss the "Farris plan." For this reason, he was careful to spell out all assumptions and document all of his analysis and computer runs fully.

SUPPLEMENT 7-1.
The Changing Face of Norfolk Street
Tom Robbins

The Lower East Side has gone through a number of well-chronicled evolutions, moving with aches and growing pains from one burgeoning group of immigrants to a new one. Most recently, the area just north of Houston Street and south of Fourteenth Street (known variously as Loisaida, the East Village, or Alphabetton depending upon perspective) has received a good deal of attention as a possible site for gentrification. Activists there have pointed to numerous examples of speculation by both large and small entrepreneurs.

So far, however, little attention has focused on the area just below East Houston Street, a stretch of turf where, even in the 1960s when large numbers of whites sought cheap apartments in the "East Village," few ventured amidst Pitt, Ridge, Attorney, or Clinton Streets where a predominantly Hispanic population resided. Building decline, landlord abandonment, urban renewal, and demolition claimed a substantial chunk of the tenements there. But the bustling activities of a troupe of housing organizers in the Pueblo Nuevo Housing and Development Association helped to intervene in the decline of dozens of multifamily buildings, as well as planning for the renovation and new construction of hundreds of apartments which will be targeted for local, low-income residents.

But the same sort of attraction exists in the Pueblo Nuevo area as in Loisaida: buildings and land are inexpensive, the area is a short walk or bus ride from City Hall and Wall Street, and, along Orchard, Ludlow, and Essex Streets, some of the best shopping bargains in the city are available, along with an old-world flavor much sought after by today's urban gentry.

Tenant organizers at Pueblo Nuevo have traditionally come to grips with landlords who have been content to watch their buildings fall apart as long as the rent checks are coming in, and even when they are not. The organizers' task has been to help tenants put together the legal and economic tools to save themselves and their building. Some of that approach has had to be refashioned, however, as attempts are made to deal with a new phenomenon—that of landlords bent on attracting a higher income breed of tenants.

Paul Stallings began purchasing buildings in the Lower East Side with a small group of investors last summer. Since then he has come to own or manage six tenements on Norfolk Street between East Houston and Stanton Streets holding over 100 apartments in all. He is now the manager and owner—or part-owner in

---

* From Tom Robbins, "The Changing Face of Norfolk Street," in *City Limits,* July 1981. Reprinted with the permission of *City Limits,* 424 West 33rd Street, New York, New York.

some cases—of every occupied building on that block as well as one large building on the next corner. He also holds a mortgage option on two other mostly abandoned structures on the block, as well as interest in purchasing the block's vacant synagogue.

Stallings's arrival on the Lower East Side has caused more than a little commotion, although he puzzles as to why this should be so. A number of residents of his buildings, as well as organizers from Pueblo Nuevo, have charged that Stallings has harassed poor, black, and Hispanic tenants out and replaced them with young white students and professionals willing to pay rents two and three times the previous level. The charges include threats, bribes, building vandalism and even a threat to tenants that the immigration department would be called to roust any illegal aliens among them.

Stallings's six buildings, it is feared, could become the beachhead from whence a general displacement of low-income neighborhood residents is launched. "In the past month," said Margaret Fournier, a housing organizer at Pueblo Nuevo for more than three years, "I've seen a completely different group of tenants in his buildings. All the new ones have been young, white, and mainly students." When Fournier first came to 184–186–188 Norfolk Street late last year, the tenant population, she says, was mainly Hispanic and black, with rents averaging $200 per month for four rooms. She estimates the average rent now at $450 per month. "Little by little," she says, "there were payoffs to tenants to get them out."

In another Stallings-owned and -run building, organizers Miguel Badillo and Victor Castro say Stallings's ownership began with a letter circulated to tenants insisting that the immigration department had ordered that no leases be signed with tenants who had no "green cards." Any illegal aliens, the notice advised, should leave the building, as the new owners didn't wish to be forced to report them.

And at the northeast corner of Norfolk and Stanton Streets, 166 Norfolk Street is now almost wholly renovated since Stallings purchased the building last year. Of the eleven tenants in the building at the time, just five remain. Some tenants claim that harassment after Stallings took over included nailing apartment doors shut and sabotaging the boiler. The building now boasts a refurbished boiler, sanded wood floors, and copious coats of new white paint.

Paul Stallings vociferously denies all the charges. Moreover, he appears genuinely hurt by some of them. Clearly, he is not cut from the same cloth as traditional Lower East Side landlords. A Wall Street lawyer until recently, he is young, optimistic about the neighborhood, and both looks the part and speaks the language of a Manhattan professional pioneering new land.

Becoming a full-time landlord was a "lifestyle" decision, says Stallings. "I'm not really a white-collar kind of person and being a Wall Street lawyer is not my style."

Without his intervention, Stallings claims at least one of his buildings would today be vacated and abandoned, save for the drug trade that flourished there before he took over. His role has been, he insists, to salvage what slumlords before him had almost destroyed. He affects little kinship with the owners who preceded him. "They just milked the buildings, that's all," he says.

The difference between him and them, he says, can be gauged by the money he has spent repairing his stock. 166 Norfolk has already cost $70,000, he says, money he hopes to recoup from the building's twenty-four studio and one-bedroom apartments. All of his investment has come from his own and other private partners' funds, none from the government, he insists. (He found one city loan program "designed to discourage.") And some of the labor involved has been his own—"I'm a pretty fair carpenter and electrician," he says—and his father is a professional contractor.

To a large extent, Stallings is the brownstone pioneer writ large: he seems to enjoy the manual work involved in running his own buildings, as well as the thought of restoring some faded gleam, and still holds a savvy eye on rising property values. His "lifestyle" shift included a sharp look around to see what areas and enterprises looked promising. Becoming a Lower East Side landlord seemed to hold both. He was not oblivious, he says dryly, to the changing patterns in the neighborhood, but he responds defensively to questions as to whether he sees himself as part of a gentrifying trend. "I don't think it's inevitable that every building down here has to become city-owned," he says. "If you define gentrification as renovating dilapidated buildings, then I'm guilty," he agrees. "But I've put my money and my sweat into stopping these places from becoming abandoned shells."

As to the impact of his ownership and the high price of his apartments, Stallings admits only to a bias toward working people as tenants and a desire to avoid welfare families. "I didn't find them responsible in the past," he says. Students, however, don't always have jobs, and many survive on a welfare system of their own. But they are apparently widely welcomed in the Norfolk Street buildings. The racial changes in the tenancy of his buildings is also a matter of dispute to Stallings, although he could name no Hispanic tenants to whom he had rented since buying the buildings and only five blacks, three of whom were roommates of whites.

Still, Stallings insists, he is being unfairly targeted. "The stench in the building right next door to 153 Norfolk (a thirty-unit building he owns) is terrible. The boiler there is always broken and I can tell you of many buildings on Clinton Avenue that are much worse. Mine may not be the greatest buildings in the world in all respects, but I haven't seen any efforts by Pueblo Nuevo to organize in any of those other buildings I'm talking about.

"If their goal is to provide the best possible services to tenants then I'm a little at a loss as to why me—I'm certainly not the worst landlord around."

Around the corner and two blocks east on Houston Street from Norfolk Street in a long open office, three Pueblo Nuevo organizers denied that Stallings was being singled out. The housing organization's involvement with the landlord and his buildings grew, they said, over a period of months as more tenants from different buildings sought their assistance. The stories the tenants and organizers relate are a far cry from the fairly passive renewal Stallings claims to be carrying out.

- In 153–155 Norfolk, a thirty-unit building, sixteen tenants recently formed an association to counter what they described in a letter to Stallings as a "vast disparity from tenant to tenant, not only in quality of service, but in tactics apparently designed to encourage or discourage tenancy." The association represents a significant change in its combination of both longtime, generally poorer and minority tenants as well as newer, better-off young whites. Some of those new tenants say they were told by Stallings that he was getting the "bad elements" out of the building. The new alliance between tenants represents a potentially major stumbling block to any plans to make further changes in the building's makeup. "We greatly resent," the tenants' letter said, "the highly illegal, at worst, and questionable, at best, tactics used to shuffle [low-income tenants] out."
- At 166 Norfolk, where tenants charged heavy-handed harassment was used to empty the building, a letter was circulated after Stallings bought the building telling tenants to leave because no services would be provided. Stallings insists that when

he bought the building it was in no shape to house anyone and there was no possible way to provide services. Tenant organizer Miguel Badillo insists that Stallings's workers damaged the boiler while it was still functionable.

· At 170 Norfolk Street, Stallings says, in the peculiar mathematical lingo of speculators, that he "owns only a small piece of a second mortgage." There, only three tenants are left and neither Stallings nor Pueblo Nuevo are attempting to get anything going. When funds are available, he said, he would like to renovate that building as well.

· 178 Norfolk is a building that has almost wholly resisted Stallings since he bought it. A rent strike has been in effect there since last fall and tenants have spent their rent monies on repairs for individual apartments. Relations there are the most stormy between tenants and landlord, and it is also another building where vacant apartments have been rented to students at rents of $292 per month for one, and $436 per month for another. The tenants, led by Maria Torres and Ramon Monte, offered several months ago to raise their rents from an average of $100 per month to $125 if Stallings would agree to a list of repairs and a promise to end harassment, including the immigration threats. The agreement remains unsigned. Stallings says he informed tenants that he had circulated the "green card" notice at the behest of the immigration department to fulfill a technicality brought on by the previous owner and that he has told tenants he would sign leases "with anyone."

· 184–188 Norfolk are in the best shape relative to Stallings's other buildings. It is where he has his small office and where his father took an apartment last year. That good condition, however, has made those buildings have the most rapid racial and economic turnover, accompanied by cash offers to tenants to move out. As in other buildings, the Pueblo Nuevo organizers have been able to show new renters previous leases held on their apartments and have shown that often the rents being charged are illegally high. That sort of openness with new renters has helped build a trust between tenants and has also led to several successful challenges to the rent levels. Stallings admits there have been overcharges, a fact he attributes to the fast-paced turnover of the buildings. The frequent moves, in turn, he attributes to the people who have been answering his ads in the *Village Voice* and the *New York Times*—two papers largely unavailable and unread in the neighborhood.

The new population, say organizers Fournier, Castro, and Badillo, is one which must double and triple up to afford the high rents, and in many, but not all cases, have been willing to accept such shortcomings as plastic over the windows, as in one apartment in 178 Norfolk where the rent is $475, because the stay is only temporary—until the end of the semester, or the next step up the ladder of career success.

Those changes hold out the prospect of a far different neighborhood, one which as Dorian Hastings, a tenant at 153 Norfolk and a recent arrival in the area, put it, "doesn't even create a neighborhood, just a lot of young, unsettled people."

Paul Stallings, along with Pueblo Nuevo, are looking toward improvements in the area. As a gesture of good faith and intentions, Stallings has suggested to Miguel Badillo that they work together on a vacant lot on the block to create a small park or playground. "He's talking about a vacant lot," responds Badillo, "while we're talking about the housing the people live in."

SUPPLEMENT 7-2.

City Is Deadbeat, Slows Foreclosings

Ron Howell

Maintaining that it is unable to manage thousands of new parcels of deadbeat real estate, the city has quietly decided to apply the brakes on foreclosures of tax-delinquent properties—meaning that buildings will be three and even four years in arrears by the time the city finally takes them over.

The slowdown has been ordered despite a 1976 law intended to speed up the acquisition of tax-delinquent buildings by allowing the city to acquire them after one year of nonpayment, rather than the three years required previously.

Community groups predict that the new policy of waiting years before seizing the buildings could leave hundreds of poorer tenants this winter at the mercy of landlords who either have no interest in their buildings or who are collecting the rent without making vital repairs to boilers and roofs.

The delay in foreclosing will likely cause many of these frustrated tenants to flee their apartments—leading to more and more abandoned buildings that will be reduced to shells by the time the city finally takes them over.

Housing officials reply that they have had to slow the rate of acquisition, despite the 1976 law, because they cannot continue to pay more than $100 million annually to care for the thousands of occupied apartment buildings that have fallen into their hands.

There are now more than 35,000 properties against which the city could begin foreclosure proceedings whenever it chooses, says Priscilla Budden, manager of the city Finance Department's central office for real estate. The vast majority are residential.

But the city hasn't even completed foreclosure on hundreds of other properties that are even further behind in taxes. Those will be almost four years in arrears when the city, according to its current schedule, finally lays claim to them.

"By waiting so long to acquire buildings, the city is violating the intent of the 1976 law passed by the City Council," says Sandy Bayer, executive director of an umbrella community group called the Task Force on City-Owned Property. "The intent was to take these buildings as quickly as possible to encourage payment of taxes and to prevent deterioration of the houses."

Nathan Leventhal, deputy mayor for operations, says the city deliberately has sought to cut back on the numbers of the properties it obtains from tax actions because it costs so much to take care of the houses.

He says also that the federal government, which provides most of the money for the occupied properties, is unhappy about the huge inventory and has demanded that it be reduced.

The city will be paying out about $115 million this year, mostly for maintenance of the 4,100 occupied buildings that it has foreclosed on over the years, according to Deputy Housing Commissioner William Eimicke.

Leventhal and Eimicke argue that the city cannot continue to be "the owner of last resort" of such buildings.

"My view is that we want to find some way of disposing of the properties we have

---

* From Ron Howell, "City Is Deadbeat, Slows Foreclosings," *Daily News,* November 19, 1980. Copyright © 1980 New York News Inc. Reprinted with permission.

before we start taking others," says Leventhal. "No one ever suggests how we're going to continue to pay for these buildings."

The Housing Preservation and Development Department has been trying to get rid of its current inventory by rehabilitating the buildings, encouraging tenants to buy them at modest prices and offering community groups money to purchase and manage them as nonprofit corporations.

But over the last two years the agency has been able to sell only 130 of the properties, officials have said.

Leventhal and Eimicke have criticized the community groups that are pressing for speedier foreclosure; they say these very groups have not been willing to purchase houses and run them for the tenants.

SUPPLEMENT 7-3.

Sales Price for Clinton Buildings Is Still a Secret
Tom Robbins

The mid-July swelter broke long enough to allow the city's Board of Estimate to bury a hot political item before it could interfere with an even hotter political primary. The Board used a much-favored tactic—nondecision and delay. It didn't even work up a sweat doing so.

The nagging question of what sales price the city will demand of tenants who have been managing their tax-foreclosed buildings came before the board's July 22nd meeting for the first time since that body approved a general policy of sale for such buildings over three years ago. A $250 price tag, according to the board's 1979 decision, should be a general figure; the housing commissioner would be allowed discretion in determining exceptions.

Since that time the board has approved housing department plans to sell some 1,932 apartments to tenants, all for the price of $250 or less apiece. But the "discretionary" loophole has grown big enough to accommodate buildings in several Manhattan neighborhoods, including Harlem, where real estate values have swelled.

The buildings closest to a showdown on the sales price issue are twelve tenements full of low-income tenants in the Clinton area of Manhattan's increasingly expensive West Side. Those ethnically diverse residents, with a median income of $5,100, have formed the cutting edge of the sales price dispute. Their fate, it is widely perceived, will determine that of other buildings approaching the point of sale to tenants, as well as of those ailing buildings just entering the city's alternative management programs.

Tenants last year formed the Clinton Mutual Housing Association, a self-described "cooperative of cooperatives providing security against displacement through home ownership." The association contains buildings which have already been sold (at the $250 price) as well as some—known as the Convention Center Six because of their proximity to that rapidly rising complex—which have been told by the city that they are not for sale, at any price.

Early this year when the twelve buildings were submitted to the city's Uniform Land Use Preview Procedure (ULURP) for sale to the tenants, without the critical

---

* From Tom Robbins, "Sale Price for Clinton Buildings Is Still a Secret," in *City Limits*, September 1982. Reprinted with permission of *City Limits*, 424 West 33rd Street, New York, New York.

price tags attached, the association went to work. The group rehearsed a careful presentation of background facts and personal testimony and pursued political support.

Residents who had never spoken before a public meeting were coached and encouraged. Being Clinton and skirting Broadway's theatre district, not a few of the tenants had some involvement with the theatre world. Mock hearings were held to gird themselves for the real thing, using lamps for microphones and family and friends for spectators. Economic and demographic data were compiled for review, and building management and rehabilitation experiences documented in a slide show.

Three times—before a community board housing committee, the board itself and in front of the City Planning Commission (which was convinced enough to recommend the apartments be sold to the tenants at an affordable price)—the tenants made their lengthy and elaborate presentation. Each one, however, was really just a dress rehearsal for their eventual date with the Board of Estimate.

Laid over from the June 24th calendar, the sales item was placed on the board's July agenda still lacking a specific price. Nor were there any breakthroughs in the political maneuverings to obtain one. Part of the tenants' successful politicking was the wooing of their local Democratic district leader, James McManus, who heads the mayor's county gubernatorial campaign. McManus, it was hoped, would get a deal with the mayor.

Instead of a price tag, the best the tenants got was a "sense of the Board" resolution introduced by Manhattan Borough President Andrew Stein to back the $250 sales figure. Stein became the most vocal supporter of the price after City Council President Carol Bellamy began muting her previously strong support sometime after the mayor announced his gubernatorial candidacy, and she became his hopeful successor. Because, under the city charter, only the city housing department can introduce a sales resolution, sympathetic board members were limited to this symbolic vote.

Yet even this symbolic affirmation of the right of low-income New Yorkers to live in neighborhoods with escalating real estate prices wasn't allowed to happen. Instead, the board, impotent in the face of the mayor's intransigence, approved the idea of selling the buildings to the tenants, without saying for how much. At the behest of the mayor's representative, the board dropped the price tag issue until October 28—well after the September gubernatorial primary and presumably far away from whatever political fallout the eventual sales terms might raise.

The board's move came after more than three hours of testimony in a chamber packed with over 200 tenants and supporters. The Clinton residents, joined at this parley by six Upper West Side tenant-managed buildings in the same fix, rolled out its prearranged speakers list and its purple and magenta "$250 for Clinton Too!" signs.

This fourth presentation was, as the occasion merited, the longest and most elaborate yet. It included, foremost, *Politics* (Manhattan Council members Ed Wallace, Carol Greitzer and an aide to Ruth Messinger spoke; so did State Senators Manfred Ohrenstein and Frantz Leichter, State Assemblyman Richard Gottfried and a representative of Congressman Ted Weiss); *Law* ("The [original board resolution] allowed for discretion by the commissioner, not this blatant discrimination."—Bonnie Brower, director of the Association of Neighborhood Housing Developers); *Religion* ("Why don't you sit down with Billy Graham and make a decision for Christ's sake!"—Father Thomas Farrelly of Sacred Heart Church); *Economics* ("The average income of a tenant in a city-owned building is $6,865.''—Ron Shiffman, Pratt Institute). Most notably, the tenants provided a steady stream of human survival and success stories, from mothers speaking with their babies slung over their shoulders, part-time actors describing their victory over the plague of burglaries that had followed them from apartment to apartment, and life-long Italian residents of an area once known as Hell's Kitchen, who told of heatless winters before they took over building management themselves.

This time around, the testimony had a rougher edge. Frustration was more visible in the words of the tenants than it had been two months before in the same chamber as they told their story to the planning commission. Several shouted vehemently, and one slapped a fallen piece of corroded roof facade in front of the discomforted board members. His building needed money for repairs, he shouted, not for mortgages.

At the close of the hearing, the mayor's representative coolly announced that ''the proper time to consider a sales price is when there is a sales resolution before us,'' and the orderliness that had marked even the earlier foot-stomping and cheering disappeared. A chant of ''We want Koch'' dissolved into a general chaos of hooting and yelling. After a few minutes, board members left the chamber.

Jesse Masyr, Borough President Stein's representative, eventually came out onto the floor to remonstrate with the crowd. Since there wasn't any support for the ''sense of the Board'' resolution from his peers, Masyr said, it would be withdrawn but reintroduced at a later date simultaneously with a sales disposition from the housing department. Could he assure them the sales resolution would come soon? No. Before the primary? No promises.

Twenty minutes later, the board reentered and, with short shrift, agreed with the mayor's representative's request to table Stein's resolution until the housing department produced a sales price—within four months' time.

Joe Restuccia, head of the Clinton association, who had shepherded tenants, community and political supporters alike through four hearings, stood off stage and shouted that the city sales unit had told him it could have sales dispositions within three weeks. Why should they wait four months? There was no response as the board went on to other business.

5 National Housing Policy Issues

Rentals, Condos, and Co-ops: Tax Expenditures and Housing Tenure

The government has many ways of encouraging businesses and individuals to invest in various economic sectors and different types of enterprises. One is by direct subsidies provided through the appropriations process; another is by indirect subsidies delivered through the federal income tax system. These latter subsidies are commonly called "tax expenditures," which the Congressional Budget Office (CBO) defines as "provisions of the tax code that provide incentives for particular kinds of activities or that give special or selective tax relief to certain groups of taxpayers."[1] In fiscal 1983, the CBO and the Joint Committee on Taxation of the Congress found that 105 provisions of the tax code met this definition (Congressional Budget Office, p. xi). Taken together, these tax expenditures resulted in a revenue loss to the federal government of more than $296 billion in fiscal 1983 and are projected to increase by 37 percent in fiscal 1988 to almost $405 billion (Congressional Budget Office, table A-1).

Nearly all businesses, individuals, and sectors of society benefit from tax expenditures. Military disability pensions are exempt from federal income taxes, as is income earned abroad by United States citizens. Exploration and development costs for oil, gas, and other fuels are subject to preferential tax treatment, as are certain kinds of reforestation expenditures in our nation's timberlands. Interest income earned on state and local government pollution control bonds is free from federal income taxes, and so is veterans' income received under the GI bill.

Although it does not account for a very large proportion of all tax expenditures, the housing sector benefits substantially from this form of government largesse. In fiscal 1983, nine separate provisions of the tax code affecting housing produced tax expenditures of $43 billion, which accounted for almost 15 percent of total tax expenditures (table 8-1). This total, which

* Based on a paper by Dennis Eisen (October 1981), whose assistance is gratefully acknowledged.
    1. *Tax Expenditures: Current Issues and Five-Year Budget Projections for Fiscal Years 1984–1988,* Congressional Budget Office, October, 1983, p. xi.

Table 8-1. Congressional Budget Office Estimates of Selected Tax Expenditures for Housing, 1983 and 1988

	Fiscal Year 1983 (Actual)	Fiscal Year 1968 (Estimated)
	(in billions of dollars)	
Deduction of mortgage interest on owner-occupied homes	$25.07	$37.95
Deduction of property taxes on owner-occupied homes	8.77	14.98
Exclusion of capital gains on home sales for persons aged 55 or older	1.26	2.35
Deferral of capital gains on home sales	3.77	7.03
Exclusion of interest on state and local government housing bonds:		
Owner-occupied	1.51	1.11
Rental housing	.87	2.88
Deduction of construction period interest and taxes	.78	1.70
Accelerated depreciation in excess of straight line for rental housing	.70	1.00
Five-year amortization of rehabilitation costs for low-income rental housing	.05	.06
Total	$42.78	$69.06

Source: Tax Expenditures: Current Issues and Five-Year Budget Projections for Fiscal Years 1984–1988, Congressional Budget Office, October, 1983; Appendix A, Table A-1.

is projected to increase by more than 60 percent to $69 billion in fiscal 1988, is dominated by two major tax subsidies to homeowners. Deduction of mortgage interest on owner-occupied homes saved American taxpayers more than $25 billion in personal income taxes in fiscal 1983, and deduction of property taxes saved them an additional $9 billion. In fiscal 1988, these two tax expenditures are projected to grow to nearly $38 billion and $15 billion, respectively.

Not all homeowners benefit from these subsidies. Low-income taxpayers, even if they own their homes, generally do not itemize their deductions. For that reason, and because of the progressive nature of the personal income tax system, homeowner benefits accrue largely to upper-income families. According to one analysis, 75 percent of these homeownership benefits in 1981 went to homeowners in the top 15 percent of the income distribution.[2] However, not all tax expenditures for housing accrue solely to the affluent. Exclusion of interest earned on state and local government bonds for rental housing, while benefiting upper-income investors, also makes possible mortgage loans below market interest rates to build low-income housing. Similarly, tax provisions governing depreciation of rental housing in general, and of low-income housing in particular, increase the relative attractiveness of these investments to equity investors and assist renters and the poor. Together, these tax expenditures totaled more than $1.5 billion in fiscal 1983.

An interesting and little-explored public policy issue involving tax expen-

2. National Low Income Housing Coalition, "Memo to Members," January 1984, p. 4.

ditures for housing concerns the recent rise in owners of multifamily units in the United States. For a variety of reasons, including high interest and inflation rates, expectations of continuing inflation, and lagging rents, the number of cooperative and condominium units nationwide increased substantially during the latter half of the 1970s. On the development side, 717,000 units, or 42 percent, of all new multifamily housing starts between 1977 and 1981 were in condominiums or cooperatives.[3] During the same period nearly half a million existing rental units were converted to co-ops and condominiums (Kerry, p. 4). In 1980 and 1981 combined, conversions exceeded the number of new, conventionally financed rental housing starts by 7,200 units (Kerry, p. 4). While the deepening national recession and volatile credit environment of the early 1980s caused a substantial decline in all housing starts and an abrupt end to the condominium conversion craze, the drop in activity in both market sectors is likely to be temporary.

A tax expenditure issue is embedded in the trend toward higher rates of multifamily-unit ownership. It has to do with whether government subsidies associated with housing cooperatives and condominiums are more or less than those that would occur if the same multifamily buildings had been built and operated or remained in use as rental housing. Subsidiary issues are how tax expenditures associated with condominiums and cooperatives vary with the incomes of their occupants and whether it is more cost-effective for the government to support low-income co-ops and condominiums or investor-owned rental housing for lower- and moderate-income families.

The impetus for a formal analysis of this issue arose out of a situation that is not uncommon in the nation's capital. During a congressional hearing on reform of the federal income tax laws, a member of Congress questioned whether Treasury would be better off with respect to tax expenditures if all co-ops were operated as rental units. Such pointed questions typically strike terror into the hearts of lobbyists everywhere, including, in this case, officials of the National Association of Housing Cooperatives (NAHC), who decided to engage a real estate analyst, Dennis Eisen, to investigate the above proposition.

With more than twenty years of experience in applying mathematical and computer techniques to problems in operations research, investment analysis, and financial planning, Eisen was exceptionally well qualified to carry out the assignment. Having served as a software development consultant and real estate analyst to various federal, state, and local government agencies as well as to numerous corporations, developers, lenders, syndicators, and investors, he had the knowledge and technical skills to complete the assignment on NAHC's urgent time schedule, and he had a reputation for being fair, impartial, and independent.

Eisen began to address the expenditure issues raised at the congressional

---

3. John P. Kerry, "Multifamily Housing in the 80's: Market Trends and Countercyclical Stimulus Options," prepared for presentation at a symposium on Countercyclical Stimulus for Multifamily Housing, General Accounting Office, June 29, 1982; Table 2, p. 4.

hearing systematically, by first enumerating the key differences in the tax treatment of housing cooperatives and condominiums and rental housing investments. Because owners of cooperative and condominium apartments are usually entitled to essentially the same federal income tax benefits, he chose to treat those two ownership forms as a single class. Condominium owners may deduct their property taxes and full interest payments on their individual mortgages, while tenant stockholders in a housing cooperative may deduct a proportionate share of the co-op's real estate taxes and interest on its blanket mortgage from their taxable income. Alternatively, while owners of rental housing can deduct their mortgage interest and property taxes (and other operating costs) from their rental (and taxable) income, they may also depreciate their buildings. While the tax expenditures associated with depreciation may be partially offset at the time of sale by the recapture provisions of the tax code, the tax treatment of capital gains realized upon sale reflects preferential treatment by the government, which increases the public costs associated with both rental and owner housing.

To proceed with his analysis, Eisen needed to define an unambiguous measure of tax expenditures to apply to both co-op/condo and rental projects. The measure he chose to use was the discounted present value of tax expenditures associated with the two housing types over seven- and fifteen-year operating periods using a 10 percent discount rate. Analysis over two holding periods was necessary to determine whether tax expenditures vary significantly with length of ownership.

Eisen realized that the analysis had to be applied to standardized projects so that neither differences in development cost nor variations in occupancy characteristics would bias his results. Using data from the Washington, D.C., metropolitan area, Eisen constructed development cost schedules for a "typical" newly constructed unit and a "typical" rehabilitated unit (table 8-2). The newly constructed (rental or co-op/condo) unit cost $62,000 (in

Table 8-2. Development Costs for New Construction and Rehabilitation Prototypes (in 1981 dollars)

	New Construction (unit costs)	Rehabilitation (unit costs)
Acquisition cost	—	$15,000
(Allocable to land)	—	(7,500)
Rehabilitation cost	—	15,000
Hard construction cost	$35,000	—
Land	10,000	—
Soft costs, excluding construction interest and property taxes	10,000	7,500
Construction period: *		
Interest	6,500	4,500
Taxes	500	500
Total	$62,000	$42,500

* Construction period is 1 year for new construction and 9 months for rehabilitation.

Table 8-3. Financing Parameters for Prototypes, Based on the Income Groups They Serve

New Construction and Rehabilitation Units	
Conventionally financed	14% interest, 30 years for 75% of value
Bond-financed for low- and moderate-income families	10.5% interest, 30 years for 90% of value

1981 dollars), of which $35,000 was for hard construction costs and $10,000 was for land. The rehabilitated (rental or co-op/condo) unit cost $42,500, including $15,000 for acquisition (including land) and $15,000 for rehabilitation (also in 1981 dollars).

Because a substantial proportion of multifamily housing starts are financed by state and local tax-exempt lending programs, Eisen decided to analyze two different financing arrangements (table 8-3). The new unit that would be aimed at the unsubsidized market would be financed with a conventional thirty-year, fixed-rate loan at a 14 percent interest rate for 75 percent of value. The new and rehabilitated units that were to be oriented to the lower-income market would be financed with thirty-year, 10.5 percent (tax-exempt bond financed) mortgage loans for 90 percent of value.

Eisen's assumptions regarding maintenance and operating costs are presented in table 8-4. Total first year operating costs were estimated to be $2,790 for the newly constructed and $2,126 for the rehabilitated unit. In both cases, Eisen assumed that operating costs would increase by 10 percent per year. To be conservative, he assumed that first-year gross rental income would be just sufficient to cover the sum of operating costs and required debt service payments, allowing for a 10 percent vacancy and bad debt rate (that is, total costs divided by a factor of 0.90) and to increase by 6.5 percent per year for the conventionally financed units. He assumed that rents for the lower-income units would increase on a dollar-for-dollar basis with operating costs. (For the low-income units, gross rent in year $t + 1$

Table 8-4. Operating Data for New Construction and Rehabilitation Rental Prototypes (in 1981 dollars)

	New Construction (per unit/year)	Rehabilitation (per unit/year)
Initial Year Costs		
Property taxes	$1,240	$850
Maintenance, replacement reserve	930	850
Utilities (public halls, spaces)	310	213
Insurance	310	213
Total	$2,790*	$2,126*

* Operating expenses increase at 10 percent per year; gross rental incomes increase at 6.5 percent per year for conventional new and rehabilitated housing and dollar-for-dollar with operating costs for low- and moderate-income housing.

Table 8-5. Miscellaneous Assumptions

Future Value: Capitalized value of net operating income using a 10.66 percent capitalization rate.

Expenses of Sale: 6 percent of the projected sales price for the rental and cooperative projects.

Refinancing Market-rate Rental Project: Borrow sufficient amount of capital in the fifth and tenth years of the loan period to bring loan to value ratio up to 85 percent (based on projected sales price). Second and third mortgage loans would be at an 18 percent interest rate with payments of interest only. No refinancing is assumed for the cooperatives or the low-income projects.

---

equals gross rent in year t plus the increase in operating expenses applicable to year $t + 1$, divided by .90.)

All of Eisen's relevant assumptions dealing with future value and disposition of the units are summarized in table 8-5. The conventionally financed new construction project is assumed to have a future value equal to the capitalized value of net operating income, using a 10.66 percent capitalization rate. Eisen "backed into" that rate with the assumption that the relationship between first-year net operating income and initial unit cost would remain constant throughout the analysis period. Since the rent increase limitation imposed on the lower-income units means that net operating income would remain constant over time, it follows that future value would always be equal to initial development cost. Selling costs were assumed to equal 6 percent of the projected sale price for the rental units. Eisen charged the same selling costs against the co-op since the transfer of shares of stock in the cooperative corporation may involve the payment of a sales commission or brokerage fee.

Rental housing investors were presumed to act to maximize their income. Therefore, Eisen assumed that they would take some portion of their accumulated equity out of their buildings by securing additional mortgage loans over their holding periods. Cash taken from their investments in that manner is free of any tax liability. For purposes of the analysis, Eisen assumed that an investor-owner of market-rate rental projects would borrow an amount of capital at the end of the fifth and tenth years of the loan period sufficient to bring the combined loan-to-value ratio up to 85 percent of the projected sales price at that time. (There would be only one refinancing in the case of the seven-year holding period.) Secured by second and third mortgages on the building, the loans would be at an 18 percent interest rate with payments of interest only. The loans would be paid in full at time of sale along with the unpaid balance of the first mortgage.

The size of the tax expenditure associated with a given provision of the Internal Revenue Code is partly a function of the taxable income of the affected individual or corporate taxpayers and their respective marginal tax rates. Eisen's assumptions regarding the taxable incomes for rental

Table 8-6. Taxable Incomes and Applicable Marginal Tax Rates for Housing/Occupancy Types

Housing/Occupancy Type*	Taxable Income Range	Marginal Tax Rate (%)
All investor-owners of rental housing	$60,000–85,600	42
Owners of market-rate new construction co-ops/condos	$24,600–29,900	25
Owners of market-rate rehabilitated co-ops/condos	$16,000–20,200	18
Owners of low-income new co-ops/condos	$5,500–7,600	12
Owners of low-income rehabilitated co-ops/condos	$3,400–5,500	11

* Assume married couple filing joint returns and tax rates in effect for calendar year 1984.

investor-owners and occupants of market-rate and lower-income co-ops and condos are presented in table 8-6. The reported incomes are net of all exemptions and itemized deductions, save for the housing-related benefits to which the respective taxpayers are entitled. While Eisen had no broadly representative income data for investor-owners or unsubsidized renters or condo/co-op owners to rely upon, he knew he could easily test the sensitivity of housing tax expenditures to varying assumptions about household and investor incomes. Though he did not have the facts at hand, Eisen knew he would have to obtain more nationally representative and reliable income data if the sensitivity analysis were to indicate that modest changes in his income assumptions could lead to different conclusions about which types of housing investments cost the government more in terms of foregone tax revenues. Thus, while Eisen's first-cut analysis assumed that all investor-owners of rental housing were in the 42 percent tax bracket and owners of new market-rate co-ops and condos were in the 25 percent bracket, those assumptions could be altered in subsequent iterations.

Eisen chose to handle the calculation of tax expenditures differently for rental and owner-occupied housing. In the latter case, he defined tax expenditures as the sum of the values of annual mortgage interest and property tax payments multiplied by the appropriate marginal tax rate discounted back to the present. Thus, for example, for a 25 percent tax bracket homeowner, a deduction of $2,000 in mortgage interest and property taxes will reduce taxes by $500. This tax expenditure, when discounted back to the present and added to those for the other years, will sum to the total tax expenditures associated with owning a co-op or condo. A similar analytic approach was used in the case of rental housing. He defined tax expenditures associated with rental production and operations as the sum of each year's taxable income multiplied by the investor's marginal tax rate discounted back to the present.

Eisen understood that neither the preferential tax treatment accorded the sale of a principal residence nor the more general issue of capital gains taxation was under review by the Congress at this time, which is why NAHC limited his assignment to analyzing tax expenditures relating to op-

Table 8-7. Tax Expenditures per Unit Associated with Rental and Cooperative Housing

| | | | | | Tax Expenditures | | | | | |
| | | | | Rental | | Co-op | | Difference | | |
Case	Type of Construction	Tenancy	Financing		7 years	15 years	7 years	15 years	7 years	15 years
1	New	Conventional	Market rate	Operations	$___	$___	$___	$___	$___	$___
				Sale	$___	$___	$___	$___	$___	$___
				Total	$___	$___	$___	$___	$___	$___
2	New	Low and moderate income	Tax exempt	Operations	$___	$___	$___	$___	$___	$___
				Sale	$___	$___	$___	$___	$___	$___
				Total	$___	$___	$___	$___	$___	$___
3	Rehabilitation	Low and moderate income	Tax exempt	Operations	$___	$___	$___	$___	$___	$___
				Sale	$___	$___	$___	$___	$___	$___
				Total	$___	$___	$___	$___	$___	$___

erations. He also knew that including the cost of capital gains benefits in his analysis could work against the interests of his client if this inclusion would raise his estimate of total tax expenditures associated with cooperatives relative to rental housing.

Eisen decided to analyze the tax treatment of capital gains in an addendum to his report. He knew that the tax expenditures associated with rental property sales could be treated conceptually in at least three ways. First, although the effective capital gains tax rate is almost always lower than the investors' marginal tax rates, one could argue that since payment of any tax at time of sale offsets some portion of the tax expenditures associated with project operations, the discounted gains tax should be deducted from the sum of the discounted tax savings due to operations.

Alternatively, one could argue that the lower capital gains tax rate is itself a subsidy that increases rather than decreases tax expenditures. The amount by which tax expenditures are raised would be the difference between the liabilities associated with taxing the gross gain on sale at an investor's marginal tax rate and the lower capital gains tax rate.

Eisen considered a third possibility, which would define the expenditures due to sale as those related to the investors' use of the depreciation provisions of the tax laws. Tax expenditures would be the difference between the sum of capital gains and recapture taxes actually paid and those that would have to be paid if all depreciation were recapturable at ordinary income tax rates. This net cost to the government would be discounted at 10 percent in the year paid and added to the tax expenditures associated with project operations.

The treatment of capital gains for homeowners could also be handled in more than one way. The tax laws allow homeowners to postpone the recognition of capital gains upon the sale of a principal residence if the proceeds are reinvested in another house, and then permanently exempts up to $125,000 in capital gains if the taxpayer is fifty-five years or older. Both the revenue loss associated with the postponed payment of the capital gains tax or its full value, in the case of older taxpayers, could be considered tax expenditures associated with the sale of cooperative and other owner housing. Alternatively, the difference between the gains tax and what the tax liability would be if the full gain on sale were taxed at the homeowner's personal income tax rates could be defined as the relevant tax expenditure.

As soon as he decided how he would treat the capital gains issue, Eisen completed his analyses (summarized in table 8-7). Based on his results, he prepared a memo to his client stating his findings and suggesting a housing strategy that the National Association of Housing Cooperative should promote on Capitol Hill.

Stimulating Multifamily Housing Production During a Recession

On April 16, 1982, Congressman Jamie Whitten (D-Miss.), chairman of the House Committee on Appropriations, asked that the General Accounting Office (GAO) assess existing federal policies relating to home construction. "The housing industry has been in a recession for more than three years," the congressman noted in his letter to the Comptroller General requesting the GAO study. With seasonally adjusted housing starts at fewer than one million per year for seven consecutive years, the failures of construction-industry-related businesses reaching 200,000 in recent years, Whitten directed the GAO to act with a sense of urgency. "The review," he said, "should include suggestions of ways in which the nation's housing industry could be revived."

Recognized housing experts were invited to assess the relative merits of several proposals to stimulate construction of multifamily housing, in a one-day symposium the GAO sponsored in response to Whitten's request. The panelists were sent a summary of several proposals to review before the symposium. The proposals suggested by the GAO staff differed on many points: the basic means of subsidy, methods of recapturing that subsidy, duration of the subsidy, lag time before implementation, and degree to which each is targeted to low- and moderate-income households. Table 9-1 summarizes key features of the major proposals, which also are discussed in the following overview.

SHALLOW TANDEM

The shallow tandem program would enable developers to borrow funds for rental housing at significant discounts, which would be absorbed initially by the Government National Mortgage Association (GNMA). The discounts, which would lower effective mortgage interest rates by as much as 4 percent, would be repaid when a project was sold or refinanced. Monthly payments on the discounted loans would be based on a sufficiently low interest rate (not lower than 11 percent) so that the operating revenues of new projects would cover the debt service satisfactorily. A balloon payment large enough to recover the discount absorbed by GNMA plus deferred interest on it (at the federal borrowing cost) would have to be repaid to the government after fifteen years or when projects were sold or refinanced. Because this proposal would require that the initial discount be repaid with interest, there might be little or no long-term direct subsidy associated with it.

---

* Based on a paper by William B. Brueggeman, "A Micro-Simulation Analysis of Options Intended to Stimulate the Production of Rental Housing," *Symposium on Countercyclical Stimulus Proposals for Multifamily Housing,* Washington, General Accounting Office, 1982, pp. 137–83.

Table 9-1. Selected Stimulus Proposals for Multifamily Rental Housing

	Basic Subsidy Mechanism	Recapture	Mortgage or Subsidy Limits	Household Targeting	Other Provisions
Shallow tandem	4% interest rate reduction by GNMA discount	15 years, full principal and interest at treasury rate	$40,000/unit	20% of units to households under 80% of median income	New construction; substantial rehabilitation; conversion to residential use
Interest reduction loan	Loan for 4% interest reduction: second lien	15 years, recapture limited to 60% of increase in value	"Modest design" $40,000/unit	Same as tandem	Same as tandem
Mortgage revenue bonds	Tax-exempt bonds	None	None	Same as tandem	15-year or longer ban on conversion to condominiums
Investment tax credit	10% credit to developers	None. Could require reduced basis and recovery through a capital gains tax	$40,000/unit	Same as tandem	None

Source: Abstracted from William J. Gainer, "Countercyclical Stimulus for Rental Housing: An Introduction," *Symposium on Countercyclical Stimulus Proposals for Multifamily Housing*, General Accounting Office, 1982, p. 10.

INTEREST REDUCTION LOAN

The interest reduction loan proposal is similar to the shallow tandem approach but involves a more explicit subsidy to developers. Developers would obtain first mortgage loans at market interest rates and simultaneously would obtain second mortgage loans from the government, equivalent to one-third of the interest requirements on the first mortgages. These second mortgages would be made available as long as current interest rates were high enough to discourage new rental production (that is, around 14 percent). Interest costs on the second liens would be compounded at the government borrowing rate but would come due as a balloon payment after fifteen years or when projects were sold or refinanced. However, amounts due to the government on second liens would be limited to 60 percent of the increase in property value over the ownership period. Because of this limitation, the government probably would not recover some portion of the subsidy.

TAX-EXEMPT MORTGAGE REVENUE BONDS

Tax-exempt mortgage revenue bonds (MRBs) have provided below-market financing for hundreds of multifamily rental units since the mid-1960s. The 1980 Mortgage Subsidy Bond Tax Act and subsequent additional measures enacted by Congress imposed stringent rules on targeting MRBs to certain income groups, imposed mortgage volume ceilings on states, and restricted the point spread issuers could set in their MRB programs. This proposal would eliminate some of those restrictions: (1) assisted projects could convert to condominium ownership once half the subsidy period had expired, but not in less than fifteen years; (2) the difference between an agency's cost of borrowing and the mortgage interest rate it charged would be increased by .25 percent to 1.75 percent (under market conditions prevailing in early 1982, that meant that tax-exempt mortgages would be available at an interest rate of 13.75 percent); and (3) the proposal would expand the definition of target areas in which restrictions would be relaxed to include those where a continuing crisis of affordable mortgage credit was jeopardizing the housing industry.

Under the MRB proposal, issuing and related marketing fees for forty-year, fixed-rate mortgage bonds would average 5 percent of the mortgage amount. The proposal also would set the amount of bond-financed mortgage loans at 65 percent of project costs to assure positive debt service coverage and the highest possible bond rating.

INVESTMENT TAX CREDIT

Another proposal would provide a 10 percent investment tax credit on direct project costs, excluding land, to developers of new and substantially rehabilitated rental housing. The investment tax credit proposal, however, would limit credits to $4,000 per unit constructed. For the project to qualify for the credit, 20 percent of its units would have to be rented to households with incomes lower than 80 percent of the area median. Of the proposals under consideration, this was the only one that would use a direct reduction in federal income taxes as an incentive to production. Projects would be selected for credits on the basis of several considerations, such as the need to alleviate housing shortages, the contribution of the project toward neighborhood development, and project costs. Federal assistance would be available to build and rehabilitate modest housing in eligible areas (as determined by objective indexes) for households lacking other reasonable and affordable alternatives. As a result of the subsidy, 20 percent of the apartments in eligible projects would be rented at prices affordable to families whose incomes did not exceed 80 percent of the area median income.

The participants in the GAO symposium were asked to come prepared to assess each of the proposals from both micro- and macroeconomic perspectives. To do so, they were asked to address as many of the following questions as possible.

Microeconomic Effects

· What are the short- and long-term costs of each alternative?
· How efficient will the subsidies be in stimulating housing production?
· Is repayment of the subsidy likely over the longer term?
· How efficiently can assistance be granted to distressed housing markets and to needy population groups?
· What effects will each proposal have on the existing stock? Will proposals cause marginal units to be removed from the rental inventory or expand the size or mix of the stock?
· If the timing the same for each alternative, or can some proposals be implemented more quickly so that they can be more effective countercyclical instruments than others?
· Do any of the alternatives substitute publicly assisted construction for what would have been private investment over the short, intermediate, or long term?

Macroeconomic Effects

· How will the alternatives affect unemployment in construction and other related industries? How will they affect the national unemployment rate?
· How will the alternatives affect inflation, including the price of housing and interest rates?
· How will changing inflation rates affect the rates of return on each project?
· How will the proposals affect the proportion of national credit and overall national borrowing that goes to housing?

As the research associate of one of the participants who has been invited to make a presentation at the symposium, you have been assigned the task of preparing a preliminary analysis of the relative merits of the various proposals. Having been thrust into this position more than once in the past,

Table 9-2. Value of New Construction Put in Place
1970–1981 (in Constant 1977 Dollars)
(Dollars in Millions)

Year	Total New Construction	Non Housing	New Housing Units	Housing as of Total
1970	$167,618	$123,745	$43,873	26.2%
1971	182,228	122,321	59,907	32.9
1972	193,998	122,344	71,654	36.9
1973	198,850	125,866	72,984	36.7
1974	170,289	116,693	53,596	31.5
1975	152,198	110,692	41,506	27.3
1976	163,457	110,573	52,884	32.4
1977	173,395	107,923	65,472	37.8
1978	181,987	116,096	65,891	36.2
1979	179,265	118,987	60,278	33.6
1980	160,696	116,626	44,070	27.4
1981	154,800	114,926	39,874	25.8

Source: Construction Reports, Series C-30, Value of New Construction Put in Place, Bureau of
the Census, Department of Commerce.

you know that no single presentation can be as comprehensive and definitive
as the session's sponsor would like, which is precisely why several experts,
with varying experiences and perspectives, will address the symposium.
This diversity should ensure that all the critical issues are covered and that
the vital elements of each proposal are given serious attention. In short, you
are aware that the GAO staff expects presenters to emphasize those evaluation criteria and economic considerations that reflect their respective experiences.

Before your mentor left town on other urgent business, he abstracted
some background information on national housing policy and the homebuilding industry, as shown in supplement 9-1, and a set of current data on
the rate and composition of housing starts (tables 9-2 through 9-5).

Your cursory analysis of the data does not conclusively indicate a rental
crisis, but it does suggest that some dramatic changes are occurring in the
housing sector. Whether such changes are cyclical or of a more permanent,
longer-term nature is not clear. Twenty-six percent of all new construction
in 1981 was residential, as opposed to about one-third during most of the
1970s. Although 35 percent of all housing starts in 1981 were multifamily,
higher than at any time since 1974, that was primarily because the single-
family housing sector was even more depressed in 1981 than the multifamily
sector. Between 1968 and 1974 (a period of higher-than-average multifamily
construction), multifamily units accounted for between 40 and 45 percent of
all housing starts. The data also point to other signs of distress. Thirty-five
percent of all rental starts were subsidized in 1977, compared to 56 percent
in 1981, while the proportion of conventionally financed units fell from 65
percent in 1977 to 44 percent in 1981. At the same time, the likelihood that

Table 9-3. Composition of Private Housing Starts for the
United States, 1965–81

Private Housing Starts
(in Thousands)

Year	Total Private	Single Family	Multifamily	Percentage of Multifamily
1965	1,473	964	509	34.5
1966	1,165	779	386	33.1
1967	1,292	844	448	34.7
1968	1,508	899	609	40.4
1969	1,467	811	656	44.7
1970	1,434	813	621	43.3
1971	2,052	1,151	901	43.9
1972	2,357	1,309	1,048	44.5
1973	2,045	1,132	913	44.6
1974	1,338	888	450	33.6
1975	1,160	892	268	23.1
1976	1,538	1,162	376	24.4
1977	1,987	1,451	536	27.0
1978	2,020	1,433	587	29.1
1979	1,745	1,194	551	31.6
1980	1,292	852	440	34.1
1981	1,087	706	381	35.0

Source: Construction Reports, Series C-20, Housing Starts, Bureau of the Census,
Department of Commerce.

Table 9-4. Comparison of Private versus Subsidized Rental Starts, 1977–81

Year	Total Rental Units Started	Private	Percentage of Private	Subsidized	Percentage of Subsidized
1977	459,800	298,500	65	161,000	35
1978	471,800	268,300	57	203,500	43
1979	392,900	202,100	51.5	190,800	48.5
1980	297,400	110,500	37	186,800	63
1981	220,000	97,300	44	122,700	56

Source: Construction Reports, Series C-20, Bureau of the Census, Department of Commerce.

multifamily construction was intended for owner rather than renter occupancy increased dramatically. In 1977, 23 percent of all multifamily starts were intended to be sold as condominium or cooperative units; by 1981, however, that figure had nearly tripled to 62 percent.

The data do suggest a crisis—if not in rental housing per se, then in investor and lender confidence because of the continuing inability of rents to keep up with increases in the cost of living or the cost of operating rental housing during the 1970s.

Table 9-5. Selected Data on Condo and Co-op Starts and Conversions in the United States, 1977–81

Year	Total Conventional Rental and Condo/ Co-op Starts	Rental		Condo/Co-op	
1977	389,500	298,500	76.6	91,000	23.4
1978	399,300	268,300	67.2	131,000	32.8
1979	375,100	202,100	53.8	173,000	46.2
1980	273,500	110,500	40.4	163,000	59.6
1981	256,300	97,300	38	159,000	62

Year	Total Conventionally Financed Rental Units	Conversions to Condo & Co-op	Net Rental Units Added to Inventory*
1977	298,500	45,527	252,973
1978	268,300	80,334	187,966
1979	202,100	150,000	52,100
1980	110,500	130,000	(19,500)
1981	97,300	85,000	12,300

* HUD estimates that 38 percent of all condos and co-ops are actually rented.

Sources: (1). *Construction Report C-20*, Bureau of the Census, Department of Commerce.

(2). *Conversion of Rental Housing To Condominiums and Cooperatives*, Office of Policy Development and Research, Department of Housing and Urban Development.

(3). Advance Mortgage Company Reports, 1980–81.

A more considered analysis of the available data and background information is necessary before you can prepare a draft paper. To help, your mentor has provided you with a set of housing production costs for a baseline case on which to develop a financial analysis (table 9-6). The $35,000 development cost is for a modest unsubsidized rental unit that would qualify for certain subsidies under the various program proposals. The base case analysis assumes a mortgage interest rate of 17 percent, a mortgage loan equal to 75 percent of value, an amortization schedule of twenty-five years, and a term to maturity of fifteen years. Before-tax cash flow and after-tax returns for this unassisted unit should be analyzed for inflation rates of 6, 8, and 10 percent (for rents and future value). The sensitivity of cash flow and after-tax returns to lower interest rates of 14, 15, and 16 percent should also be determined (complete table 9-7).

The simulation of operating results under alternative interest and inflation rate scenarios indicates that at very high interest rates, as long as inflation rates remain in the 8 to 10 percent range, after-tax rates of return are quite adequate, but negative before-tax cash flows would discourage lenders from financing new rental projects. "As the interest rate is lowered, both before- and after-tax returns on investment increase and the number of years that negative cash flow occur declines."[1] In short, your analysis shows that with

1. William B. Brueggeman, "A Micro-Simulation Analysis of Options Intended to Stimulate the Production of Rental Housing." *Symposium on Countercyclical Stimulus Proposals for Multifamily Housing*, General Accounting Office, 1982, p. 148.

Table 9-6. Development of Operating Cost Data for Baseline Case

Development Costs:

Land	9.4%
Direct costs	72.1
Soft costs	7.0
Interest	8.0
Property taxes	.5
Loan fee	3.0
Total development cost	100.0%
Development cost/unit	$35,000

Financing:

Permanent mortgage loan as percent of value	75.0%
Interest rate	17.0%
Amortization	25 years
Term to maturity	15 years

Operating Data:

Development period	1 year
Normal vacancy	5%
Operating expenses	35% (increasing to 45% over period of analysis)
Selling expenses	5.5%
Ratio of rent to total development cost	13.7%
Holding period	15 years

Tax Treatment:
- Direct costs—depreciated over 15 years and 175% of straight-line
- Soft costs—2% expensed during construction period, remainder amortized over 15 years
- Construction interest and property taxes during construction period—amortized over 10 years
- Loan fee—amortized over life of mortgage
- Investor tax rate—44%
- Project description—Garden apartment development, 150 units, average area = 750–800 square feet per unit, suburban location in a large metropolitan area

Source: Based on figures from William Brueggeman, in "A Micro-Simulation Analysis of Options Intended to Stimulate the Production of Rental Housing," *Symposium on Countercyclical Stimulus Proposals in Multifamily Housing,* General Accounting Office, 1982, p. 143.

lower interest rates, new unsubsidized development is more likely to occur at all inflation rates.

To simulate the effects on production of each program alternative, it is first necessary to define a yield requirement below which equity investors generally will not risk their personal funds. The literature and your own research experience indicate that after-tax yield requirements range between 15 and 20 percent of initial equity. To determine how large a subsidy would be necessary to induce new production for 15, 17, and 20 percent equity yield requirements, you program your simulation model to produce a positive cash flow in each year of operation while providing investors with

Table 9-7. Simulation Results for Base Case
(Keyed to Data in Table 9-6)

Baseline Case	Rate of Inflation	Rate of Return Before Tax	Rate of Return After Tax	Years of Negative Before-Tax Cash Flow
Interest rate = 17%	6%	——	——	——
	8%	——	——	——
	10%	——	——	——
Interest rate = 16%	6%	——	——	——
	8%	——	——	——
	10%	——	——	——
Interest rate = 15%	6%	——	——	——
	8%	——	——	——
	10%	——	——	——
Interest rate = 14%	6%	——	——	——
	8%	——	——	——
	10%	——	——	——

the necessary after-tax yields on equity for the base case project. You then estimate the subsidy needed to stimulate new rental production by taking the sum of the differences between after-tax cash flows in each operating period and in the year of sale for the subsidized and unsubsidized base case projects, and discount them back to the present at the required equity rate of return. When divided by the cost of the base case unit, the discounted subsidy is converted to the minimum subsidy required to induce production, stated as a percentage of development cost. The results of your analysis for three different equity yield requirements and inflation rates are presented in table 9-8. The table shows, for example, that if inflation is anticipated to be 8 percent and equity investors require a 17 percent return, it would take a subsidy equal to 2.5 percent of development costs, or $875 (2.5 percent × $35,000) to make the project financially attractive. Your analysis shows that at lower equity return requirements or at higher inflation rates, no direct subsidies would be needed to stimulate new production.

The next step in your analysis is to translate each of the stimulus proposals into direct subsidies implied by their respective designs, discount and translate them into subsidies as a percent of development cost, and compare them to the minimum subsidies needed to induce new production. This final comparison will enable you to determine which stimulus proposals are likely to be too small to encourage investors to build new rental housing under today's cost and market conditions and which are likely to provide more assistance than necessary to stimulate building activity.

Realizing that your mentor will want to provide an overview of your results at the symposium, you summarize your analysis in a chart that shows

Table 9-8. **Estimates of Subsidy as a Percentage of
Development Cost Needed to Induce New
Rental Housing Development**

Required After-Tax Return on Equity to Investors	Minimum Subsidy Cost as Percentage of Development Cost		
	Inflation Rate		
	6%	8%	10%
15%	6%	*	*
17%	9	2.5	*
20%	12.7	7.9	1.4

Note: A 17 percent mortgage interest rate is assumed in this chart.

  * At this combination of equity yield and inflation rate, no direct subsidy should be needed to stimulate production.

Source: William B. Brueggeman, "A Micro-Simulation Analysis of Options Intended to Stimulate the Production of Rental Housing," *Symposium on Countercyclical Stimulus Proposals for Multifamily Housing,* General Accounting Office, 1982, p. 152.

the following for the base case and each program option: after-tax return on investment; years of negative before-tax cash flow; the discounted subsidy as a percent of development cost; and the difference between the minimum subsidy needed to induce new construction and the subsidy provided for in each stimulus proposal (table 9-9).

In addition to assessing the stimulus proposals quantitatively, it is important that you also evaluate them in qualitative terms. Although you will complete more detailed analysis later, a good way to organize your thoughts now is to compare the proposals according to the qualitative criteria suggested by your boss (table 9-10).

To be effective, a countercyclical program must produce housing that would not be built otherwise or must speed up production as quickly as possible. If programs take too long to be implemented, the stimulus to the market is lost and the subsidy may simply be substituted for private capital that eventually would have been invested in housing during a general economic recovery. Even worse, depending on its size, an ill-timed countercyclical program that acts cyclically may even force rental prices upward by increasing the short-run demand for land, labor, and capital at a time when the rate of new construction already has risen substantially. For that reason, it is also important to assess the time frame for the implementation of proposals put forth by the GAO staff (table 9-11).

Once you have completed all your simulation runs (tables 9-7 through 9-9) and your qualitative assessments (table 9-10), you will be able to draft your paper. In preparing to write the paper, you are reminded of your mentor's caution not to lose sight of the forest for the trees, which you interpret to mean that you should not get lost in the numbers but should be prepared to explain how the different stimulus proposals cause variations in

Table 9-9. Estimates of Rates of Return, Cash Flow Patterns, and Subsidy Costs for Program Options

Program Options	Inflation Rate (Percent)	After-Tax Return On Investment	Years of Negative Cash Flow	Discounted Subsidy as Percentage of Development Cost	Excess (+) or Deficiency (−) of Stimulus Proposal Subsidy over Minimum Needed to Induce Production*
Base Case (from table 9-7, assuming 17% interest)	6	—		0	6.0%
	8	—		0	0
	10	—		0	0
Shallow tandem	6	11.4	3	-0.3	-6.3
	8	17.3	2	-0.8	-0.8
	10	21.6	1	-1.1	-1.1
Interest-rate subsidy	6	16.0	0	5.0	-1.0
	8	19.4	0	3.5	+3.5
	10	22.6	0	1.9	+1.9
Tax-exempt financing	6	16.9	0	5.3	-0.7
	8	20.0	0	5.3	+5.3
	10	23.0	0	5.6	+5.6
Investment tax credit	6	19.0	9	6.9	+0.9
	8	23.3	6	6.9	+6.9
	10	27.3	4	6.9	+6.9

* From table 9-8; assumes a 17% after-tax equity yield in minimum subsidy calculation.

Note: A negative discounted subsidy implies that the shallow-tandem subsidy actually imposes a net cost on developers. This is due to the loss of the tax deduction on mortgage interest during operations and the recapture of the subsidy with interest at the end of the holding period. Since the net cost to the developer is equal to 0.3% of development cost under a 6% inflation situation and a subsidy equal to 6% of development cost is needed to stimulate production in the base case, the deficiency of the shallow-tandem subsidy stimulus proposal over minimum needed to stimulate production is −6.3%.

Table 9-10. Comparing the Rental Housing Alternatives: Advantages and Disadvantages

	Speed of Impact	Delivery System	Administrative Simplicity	Subsidy Depth	Budgetary Impact	Before-tax Return	After-tax Return	Potential Stimulus	Cost Effectiveness
Shallow tandem									
Interest reduction cost									
Mortgage revenue bonds									
Investment tax credit									

Source: *Analysis of Options for Aiding the Homebuilding and Forest Products Industries*, General Accounting Office, August 1982, pp. 79, 83.

**Table 9-11. Implementation Time Frames for Housing Stimulus
Programs Depend on Their Complexity**

	Simple/Fast Implementation	*Moderately Complex*	*Complex/Slow Implementation*
Possible Characteristics	Current program (used before)	Modification of past program	Entirely new program
	Apparatus in place	Apparatus in place	Apparatus must be developed
	Simple targeting rules or no targeting	More complex targeting	Complex procedures
	Well understood by users	Some uncertainties	Not understood by users
Time Estimates Planning/writing regulations	2 weeks	2–4 weeks	30 days
Internal clearance	2–3 weeks	2–4 weeks	6 weeks
OMB clearance	10 days	20 days	20–30 days
Procedural steps (with congressional waivers)	1 week	1 week	1 week
Field implementation	1 day	10 days	60 days
Market response	2 months	3–9 months	3–9 months
Total time	4 months	5–11 months	9–15 months

Source: Analysis of Options for Aiding the Homebuilding and Forest Products Industries, Genral Accounting Office, 1982,
   p. 32.

project performance and why their respective costs may differ for different
inflation rates and from each other. It is also well to keep in mind your
mentor's admonition to disregard the politics of the moment and not to
worry about whether the administration and Congress are prepared to enact
a countercyclical measure to aid the industry and ease the nation's housing
problems at this time. Cyclical problems have plagued the industry for years
and are likely to recur in the future. The more advanced thought that can be
given to the problems, the more likely it is that a set of cost-effective program responses can be developed and will be available for use in the event
of similar housing production crises in the future.

SUPPLEMENT 9-1.

Conditions in the Homebuilding Industry

The homebuilding industry is in the fourth year of a deep recession. Construction starts in 1981 reached their lowest levels since 1946, with little relief in sight. Unemployment among construction workers accounts for one-tenth of the nation's jobless total and is twice the national average. This is particularly disturbing since problems in the homebuilding industry affect other sectors of the economy. In particular, the housing recession has depressed the forest products industry, where production and employment have declined since 1978.

In an April 26, 1982, letter to us, the chairman, House Committee on Appropriations, expressed concern over the nation's continuing economic recession. The chairman stated that the protracted recession in the housing industry and the effect of monetary and fiscal policies on interest rates were of major importance to the nation's economic health and requested us to conduct two comprehensive reviews dealing with these issues. The first review was to involve an assessment of existing federal policies relating to home construction, including a discussion of alternatives for reviving the homebuilding and forest products industries. The second review was to be an analysis of the nation's monetary and fiscal policies, including suggestions for change. This report contains the results of the first of these reviews. The other study, which is entitled "An Analysis of Fiscal and Monetary Policies" (GAO/PAD-82-45), is being issued simultaneously.

THE HOMEBUILDING INDUSTRY: A KEY TO THE NATION'S ECONOMY

The homebuilding industry is important to the nation's overall economic well-being for several reasons. Residential construction is a major industry, usually accounting for 4 to 5 percent of the gross national product (GNP). Before the current recession, it provided employment for about 3 million workers. The level of homebuilding affects other industries, including lumber, masonry, steel, glass, and consumer durables. For example, softwood lumber used for residential construction declined from 18.5 billion board feet in 1978 to 9.4 billion board feet in 1981. At its peak, residential construction has consumed over 40 percent of the nation's softwood lumber output. Finally, the homebuilding industry has tended to behave countercyclically—that is, to counterbalance the ups and downs of the economic cycle. Historically, the industry has often preceded the rest of the economy into both recessionary downturns and periods of growth.

Homebuilding has often behaved countercyclically because of its sensitivity to the cost and availability of credit, coupled with its size and effects on other economic sectors. During inflationary periods the demand for credit rises, driving up interest rates. This is often accompanied by restrictive monetary policy, which is designed to reduce inflation by further tightening the availability of credit. Because both the homebuilder and home buyer rely heavily on credit, the result is a housing downturn that spreads to other sectors of the economy. The general economic downturn that follows usually has been accompanied by easier credit conditions and lowered interest rates. As this occurs, the housing industry revives rapidly and leads the way out

---

* "Conditions in the Homebuilding Industry," from *Analysis of Options for Aiding the Homebuilding and Forest Products Industries*, U.S. General Accounting Office, Washington, D.C., August 31, 1982.

of the recession. Although this pattern has been characteristic of previous recessions, financial deregulation and a variety of changes in the economy have led many people to doubt that the present homebuilding cycle will follow the historical pattern.

CURRENT HOMEBUILDING CYCLE MORE SEVERE THAN PRECEDING ONES

The present homebuilding cycle has been the longest in a series of peaks and troughs that have occurred since World War II. The average cycle has been about four years in length and has involved a decline from peak to trough of nearly 40 percent. The current cycle began in February 1975, reached its peak in June 1978, and has fallen by nearly 50 percent since then.

In most cycles, a recession has led to a decline in credit demand and interest rates. However, in the current cycle interest rates have remained high despite the general economic recession. In addition, many other economic signs are different from those of past recessions. Real interest rates are higher, and the percentage of income spent on housing has risen considerably. Signs such as these cast doubt on the likelihood that homebuilding will lead the way out of the present recession. The economic climate of the late 1970s has caused housing starts to fall and construction unemployment to rise.

THE COST OF CYCLICAL INSTABILITY

Cyclical instability in residential construction is costly. When housing production is expanding rapidly, new and inexperienced firms enter the field, new and unskilled workers are recruited, building materials and sites may temporarily be in short supply, and existing supplies increase in price. When housing production turns downward, workers are often discharged and unemployment rises. This, in turn, results in lost tax revenue and increased unemployment expenses.

Because of the cyclical variations in the housing industry, many construction firms are reluctant to invest more capital than absolutely necessary in training workers or in devising cheaper construction methods. In addition, the capital and managerial assets of builders are not fully employed a large part of the time. According to one study, Marion Clawson's "Shelter in America: An Interpretive Overview,"[1] homebuilding fluctuations may have cost the nation an average of $20 to $25 billion annually since 1950. While such a figure is difficult to verify, it seems clear that government, industry, and individuals all pay a part of the cost of cyclical instability in the homebuilding industry.

FEDERAL POLICY HAS SHAPED THE HOMEBUILDING INDUSTRY

The federal government's involvement in housing programs began during the Great Depression of the 1930s. Over the succeeding years, the influence of federal policies on the homebuilding industry grew to the point where a 1974 National Housing Policy Review report stated that "today there is not a single significant aspect of the vast, diverse, and complex housing market that is not affected by governmental action in one form or another."[2] The nature of federal housing policy

1. Marion Clawson, "Shelter in America: An Interpretive Overview" (Washington, D.C.: Resources for the Future, 1982).
2. "Housing in the Seventies: A Report of the National Housing Policy Review," Department of Housing and Urban Development (Washington, D.C.: 1974), p. 1.

has changed during the eight years following the National Housing Policy Review report, but the influence of the federal government on the homebuilding industry is still pervasive. For example, a recent federal report estimated that in 1981 government or government-related agencies held $101 billion in mortgages (9 percent of all residential mortgages) and insured or guaranteed another $281 billion (24 percent of all mortgages).[3]

In response to the collapse of the housing industry in the 1930s, the federal government devised two major policies that are still in place. First, the government decided to restructure the home financing system by creating institutions to provide mortgage insurance, insurance for banks and savings and loan associations, and a permanent secondary mortgage market. This restructuring resulted in the acceptance of long-term, low down payment, fully amortizing mortgages and the creation of a system to provide capital for the mortgage market. The second major policy to arise out of the Great Depression was the federal government's decision to subsidize housing for low-income families. This decision was first embodied in the public housing program authorized in 1937.

The seeds of government involvement planted in the 1930s took root during the ensuing years. Numerous federal programs germinated and grew to fruition as public acceptance of the government's role in housing became entrenched. Construction of low- and moderate-income rental housing and owner-occupied dwellings received increasing support through a wide range of subsidy and tax-incentive programs.

Several of the institutions created in the 1930s have continued to implement federal housing policy. For example, the Federal Home Loan Bank Board (FHLBB), created in 1932, has for years helped provide guidance and an expanded source of credit to institutions that make long-term mortgage loans. The Federal Housing Administration (FHA), created in 1934 to insure long-term home mortgage loans for new construction, resale, and rehabilitation, has long provided a leadership role in addressing housing needs by insuring several types of mortgages and maintaining housing standards for properties with FHA-insured mortgages. The Federal National Mortgage Association (FNMA), created in 1938, has improved the flow of mortgage capital to areas of scarcity from areas of abundance by helping to provide a secondary mortgage market.

In 1949, major housing legislation provided a national goal that still endures today: "a decent home and suitable living environment for every American family." To help achieve this goal, additional federal programs were created and the flow of federal funds into housing was increased.

The 1949 national housing goal has remained a source of direction for federal policy. However, other economic and social concerns have also helped shape the federal government's programs and policies. For example, homebuilding has long been considered a stabilizing force in the economy. As a result, the federal government has taken special action to stimulate the housing industry for the purpose of providing employment and stimulating the economy during recession.

In 1968 the Congress decided that progress toward achieving the 1949 national goal was too slow. The resulting legislation established a production schedule for the construction or rehabilitation of 26 million housing units over the following decade. New federal programs were set up to help meet the housing needs of low- and moderate-income families, including greater financial assistance for homeown-

---

3. "The Report of the President's Commission on Housing," President's Commission on Housing (Washington, D.C.: 1982), p. 160.

ership and rental housing. The number of housing units produced following the 1968 legislation rose by 65 percent over the three-year period from 1970 to 1973.

The federal government has attempted to soften the fluctuations by stimulating the industry at low points in the cycle. For example, the Emergency Home Purchase Assistance Act of 1974 attempted to stabilize the housing market against cyclical downturns by increasing the supply of subsidized mortgage credit, thereby increasing new home sales. When we reviewed the program four years later, we concluded that it did result in additional housing starts and employment, but at considerable cost. In another instance, the government attempted to stimulate housing and reduce builders' inventories under the Tax Reduction Act of 1975 by offering a tax credit of up to $2,000 for the purchase of a principal residence. However, a 1975 Department of Housing and Urban Development (HUD) study concluded that "the tax credit has had little impact on the sales of new one-family houses."[4] The debate over the success of this initiative still continues.

By the end of the 1970s, the major agencies involved in implementing the federal programs included HUD; the Farmers Home Administration, Department of Agriculture; the Bureau of Indian Affairs, Department of the Interior; the Veterans Administration (VA); FHLBB; the Department of Defense; FNMA; and the Federal Home Loan Mortgage Corporation (FHLMC). These agencies administered the wide range of programs and activities related to providing mortgage insurance and guarantees, direct loans, grants, and other subsidies for the support of federal housing policy.

4. Duane McGough, "Assessment of the Housing Market Impact of the Five Percent Tax Credit on New Home Purchases" (Washington, D.C.: HUD, 1975), p. 37.

PART TWO

Readings in Finance
and Investment Analysis

⑥ Fundamentals of Finance and Investment Analysis

Development of Compound Interest Tables

Paul F. Wendt and Alan R. Cerf

In order to understand real estate investments and related financial instruments, facility in dealing with compound interest is desirable. This article is designed to further an understanding of the use of compound interest tables and of the formulas underlying these tables. No previous study of compound interest is assumed.

Simple Interest

Simple interest, that is, interest for a single time period, must be distinguished from compound interest. For example, if Barnes loans Jones $10,000.00 at 6 percent for three years and collects the interest annually, the interest is $600.00 each year. Note that the principal of the loan is $10,000.00 at the beginning of each year, since the $600.00 is paid to Barnes at the end of each year.

Compound Interest

Compound interest reflects the fact that if interest is not withdrawn at the end of each earning period, it is added to the previous capital amount and thereafter becomes part of the accumulation on which the next interest charge is calculated. Amounts that are not withdrawn do not lie idle. Rather, they become part of the principal on which future interest is calculated.

The example below shows the growth of $10,000.00 invested at 6 percent and compounded annually for three years. Interest is not withdrawn but rather becomes part of the principal.

Investment beginning of year 1	$10,000.00
Increase during year 1 (6% of $10,000.00)	600.00
Balance beginning of year 2	$10,600.00
Increase during year 2 (6% of $10,600.00)	636.00
Balance beginning of year 3	$11,236.00
Increase during year 3 (6% of $11,236.00)	674.16
	$11,910.16

If we multiply 1.06 for the first year by 1.06 for the second year, we arrive at the amount to which one dollar invested at 6 percent would accumulate in two years. Multiplying this amount again by 1.06, we obtain the compound interest that one dollar would accumulate in three years at 6 percent interest compounded annually. This is expressed as $(1.06)^3$, which amounts to 1.191016. When we multiply this factor by $10,000.00, we have a total of $11,910.16, which is the amount determined above.

The compound amount of one dollar at different rates of interest and for various periods is presented in column 1 of the compound interest tables. To calculate the amount of any investment earning a specified interest rate compounded annually for a specified number of years, all that is necessary is to multiply the value of the investment by the compound amount of the dollar factor in the proper table.

For example, what would $20,000.00 amount to in five years if it were invested at 6 percent interest compounded annually? Look in the 6 percent annual compound interest table for the factor in column 1 for five periods, which is 1.338226. Then $20,000.00 (1.338226) = $26,764.52.

If we assume the interest is compounded quarterly, as in some savings institutions, we would look in the table with interest compounded quarterly. For example, look in column 1 in the quarterly compound interest tables for six percent and for three years. The factor is 1.195618, and $10,000.00 times 1.195618 = $11,956.18.

Note that compounding quarterly makes the investment grow faster than if it is compounded annually. The computation of the 1.195618 factor is determined by:

$$S = (1 + .015)^{12}$$

The annual rate is 6 percent, so the quarterly interest rate is one-fourth of this or 1.5 percent. Interest rates are generally expressed in annual terms. To determine interest rates for periods less than a year, the annual interest rate is divided by the number of compounding periods in the year. In each of the three years, interest is compounded four times, so the number of periods now becomes twelve instead of three.

In detail, the computation for the first year of the quarterly compounding is as follows:

Investment beginning year 1	$10,000.00
Interest at .015 for first quarter	150.00
Balance beginning second quarter	$10,150.00
Interest at .015 for second quarter	152.25
Balance beginning third quarter	$10,302.25
Interest at .015 for third quarter	154.53
Balance beginning of fourth quarter	$10,456.78
Interest at .015 for fourth quarter	156.86
Balance end of fourth quarter	$10,613.64

We can express the above by saying $10,000.00 compounded quarterly at an annual rate of 6 percent amounts to $10,613.64 at the end of the year.

The table below shows the rates and periods, starting from 6 percent compounded annually for three years.

Compounding	Interest Rate	Periods
Annual	.06	3
Semiannual	.03	6
Quarterly	.015	12
Monthly	.005	36

To obtain the monthly number of periods, we multiplied by 12 since there are twelve separate periods. The annual rate of 6 percent is divided by 12 to obtain the monthly rate of one-half of one percent.

Values Outside Tables

A problem may be encountered where n is larger than the number of periods listed in the table. This may be solved as shown by the following:

Assume the limit of the table is fifty years and we need the amount of $10,000.00 at 6 percent interest compounded annually for seventy years.

$$S = \$10,000.00 \ (1.06)^{70} =$$
$$\$10,000.00 \ (1.06)^{50} \times (1.06)^{20} =$$
$$\$10,000.00 \ (18.420154) \times (3.207135) =$$
$$\$59,075.99$$

The factors for $(1.06)^{50}$ and $(1.06)^{20}$ can be read directly from the table. The factor $(1.06)^{70}$ can be obtained by multiplying $(1.06)^{50}$ by $(1.06)^{20}$.

The time line below shows the results of the annual compounding of $10,000.00 invested at 6 percent for three years, which amounted to $11,910.16.

Values	$10,000.00	$10,600.00	$11,236.00	$11,910.16
End of Year	1	2	3	

Note that the principal value of $10,000.00 at the beginning grew at 6 percent compounded annually to $11,910.16.

We can also say that $10,000.00 is the present value of $11,910.16 three years hence at 6 percent. Recall that to arrive at $11,910.16, we multiplied $10,000.00 by 1.191016 or $(1.06)^3$. We can determine that $10,000.00 is the present value of $11,910.16 at 6 percent interest for three years by the reverse process. The amount $11,910.16 can be divided by 1.06 three times in succession or by $(1.06)^3$.

Note that for any given interest rate per period the amount of any given amount at some future date can be determined by multiplying by $(1 + i)^n$. Conversely, the present value of any given future amount can be determined by dividing by $(1 + i)^n$.

FORMULAS FOR ACCUMULATION AND DISCOUNTING[1]
Algebraically, the above can be summarized as follows:

Let: i = rate of interest per period
n = number of periods
S = compound amount

Period 1
Interest on \$1 is $(1 \times i)$ or i, and the compound amount is $(1 + i)$
Period 2
$(1 + i) + i(1 + i) = (1 + i)(1 + i) = (1 + i)^2$
Period 3
$(1 + i)^2 + i(1 + i)^2 = (1 + i)^2 (1 + i) = (1 + i)^3$
Period 4
$(1 + i)^3 + i(1 + i)^3 = (1 + i)^3 (1 + i) = (1 + i)^4$
n^{th} Period
$(1 + i)^{n-1} + i(1 + i)^{n-1} = (1 + i)^{n-1}(1 + i) = (1 + i)^n$
General Formula for Compound Amount of \$1
$S = P(1 + i)^n$
General Formula for Present Value Reversion of \$1
The present value can be determined as follows:
The general formula for determination of amount was as above:
$S = P(1 + i)^n$
where P equals the principal amount.

$$\text{Solving for P:} \quad P = \frac{S}{(1 + i)^n} \quad \text{or} \quad S\left\{\frac{1}{(1 + i)^n}\right\}$$

The factor $\dfrac{1}{(1 + i)^n}$ is found in column 4 of the compound interest tables. It is designated sometimes as v^n, representing the valuation of a residual amount.

For example, a supermarket enters into a sale and leaseback agreement with an insurance company. The insurance company wishes to determine the present value of its interest in the land and building fifty years hence assuming money is worth 7 percent, compounded annually, and the land and building will be worth \$100,000.00 in fifty years.

1. The author has drawn upon the following text in this section: M. Moonitz and L. Jordan, *Accounting, An Analysis of Its Problems*, vol. I (Holt, Rinehart and Winston, 1963), pp. 553–76.

$$\text{Present value equals } \$100,000.00 \left\{ \frac{1}{(1.07)^{50}} \right\}$$

Referring to the factor, $\dfrac{1}{(1 + i)^n}$ at 7 percent for fifty years equals

$\dfrac{1}{(1.07)^{50}} = .033948$. So the present value is $\$100,000.00 \ (.033948) =$

$\$3,394.80$.

Practice Problems

Here are some examples of accumulating and discounting. Try them out and check your answers.

Example 1: Brown loans $20,000.00 at 8 percent compounded annually for five years. Interest and principal are due at the end of the contract. How much will he receive at the end of five years?

The problem may be expressed as: $S = \$20,000.00 \ (1.08)^5$. Looking at the annual compound interest table for 8 percent, we find $(1.08)^5$ equals 1.469328, and $\$20,000.00 \ (1.469328) = \$29,386.56$.

Example 2: Investor Greene places $30,000.00 in a savings institution which compounds interest quarterly at 5 percent. What amount will he have at the end of three years?

$$S = (1.0125)^{12}$$
$$\text{where } i = .05 \div 4 = .0125$$
$$\text{and } n = 3 \times 4 = 12$$

Looking at the quarterly compound interest table for 5 percent, we find:

$$(1.0125)^{12} = 1.160755$$
$$\$30,000.00 \ (1.160755) = \$34,822.65$$

Example 3: As part of the selling price for the sale of a duplex, Armstrong receives a $10,000.00 6 percent note for three years, four months, with interest compounded monthly. Interest and principal are paid at maturity. What is the value of the note at maturity with interest?

$$\text{This may be expressed as: } S = (1.005)^{40}$$
$$\text{where } i = .06 \div 12 = .005$$
$$\text{and } n = (3 \times 12) + 4 = 40$$

Referring to the monthly 6 percent compound interest table, there is no column for forty months, but for three years:

$$(1.005)^{36} = 1.196681, \text{ and for four months } (1.005)^4 = 1.020151$$
$$\text{Thus, } S = \$10,000.00 \ (1.196681) \ (1.020151) = \$12,207.95$$

Example 4: A financial institution estimates that property it owns will be worth $200,000.00 at the end of the present lease in thirty years. Money is considered to be worth 6.5 percent compounded annually. What is the present value of this property?

$$\text{Present value} = \$200,000.00 \left\{ \frac{1}{(1.065)^{30}} \right\}$$

$$\$200,000.00 \ (.151186) = \$30,237.20$$

Ordinary Annuity

An ordinary annuity is a series of individual payments of equal amounts that are paid or received at the end of each of a number of successive periods of equal length. The amount of an ordinary annuity, then, is the total accumulation resulting from the periodic payments and interest on each of these payments.

A diagram of an ordinary annuity of $1 per period for four periods would appear as follows:

	$1.00	$1.00	$1.00	$1.00
Period	1	2	3	4

Note that an ordinary annuity is an annuity in which payments are made at the *end* of the period. Later, we will study a series of payments which are made at the beginning of each period. Such an annuity is called an "annuity due."

The formula for the compound annuity of $1 flows directly from the formula for the compound amount of $1. The amount of the annuity is the sum of the compound amounts of the several payments each accumulated to the end of the term. Assume an interest rate of 6 percent and an annuity of four payments. Then the first payment earns interest for three years, the second payment for two years, the third for one year, and the fourth does not earn any interest.

This can be shown as: $S_{\overline{n}|} = (1.06)^3 + (1.06)^2 + (1.06)^1 + 1.00$

Referring to the tables for the amount of $1:

$$(1.06)^3 = 1.191016$$
$$(1.06)^2 = 1.123600$$

Thus, we can substitute the values in the above formula and write:

$$S_{\overline{n}|} = 1.191016 + 1.123600 + 1.060000 + 1.00 = \$4.374616$$

Algebraically, this may be expressed as:

$$S_{\overline{n}|} = \frac{(1 + i)^n - 1}{i}$$

The process of accumulation of an ordinary annuity of $10,000.00 for four periods at 6 percent compounded annually is shown below:

End of Period	Interest on Balance	Receipt	Total Increase	Accumulated Total
1	—	$10,000.00	—	$10,000.00
2	$600.00	10,000.00	$10,600.00	20,600.00
3	1,236.00	10,000.00	11,236.00	31,836.00
4	1,910.16	10,000.00	11,910.16	43,746.16

The above indicates that if we deposited $10,000.00 at the end of each year for four years and money was compounded at 6 percent annually, the value of the series of payments at the end of the four years would be $43,746.16.

This annuity could be expressed in another manner. Recall our computation of the amount of $1 at a given rate of interest at a given number of periods in the future:

$$S = (1 + i)^n$$

The accumulation could be determined using this formula for each payment as follows:

Period 1 $10,000.00 (1.06)^3 = $10,000.00 (1.191016) = $11,910.16
Period 2 $10,000.00 (1.06)^2 = $10,000.00 (1.123600) = $11,236.00
Period 3 $10,000.00 (1.06) = $10,000.00 (1.060000) = $10,600.00
Period 4 $10,000.00 (1.00) = $10,000.00 (1.000000) = $10,000.00
Total $43,746.16

Note the first payment that is made at the end of period one draws interest for the three remaining periods. The payment made at the end of period four draws no interest.

The amount of $43,746.16 can be easily determined by looking up the accumulation of $1 per period at 6 percent for four periods in column 2 of the tables. This amount of $4.374616 is then multiplied by $10,000.00 to obtain the answer.

Annuity Due

An annuity due is an annuity in which each payment is due at the beginning instead of the end of the period. A diagram of an ordinary annuity of $10,000.00 for four periods looks like this:

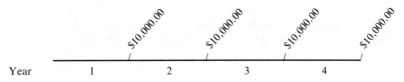

A diagram of an annuity due looks like the one below:

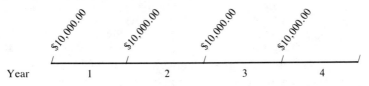

In order to calculate the amount of an annuity due, calculate the amount of an ordinary annuity for one more than the actual number of periods and subtract the last payment. This last payment will not be received, since by definition payments are made at the beginning of the period.

The formula for the amount of an annuity due of $P per period is as follows:

$$S_{\overline{n}|} \text{ due} = P\left\{\frac{(1 + i)^{n+1} - 1}{i}\right\} - P$$

For an annuity due of $10,000.00 per period at 6 percent for four periods, the formula would be:

$$S_{\overline{n}|} \text{ due} = \$10,000.00 \left\{\frac{(1.06)^5 - 1}{.06}\right\} - \$10,000.00$$

By reference to column 2 of our tables:

$$\frac{(1.06)^5 - 1}{.06} = 5.637093$$

Then, $S_{\overline{n}|}$ due = $10,000.00 (5.637093) − $10,000.00 = $46,370.93.

Examples of Annuities

Some examples of computations involving ordinary annuities and annuities due follow. Try each and then check the solution by reference to the tables.

Example 1: Reagan deposits $20,000 at the end of each year for ten years in an investment account which earns 7 percent interest compounded annually. What is the value of Reagan's investment account at the end of the ten years?

$$S_{\overline{n}|} = \$20,000.00 \left\{ \frac{(1.07)^{10} - 1}{.07} \right\}$$

By reference to column 2 of the tables:

$$S_{\overline{n}|} = \$20,000.00 \ (13.494423) = \$276,328.96$$

Example 2: Assume the same facts as in the above except that the $20,000.00 was deposited at the beginning of each period rather than at the end of the period. Now we have:

$$S_{\overline{n}|} \ \text{due} = \$20,000.00 \left\{ \frac{(1.07)^{11} - 1}{.07} \right\} - \$20,000.00$$

Column 2 of the tables gives 15.783599 as the value for an ordinary annuity of eleven periods.

$$\$20,000.00 \ (15.783599) - \$20,000.00 = \$315,671.98 - \$20,000.00 = \$295,671.98$$

Example 3: Martin has an account in a savings institution that pays five percent compounded quarterly. He deposits $5,000.00 in the account at the end of each quarter for three years. How much does he have in his account at the end of three years?

$$S_{\overline{n}|} = \$5,000.00 \left\{ \frac{(1.0125)^{12} - 1}{.0125} \right\}$$

Reference to column 2 of the tables for 5 percent compounded quarterly gives us a value of 12.860361. Therefore:

$$\$5,000.00 \ (12.860361) = \$64,301.81$$

Present Value of an Annuity

The present value of an annuity is the sum of the present values of the several payments, each discounted at the designated interest rate to the beginning of the term.

The present value of an ordinary annuity flows from the values of the present value of $1 which, recall, was:

$$a_{\overline{n}|} = \frac{1}{(1 + i)^n}$$

For example, assume the determination of the present value of an ordinary annuity of $1 per period for four periods at 6 percent. On a line diagram this may be shown as:

	$1	$1	$1	$1
Period	1	2	3	4

This may be expressed as shown below. Note the $1 to be received in a year is discounted for one period; the $1 to be received in two years is discounted for two years; and so forth.

$$a_{\overline{n}|} = \frac{1}{(1.06)^1} + \frac{1}{(1.06)^2} + \frac{1}{(1.06)^3} + \frac{1}{(1.06)^4}$$

Referring to the tables for the present value of $1 at 6 percent, we can substitute the values in the above formula and write:

$$a_{\overline{n}|} = .943396 + .889996 + .839619 + .792094 = \$3.465105$$

Algebraically, the formula for the present value of an ordinary annuity of $1 may be expressed as:

$$a_{\overline{n}|} = \frac{1 - \dfrac{1}{(1 + i)^n}}{i}$$

Values for this formula are presented in column 5 of the compound interest tables. The $a_{\overline{n}|}$ is merely a symbol for the present value of an annuity of $1.

To illustrate the use of these tables, assume a lease agreement requiring an annual rental of $10,000.00 for twenty years. The tenant desires to pay the entire lease obligation in advance and the landlord allows a discount at the rate of seven percent compounded annually for the advance payment. Assume rental payments are due at the end of the year. Then:

$$a_{\overline{n}|} = \$10,000.00 \left\{ \frac{1 - \dfrac{1}{(1.07)^{20}}}{.07} \right\}$$

Column 5 of the tables gives the factor for an annuity of $1 for the required periods and interest rate.

$$\$10,000.00 \,(10.594014) = \$105,940.14$$

Present Value of an Annuity Due

If payments are made at the beginning rather than the end of the period, then the series of payments becomes an annuity due. The formula for the present value of an annuity due is:

$$a_{\overline{n}|} \text{ due } = R \left\{ \frac{1 - \dfrac{1}{(1 + i)^{n-1}}}{i} \right\} + R$$

The present value of an ordinary annuity is calculated for one less than the actual number of periods and one payment (R) is added. This first payment is made immediately at the beginning of the first period and, therefore, requires no discounting.

Assume for example a lease agreement, as in the previous example, except assume payments are made at the beginning of the period. Thus the present value of a series of twenty annual payments of $10,000.00 made at the beginning of each year at 7 percent compounded annually is to be determined. This may be shown as:

$$a_{\overline{n}|} \text{ due } = \$10,000.00 \left\{ \frac{1 - \dfrac{1}{(1.07)^{19}}}{.07} \right\} + \$10,000.00$$

By reference to the tables we have:

$$\$10,000.00 \ (10.335595) + \$10,000.00 = \$113,355.95$$

Examples of Present Value Calculations

Here are some examples of the determination of present values of ordinary annuities and of annuities due. Try each and then check the result to the answers provided.

Example 1: Assume $5,000 a year is the income for 10 years for a net lease payable at the end of each year. What is its present value at 6 percent per annum?

This may be expressed as:

$$a_{\overline{n}|} = \$5,000.00 \left\{ \frac{1 - \dfrac{1}{(1.06)^{10}}}{.06} \right\}$$

$$a_{\overline{n}|} = \$5,000.00 \ (7.360087) = \$36,800.43$$

Example 2: A financial institution leases land and a building to a supermarket at $20,000.00, payable at the end of each year for thirty years. It is estimated that the residual value of the property in thirty years will be $100,000.00. What is the present value of the lease and the residual value at 8 percent discounted annually?

Note there is a computation required for both the present value of an annuity and the present value of the reversion at the end of the period. This can be expressed as follows:

$$\$20,000.00 \left\{ \frac{1 - \dfrac{1}{(1.08)^{30}}}{.08} \right\} + \$100,000.00 \left\{ \frac{1}{(1.08)^{30}} \right\}$$

By reference to column 5 and column 4 of the tables:

$$\$20,000.00 \ (11.257783) + \$100,000.00 \ (.099377) =$$
$$\$225,155.66 + \$9,937.70 = \$235,093.36$$

Example 3: What is the present value of a net lease of $4,000.00 per year for eight years with rentals paid at the beginning of the year, assuming an annual interest rate of 6 percent compounded annually?

This may be expressed as:

$$\$4,000.00 \left\{ \frac{1 - \dfrac{1}{(1.06)^{7}}}{.06} \right\} + \$4,000.00$$

Here, there is an annuity due, since the rent is paid at the beginning of each year. Thus:

$$\$4,000.00 \ (5.582381) + \$4,000.00 = \$26,329.52$$

Sinking Fund Payments

Periodic payments may be made into a fund in order to accumulate to a certain amount at a given future date and at a specified interest rate. These payments are often referred to as "sinking fund payments."

For example, it may be necessary, assuming a 5 percent interest rate, to have $100,000.00 available in ten years. What equal annual deposit will accumulate to $100,000.00 in ten years at 5 percent compounded annually? A line diagram would appear as follows:

	R	R	R	R	R	R	R	R	R	R
Year	1	2	3	4	5	6	7	8	9	10

$n = 10$ $i = .05$ Total Fund $= \$100,000.00$

The sum of the level payments plus interest on each payment will amount to $100,000.00 in ten years. Reference to the tables in column 2 gives the amount of an annuity of $1 at 5 percent compounded annually for ten years to be 12.577893. We can then determine the periodic deposit by dividing $100,000.00 by 12.577893. The result is $7,950.50 which is the periodic annual deposit required at 5 percent which will amount to $100,000.00 in ten years.

Basically, we are solving for R in the following formula, where R equals the periodic deposit of an ordinary annuity.

$$S_{\overline{n}|} = R \left\{ \frac{(1 + i)^n - 1}{i} \right\}$$

To solve for R, we can look up the value for the amount of an annuity of $1 at a given interest rate and number of periods and then solve for R by simple division, as above.

However, sinking fund factors are presented directly in column 3 of the compound interest tables. These factors are the reciprocals of the amounts in column 2. When these tables are available, the periodic deposit can be determined by multiplying the appropriate factor in column 3 by the amount the fund will accumulate to at the end of the specified time period. This is illustrated in the following example:

Example: An investor desires to build a replacement fund of $40,000.00 in ten years. How much would he have to invest monthly at an annual interest rate of 5 percent assuming interest is compounded monthly?

Reference to column 3 in the monthly compound interest table for 120 months gives a factor of .006440.

$$\$40,000.00 \ (.006440) = \$257.60$$

Thus, an investor would have to deposit $257.60 each month for ten years in a savings institution that pays 5 percent interest compounded monthly in order to have $40,000.00 at the end of ten years.

Assume tables were available for amounts of ordinary annuities but *not* for sinking fund payments. The answer then could be determined by dividing the $40,000.00 by the amount of an annuity of $1 for the proper number of periods and the specified interest rate. The amount of an ordinary annuity of $1 for 120 periods at an annual interest rate of 5 percent compounded monthly is 155.282279. If we divide $40,000.00 by 155.282279, the result is $257.60.

Loan Amortizaton Payments

A common problem is to determine the level periodic installment that will amortize a loan. For example, in a mortgage on a home a level monthly payment is usually made which will amortize the loan in a certain time period at the specified interest rate.

For example, assume that we wanted to determine what equal annual payment would amortize a loan of $100,000.00 received at the beginning of a period in ten annual payments at 6 percent. A diagram of this problem would appear as follows:

```
                        R    R    R    R    R    R    R    R    R    R
Loan                 ___/____/____/____/____/____/____/____/____/____/
$100,000.00   Year     1    2    3    4    5    6    7    8    9    10
                                n = 10                 i = .06
```

Note the amount of the loan is the present value of an ordinary annuity. Here the $100,000.00 is the present value of an ordinary annuity of ten annual payments at 6 percent, and the problem is to determine the amount of the periodic payment. Column 6 of the tables gives the periodic installment that will amortize a loan of $1 in ten periods at 6 percent to be .135868. If we multiply $100,000.00 by .135868, we get the required annual payment of $13,586.80.

Many tables do not have the loan amortization factors. However, the answer can readily be determined by using the table for the present value of an ordinary annuity (column 5). The amortization factors (column 6) are reciprocals of the factors in column 5.

To illustrate, assume the same problem as above. Reference to column 5 gives the present value of an ordinary annuity of $1 a period for ten periods at 6 percent to be 7.360087. If we divide the $100,000.00 loan by 7.360087, the result is $13,586.80, which is the required annual payment to amortize the loan.

Relationship of Columns

The relationship of the amounts in the various columns will be demonstrated using the example below of an interest rate of 10 percent and data for five periods.

The first column is the amount to which an investment of $1 will grow in n periods at 10 percent. This column is, of course, determined through the use of the formula $(1 + i)^n$.

Periods	1 Amount of $1 at Compound Interest	2 Accumulation of $1 per Period	3 Sinking Fund Factor	4 Present Value Reversion of $1	5 Present Value Ordinary Annuity $1 per Period	6 Installment to Amortize $1
1	1.100000	1.000000	1.000000	.909091	.909091	1.100000
2	1.210000	2.100000	.476190	.826446	1.735537	.576190
3	1.331000	3.310000	.302115	.751315	2.486852	.402115
4	1.464100	4.641000	.215471	.683013	3.169865	.315471
5	1.610510	6.105100	.163798	.620921	3.790786	.263798

The second column gives the amounts to which a series of individual payments of $1 per period will amount to at an interest rate of 10 percent per period. These are the figures for an ordinary annuity in which payments are made at the end of the period.

The second column starts with 1.000000, and each successive period adds the corresponding factor from the first column of the table. For example:

$$\text{Period } 1 = 1.000000 \qquad\qquad\quad = 1.000000$$
$$\text{Period } 2 = 1.000000 + 1.100000 = 2.100000$$
$$\text{Period } 3 = 2.100000 + 1.210000 = 3.310000$$

Returning to the basic formula, the basis for construction of column 2 is as follows:

Period 1 $1
Period 2 $1 + (1 + i)$
Period 3 $1 + (1 + i) + (1 + i)^2$
Period 4 $1 + (1 + i) + (1 + i)^2 + (1 + i)^3$
Period 5 $1 + (1 + i) + (1 + i)^2 + (1 + i)^3 + (1 + i)^4$

The first column shows the growth of $1 at 10 percent interest per period. The second column presents the accumulation of a series of payments of $1 made at the end of each period. Each deposit earns interest for one period less than the one which precedes it.

The third column presents the periodic installment which will accumulate to $1 in n periods at 10 percent. These figures are often referred to as sinking fund factors. Note that the third column is a tabulation of the reciprocals of column 2. A deposit of .163798 per period would amount to $1.000000 in five periods at 10 percent. Division of 1 by 6.105100 (factor in column 2 for n = 5) yields .163798. Stated in another way, $1 is divided by the amount of an ordinary annuity for the specified interest rate and number of periods. This may be shown as the following for n periods:

$$\frac{1}{1 + (1 + i) + (1 + i)^2 \ldots (1 + i)^n}$$

The fourth column represents the present values of $1 at 10 percent deferred n periods in the future. These are the discounted values of $1 to be paid or collected n periods from the present. Note the fourth column is a tabulation of the reciprocals of corresponding factors in the first column.

Assume that unimproved land was purchased for $10,000.00 today and held for three years. It would have to be sold for $13,310.00 to produce a yield of 10 percent. The factor 1.331000 is found in column 1 of the table at n = 3. Thus the present value of $13,310.00 in three years at 10 percent is $10,000.00. This can be determined by dividing $13,310.00 by the factor

1.331000 or by multiplying $13,310.00 by the reciprocal of 1.331000 which is .751315.

$$\frac{1}{1.331} = .751315, \text{ or, } .1751315 \times \$13,310.00 = \$10,000.00$$

Recall the formula for the present value of $1 is:

$$\frac{1}{(1 + i)^n}$$

The fifth column presents the present values of an annuity. These figures are the sum of the present values of the several payments, each discounted at the designated interest rate to the beginning of the term. These values are sometimes referred to as *Inwood coefficients*.

Each payment is one period further removed from the present than its predecessor. The fifth column may be produced by adding the factors in the fourth column and entering the subtotal in the fifth column.

Period 1   .909091 +   0 =   .909091
Period 2   .909091 + .826446 = 1.735537
Period 3   1.735537 + .751315 = 2.486852

The present value of an ordinary annuity of $1 per period for n periods may be represented by the progression:

$$\frac{1}{(1 + i)} + \frac{1}{(1 + i)^2} + \frac{1}{(1 + i)^3} \cdots \frac{1}{(1 + i)^n}$$

The sixth column is a tabulation of the reciprocals of the corresponding factors in the fifth column. These are the factors that are employed for calculating the periodic installment in level payment mortgage contracts in which the principal amount is to be amortized over the term of the contract. In such a contract the lender is purchasing the right to collect a series of future, level, periodic installments from the borrower. These installments comprise an ordinary annuity and the amount of the loan is the present value of the annuity at the contract rate of interest. The installment required per dollar of loan may be determined by dividing 1 by the present value of an ordinary annuity of $1 per period at the specified interest rate.

For example, assume a loan of $1,000,000.00 which is to be amortized by five level, annual installments at 10 percent interest. Column 6 of the table at n = 5 gives a factor of .263798 per dollar of loan. Multiplying this factor of .236798 by $1,000,000.00 the level, annual payment to amortize the loan would be $263,798.00.

Table 10-1. Sample Amortization Table

			$10,000.00 Loan	
Monthly Amortization			Monthly Payment	
5.00 Percent Interest			$106.07	

Year	Month	Balance (in dollars)	Principal (in dollars)	Interest (in dollars)
1	1	9935.601151	64.398849	41.666667
	2	9870.933974	64.667177	41.398338
	3	9805.997351	64.936624	41.128892
	4	9740.790158	65.207193	40.858322
	5	9675.311268	65.478890	40.586626
	6	9609.559550	65.751718	40.313797
	7	9543.533866	66.025684	40.039831
	8	9477.233075	66.300791	39.764724
	9	9410.656031	66.577044	39.488471
	10	9343.801583	66.854448	39.211067
	11	9276.668574	67.133009	38.932507
	12	9209.255844	67.412730	38.652786
2		8378.055717	831.200127	441.586056
3		7504.329814	873.725903	399.060280
4		6585.902435	918.427379	354.358804
5		5620.486568	965.415867	307.370316
6		4605.678193	1014.808375	257.977808
7		3538.950296	1066.727897	206.058286
8		2417.646575	1121.303721	151.482462
9		1238.974828	1178.671747	94.114436
10		− 0.000003	1238.974831	33.811352

DEVELOPMENT OF LOAN AMORTIZATION TABLES

In the above section, the method of determining a level payment that would amortize a loan of a given amount over a certain number of periods at a specified interest rate was explained. A portion of each level payment applies to interest and the remainder to reduction of the principal balance on the loan. Amortization tables indicate the principal balance of the loan at the end of each period and the amount of the payments that are applied to principal and to interest.

An example of a table presenting monthly balances for the first year and annual balances thereafter appears on table 10-1.[2] The table is for a $10,000.00 loan at five percent annual interest for ten years. The level monthly payment to amortize such a loan is $106.07.

2. The computer program for the determination of the numerical values of the amortization tables was developed and run at the University of California, Berkeley. The authors are indebted to David Moffett and C. A. Prentice for their work in this regard.

The level monthly payment can be determined directly by multiplying the factor from column 6 of the compound interest tables by $10,000.00. Alternatively, it may be computed by multiplying the reciprocal of the present value of an ordinary annuity of $1 per month at 5 percent per annum for 120 periods by $10,000.00. The present values of ordinary annuities are in column 5 of the compound interest table.

The loan amortization table is derived as follows:

Beginning balance of loan	$10,000.00
Interest for one year .05($10,000.00) = $500.00	
Monthly interest $500.00 ÷ 12 = $41.666667	
Applied to principal $106.07 − $41.67 =	64.40
Balance at the end of month	$ 9,935.60

Only annual summaries of monthly amortization are presented here. If a balance is desired within a specified year, all that is necessary is to start with the balance at the beginning of the year and calculate the yearly interest. Divide by 12 to obtain the monthly interest, and the balance of the monthly payment is allocated to principal and deducted from the principal balance. Proceed until the desired point is reached.

The amortization tables that follow show annual summaries of monthly amortization for a variety of interest rates.

Compound Interest Problem Set

Michael A. Stegman

1. The rental management company you work for pays a bonus of $50, $100, or $150 for every tenant you sign to a new or renewal one-, two-, or three-year lease, respectively. Assume that your lease-signing record over the past five years is as depicted below; that you receive bonuses at the end of the year in which you earn them; and that all bonuses are deposited into your personal savings account, which earns 8.5 percent interest, compounded annually. What would your bank balance be at the end of the period?

2. A. What periodic level payment will amortize a $50,000, thirty-year mortgage loan at 13 percent interest? Calculate separate answers, assuming annual and monthly payment periods, and explain why the sum of the twelve monthly payments does not equal one annual payment.

B. What is the present value of the monthly payments on a $35,000, thirty-year mortgage at 9 percent interest?

C. Using column 5 (Present Value of an Ordinary Annuity) of the tables, calculate the unpaid principal on a $50,000, 9 percent, thirty-three-year mortgage after eighteen years of the loan period. Assume monthly payments. Replicate your results, using column 2 of the ordinary annuity tables (Amount of $1 Per Period).

			Year		
Number of	1	2	3	4	5
1-year leases	20	20	20	20	20
2-year leases	15	15	15	15	30
3-year leases	5	0	5	10	15
Total	40	35	40	45	65

D. Construct a schedule showing the breakdown of monthly payments to principal and interest for the first five months of the loan period for a $50,000, 9 percent, ten-year mortgage.

3. Assume that the federal government has made a large volume of 9 percent, thirty-year mortgage loans to eligible homeowners and rental housing investors in order to encourage higher rates of homeownership and rental housing production. Because of the substantial budgetary impact of holding all of these loans in portfolio, the government decides to sell its mortgage portfolio on the open market. If, at the time of sale, market interest rates are 13 percent for investments of similar risk and liquidity, for how much could the government's $100 million, 9 percent loan portfolio be sold?

* Designed to be used in conjunction with *Development of Compound Interest Tables* by Wendt and Cerf. The compound interest tables and other data needed to complete this problem set follow problem 11.

4. A buyer has $23,000 to use for a down payment. He has narrowed his choices to two virtually identical houses. The principal differences between the two houses concern financing arrangements and price. One house is priced at $60,000 and can be financed with a fixed-rate, 13 percent, thirty-year first mortgage loan. The other house has an assumable loan of $43,833. The interest rate on this thirty-year assumable loan, which has a remaining term of twenty-six years, is 8 percent. The asking price for this house is $66,833, the premium reflecting the desirable financing opportunity.

A. As the potential buyer, which of the two houses would you purchase, assuming that, in either case, your down payment would be the same?

B. Would your decision change if your analysis considered after-tax mortgage costs and you were in the 32 percent tax bracket?

C. In what way, if any, would your intended length of stay in your new house affect your investment decision?

5. In 1984, Congress amended the Internal Revenue Code by increasing the minimum period over which owners of all non–low-income housing and other real estate must depreciate their properties from fifteen to eighteeen years. (The law still permits investor-owners to use an accelerated depreciation rate equal to 175 percent of the straight-line rate.) If the average investor is in the 42 percent tax bracket, calculate the magnitude of the reduction in tax benefits resulting from the lengthening of the depreciation schedule for a property having an original basis of $15,000. Use a 10 percent discount rate.

6. The Internal Revenue Code permits investors in qualified low-income housing projects to depreciate their properties at twice the straight-line rate over a fifteen-year period. The tax code also provides for the "recapture" of excess depreciation at ordinary income tax rates at the time of sale. (Excess depreciation is the difference between the total depreciation taken and the amount that would have been taken were the property being depreciated at a straight-line rate.) The recapture rate declines by 1 percent a month beginning with the 101st month of ownership.

A. Assume that a qualifying low-income property with a $150,000 depreciable base has been held for a period of 122 months, and that the investor-owner is in the 42 percent tax bracket. Using a 10 percent discount rate, determine the value of the accelerated depreciation provisions of the tax code.

B. Determine the value of the accelerated depreciation provisions of the code, assuming a ninety-nine-month holding period.

7. As indicated in question 5, the tax code also permits investors in non–low-income housing to depreciate their properties on an accelerated schedule, although the accelerated rate is more modest. More important, more stringent recapture rules apply. In the case of non–low-income housing investments, all excess depreciation is recaptured regardless of how long the property is held. Given these more stringent recapture rules, determine the following:

A. The value of the accelerated depreciation provisions of the tax code for an investor in the 42 percent tax bracket who holds the property having a $150,000 basis for a period of five years. (Use a 10 percent discount rate.)

B. The value of these same provisions for an eighteen-year holding period.

8. Another tax benefit associated with the ownership of income-producing real estate is the conversion of ordinary income into capital gains, since the latter are taxed at lower rates than the former. (Sixty percent of a long-term capital gain is excluded from any tax liability; the remaining 40 percent is added to ordinary income and taxed at personal income tax rates.)

A. Assume that a taxpayer in the 42 percent bracket acquires and holds a property for five years and then sells it for $170,000, the same price he paid for it. If the original basis of the property was $150,000 and the investor-owner depreciated the property under the eighteen-year accelerated cost recovery system (which is equivalent to 175 percent of the straight-line rate), calculate the value of the income conversion provision of the tax code. (Use a 10 percent discount rate.)

B. What is the value of these same provisions if the property were held ten years and then sold at the same price?

9. Using the following data for a low-income housing project, determine the investor-owner's tax liability in the year of sale if the project is sold for its outstanding mortgage balance.

Original development cost	$1,150,000
Initial project mortgage	$1,100,000
Mortgage term	30 years
Mortgage interest rate	13 percent
Depreciable base	$1,000,000
Holding period	48 months
Investor tax bracket	42 percent

How does your answer illustrate the riskiness of assisted housing investments and the financial danger of an early mortgage foreclosure or distressed sale?

10. Using a community development block grant and locally generated funds, a municipality has created a housing assistance program that provides subsidies of up to $15,000 per housing unit to rehabilitate or develop new housing for lower- and moderate-income families. The program rules allow the subsidy to be used in a variety of ways. Using the project data presented below, answer questions A through H.

PROJECT DATA

Total development cost per unit	$40,000
Market interest rate	13 percent
Mortgage term	30 years
Maintenance and operating costs/unit, including real estate taxes and utilities	$95/month
Minimum equity requirement (before applying the subsidy)	10 percent of total development cost

A. Assuming that the average unit will be vacant 5 percent of the time and that the investment should provide a 10 percent, before-tax cash flow to the property owner, what is the monthly rent needed to make the project viable?

B. If a family must pay 30 percent of gross income for rent, what is the minimum income limit implied by your response to question A, above?

C. By how much would the effective interest rate on the private loan be lowered if the full subsidy were used to reduce borrowing costs through a one-time grant to the originating lender?

D. If the full subsidy were used to reduce development cost, by how much could rents and maximum income limits be reduced?

E. If local officials wanted to preserve the original subsidy capital and use only the interest generated from its investment in no-risk, long-term government securities to subsidize rents, by how much could rents and income limits be reduced if the $15,000 subsidy could be invested at 8.5 percent a year, compounded monthly?

F. If available subsidy funds were used to provide a fifteen-year rent subsidy, after which the owner would be allowed to rent the apartment at market rates to unassisted families, by how much could rents and maximum income limits be lowered if all available assistance funds were to be consumed over the fifteen-year subsidy period and the unexpended annual balance could earn 8.5 percent interest, compounded monthly?

G. If the subsidy were used to provide a $15,000, 4 percent, second mortgage loan that would have a ten-year term and be amortized over a thirty-year period, by how much could rents and income limits be reduced?

H. Which of the above subsidy alternatives described in items C through G above do you prefer, and why?

11. Presented below are development cost data for a 180-unit multifamily project. The question is whether the project is feasible at current interest rates, and, if not, by how much rates would have to fall for the project to become feasible. Make any necessary assumptions to complete the analysis as long as they are realistic and can be supported.

PROJECT DATA INCOME

Number of Dwellings	Monthly Rents
24 Studios	$239
60 1-Bedroom	$319
96 2-Bedroom	$382
Total monthly operating costs	$21,050

DEVELOPMENT AND CONSTRUCTION COST DATA

Raw land	456,372 square feet
Raw land cost	$2.10/square foot
Land improvement cost	$120,000
Gross residential floor area	159,560 square feet
Construction cost of main residential area	$22.50/square foot
Accessory building cost	$50,000
Other costs	$1,202,000

Mortgage terms: 25 years, 14 percent interest
Mortgage request: 80 percent of total project replacement cost

Table 11-1. Monthly Compound Interest Tables

8.00%   Effective Rate 0.667   8.00%

	1 Amount of $1 at Compound Interest	2 Accumulation of $1 Per Period	3 Sinking Fund Factor	4 Present Value Reversion of $1	5 Present Value Ord. Annuity $1 Per Period	6 Installment to Amortize $1	
Months							
1	1.006667	1.000000	1.000000	0.993377	0.993377	1.006667	
2	1.013378	2.006667	0.498339	0.986799	1.980176	0.505006	
3	1.020134	3.020044	0.331121	0.980264	2.960440	0.337788	
4	1.026935	4.040178	0.247514	0.973772	3.934212	0.254181	
5	1.033781	5.067113	0.197351	0.967323	4.901535	0.204018	
6	1.040673	6.100893	0.163910	0.960917	5.862452	0.170577	
7	1.047610	7.141566	0.140025	0.954553	6.817005	0.146692	
8	1.054595	8.189176	0.122112	0.948232	7.765237	0.128779	
9	1.061625	9.243771	0.108181	0.941952	8.707189	0.114848	
10	1.068703	10.305396	0.097037	0.935714	9.642903	0.103703	
11	1.075827	11.374099	0.087919	0.929517	10.572420	0.094586	
12	1.083000	12.449926	0.080322	0.923361	11.495782	0.086988	
Years							**Months**
1	1.083000	12.449926	0.080322	0.923361	11.495782	0.086988	12
2	1.172888	25.933190	0.038561	0.852596	22.110544	0.045227	24
3	1.270237	40.535558	0.024670	0.787255	31.911806	0.031336	36
4	1.375666	56.349915	0.017746	0.726921	40.961913	0.024413	48
5	1.489846	73.476856	0.013610	0.671210	49.318433	0.020276	60
6	1.613502	92.025325	0.010867	0.619770	57.034522	0.017533	72
7	1.747422	112.113308	0.008920	0.572272	64.159261	0.015586	84
8	1.892457	133.868583	0.007470	0.528414	70.737970	0.014137	96
9	2.049530	157.429535	0.006352	0.487917	76.812497	0.013019	108
10	2.219640	182.946035	0.005466	0.450523	82.421481	0.012133	120
11	2.403869	210.580392	0.004749	0.415996	87.600600	0.011415	132
12	2.603389	240.508387	0.004158	0.384115	92.382800	0.010825	144
13	2.819469	272.920390	0.003664	0.354677	96.798498	0.010331	156
14	3.053484	308.022574	0.003247	0.327495	100.875784	0.009913	168
15	3.306921	346.038222	0.002890	0.302396	104.640592	0.009557	180
16	3.581394	387.209149	0.002583	0.279221	108.116871	0.009249	192
17	3.878648	431.797244	0.002316	0.257822	111.326733	0.008983	204
18	4.200574	480.086128	0.002083	0.238063	114.290596	0.008750	216
19	4.549220	532.382966	0.001878	0.219818	117.027313	0.008545	228
20	4.926803	589.020416	0.001698	0.202971	119.554292	0.008364	240
21	5.335725	650.358746	0.001538	0.187416	121.887606	0.008204	252
22	5.778588	716.788127	0.001395	0.173053	124.042099	0.008062	264
23	6.258207	788.731114	0.001268	0.159790	126.031475	0.007935	276
24	6.777636	866.645333	0.001154	0.147544	127.868388	0.007821	288
25	7.340176	951.026395	0.001051	0.136237	129.564523	0.007718	300
26	7.949407	1042.411042	0.000959	0.125796	131.130668	0.007626	312
27	8.609204	1141.380571	0.000876	0.116155	132.576786	0.007543	324
28	9.323763	1248.564521	0.000801	0.107253	133.912076	0.007468	336
29	10.097631	1364.644687	0.000733	0.099033	135.145031	0.007399	348
30	10.935730	1490.359449	0.000671	0.091443	136.283494	0.007338	360
31	11.843390	1626.508474	0.000615	0.084435	137.334707	0.007281	372
32	12.826385	1773.957801	0.000564	0.077964	138.305357	0.007230	384
33	13.890969	1933.645350	0.000517	0.071989	139.201617	0.007184	396
34	15.043913	2106.586886	0.000475	0.066472	140.029190	0.007141	408
35	16.292550	2293.882485	0.000436	0.061378	140.793338	0.007103	420
36	17.644824	2496.723526	0.000401	0.056674	141.498923	0.007067	432
37	19.109335	2716.400273	0.000368	0.052330	142.150433	0.007035	444
38	20.695401	2954.310082	0.000338	0.048320	142.752013	0.007005	456
39	22.413109	3211.966288	0.000311	0.044617	143.307488	0.006978	468
40	24.273386	3491.007831	0.000286	0.041197	143.820392	0.006953	480

Table 11-2. Annual Compound Interest Tables
8.50%   **Effective Rate 8.50**   **8.50%**

	1 Amount of $1 at Compound Interest	*2* Accumulation of $1 Per Period	*3* Sinking Fund Factor	*4* Present Value Reversion of $1	*5* Present Value Ord. Annuity $1 Per Period	*6* Installment to Amortize $1
Years						
1	1.085000	1.000000	1.000000	0.921659	0.921659	1.085000
2	1.177225	2.085000	0.479616	0.849455	1.771114	0.564616
3	1.277289	3.262225	0.306539	0.782908	2.554022	0.391539
4	1.385859	4.539514	0.220288	0.721574	3.275597	0.305288
5	1.503657	5.925373	0.168766	0.665045	3.940642	0.253766
6	1.631468	7.429030	0.134607	0.612945	4.553587	0.219607
7	1.770142	9.060497	0.110369	0.564926	5.118514	0.195369
8	1.920604	10.830639	0.092331	0.520669	5.639183	0.177331
9	2.083856	12.751244	0.078424	0.479880	6.119063	0.163424
10	2.260983	14.835099	0.067408	0.442285	6.561348	0.152408
11	2.453167	17.096083	0.058493	0.407636	6.968984	0.143493
12	2.661686	19.549250	0.051153	0.375702	7.344686	0.136153
13	2.887930	22.210936	0.045023	0.346269	7.690955	0.130023
14	3.133404	25.098866	0.039842	0.319142	8.010097	0.124842
15	3.399743	28.232269	0.035420	0.294140	8.304237	0.120420
16	3.688721	31.632012	0.031614	0.271097	8.575333	0.116614
17	4.002262	35.320733	0.028312	0.249859	8.825192	0.113312
18	4.342455	39.322995	0.025430	0.230285	9.055476	0.110430
19	4.711563	43.665450	0.022901	0.212244	9.267720	0.107901
20	5.112046	48.377013	0.020671	0.195616	9.463337	0.105671
21	5.546570	53.489059	0.018695	0.180292	9.643628	0.103695
22	6.018028	59.035629	0.016939	0.166167	9.809796	0.101939
23	6.529561	65.053658	0.015372	0.153150	9.962945	0.100372
24	7.084574	71.583219	0.013970	0.141152	10.104097	0.098970
25	7.686762	78.667792	0.012712	0.130094	10.234191	0.097712
26	8.340137	86.354555	0.011580	0.119902	10.354093	0.096580
27	9.049049	94.694692	0.010560	0.110509	10.464602	0.095560
28	9.818218	103.743741	0.009639	0.101851	10.566453	0.094639
29	10.652766	113.561959	0.008806	0.093872	10.660326	0.093806
30	11.558252	124.214725	0.008051	0.086518	10.746844	0.093051
31	12.540703	135.772977	0.007365	0.079740	10.826584	0.092365
32	13.606663	148.313680	0.006742	0.073493	10.900078	0.091742
33	14.763229	161.920343	0.006176	0.067736	10.967813	0.091176
34	16.018104	176.683572	0.005660	0.062429	11.030243	0.090660
35	17.379642	192.701675	0.005189	0.057539	11.087781	0.090189
36	18.856912	210.081318	0.004760	0.053031	11.140812	0.089760
37	20.459750	228.938230	0.004368	0.048876	11.189689	0.089368
38	22.198828	249.397979	0.004010	0.045047	11.234736	0.089010
39	24.085729	271.596808	0.003682	0.041518	11.276255	0.088682
40	26.133016	295.682536	0.003382	0.038266	11.314520	0.088382
41	28.354322	321.815552	0.003107	0.035268	11.349788	0.088107
42	30.764439	350.169874	0.002856	0.032505	11.382293	0.087856
43	33.379417	380.934313	0.002625	0.029959	11.412252	0.087625
44	36.216667	414.313730	0.002414	0.027612	11.439864	0.087414
45	39.295084	450.530397	0.002220	0.025448	11.465312	0.087220
46	42.635166	489.825480	0.002042	0.023455	11.488767	0.087042
47	46.259155	532.460646	0.001878	0.021617	11.510384	0.086878
48	50.191183	578.719801	0.001728	0.019924	11.530308	0.086728
49	54.457434	628.910984	0.001590	0.018363	11.548671	0.086590
50	59.086316	683.368418	0.001463	0.016924	11.565595	0.086463

Table 11-3. Monthly Compound Interest Tables

9.00%   **Effective Rate 0.750**   9.00%

	1 Amount of $1 at Compound Interest	*2* Accumulation of $1 Per Period	*3* Sinking Fund Factor	*4* Present Value Reversion of $1	*5* Present Value Ord. Annuity $1 Per Period	*6* Installment to Amortize $1	
Months							
1	1.007500	1.000000	1.000000	0.992556	0.992556	1.007500	
2	1.015056	2.007500	0.498132	0.985167	1.977723	0.505632	
3	1.022669	3.022556	0.330846	0.977833	2.955556	0.338346	
4	1.030339	4.045225	0.247205	0.970554	3.926110	0.254705	
5	1.038067	5.075565	0.197022	0.963329	4.889440	0.204522	
6	1.045852	6.113631	0.163569	0.956158	5.845598	0.171069	
7	1.053696	7.159484	0.139675	0.949040	6.794638	0.147175	
8	1.061599	8.213180	0.121756	0.941975	7.736613	0.129256	
9	1.069561	9.274779	0.107819	0.934963	8.671576	0.115319	
10	1.077583	10.344339	0.096671	0.928003	9.599580	0.104171	
11	1.085664	11.421922	0.087551	0.921095	10.520675	0.095051	
12	1.093807	12.507586	0.079951	0.914238	11.434913	0.087451	
Years							**Months**
1	1.093807	12.507586	0.079951	0.914238	11.434913	0.087451	12
2	1.196414	26.188471	0.038185	0.835831	21.889146	0.045685	24
3	1.308645	41.152716	0.024300	0.764149	31.446805	0.031800	36
4	1.431405	57.520711	0.017385	0.698614	40.184782	0.024885	48
5	1.565681	75.424137	0.013258	0.638700	48.173374	0.020758	60
6	1.712553	95.007028	0.010526	0.583924	55.476849	0.018026	72
7	1.873202	116.426928	0.008589	0.533845	62.153965	0.016089	84
8	2.048921	139.856164	0.007150	0.488062	68.258439	0.014650	96
9	2.241124	165.483223	0.006043	0.446205	73.839382	0.013543	108
10	2.451357	193.514277	0.005168	0.407937	78.941693	0.012668	120
11	2.681311	224.174837	0.004461	0.372952	83.606420	0.011961	132
12	2.932837	257.711570	0.003880	0.340967	87.871092	0.011380	144
13	3.207957	294.394279	0.003397	0.311725	91.770018	0.010897	156
14	3.508886	334.518079	0.002989	0.284991	95.334564	0.010489	168
15	3.838043	378.405769	0.002643	0.260549	98.593409	0.010143	180
16	4.198078	426.410427	0.002345	0.238204	101.572769	0.009845	192
17	4.591887	478.918252	0.002088	0.217775	104.296613	0.009588	204
18	5.022638	536.351674	0.001864	0.199099	106.786856	0.009364	216
19	5.493796	599.172747	0.001669	0.182024	109.063531	0.009169	228
20	6.009152	667.886870	0.001497	0.166413	111.144954	0.008997	240
21	6.572851	743.046852	0.001346	0.152141	113.047870	0.008846	252
22	7.189430	825.257358	0.001212	0.139093	114.787589	0.008712	264
23	7.863848	915.179777	0.001093	0.127164	116.378106	0.008593	276
24	8.601532	1013.537539	0.000987	0.116258	117.832218	0.008487	288
25	9.408415	1121.121937	0.000892	0.106288	119.161622	0.008392	300
26	10.290989	1238.798494	0.000807	0.097172	120.377014	0.008307	312
27	11.256354	1367.513924	0.000731	0.088839	121.488172	0.008231	324
28	12.312278	1508.303750	0.000663	0.081220	122.504035	0.008163	336
29	13.467255	1662.300631	0.000602	0.074254	123.432776	0.008102	348
30	14.730576	1830.743483	0.000546	0.067886	124.281866	0.008046	360
31	16.112406	2014.987436	0.000496	0.062064	125.058136	0.007996	372
32	17.623861	2216.514743	0.000451	0.056741	125.767832	0.007951	384
33	19.277100	2436.946701	0.000410	0.051875	126.416664	0.007910	396
34	21.085425	2678.056697	0.000373	0.047426	127.009850	0.007873	408
35	23.063384	2941.784473	0.000340	0.043359	127.552164	0.007840	420
36	25.226888	3230.251735	0.000310	0.039640	128.047967	0.007810	432
37	27.593344	3545.779215	0.000282	0.036241	128.501250	0.007782	444
38	30.181790	3890.905350	0.000257	0.033133	128.915659	0.007757	456
39	33.013050	4268.406696	0.000234	0.030291	129.294526	0.007734	468
40	36.109902	4681.320272	0.000214	0.027693	129.640902	0.007714	480

Table 11-4. Annual Compound Interest Tables

9.00%   Effective Rate 9.00   9.00%

	1 Amount of $1 at Compound Interest	2 Accumulation of $1 Per Period	3 Sinking Fund Factor	4 Present Value Reversion of $1	5 Present Value Ord. Annuity $1 Per Period	6 Installment to Amortize $1
Years						
1	1.090000	1.000000	1.000000	0.917431	0.917431	1.090000
2	1.188100	2.090000	0.478469	0.841680	1.759111	0.568469
3	1.295029	3.278100	0.305055	0.772183	2.531295	0.395055
4	1.411582	4.573129	0.218669	0.708425	3.239720	0.308669
5	1.538624	5.984711	0.167092	0.649931	3.889651	0.257092
6	1.677100	7.523335	0.132920	0.596267	4.485919	0.222920
7	1.828039	9.200435	0.108691	0.547034	5.032953	0.198691
8	1.992563	11.028474	0.090674	0.501866	5.534819	0.180674
9	2.171893	13.021036	0.076799	0.460428	5.995247	0.166799
10	2.367364	15.192930	0.065820	0.422411	6.417658	0.155820
11	2.580426	17.560293	0.056947	0.387533	6.805191	0.146947
12	2.812665	20.140720	0.049651	0.355535	7.160725	0.139651
13	3.065805	22.953385	0.043567	0.326179	7.486904	0.133567
14	3.341727	26.019189	0.038433	0.299246	7.786150	0.128433
15	3.642482	29.360916	0.034059	0.274538	8.060688	0.124059
16	3.970306	33.003399	0.030300	0.251870	8.312558	0.120300
17	4.327633	36.973705	0.027046	0.231073	8.543631	0.117046
18	4.717120	41.301338	0.024212	0.211994	8.755625	0.114212
19	5.141661	46.018458	0.021730	0.194490	8.950115	0.111730
20	5.604411	51.160120	0.019546	0.178431	9.128546	0.109546
21	6.108808	56.764530	0.017617	0.163698	9.292244	0.107617
22	6.658600	62.873338	0.015905	0.150182	9.442425	0.105905
23	7.257874	69.531939	0.014382	0.137781	9.580207	0.104382
24	7.911083	76.789813	0.013023	0.126405	9.706612	0.103023
25	8.623081	84.700896	0.011806	0.115968	9.822580	0.101806
26	9.399158	93.323977	0.010715	0.106393	9.928972	0.100715
27	10.245082	102.723135	0.009735	0.097608	10.026580	0.099735
28	11.167140	112.968217	0.008852	0.089548	10.116128	0.098852
29	12.172182	124.135356	0.008056	0.082155	10.198283	0.098056
30	13.267678	136.307539	0.007336	0.075371	10.273654	0.097336
31	14.461770	149.575217	0.006686	0.069148	10.342802	0.096686
32	15.763329	164.036987	0.006096	0.063438	10.406240	0.096096
33	17.182028	179.800315	0.005562	0.058200	10.464441	0.095562
34	18.728411	196.982344	0.005077	0.053395	10.517835	0.095077
35	20.413968	215.710755	0.004636	0.048986	10.566821	0.094636
36	22.251225	236.124723	0.004235	0.044941	10.611763	0.094235
37	24.253835	258.375948	0.003870	0.041231	10.652993	0.093870
38	26.436680	282.629783	0.003538	0.037826	10.690820	0.093538
39	28.815982	309.066463	0.003236	0.034703	10.725523	0.093236
40	31.409420	337.882445	0.002960	0.031838	10.757360	0.092960
41	34.236268	369.291865	0.002708	0.029209	10.786569	0.092708
42	37.317532	403.528133	0.002478	0.026797	10.813366	0.092478
43	40.676110	440.845665	0.002268	0.024584	10.837950	0.092268
44	44.336960	481.521775	0.002077	0.022555	10.860505	0.092077
45	48.327286	525.858734	0.001902	0.020692	10.881197	0.091902
46	52.676742	574.186021	0.001742	0.018984	10.900181	0.091742
47	57.417649	626.862762	0.001595	0.017416	10.917597	0.091595
48	62.585237	684.280411	0.001461	0.015978	10.933575	0.091461
49	68.217908	746.865648	0.001339	0.014659	10.948234	0.091339
50	74.357520	815.083556	0.001227	0.013449	10.961683	0.091227

Table 11-5. Annual Compound Interest Tables

10.00%   **Effective Rate 10.00**   10.00%

	1 Amount of $1 at Compound Interest	2 Accumulation of $1 Per Period	3 Sinking Fund Factor	4 Present Value Reversion of $1	5 Present Value Ord. Annuity $1 Per Period	6 Installment to Amortize $1
Years						
1	1.100000	1.000000	1.000000	0.909091	0.909091	1.100000
2	1.210000	2.100000	0.476190	0.826446	1.735537	0.576190
3	1.331000	3.310000	0.302115	0.751315	2.486852	0.402115
4	1.464100	4.641000	0.215471	0.683013	3.169865	0.315471
5	1.610510	6.105100	0.163797	0.620921	3.790787	0.263797
6	1.771561	7.715610	0.129607	0.564474	4.355261	0.229607
7	1.948717	9.487171	0.105405	0.513158	4.868419	0.205405
8	2.143589	11.435888	0.087444	0.466507	5.334926	0.187444
9	2.357948	13.579477	0.073641	0.424098	5.759024	0.173641
10	2.593742	15.937425	0.062745	0.385543	6.144567	0.162745
11	2.853117	18.531167	0.053963	0.350494	6.495061	0.153963
12	3.138428	21.384284	0.046763	0.318631	6.813692	0.146763
13	3.452271	24.522712	0.040779	0.289664	7.103356	0.140779
14	3.797498	27.974983	0.035746	0.263331	7.366687	0.135746
15	4.177248	31.772482	0.031474	0.239392	7.606080	0.131474
16	4.594973	35.949730	0.027817	0.217629	7.823709	0.127817
17	5.054470	40.544703	0.024664	0.197845	8.021553	0.124664
18	5.559917	45.599173	0.021930	0.179859	8.201412	0.121930
19	6.115909	51.159090	0.019547	0.163508	8.364920	0.119547
20	6.727500	57.274999	0.017460	0.148644	8.513564	0.117460
21	7.400250	64.002499	0.015624	0.135131	8.648694	0.115624
22	8.140275	71.402749	0.014005	0.122846	8.771540	0.114005
23	8.954302	79.543024	0.012572	0.111678	8.883218	0.112572
24	9.849733	88.497327	0.011300	0.101526	8.984744	0.111300
25	10.834706	98.347059	0.010168	0.092296	9.077040	0.110168
26	11.918177	109.181765	0.009159	0.083905	9.160945	0.109159
27	13.109994	121.099942	0.008258	0.076278	9.237223	0.108258
28	14.420994	134.209936	0.007451	0.069343	9.306567	0.107451
29	15.863093	148.630930	0.006728	0.063039	9.369606	0.106728
30	17.449402	164.494023	0.006079	0.057309	9.426914	0.106079
31	19.194342	181.943425	0.005496	0.052099	9.479013	0.105496
32	21.113777	201.137767	0.004972	0.047362	9.526376	0.104972
33	23.225154	222.251544	0.004499	0.043057	9.569432	0.104499
34	25.547670	245.476699	0.004074	0.039143	9.608575	0.104074
35	28.102437	271.024368	0.003690	0.035584	9.644159	0.103690
36	30.912681	299.126805	0.003343	0.032349	9.676508	0.103343
37	34.003949	330.039486	0.003030	0.029408	9.705917	0.103030
38	37.404343	364.043434	0.002747	0.026735	9.732651	0.102747
39	41.144778	401.447778	0.002491	0.024304	9.756956	0.102491
40	45.259256	442.592556	0.002259	0.022095	9.779051	0.102259
41	49.785181	487.851811	0.002050	0.020086	9.799137	0.102050
42	54.763699	537.636992	0.001860	0.018260	9.817397	0.101860
43	60.240069	592.400692	0.001688	0.016600	9.833998	0.101688
44	66.264076	652.640761	0.001532	0.015091	9.849089	0.101532
45	72.890484	718.904837	0.001391	0.013719	9.862808	0.101391
46	80.179532	791.795321	0.001263	0.012472	9.875280	0.101263
47	88.197485	871.974853	0.001147	0.011338	9.886618	0.101147
48	97.017234	960.172338	0.001041	0.010307	9.896926	0.101041
49	106.718957	1057.189572	0.000946	0.009370	9.906296	0.100946
50	117.390853	1163.908529	0.000859	0.008519	9.914814	0.100859

Table 11-6. Monthly Compound Interest Tables

13.00%   Effective Rate 1.083   13.00%

	1 Amount of $1 at Compound Interest	2 Accumulation of $1 Per Period	3 Sinking Fund Factor	4 Present Value Reversion of $1	5 Present Value Ord. Annuity $1 Per Period	6 Installment to Amortize $1	
Months							
1	1.010833	1.000000	1.000000	0.989283	0.989283	1.010833	
2	1.021784	2.010833	0.497306	0.978680	1.967963	0.508140	
3	1.032853	3.032617	0.329748	0.968192	2.936155	0.340581	
4	1.044043	4.065471	0.245974	0.957815	3.893970	0.256807	
5	1.055353	5.109513	0.195713	0.947550	4.841520	0.206547	
6	1.066786	6.164866	0.162210	0.937395	5.778915	0.173043	
7	1.078343	7.231652	0.138281	0.927349	6.706264	0.149114	
8	1.090025	8.309995	0.120337	0.917410	7.623674	0.131170	
9	1.101834	9.400020	0.106383	0.907578	8.531253	0.117216	
10	1.113770	10.501854	0.095221	0.897851	9.429104	0.106055	
11	1.125836	11.615624	0.086091	0.888229	10.317333	0.096924	
12	1.138032	12.741460	0.078484	0.878710	11.196042	0.089317	
Years							**Months**
1	1.138032	12.741460	0.078484	0.878710	11.196042	0.089317	12
2	1.295118	27.241655	0.036708	0.772130	21.034112	0.047542	24
3	1.473886	43.743348	0.022861	0.678478	29.678917	0.033694	36
4	1.677330	62.522811	0.015994	0.596185	37.275190	0.026827	48
5	1.908857	83.894449	0.011920	0.523874	43.950107	0.022753	60
6	2.172341	108.216068	0.009241	0.460333	49.815421	0.020074	72
7	2.472194	135.894861	0.007359	0.404499	54.969328	0.018192	84
8	2.813437	167.394225	0.005974	0.355437	59.498115	0.016807	96
9	3.201783	203.241525	0.004920	0.312326	63.477604	0.015754	108
10	3.643733	244.036917	0.004098	0.274444	66.974419	0.014931	120
11	4.146687	290.463399	0.003443	0.241156	70.047103	0.014276	132
12	4.719064	343.298242	0.002913	0.211906	72.747100	0.013746	144
13	5.370448	403.426010	0.002479	0.186204	75.119613	0.013312	156
14	6.111745	471.853363	0.002119	0.163619	77.204363	0.012953	168
15	6.955364	549.725914	0.001819	0.143774	79.036253	0.012652	180
16	7.915430	638.347406	0.001567	0.126336	80.645952	0.012400	192
17	9.008017	739.201542	0.001353	0.111012	82.060410	0.012186	204
18	10.251416	853.976825	0.001171	0.097548	83.303307	0.012004	216
19	11.666444	984.594826	0.001016	0.085716	84.395453	0.011849	228
20	13.276792	1133.242353	0.000882	0.075319	85.355132	0.011716	240
21	15.109421	1302.408067	0.000768	0.066184	86.198412	0.011601	252
22	17.195012	1494.924144	0.000669	0.058156	86.939409	0.011502	264
23	19.568482	1714.013694	0.000583	0.051103	87.590531	0.011417	276
24	22.269568	1963.344717	0.000509	0.044904	88.162677	0.011343	288
25	25.343491	2247.091520	0.000445	0.039458	88.665428	0.011278	300
26	28.841716	2570.004599	0.000389	0.034672	89.107200	0.011222	312
27	32.822810	2937.490172	0.000340	0.030467	89.495389	0.011174	324
28	37.353424	3355.700690	0.000298	0.026771	89.836495	0.011131	336
29	42.509410	3831.637843	0.000261	0.023524	90.136227	0.011094	348
30	48.377089	4373.269783	0.000229	0.020671	90.399605	0.011062	360
31	55.054699	4989.664524	0.000200	0.018164	90.631038	0.011034	372
32	62.654036	5691.141761	0.000176	0.015961	90.834400	0.011009	384
33	71.302328	6489.445641	0.000154	0.014025	91.013097	0.010987	396
34	81.144365	7397.941387	0.000135	0.012324	91.170119	0.010969	408
35	92.344923	8431.839055	0.000119	0.010829	91.308095	0.010952	420
36	105.091522	9608.448184	0.000104	0.009516	91.429337	0.010937	432
37	119.597566	10947.467591	0.000091	0.008361	91.535873	0.010925	444
38	136.105914	12471.315170	0.000080	0.007347	91.629487	0.010914	456
39	154.892951	14205.503212	0.000070	0.006456	91.711747	0.010904	468
40	176.273210	16179.065533	0.000062	0.005673	91.784030	0.010895	480

Table 11-7. Annual Compound Interest Tables

13.00%   **Effective Rate 13.00**   13.00%

	1 *Amount of $1* *at Compound* *Interest*	*2* *Accumulation* *of $1* *Per Period*	*3* *Sinking* *Fund* *Factor*	*4* *Present Value* *Reversion* *of $1*	*5* *Present Value* *Ord. Annuity* *$1 Per Period*	*6* *Installment* *to* *Amortize $1*
Years						
1	1.130000	1.000000	1.000000	0.884956	0.884956	1.130000
2	1.276900	2.130000	0.469484	0.783147	1.668102	0.599484
3	1.442897	3.406900	0.293522	0.693050	2.361153	0.423522
4	1.630474	4.849797	0.206194	0.613319	2.974471	0.336194
5	1.842435	6.480271	0.154315	0.542760	3.517231	0.284315
6	2.081952	8.322706	0.120153	0.480319	3.997550	0.250153
7	2.352605	10.404658	0.096111	0.425061	4.422610	0.226111
8	2.658444	12.757263	0.078387	0.376160	4.798770	0.208387
9	3.004042	15.415707	0.064869	0.332885	5.131655	0.194869
10	3.394567	18.419749	0.054290	0.294588	5.426243	0.184290
11	3.835861	21.814317	0.045841	0.260698	5.686941	0.175841
12	4.334523	25.650178	0.038986	0.230706	5.917647	0.168986
13	4.898011	29.984701	0.033350	0.204165	6.121812	0.163350
14	5.534753	34.882712	0.028667	0.180677	6.302488	0.158667
15	6.254270	40.417464	0.024742	0.159891	6.462379	0.154742
16	7.067326	46.671735	0.021426	0.141496	6.603875	0.151426
17	7.986078	53.739060	0.018608	0.125218	6.729093	0.148608
18	9.024268	61.725138	0.016201	0.110812	6.839905	0.146201
19	10.197423	70.749406	0.014134	0.098064	6.937969	0.144134
20	11.523088	80.946829	0.012354	0.086782	7.024752	0.142354
21	13.021089	92.469917	0.010814	0.076798	7.101550	0.140814
22	14.713831	105.491006	0.009479	0.067963	7.169513	0.139479
23	16.626629	120.204837	0.008319	0.060144	7.229658	0.138319
24	18.788091	136.831465	0.007308	0.053225	7.282883	0.137308
25	21.230542	155.619556	0.006426	0.047102	7.329985	0.136426
26	23.990513	176.850098	0.005655	0.041683	7.371668	0.135655
27	27.109279	200.840611	0.004979	0.036888	7.408556	0.134979
28	30.633486	227.949890	0.004387	0.032644	7.441200	0.134387
29	34.615839	258.583376	0.003867	0.028889	7.470088	0.133867
30	39.115898	293.199215	0.003411	0.025565	7.495653	0.133411
31	44.200965	332.315113	0.003009	0.022624	7.518277	0.133009
32	49.947090	376.516078	0.002656	0.020021	7.538299	0.132656
33	56.440212	426.463168	0.002345	0.017718	7.556016	0.132345
34	63.777439	482.903380	0.002071	0.015680	7.571696	0.132071
35	72.068506	546.680819	0.001829	0.013876	7.585572	0.131829
36	81.437412	618.749325	0.001616	0.012279	7.597851	0.131616
37	92.024276	700.186738	0.001428	0.010867	7.608718	0.131428
38	103.987432	792.211014	0.001262	0.009617	7.618334	0.131262
39	117.505798	896.198445	0.001116	0.008510	7.626844	0.131116
40	132.781552	1013.704243	0.000986	0.007531	7.634376	0.130986
41	150.043153	1146.485795	0.000872	0.006665	7.641040	0.130872
42	169.548763	1296.528948	0.000771	0.005898	7.646938	0.130771
43	191.590103	1466.077712	0.000682	0.005219	7.652158	0.130682
44	216.496816	1657.667814	0.000603	0.004619	7.656777	0.130603
45	244.641402	1874.164630	0.000534	0.004088	7.660864	0.130534
46	276.444784	2118.806032	0.000472	0.003617	7.664482	0.130472
47	312.382606	2395.250816	0.000417	0.003201	7.667683	0.130417
48	352.992345	2707.633422	0.000369	0.002833	7.670516	0.130369
49	398.881350	3060.625767	0.000327	0.002507	7.673023	0.130327
50	450.735925	3459.507117	0.000289	0.002219	7.675242	0.130289

Table 11-8. Monthly Compound Interest Tables

14.00%   Effective Rate 1.167   14.00%

	1 Amount of $1 at Compound Interest	2 Accumulation of $1 Per Period	3 Sinking Fund Factor	4 Present Value Reversion of $1	5 Present Value Ord. Annuity $1 Per Period	6 Installment to Amortize $1	
Months							
1	1.011667	1.000000	1.000000	0.988468	0.988468	1.011667	
2	1.023469	2.011667	0.497100	0.977069	1.965537	0.508767	
3	1.035410	3.035136	0.329475	0.965801	2.931338	0.341141	
4	1.047490	4.070546	0.245667	0.954663	3.886001	0.257334	
5	1.059710	5.118036	0.195387	0.943654	4.829655	0.207054	
6	1.072074	6.177746	0.161871	0.932772	5.762427	0.173538	
7	1.084581	7.249820	0.137934	0.922015	6.684442	0.149601	
8	1.097235	8.334401	0.119985	0.911382	7.595824	0.131651	
9	1.110036	9.431636	0.106026	0.900872	8.496696	0.117693	
10	1.122986	10.541672	0.094862	0.890483	9.387178	0.106528	
11	1.136088	11.664658	0.085729	0.880214	10.267392	0.097396	
12	1.149342	12.800745	0.078120	0.870063	11.137455	0.089787	
Years							**Months**
1	1.149342	12.800745	0.078120	0.870063	11.137455	0.089787	12
2	1.320987	27.513180	0.036346	0.757010	20.827743	0.048013	24
3	1.518266	44.422800	0.022511	0.658646	29.258904	0.034178	36
4	1.745007	63.857736	0.015660	0.573064	36.594546	0.027326	48
5	2.005610	86.195125	0.011602	0.498601	42.977016	0.023268	60
6	2.305132	111.868425	0.008939	0.433815	48.530168	0.020606	72
7	2.649385	141.375828	0.007073	0.377446	53.361760	0.018740	84
8	3.045049	175.289927	0.005705	0.328402	57.565549	0.017372	96
9	3.499803	214.268826	0.004667	0.285730	61.223111	0.016334	108
10	4.022471	259.068912	0.003860	0.248603	64.405420	0.015527	120
11	4.623195	310.559535	0.003220	0.216301	67.174230	0.014887	132
12	5.313632	369.739871	0.002705	0.188195	69.583269	0.014371	144
13	6.107180	437.758319	0.002284	0.163742	71.679284	0.013951	156
14	7.019239	515.934780	0.001938	0.142466	73.502950	0.013605	168
15	8.067507	605.786272	0.001651	0.123954	75.089654	0.013317	180
16	9.272324	709.056369	0.001410	0.107848	76.470187	0.013077	192
17	10.657072	827.749031	0.001208	0.093834	77.671337	0.012875	204
18	12.248621	964.167496	0.001037	0.081642	78.716413	0.012704	216
19	14.077855	1120.958972	0.000892	0.071034	79.625696	0.012559	228
20	16.180270	1301.166005	0.000769	0.061804	80.416829	0.012435	240
21	18.596664	1508.285522	0.000663	0.053773	81.105164	0.012330	252
22	21.373928	1746.336688	0.000573	0.046786	81.704060	0.012239	264
23	24.565954	2019.938898	0.000495	0.040707	82.225136	0.012162	276
24	28.234683	2334.401417	0.000428	0.035417	82.678506	0.012095	288
25	32.451308	2695.826407	0.000371	0.030815	83.072966	0.012038	300
26	37.297652	3111.227338	0.000321	0.026811	83.416171	0.011988	312
27	42.867759	3588.665088	0.000279	0.023328	83.714781	0.011945	324
28	49.269718	4137.404360	0.000242	0.020296	83.974591	0.011908	336
29	56.627757	4768.093468	0.000210	0.017659	84.200641	0.011876	348
30	65.084661	5492.970967	0.000182	0.015365	84.397320	0.011849	360
31	74.804537	6326.103143	0.000158	0.013368	84.568442	0.011825	372
32	85.975998	7283.656968	0.000137	0.011631	84.717330	0.011804	384
33	98.815828	8384.213826	0.000119	0.010120	84.846871	0.011786	396
34	113.573184	9649.130077	0.000104	0.008805	84.959580	0.011770	408
35	130.534434	11102.951488	0.000090	0.007661	85.057645	0.011757	420
36	150.028711	12773.889539	0.000078	0.006665	85.142966	0.011745	432
37	172.434303	14694.368869	0.000068	0.005799	85.217202	0.011735	444
38	198.185992	16901.656479	0.000059	0.005046	85.281792	0.011726	456
39	227.783490	19438.584900	0.000051	0.004390	85.337989	0.011718	468
40	261.801139	22354.383359	0.000045	0.003820	85.386883	0.011711	480

7 Evaluating Investment Decisions

An Investment Analysis Approach to Public Incentives for Private Development

Richard J. Roddewig and Jared Shlaes

Every real estate feasibility study tries to answer three critical questions:

- Will gross income be large enough to cover operating expenses and debt service costs and provide a satisfactory cash return to equity investors?
- How much debt financing will the net operating income support, and on what terms?
- How much investors' equity will be needed, and what return on investment will this project provide to investors both before and after considering federal income taxes?

Planners attempting to answer these questions will likely be presented with a developer's pro forma—a one-year analysis of income, expenses, debt service, pre-tax cash flow, and perhaps even after-tax cash flow in the first full year after project completion. They should also review the developer's five-, ten- or fifteen-year forecast of annual income, expenses, debt service, pre-tax cash flow, taxable income, and after-tax cash flow. This long-range forecast may present a more complete picture of project feasibility. Included should be a summary of the income tax aspects of the project: tax bracket of investors, depreciation method and rate, and tax consequences at sale or upon refinancing in the future.

THE INCOME/EXPENSE FEASIBILITY ANALYSIS

Most redevelopment projects involve long-term investments in income producing real estate. The developer builds or rehabilitates an income producing structure such as an office building, shopping center, or apartment building; leases out the space for an expected holding period; and

* Richard J. Roddewig and Jared Shlaes, "An Investment Analysis Approach to Public Incentives for Private Development," from *Analyzing the Economic Feasibility of a Development Project: A Guide for Planners,* Planning Advisory Service, report no. 30, 1983. Reprinted by permission of the American Planning Association, Washington, D.C.

plans someday to sell the project to someone else. The feasibility analysis must not only consider current rents but also future rents during the project's life, as well as the likely proceeds of an eventual sale or refinancing.

Other redevelopment projects may involve shorter-term investments such as construction and sale of single-family homes, townhouses, or condominiums. The benefits from public incentives provided these projects (for example, land cost writedowns, low-interest construction loans, financing assistance to unit purchasers, etc.) are often easier to measure than in long-term projects. This report will focus exclusively on the more complicated problems presented when long-term, income-producing projects seek public incentives. It is a complex subject, but the examples that follow the discussion will cover projects that are familiar to you and will make the financial analysis clearer.

First, the developer or his consultants determine current rents with the help of a "market study." They search the area where the project is located for similar projects. The rents in those similar buildings are determined and adjusted to account for any differences in location, design, layout, construction, age, condition, and amenities provided.

Other buildings may also be the source of information for the developer's estimates of vacancy and current operating expenses. Rents of comparable projects may be easier to determine than expenses because developers and managers are often less willing to share expense information than rental information with the general public. Fortunately, developers also have access to general sources of expense information such as the Building Owners and Managers Association (BOMA) International, which publishes an annual survey of income and expenses in downtown and suburban office buildings across the United States and Canada, broken down by city, building size, and building age. The Institute of Real Estate Management (IREM) publishes similar information for large- and small-scale apartment building projects. The Urban Land Institute (ULI) also provides income and expense data on actual projects in a case study format, as well as generalized information on shopping centers. The International Council of Shopping Centers (ICSC) also provides for shopping centers what BOMA and IREM provide for office and apartment buildings. But generally the best source of information is other similar buildings about which the developer has good data.

Careful adjustments must be made from the experience of other buildings to the project in question. Slight differences in location, for example, may mean major differences in assessed valuation and property taxes. Differences in mechanical systems, window treatment, and insulation can create sizeable variations in utility costs between one building and another. Energy as well as repair and maintenance costs may also vary dramatically with building age, design, construction, condition, location, orientation, and tenancy. The size and layout of a building may affect operating costs per square foot or per unit; some sizes are more efficient than others, and the same building maintenance and security staff necessary to operate a 100,000-square-foot building may also be able to handle a good deal more.

A thorough market study will also consider a good deal more than current rents and expenses. Past trends and current market conditions will be analyzed to predict the period of time it will take the new or rehabilitated space to be leased, the typical length of lease that can be expected, likely tenant turnover rate, vacancy rate, and increases in future rents and expenses that can be expected. If current market conditions require temporary rent concessions, the market study might also analyze the type and magnitude of concession most likely to attract tenants.

Once current income, vacancy, expenses, absorption, and turnover have been determined, net operating income (NOI) (sometimes called *stabilized NOI* if calculated on the basis of full or "normal" occupancy levels) can be calculated. This is simply the cash left in any year when annual operating expenses are deducted from gross revenues after making provision for expected loss of revenues from vacancy and uncollected rent.

The determination of stabilized net operating income is only a starting point in the income/expense analysis. It provides a one-year picture of a project, but it says nothing about income and expenses in future years and in most cases tells little about the start-up period that preceded the first full year of operation. It does provide some insight into the *operating ratio*, the relationship between total operating expenses and effective gross income. (See table 12-1.) If that operating ratio is too high in comparison to other projects, the developer may conclude that the project does not work; the higher the operating ratio, the lower will be net operating income, the greater the risk of mortgage loan default, or, as we shall explain, the smaller the mortgage that can be placed on the property.

The income and expenses in the months or years prior to the first stabilized year are important also. The developer's market study will try to predict demand for the space being planned and predict how long it will take to rent the proposed space. The absorption rate is typically estimated on the basis of the history of other similar projects in the community. On the average, how much space of this type has been added per year during the recent past? How long has it taken other projects of this size to fill up? Are there any peculiarities in the marketplace today, such as an oversupply of comparable projects under way, that make past history less relevant than

Table 12-1. Components of a Typical Pro Forma

	Gross revenues
Less:	Vacancy and collection loss
	Effective gross income
Less:	Operating expenses
	Net operating income
Less:	Debt service (mortgage principal and interest)
	Pre-tax cash flow
Plus:	Amortization of principal
Less:	Depreciation (accelerated cost recovery)
	Taxable income

current market conditions? The developer will make a forecast about the absorption rate and factor that into a five-year, ten-year, or even sometimes fifteen-year forecast of annual income and expenses beginning on the date of project inception and ending at some future date—often on the date the project is assumed to be sold to someone else.

Recent history of other comparable projects is also the starting place for a forecast of future income and expenses. How fast have rents been going up in comparable projects in the past few years? Are the conditions that caused those increases still present, or have they changed to suggest that lower rents might be expected? How fast have expenses been going up? Will they continue to increase at the same rate, or are there factors, such as a slackening in the price increases for utilities, that will lower the future rate of increase? What about labor costs? Will unions get more demanding in the immediate future? Will major mechanical systems require increased maintenance and repair in later years? Will property taxes increase more rapidly as cash-strapped local governments look for more revenues, or will they decrease as a result of citizen tax revolts or a shift in local tax policies?

The purpose of an income and expense forecast is not to pin down the actual net operating income for every future year, but rather to come up with a reasonable and acceptable set of predictions upon which to base the investment decision. Investing in real estate is sometimes said to be no more than "buying a set of assumptions about the future." To measure return on investment in a real estate project over a period of years, some of the uncertainty associated with the future must be dealt with by clarifying and studying those assumptions realistically.

FINANCIAL FEASIBILITY ANALYSIS

Few developers can complete a project using only their own money. Most of them look to mortgage lenders and to equity investors for a major share of project financing, partly because developers generally do not have all the cash needed to swing the real estate project and partly for another, somewhat more profound reason as well. By borrowing some of the funds needed to complete a project from a mortgage lender at a fixed rate of interest, the developer may be able to increase both the pre-tax and the after-tax returns paid to the other equity investors in the project. Using a lender's money to complete a real estate project is called *leveraging*. The greater the ratio of borrowed funds to funds supplied by equity investors, the greater the financial and income tax leverage in the project.

Financial leveraging can have either a positive or a negative impact on the rate of return to the equity in a project. Consider the following example. A developer spends $1 million to construct an apartment building. Total annual effective gross income is $200,000. Stabilized operating expenses in the first full year are $100,000, so that stabilized net operating income is $100,000, and the total annual return to the developer in the first full year of operation on the $1 million cost of the project is 10 percent. This return on total cash invested in a project is often called the "cash-on-cash return."

Table 12-2. Positive Financial Leverage

Property cost	$1,000,000
Less: Mortgage loan	800,000
Developer's cash or equity required	$ 200,000
Anticipated rental income	200,000
Anticipated operating expenses	100,000
Net operating income available for debt service and return on equity	$ 100,000
Less: Debt service requirement (@ 7.73% constant)	61,850
Cash return on equity	$ 38,150
Percentage return on equity (before income taxes)	19.08%

Fifteen or twenty years ago, it might have been possible for this developer to borrow $800,000 of the total project cost from a traditional mortgage lender at a 6 percent interest rate payable in self-amortizing installments over twenty-five years or longer. Every dollar of project cost is generating a 10-percent annual return, but the developer has borrowed $800,000 of that cost from a lender to whom he pays only a 6 percent return (actually he pays slightly more than 6 percent of total project cost every year in order to repay the original principal by the end of the twenty-five-year period). On every dollar of project cost supplied by the mortgage lender, the developer gets to keep the difference between the 6 percent or so paid back to the lender and the 10 percent generated in the form of net operating income. The effect is to boost the return on the remaining $200,000 in project costs supplied by the developer or his equity investors to over 19 percent. That is "positive leverage," and how it works is shown in table 12-2.

Long-term fixed-rate mortgages at 6 percent are a thing of the past. Any interest rate above 10 percent on this particular project creates negative financial leverage. If the interest rate on the $800,000 loan is fixed at 11 percent over the same twenty-five-year period, the return on equity provided by the developers or others is reduced to less than 3 percent. (See table 12-3.)

Table 12-3. Financial Leverage Reducing Rate of Return

Property cost	$1,000,000
Less: Mortgage loan	800,000
Developer's cash or equity required	$ 200,000
Net operating income	100,000
Less: Debt service requirement (@ 11.76% constant)	94,090
Cash return on equity	$ 5,910
Percentage return on equity (before income taxes)	2.96%

Still, developers often find a need to borrow funds from mortgage lenders for a number of reasons. Most developers lack the available funds to build out of their own pockets during times of high interest rates as well as low. Some projects benefit from positive leveraging even when interest rates are high, and real estate projects may still be attractive in comparison with non-real estate investments.

But the most important reasons to borrow from a mortgage lender, even in times of high interest rates, result from the long-term nature of real estate ownership, the widespread belief in continuing inflation, and the favorable tax treatment accorded real estate under federal and state income-tax laws. The return on equity may be low in the first year of operations, but if net operating income continues to go up as a result of inflation in rents, returns to equity investors in later years may be much higher than the initial cash-on-cash return indicates. The developer may thus be able to find equity investors even for projects that show negative leveraging in the early years if equity returns over the life of the project are high enough to be attractive. If net operating income increases during the project's holding period, the "reversion," the price that can be expected upon a future sale, will also be higher than the original cost and provide an additional element of return to equity investors.

How does a mortgage lender decide how big a loan to make? The track record of the developer is one factor to be considered. A developer with a history of successful projects that have net operating income in keeping with initial forecasts will be considered a relatively good risk for future real estate projects.

Value is another factor. Traditionally, lenders have looked to the value of the project in deciding how big a mortgage to commit. The lender's security is usually only the project itself.[1] If the developer defaults on the mortgage loan and the lender forecloses on the property, the lender wants to be able to sell the property for enough money to pay back the remaining mortgage principal and any accrued but unpaid interest owed by the developer. The value of the property is therefore a critical factor. The traditional rule has been for a mortgage lender to provide no more than 70 to 90 percent of value. The relationship between the size of the mortgage loan and the total project cost (or value) is called the *loan-to-value ratio,* and it may be limited by law or regulation to a set percentage.

When interest rates are high, as in the recent past, a reasonable loan-to-value ratio may result in unaffordable annual debt service costs that exceed the net operating income generated by the project. Recognizing this, lenders have become increasingly interested in the net operating income that can be expected. Unless the developer and the equity investors are willing to pro-

---

1. Investors in real estate generally try to avoid personal liability for loans whenever possible. Non-recourse debt, an obligation secured by the real estate asset and not by the personal assets of the developer or his investors, may be preferable for other tax reasons also. Some lenders insist on personal liability by some or all partners and may, in return, lower the interest rate on the loan.

vide adequate guarantees that mortgage payments will be made, the lender wants assurances that NOI will exceed the annual debt service cost by a significant margin.

The relationship between debt service and net operating income is expressed by the *debt coverage ratio,* defined as

$$\text{Debt Coverage Ratio} = \frac{\text{Net Operating Income}}{\text{Annual Debt Service}}$$

The ratio required varies depending upon the type of project, the character of the developer, the developer's relationship with the lender, and the lender's assessment of the risks involved in a particular project proposal. Generally, the riskier a lender considers a project, the higher the debt coverage ratio required. The lender wants a thicker cushion between forecast net operating income and the annual cost of the debt service to allow for errors and bad luck.

Typical or average debt coverage ratios required by lenders on real estate projects change from time to time, as do the terms on which loans can be made. Large institutional lenders, for example, may lower their requirements when lending on office buildings in a year when office demand is strong, only to raise them sharply the following year if the office market seems likely to be overbuilt and new projects look less certain of success. Some indication of the range of variation is provided by the American Council of Life Insurance, which publishes quarterly and annual information on mortgage commitments of $100,000 and more made by the twenty largest life insurance companies in the United States. Their information on the loan-to-value and debt coverage ratios for a variety of real estate projects in 1982 is shown in table 12-4.

Since the banking system reorganization of the 1930s, mortgages typically have been repayable in fixed monthly, quarterly, or annual installments. Ordinarily, each payment includes a partial repayment of the original amount borrowed—the *mortgage principal*—and an interest payment on the outstanding principal balance. The partial repayment of principal is called *amortization.* Because the payments are constant—that is, they do

Table 12-4. American Council of Life Insurance: 1982 Loan Statistics

Property Type	Number of Loans	Interest Rate	Loan-to-Value Ratio	Debt Coverage Ratio
Conventional apartments	83	13.94%	63.7	1.31
Shopping center (five or more stores)	56	14.15	66.1	1.38
Office building	320	14.25	67.6	1.33
Commercial warehouse	23	13.91	70.1	1.21
Industrial warehouse	104	14.41	64.9	1.25

Source: American Council of Life Insurance, *Investment Bulletin No. 852,* May 2, 1983.

not change over the life of the mortgage—as each installment payment is made, the amount of the loan balance is reduced. This means that for the next installment payment, the interest component will be lower while the amortization component will be higher. By the final years of the repayment schedule, the bulk of each installment is a principal repayment while only a small portion is interest on the unpaid balance. This has income tax consequences, which will be discussed later, but the important point is that each installment mortgage payment includes an amortization of principal component, so that the total periodic payment is higher than would be required merely to cover interest on the original mortgage loan.

Once the size of the mortgage loan, the annual interest rate, and the amortization term are known, the mortgage lender consults mortgage schedule tables or a computer to determine the fixed periodic payment required to cover the interest due and to amortize the entire mortgage loan over its term. Table 12-5 shows an "amortization schedule" for an $800,000 mort-

Table 12-5. Mortgage Amortization Schedule

Principal is $800,000.00 at 11.000% for 25 Years

Year	Interest	Amortization	Princ. Balance
1	$87,683.36	$6,407.44	$793,592.56
2	86,941.89	7,148.91	786,443.65
3	86,114.63	7,976.17	778,467.48
4	85,191.62	8,899.18	769,568.30
5	84,161.83	9,928.97	759,639.33
6	83,012.87	11,077.93	748,561.40
7	81,730.93	12,359.87	736,201.53
8	80,300.68	13,790.12	722,411.41
9	78,704.89	15,385.91	707,025.50
10	76,924.45	17,166.35	689,859.15
11	74,937.97	19,152.83	670,706.32
12	72,721.62	21,369.18	649,337.14
13	70,248.81	23,841.99	625,495.15
14	67,489.85	26,600.95	598,894.20
15	64,411.61	29,679.19	569,215.01
16	60,977.17	33,113.63	536,101.38
17	57,145.31	36,945.49	499,155.89
18	52,870.02	41,220.78	457,935.11
19	48,099.99	45,990.81	411,944.30
20	42,777.98	51,312.82	360,631.48
21	36,840.14	57,250.66	303,380.82
22	30,215.15	63,875.65	239,505.17
23	22,823.53	71,267.27	168,237.90
24	14,576.55	79,514.25	88,723.65
25	5,367.15	88,723.65	0.00
TOTALS	$1,552,270.00	$800,000.00	

Source: Computer-developed on Real Estate Analytical Package (REAP), Shlaes & Young Information Systems, Inc., Chicago, Illinois.

gage loan at an interest rate of 11 percent for an amortization term of twenty-five years.

The *mortgage constant* is simply an expression of the relationship between the annual installment payments and the original mortgage loan amount. On the $800,000 loan shown in table 12-5, the total annual interest and principal payment is $94,090.80, so the mortgage constant is $94,090.80 divided by 800,000, or 11.76 percent. In other words, the annual installment payments of principal and interest are equal to 11.76 percent of the original mortgage loan amount. The mortgage constant tells the developer what the total annual cost of debt service on the project will be.

Using accepted loan-to-value and debt coverage ratios, current interest rates, and currently available terms on mortgage loans, both the developer and the lender can calculate the size of the mortgage loan that any particular project will support. Consider once again our $1 million project that generates $100,000 in net operating income available for debt service and return on equity. If the mortgage lender demands a debt coverage ratio of 1.35, the developer knows that the annual debt service cost that can be supported by this project is $100,000 divided by 1.35 or $74,000. At an interest rate of 13 percent and an amortization term of twenty-five years, that amount of debt service will repay a mortgage principal of only $546,770. Our developer would have to find about $453,230 somewhere else, probably from equity investors.

EQUITY FEASIBILITY ANALYSIS

Real estate competes with other types of investments for capital, and one real estate project competes with another for the limited number of equity investors interested in real estate. This means that every real estate venture must not only provide a return competitive with other types of investments, such as savings accounts, money market funds, stocks, and bonds, but also must match the return promised by other developers in similar projects.

The return must also take into account the special risks associated with real estate. An investor in real estate could instead put his or her money into a fixed-rate savings account at a savings and loan and receive 5.5 percent annual interest, insured by the Federal Savings and Loan Insurance Corporation up to $100,000. Or the investor could put the money into a six-month, one-year, two-year, or perhaps even a three-year savings certificate at a savings and loan or a commercial bank at a fixed rate of interest quoted in advance and insured by the federal government, or could purchase a long-term corporate bond at a predetermined interest rate if held to maturity. Perhaps the corporate bond is not as secure as the bank investments, but seldom do large American corporations fail to meet their bonded indebtedness. That risk of failure will be built into the rating that the bond has and the interest rate it carries.

Real estate is often a riskier investment than any of these and is usually much less liquid. It cannot be sold or cashed in like a share of listed stock or a savings account, and it tends to come in big chunks, which makes investment diversification hard to achieve. Often the return to the real estate investor will vary dramatically from what was expected when the project began, sometimes for the worse. While the risks of failure—or at least of the returns being different than expected—can be high, so often are the possibilities that the return will be greater than predicted on the date of project initiation.

Real estate developers and investors need analytical tools to measure return on equity and compare alternate investments. Three such tools are in common use: cash-on-cash return, discounted present value, and internal rate of return.[2]

Cash-on-cash return is the mathematical result of dividing income in any current or future year by the amount of cash invested in the project. If the project is leveraged by a mortgage, cash-on-cash return typically is measured by dividing pre-tax cash flow by equity. (See table 12-1.) This measure of return may be quite low in the early years, but the effect of inflation on rents may increase net operating income, and consequently pre-tax cash flow in later years, and gradually increase the annual cash-on-cash return.

The yearly cash-on-cash returns from one real estate project can be compared to another to rank investment opportunities. However, the method has its drawbacks. All that the investor sees is either a one-year stabilized income and expense forecast or at best a series of annual forecasts, perhaps with some expression of the relationship between the proceeds of sale in some future year, the reversion, and the original equity investment as well. It does not take into consideration the timing of those cash returns. The return on an investment in real estate is in the form of a series of annual cash flows and a *reversion* at the end of the investment period when the project is sold to someone else. Some method is necessary for comparing two quite different scenarios for the future that vary in the timing and size of the future cash flows. Consider the two cash flow forecasts shown in table 12-6, each of which requires a $15,000 investment in the first year.

Which investment is the better one, assuming the risk in each is the same? Is it simply Investment 1 because it returns a total accumulated cash flow of $1,750 more than Investment 2? The answer is not that simple because of two fundamental principles of long-term investment: more is better than less and sooner is better than later. Those two rules express the time/value component in any real estate investment. One dollar today is worth more than one dollar promised one year from now because of the opportunity to invest the dollar received today in some other productive asset, such as a savings account, with a rate of return that will increase its value to something more than one dollar within one year. The corollary to that principle is that a dollar promised one year from now, or two years from now, is worth less than a dollar in hand today; you would hardly pay a full dollar

---

2. Many real estate developers and syndicators also stress the payback period, the amount of time it takes for the original cash investment to be returned, or the ratio between total tax deductions generated by the project and the cash investment. These are not as important as the other three measures of return.

Table 12-6. Annual Cash Flow: Initial Investment of $15,000

Year	Investment 1: Annual Cash Flow	Present Value @ 13% D.R.	Investment 2: Annual Cash Flow	Present Value @ 13% D.R.
1	$1,000	$885	$1,500	$1,327
2	1,100	861	1,500	1,175
3	850	589	1,500	1,040
4	1,400	859	1,500	920
5	1,600	868	1,500	814
6	1,200	576	1,500	720
7	1,700	723	1,500	638
8	1,900	715	1,500	564
9	1,400	466	1,500	499
10	2,100	619	1,500	442
Reversion	27,500	8,101	25,000	7,365
Total Accumulated Cash Flow	$41,750	$15,262	$40,000	$15,504
Net Present Value Assuming $15,000 Initial Investment		$262		$504

today for the promise of a dollar back a year from now. The rate used to adjust promised future dollars to their present value is called the "discount rate." Two alternative streams of income available to an investor can be analyzed and compared by reducing them to a present value at a common discount rate. Other things being equal, the alternative with the higher present value is the better investment.

Assume that the appropriate discount rate to apply to the alternative streams of income set out in table 12-6 is 13 percent—the rate of return that could be obtained today by the investor in another project of comparable risk. Investment 1 has a present value of $15,262. Investment 2 has a present value of $15,504. If the risks of each project are the same, Investment 2 is the better one when the time/value relationship of money is considered.

This discounting of a future stream of income to a present value at a specified discount rate is called the *discounted present value* method of investment analysis. When the initial investment of $15,000 is subtracted from the present value, the resulting number is called the *net present value* (NPV). Table 12-6 shows both the present value and the net present value of Investment 1 and Investment 2 at 13 percent discount rate.

The internal rate of return (IRR) method of calculating feasibility is in many ways similar to the net present value method and often produces the same result. The difference is conceptually important but may mean little in practice. In the internal rate of return analysis, the investor is searching for a common discount or yield rate that will reduce each future annual cash flow, including the reversion to the original equity investment. Net present value, in contrast, is based on an investor's preselection of a particular discount or yield rate. The internal rate of return method results in a discount rate that then can be compared to the rate, or *yield,* as it is sometimes called, provided by other types of projects, and the investor can select the project providing the highest IRR, assuming that the risks of each project are equal.

Using the same example set out in Table 12-6, Investment 1 has an internal rate of return of 13.25 and Investment 2 has an internal rate of return of 13.53. The second investment is superior, and that corresponds to the result of our net present value calculation. The two methods usually do give the same advice about whether an investment is a good one. There are some mathematical peculiarities involved with the internal rate of return method, however, that mean the often "more reliable" NPV also should be looked at before a decision is made.

There are at least two lines in a cash flow forecast to which the IRR and NPV methods can be applied. One is the pre-tax cash flow generated annually and at date of reversion, and the second is the cash flows generated after the effects of the Internal Revenue Code are considered. The income tax code has a significant effect on the attractiveness of real estate as an investment. This effect has a major bearing on feasibility and must be understood by planners as well as real estate investors if they are to understand the needs of a development project.

A tax shelter in real estate consists of two principal components. The first is the opportunity to take *depreciation deductions* (now called by the tax code *accelerated cost recovery* or ACRS) on a large portion of the cost of the real estate project. The second element is the opportunity to convert ordinary income to capital gain that is taxed at a lower rate at a later date. Each of these elements needs careful consideration.[3]

Depreciation, or accelerated cost recovery as it is called in the Economic Recovery Tax Act of 1981 (ERTA), is an annual deduction from income allowed by the Internal Revenue Code to reflect the using up of an investment. It is not an actual out-of-pocket expenditure but an accounting entry that reflects a judgment by Congress that real estate has a useful life over which it is used up. The deductions are allowed only on income-producing properties or properties used in a trade or business, such as office buildings, apartment complexes, hotels, and warehouses.

The amount of the investment in a real estate project that can be depreciated is called the *depreciable basis.* Land is assumed to hold its value over time and cannot be depreciated, so a developer acquiring a site and constructing a new building can only depreciate the cost to build the structure and not the price paid for the land. Likewise, a developer acquiring an existing building must allocate a portion of the purchase price to undepre-

---

3. The deduction of mortgage interest payments from otherwise taxable income is a benefit, but not truly an element, of tax shelter. It simply reduces the out-of-pocket costs of the interest actually paid by allowing that interest to offset some income that would otherwise be taxed. Unlike depreciation deductions, interest deductions represent a real out-of-pocket expenditure.

Net Present Value and Internal Rate of Return

Net present value calculations provide a way of comparing the present value of the cash investments in a real estate development project with the present value of the cash receipts from it. First, the investor must understand the concept of *present value*. For example, suppose the investor wants to calculate the value today (present value) of $100 one year from today. If an interest rate of five percent is expected during the year, an investment of $95.24 today will be equal to $100 a year from now (1.05 × $95.24 = $100). Hence, the *present* value of $100 one year from now at five percent is $95.24. It is possible to generalize the calculation to any point in the future and any rate of interest.

Summing up the present value of all future cash flows from a project and subtracting the amount of the initial cash investment from the result will tell the investor whether or not the initial cash investment is desirable. This process represents a net present value calculation. When making a net present value calculation, an investor should always select a rate (the discount rate or hurdle rate) equal to his minimum acceptable rate of return. If the calculation results in a positive net present value, the rate of return to the investor is higher than the minimum acceptable, and the investment is worthwhile. A negative net present value means the rate of return is lower than the minimum acceptable to the particular investor.

The formula for the calculation is:

$$NPV = \frac{CF_1}{(1 + i)} + \frac{CF_2}{(1 + i)^2} + \cdots + \frac{CF_n}{(1 + i)^n} - C =$$

$$\sum_{t=1}^{n} CF_t \frac{1}{(1 + i)^t} - C$$

CF_1 = Cash flow in the first year
CF_2 = Cash flow in the second year, etc.
i = Discount rate
C = Initial cash investment

The internal rate of return calculation allows an investor to determine the discount rate that reduces a future stream of cash flows to the initial cash investment. In other words, the internal rate is the rate that makes the present value of all the future cash flows equal to the initial cash outlay. If the rate equals or exceeds a minimum desired rate of return, then the project is acceptable. The generalized equation for the internal rate of return is as follows:

$$\text{Cost} = \sum_{t=1}^{n} (CF)_t \frac{1}{(1 + k)^t}$$

CF = Cash flow
Cost = Initial cash investment
k = Discount rate (internal rate of return)

Solving the equation for *k* when all the other factors are known results in the internal rate of return.

ciable land. Once that allocation is made, the developer and the investors may depreciate the entire remaining cost of the project whether they have put up their own funds for the project or borrowed them from a mortgage lender.

To determine the amount of the annual depreciation deduction, the useful life of the project, over which the depreciation deductions will be taken, must be determined. Prior to 1981, complicated rules determined the appropriate useful life of any particular real estate project. Those rules were simplified by ERTA, which now allows a fifteen-year cost recovery period for any type of investment real estate and an optional thirty-five-year or forty-five-year useful life if preferred. Most development projects elect the fifteen-year recovery period in order to maximize the annual depreciation deduction.

There is also some choice under ERTA in the selection of the rate of depreciation. Straight-line cost recovery allows the owner/investor to take the same depreciation deduction each year throughout the useful life of a property. Accelerated cost recovery allows the owner/investor to take larger depreciation deductions in the early years of a real estate project, roughly equivalent to those produced by the old 175 percent declining balance method, and gradually to decrease the annual deduction until an automatic switch-over to the straight-line rate occurs in a later year.

Consider again a developer who undertakes a $1 million project to construct and operate an apartment building. The site costs $100,000, which must be deducted from total project cost to determine the depreciable basis. If a fifteen-year useful life and straight-line depreciation are selected, the developer will be entitled to a $60,000 depreciation deduction each year for fifteen years. If, instead, the accelerated cost recovery method is used, a $108,000 deduction can be taken in the first year, a $90,000 deduction in the second year, and so on according to a prescribed schedule set out by the Internal Revenue Code. Table 12-7 compares the alternative straight-line and accelerated depreciation schedules available to this developer and his or her investors.

Accelerated cost recovery is not automatically preferable to straight-line. The same principles of discounted cash flow analysis can be used to compare the alternative depreciation possibilities. The tax code also imposes some later surcharges on the use of accelerated cost recovery in the form of recapture of accelerated depreciation upon sale of the real estate project. The surcharges are higher on commercial projects such as office buildings than they are on residential income-producing projects such as apartment buildings, with the result that most office building projects under today's tax code use straight-line rather than accelerated cost recovery.[4]

The second component of the tax shelter available to real estate is the

4. The excess of accelerated depreciation over a straight-line also is a tax preference item that may be subject to a 15 percent add-on minimum tax or an alternative minimum tax equal to 10 to 20 percent of the income items that qualify.

Table 12-7. Depreciation Schedules: $900,000 Depreciable Basis

	Straight-Line Cost Recovery		Accelerated Cost Recovery	
Year	Amount	Percent of Original Depreciable Basis	Amount	Percent of Original Depreciable Basis
1	$60,000	6.67%	$108,000	12%
2	60,000	6.67	90,000	10
3	60,000	6.67	81,000	9
4	60,000	6.67	72,000	8
5	60,000	6.67	63,000	7
6	60,000	6.67	54,000	6
7	60,000	6.67	54,000	6
8	60,000	6.67	54,000	6
9	60,000	6.67	54,000	6
10	60,000	6.67	45,000	5
11	60,000	6.67	45,000	5
12	60,000	6.67	45,000	5
13	60,000	6.67	45,000	5
14	60,000	6.67	45,000	5
15	60,000	6.67	45,000	5
Total	$900,000	100.00%*	$900,000	100%

* Due to rounding off of figures, the total is not 100 percent.

opportunity to convert ordinary income to capital gain and defer the taxes until the project is sold. The American income tax system is progressive; taxpayers with higher incomes pay a higher percentage of their incomes in taxes. Currently the maximum tax rate (or bracket) is 50 percent. That does not mean that a person earning $200,000 per year pays $100,000 in taxes, but that the last increment of total income is taxed at a 50 percent rate. As income increases, a taxpayer moves into an ever-higher marginal tax bracket until the 50 percent rate is reached.[5]

Some types of incomes are taxed at rates less than these. Gain from the sale of income-producing real estate held for longer than one year is one such capital gain item. A full 60 percent of the gain may be excluded from income before determining the taxes that must be paid. For a taxpayer in the 50 percent bracket, that means the current maximum tax that can be paid on a capital gain is 20 percent (100 percent minus 60 percent times 50 percent).

In order to calculate the capital gain and the taxes due at sale, the original basis and the accumulated depreciation deductions taken during the holding period must be known. Consider again the $1 million apartment building project with an allocation to land of $100,000 and a depreciable basis of $900,000. Assume that the developer and his investors are taking straight-

5. As a result of changes made by the Economic Recovery Tax Act of 1981 (ERTA), the tax brackets are now adjusted annually for inflation so that taxpayers will not be forced into ever-higher tax brackets simply by the effect of inflation on their income.

Table 12-8. Determining Tax Consequences of Sale

Original project cost	$1,000,000
Less: Total depreciation	600,000
Adjusted basis at sale	$ 400,000
Net sales price	$1,000,000
Less: Adjusted basis	400,000
Total taxable gain	$ 600,000
Less: 60 percent capital gain exclusion	360,000
Gain included in income	$ 240,000
Tax (50 percent bracket)	$ 120,000

line cost recovery on a fifteen-year useful life schedule. (See table 12-7.) Every year the owners are entitled to a $60,000 depreciation deduction. If all of them are in the 50 percent maximum tax bracket, that may save them annually a combined $30,000 in taxes that would otherwise have to be paid to the federal government. If they decide to sell the apartment building after holding it for ten years, their total accumulated annual tax savings from the depreciation deductions will be $300,000, since the total deductions are $600,000. When they sell the project, however, some of that tax savings is repaid because every dollar in depreciation deduction reduces the depreciable basis, and it is the depreciable basis, now reduced to $300,000, that is used to calculate taxable gain at sale. The taxable gain at sale is the difference between the sales price (less any expenses of sale) and the taxpayer's adjusted basis in the property, as reduced by total depreciation deductions taken during the time the project was held.

If the developer and his investors sell this project for $1 million at the end of ten years, the tax consequences of the sale are as shown in table 12-8. The taxpayers have sheltered $300,000 in taxes that would otherwise have been paid over those ten years, but, at sale, they must repay $120,000 of those accumulated tax savings. There may be additional add-on minimum tax payments due as well, if the taxpayers have elected to use an accelerated form of depreciation, and an alternative minimum tax (a surcharge on some types of investments such as real estate) due on the 60 percent of the total gain excluded from income.

Criteria for Investment Decision Making

Daniel E. Page

During the past decade, real estate has received widespread attention as an attractive investment. An increased awareness of how to make the investment decision has accompanied this interest, and substantial advances have been made in the theory of the investment decision.[1] However, little attention has been given to how the practitioner actually makes the investment decision.

In mid-1972, Robert J. Wiley surveyed real estate investment trusts (REITs), real estate corporations, and insurance companies to see how real estate investors were making investment decisions.[2] In 1982, Edward J. Farragher examined the quantitative investment decision-making tools used by real estate investors.[3] Many changes have taken place in the institutional and economic structure of society since Wiley's study. The purpose of this article is to reexamine the real estate investor's decision-making process. This study not only updates Wiley's study but expands into other areas, such as the use of ratio analysis in decision making and the impact of the Economic Recovery Tax Act of 1981 (ERTA).

DATA BASE

Questionnaires were sent to 85 REITs, 100 real estate companies, and 125 insurance companies, a group of investors who could be classified as sophisticated real estate investors. The usable response rate was 33 percent, including thirty-one REITs, forty-five insurance companies, and twenty-five real estate corporations.

Table 13-1 provides information on the size of the respondents' real estate portfolios and the types of property held: 91 percent of the respondents held at least $5 million in real estate, and 56 percent held over $50 million. The major investments of each category were: REITs, shopping centers, office buildings, and real estate corporations, land.

DECISION-MAKING CRITERIA

In this section, criteria for investment decision making are examined, the use of rules of thumb and discounted cash flow models before and after

* Daniel E. Page, "Criteria for Investment Decision Making: An Empirical Study," in *The Appraisal Journal*, October 1983. Copyright © 1983 by *The Appraisal Journal*, Chicago, Illinois. Reprinted by permission.

1. Techniques for the evaluation of real estate investments range from rules of thumb, to discounted cash flow models, to computer simulation models. For a discussion of these techniques, see Austin Jaffe and C. F. Sirmans, *Real Estate Investment Decision Making* (Englewood Cliffs, N.J.: Prentice-Hall, 1982), chap. 16–20.

2. Robert J. Wiley, "Real Estate Investment Analysis: An Empirical Study," *The Appraisal Journal* (October 1976): 586–595.

3. Edward J. Farragher, "Investment Decision-Making Practices of Equity Investors in Real Estate," *The Real Estate Appraiser and Analyst* (Summer 1982): 36–41.

Table 13-1. Size and Type of Real Estate Portfolio

Market Value of Portfolio	Percentage of 31 REITs	Percentage of 45 Insurance Companies	Percentage of 25 Real Estate Corporations	Percentage of 101 Respondents
Under $500,000	4	2	0	2
$500,000 to $5 million	4	12	0	7
$5 million to $25 million	26	24	25	25
$25 million to $50 million	11	0	38	11
$50 million to $100 million	22	21	6	19
Over $100 million	33	41	31	37
Type of Property Held				
Apartments	19	7	12	13
Office buildings	17	32	7	18
Shopping centers	23	13	6	14
Single-family housing	5	9	16	10
Hotels/motels	9	6	11	9
Industrial/commercial	12	17	3	11
Land	9	7	39	18
Other	8	8	5	7

taxes are explored, and the use of ratio analysis and the treatment of risk in investment decision making is examined.

Before-Tax Investment Criteria

Table 13-2 lists responses of various decision-making criteria used on a before-tax basis; 95 percent of the respondents indicated that they used some form of before-tax measure. Many investors cited the use of several techniques. The two most popular rules of thumb were the equity dividend rate (EDR) (33 percent) and the overall capitalization rate (25 percent). However, the most often cited technique was a discounted cash flow technique, the before-tax internal rate of return (IRR) (57 percent).

Wiley found that the most used before-tax technique was the EDR. One reason an investor might switch from the EDR to a before-tax IRR is an increased awareness of the time value of money. Before 1972, inflation was growing at a slow to moderate pace. Beginning in the mid-1970s, inflation began to increase rapidly, making it necessary to account for the time value of money which the EDR does not do.

After-Tax Investment Criteria

Table 13-3 lists the after-tax investment criteria. The 74 percent using an after-tax measure represents a substantial increase from the 54 percent Wiley found. Excluding REITs, which generally do not pay any federal taxes and therefore may not use an after-tax measure, 85 percent of the respondents use an after-tax measure.

Table 13-2. Before-tax Investment Criteria

Before-tax Measure	Percentage of 31 REITs	Percentage of 45 Insurance Companies	Percentage of 25 Real Estate Corporations	Percentage of 101 Respondents
Rules of Thumb				
Payback period	7	17	6	12
Net income multiplier[a]	7	17	19	14
Gross income multiplier[b]	0	5	13	5
BTCF multiplier[c]	15	15	6	13
Overall capitalization rate[d]	26	66	25	45
Equity dividend rate[e]	26	39	31	33
Other	4	7	0	5
Discounted Cash Flow Method				
Before-tax IRR	48	66	50	57
No Before-tax Measure Used	4	3	13	5

a. Net income multiplier = Total investment ÷ Net operating income
b. Gross income multiplier = Total investment ÷ Gross income
c. Before-tax cash flow multiplier = Equity investment ÷ BTCF
d. Overall capitalization rate = Net operating income ÷ Total investment
e. Equity dividend rate = BTCF ÷ Equity investment

Table 13-3. After-tax Investment Criteria

After-tax Measure	Percentage of 31 REITs	Percentage of 45 Insurance Companies	Percentage of 25 Real Estate Corporations	Percentage of 101 Respondents
Rules of Thumb				
Payback period	6	13	7	11
After-tax rate[a]	0	29	0	17
After-tax multiplier[b]	17	11	14	14
Discounted Cash Flow Techniques				
Net present value	6	18	36	20
Internal rate of return	22	61	43	50
Financial management rate of return	0	16	7	11
Profitability index	0	3	7	3
Tax Shelter Benefits	11	11	0	9
Other	6	3	7	5
No After-tax Measure Used	50	13	21	26

a. After-tax rate = After = tax cash flow ÷ Equity investment
b. After-tax cash flow multiplier = Equity investment ÷ After-tax cash flow

An after-tax rate (ATR) was most popular with REITs and real estate corporations, while insurance companies preferred an after-tax cash flow multiplier. The net present value (NPV) and internal rate of return (IRR) were the most popular discounted cash flow techniques. The IRR was the most frequently used of all after-tax measures.

Table 13-4. Ratio Analysis in Investment Decision Making

Do you use ratio analysis?	Percentage of 31 REITs	Percentage of 45 Insurance Companies	Percentage of 25 Real Estate Corporations	Percentage of 101 Respondents
Yes	72	78	47	70
No	28	22	53	30
Types of Ratios Used				
Leverage Ratios				
Mortgage debt to property value[a]	47	34	20	36
Debt coverage[b]	21	40	20	44
Default ratio[c]	21	29	20	25
Total asset turnover[d]	5	6	10	6
Operating expense ratio[e]	26	23	10	22
Profitability Ratios				
Profit margin	0	0	10	2
Return on total investment	5	20	20	16
Return on equity	11	43	30	31
Other Ratios Used	21	14	20	17

a. Mortgage debt to property value = Mortgage outstanding ÷ property value
b. Debt coverage = Net operating income ÷ Debt service
c. Default ratio = Operating expense + debt service ÷ Gross income
d. Total asset turnover = Gross income ÷ Property value
e. Operating expense ratio = Operating expenses ÷ Gross income

Wiley's study found that the ATR was the most popular technique. The switch from the ATR to the IRR may be due to the time value of money component captured in the IRR method. Farragher also found that the IRR was the most popular evaluation technique.

Ratio Analysis in Investment Decision Making

Seventy percent of all respondents used ratio analysis in their decision making process. Table 13-4 lists common leverage and profitability ratios and the percentage of respondents that use each. The most popular leverage ratios were the debt coverage ratio (44 percent) and the default ratio (25 percent). Return on equity (31 percent) and return to equity on total investment (16 percent) were the most frequently cited profitability ratios. The results suggest that investors are very concerned with the overall profitability of the project and how well they can cover debt service.

Risk Adjustment Techniques

Handling projects that are above normal risk is difficult. Table 13-5 lists various risk adjustments and the percentage of respondents that use each type. Twenty-three percent of the respondents indicated that they did not quantify increases in risk. The three most popular techniques for adjusting risk were: 1) adjusting downward the cash flows expected from the project

Table 13-5. Risk Adjustment Techniques

Risk Adjustment Technique	Percentage of 31 REITs	Percentage of 45 Insurance Companies	Percentage of 25 Real Estate Corporations	Percentage of 101 Respondents
Adjust upward the required rate of return for the project	33	28	31	30
Adjust downward the cash flows expected from the project	33	40	44	39
Use decision trees	4	0	0	1
Use sensitivity analysis	26	20	13	20
Use probability distributions	0	5	19	6
Other adjustments	0	8	0	4
No explicit adjustments for uncertainty	19	30	13	23

(39 percent); 2) adjusting upward the required rate of return (30 percent); and 3) the use of sensitivity analysis (20 percent).

Labeling the investor portfolios as small (less than 5 million), medium (from $5 million to $100 million), and large (over $100 million) yields some interesting results. Of the small firms, 42 percent made no adjustment for risk. The favorite method for medium firms was adjusting downward the cash flow expected from the project (51 percent). Adjusting upward the required rate of return was the most popular method for large firms (38 percent).

Use of sensitivity analysis has also increased since Wiley's study. Fourteen percent of the small firms reported using sensitivity analysis as did 16 percent of medium firms, and 28 percent of large firms. This result is probably due to increased access to computers.

COMPUTER USAGE

Wiley found that only 14 percent of his respondents used a computer in their decision making and noted that computer usage would probably increase in the future. Wiley was correct in his prediction. Of the investors responding to this study, 57 percent reported using the computer in decision making.

The three most popular ways of using the computer (see table 13-6) were: 1.) computing rates of return, 82 percent; 2.) calculating cash flows, 71 percent; and 3.) forecasting, 50 percent. With the microcomputer boom, it is no surprise that 58 percent of the respondents reported using microprocessors, while 21 percent reported using both a micro- and large mainframe computer.

Separating investor portfolios by size also illustrates an increase in computer usage since the time of Wiley's study. Thirty-eight percent of small firms reported using the computer as compared to 14 percent in Wiley's study; 52 percent of medium firms used computers as compared to Wiley's

Table 13-6. Computer Usage

Do you use a computer?	Percentage of 31 REITs	Percentage of 45 Insurance Companies	Percentage of 25 Real Estate Corporations	Percentage of 101 Respondents
Yes	56	62	50	57
No	44	38	50	43
Ways Computer is Used				
Simulations	25	33	33	31
Forecasting	75	29	44	50
Computing rates of return	75	92	67	82
Regression analysis	0	13	11	8
Calculating cash flows	69	71	78	71
Other	6	13	11	10
Type of Computer Used				
Large mainframe	32	19	0	21
Microcomputer	63	45	100	58
Both	5	36	0	21

25 percent; and 69 percent of large firms used computers as compared to Wiley's 43 percent. The chief use of the computer by all sizes of firms was in computing rates of return.

IMPACT OF THE ECONOMIC RECOVERY TAX ACT

The passage of the Economic Recovery Tax Act (ERTA) in August 1981 was the most comprehensive revision of the tax law since 1954. The ERTA was designed to reduce the federal tax burden of individuals and businesses, thereby putting more money into the private sector. It affected real estate investors by changing depreciation schedules and altering the way certain items, such as excess depreciation, were taxed.

This study answers three questions concerning the ERTA: 1) Which investments have become more attractive since the passage of the ERTA? 2) Has the holding period used to base investment analysis changed? 3) Has the ERTA stimulated more investment in real estate? Tables 13-7 and 13-8 show the responses to these questions. The most popular holding period before and after the passage of the ERTA was ten years. This suggests that eliminating the previous depreciation schedule and implementing the accelerated cost recovery system (ACRS) did not affect the holding period typically assumed in the respondents' investment analysis. (The majority [73 percent] of the respondents also used the straight-line method of depreciation after ERTA.)

Table 13-8 indicates that the ERTA did not change the respondents' interests from one type of real estate investment to another. In fact, 84 percent

Table 13-7. Holding Periods Before and After ERTA

Holding Period Before ERTA	Percentage of 31 REITs	Percentage of 45 Insurance Companies	Percentage of 25 Real Estate Corporations	Percentage of 101 Respondents
5 years	33	0	47	20
10 years	48	58	20	48
15 years	11	24	7	16
20 years	0	16	7	9
Life of tax shelter	7	3	13	6
Other time periods	15	11	13	13
Holding Period After ERTA				
5 years	37	0	40	20
10 years	33	66	20	46
15 years	15	21	13	18
Life of tax shelter	4	8	13	8
Other time period	22	13	13	16

Table 13-8. Investment Interests After ERTA

Investment Interests After ERTA	Percentage of 31 REITs	Percentage of 45 Insurance Companies	Percentage of 25 Real Estate Corporations	Percentage of 101 Respondents
Residential	8	5	12	7
Nonresidential	0	18	24	13
Low-income property	4	0	0	1
Did not affect interests	88	77	64	79
Did ERTA stimulate more investment in real estate?				
Yes	15	18	13	16
No	85	82	87	84

reported that the ERTA did not stimulate them to increase their real estate investments. This result is not surprising for REITs because they do not pay taxes and for real estate corporations because they are in the real estate business. It is somewhat surprising for insurance companies; one might conclude they would be more interested in residential property since the passage of the ERTA.

CONCLUSION

Table 13-9 compares the major results of this study to those of Wiley in 1972 and Farragher in 1982. The current study shows that more investors, including REITs, are using after-tax discounted cash flow measures. This

Table 13-9. Comparison of Investment Studies

Criteria Most Often Used	Studies		
	Wiley (1972)	Farragher (1982)	Page (1982–83)
Before-tax Measure	Equity dividend rate	N/A	Before-tax IRR
After-tax Measure			
Percent using after-tax measure	54%	N/A	74%
Method used	After-tax rate	IRR	IRR
Ratio Analysis			
Percent using ratio analysis	N/A	N/A	70%
Leverage ratios	N/A	N/A	Debt coverage
Profitability ratios	N/A	N/A	Return on equity
Risk Adjustment	Adjust downward	No method used	Adjust downward
Techniques	cash flows	primarily	cash flows
Computer Usage			
Percentage that use computer	14%	N/A	58%
Computer primarily used for	Computing rates of return	N/A	Computing rates of return
Type of computer used most often	N/A	N/A	micro
Impact of ERTA			
Holding period before ERTA	None specifically stated	N/A	10 years
Holding period after ERTA	N/A	N/A	10 years
Investment interests after ERTA	N/A	N/A	Interests not affected
Did ERTA stimulate more real estate investment?	N/A	N/A	No

implies that investors are realizing the importance of depreciation and other tax-shelter benefits of real estate. They are also more aware of inflation. Investors frequently use ratio analysis in making real estate investment decisions. They emphasize debt coverage and return on equity. The majority of investors are either adjusting the cash flows downward or the required rate of return upward when projects have above-normal risk. The facility of microcomputers has prompted increased investor use of them in making decisions, predominantly in calculating rates of return. The ERTA of 1981 has neither changed the holding period on which most investors base their analysis, nor has it changed investment interests or stimulated more investment in real estate.

The Internal Rate of Return: A Misleading Concept for the Average Real Estate Investor

W. B. Martin

The measures of profit used to evaluate real estate investments range from the unsophisticated gross income multiplier to sophisticated discounted cash-flow measures like the internal rate of return (IRR). Surveys indicate that IRR is widely used in the corporate business world. In many firms, IRR is used to help allocate capital among a variety of competing capital investment projects—almost always under capital rationing conditions (that is, there are more projects than there is capital).

In real estate, the use of IRR does not appear to be nearly as widespread. Surveys indicate that it is used primarily by large, sophisticated investors like life insurance companies and real estate investment trusts. Nevertheless, real estate publications feature numerous articles advocating the use of IRR to evaluate real estate deals. And the IRR technique is being taught in real estate courses and seminars across the country.

The IRR is often touted as being superior to other measures of profitability, like the "cap" and cash-on-cash rates, because it has two features that the other measures do not: it recognizes the time value of money and it recognizes reversion, or sales proceeds (value appreciation). Unfortunately, the real estate professional who looks to IRR to help him decide whether a real estate investment opportunity is good or bad is using a technique that is full of pitfalls. IRR calculations may send misleading signals even to large, sophisticated investors, and in the hands of smaller, less sophisticated investors they can be downright dangerous.

Real Estate Review has published many articles that have contained IRR calculations based on hypothetical projects. We offer another such calculation merely so that we can analyze the implications of its components. The property in our example is a twenty-unit apartment building. All units have two bedrooms. We have the following financial data:

· Current rents are $300 per month.
· Operating costs are 35 percent of gross possible income.
· The purchase price is $400,000.
· The buyer must put $100,000 down, and the seller will finance $300,000 at 12 percent for thirty years.
· The building will be depreciated straight line over fifteen years.
· Closing costs are ignored.

* W. B. Martin, "IRR Misleads the Average Real Estate Investor," in *Real Estate Review*, vol. 12, no. 13, Fall 1982. Copyright © 1982 by Warren, Gorham and Lamont, Boston, Massachusetts. Reprinted by permission.

In order to develop cash-flow projections over the holding period, we must make the following assumptions:

· Vacancies will average 5 percent of gross possible income.
· Operating costs will rise by 10 percent per year.
· Rents will rise by 7 percent per year.
· The purchaser's tax bracket is 50 percent.
· Land value is $50,000.
· The property will be sold at the end of four years.
· The selling price will be based on the same capitalization rate that prevailed at the time of purchase (10.8 percent).
· Selling expenses will be 3 percent of the selling price.
· The owners will cash out of the deal when they sell the property. (There will be no seller financing.)

The four-year cash-flow projection produced by these assumptions is shown in table 14-1.

The IRR is simply a number that solves an equation. It is the interest rate (or yield) that equates the present value of the expected cash inflows from an investment to the initial cash outlay. A hand calculator can be used to calculate the IRR from table 14-1. That IRR on an initial cash outlay of $100,000 is 20.62 percent per year after taxes.

THE REINVESTMENT RATE PROBLEM

The IRR of 20.62 percent can be interpreted two ways. One is that the 20.62 percent is simply the annual yield on the initial $100,000 equity and has nothing to do with whether the cash flows are reinvested. The other interpretation considers the deal as part of a continuous investment process (that is, a wealth-building process) in which the investor is engaged, and as a result the investor's wealth position will "decline" if the annual cash flows are reinvested in any investment that yields less than 20.62 percent per year.

Table 14-1. Cash-Flow Projection for IRR Calculation

	First Year	Second Year	Third Year	Fourth Year
Gross possible income	$72,000	$77,040	$82,433	$88,203
Vacancy allowance	3,600	3,852	4,122	4,410
Operating costs	25,200	27,720	30,492	33,541
Net operating income	$43,200	$45,468	$47,819	$50,252
Interest on mortgage	36,000	35,851	35,684	35,497
Depreciation	23,333	23,333	23,333	23,333
Taxable income	($16,133)	($13,716)	($11,198)	($ 8,578)
Taxes saved	$ 8,067	$ 6,858	$ 5,599	$ 4,289
Cash flow after taxes	$14,024	$15,083	$16,175	$17,298

Notes: (1) The net proceeds from the sale at the end of four years is $128,308.
(2) The IRR is 20.62 percent.

The *decline* in wealth is somewhat abstract since it is relative to the wealth that would have been accumulated had the $100,000 been invested risk-free at 20.62 percent (after tax) and left for four years, with interest compounded annually. If this had been possible, the accumulated dollars would have been $211,678 [$100,000 (1.2062)^4 = $211,678]. Likewise, if the annual cash flows from the apartment deal are reinvested at the end of each year at a 20.62 percent after-tax yield, then the accumulated wealth of the investor would be $211,678.

COMPONENTS OF IRR

The IRR can be analyzed further by partitioning it into cash flow, tax benefits, and value appreciation components. This has been done in table 14-2.

Perhaps the investor would be distressed to note that 61 percent of the IRR is expected to come from value appreciation (from the net sales proceeds). The implications of this fact will be examined later.

The average investor might conclude that this property is a good deal. If he pays $400,000 for the property, he earns an attractive 20.62 percent. Who wouldn't like to invest $100,000 and earn 20.62 percent after taxes? But the average investor can also undertake a simple calculation to discover that his cash-on-cash yield is only 5.96 percent before taxes and 14 percent after taxes. If the market indicated that the before-tax cash-on-cash yield should be about 9 percent, the property's value, given the financing offered, would be about $367,000, and not $400,000. So which indicator should the investor believe?

CRITIQUE

The potential danger inherent in the use of the IRR to analyze our hypothetical property lies in the assumptions that we had to make in order to create the multiyear cash-flow projections. We made assumptions about future income, expenses, vacancies, tax benefits, and value appreciation. Who really knows what the income and expenses will be and what vacancy problems might be encountered three, four, or five years down the road? We are on even less firm ground when we start to guess what the property might sell for four or five years in the future.

Table 14-2. IRR Partitioned Into Cash Flow, Tax Benefits, and Value Appreciation Components

Component	Partitioned IRR (%)	Component as a Percentage of Total IRR (%)
Cash flow	4.69	23
Tax benefits	3.43	17
Value appreciation	12.50	61
Total	20.62	100

Rent levels and vacancies are determined ultimately by the supply and demand for space. The changes in these variables are heavily influenced by location (whether improving or declining), by competition in the area, and by the state of the economy. Operating expenses may be more stable, and we may be relatively safe in assuming a rate of inflation for management fees, utilities, property taxes, insurance, and maintenance costs. Tax benefit projections make assumptions about future tax laws and about the investor's future tax bracket.

Although value appreciation is certainly a major potential benefit, it is the most difficult to estimate with any degree of confidence.

Another criticism of IRR is its assumption that the seller will cash out when the property is sold. The average investor is frequently involved with properties that require seller financing, and upon sale, the seller merely receives a down payment. Today he may have to take back a mortgage at a below-market rate.

HOW MOST INVESTORS ANALYZE PROPERTY

Real estate prices are set by the market. No analytical technique can substitute for knowledge of the market for a particular type of property. No investor is justified in paying more for a property than what most other buyers would pay—even if IRR analysis indicates that a higher price is possible.

The average investor ordinarily puts the property through a rather simple, yet market oriented, screening process that involves finding answers to the following questions:

· *Location analysis.* What trends are evident in the area? Is the location generally acceptable? Is the area overbuilt?
· *Income/expense analysis.* Does there appear to be potential for increasing rents over time? Who pays the utilities? Do the expenses on the seller's statement appear to be reasonable?
· *Capitalization rate.* Is the capitalization rate in line with the market?
· *Cash-on-cash.* Is the first year cash-on-cash in line with the market? If not, should the seller be compelled to modify either price or financing terms?
· *Physical condition.* Is there something physically wrong with the property? Is it serious? Is it curable?
· *Seller's motivation.* Is the seller really motivated to sell, or has he merely overpriced the property in hopes of trapping an investor who is using the IRR to justify paying above-market prices?

This typical analysis focuses on the first year. The average investor usually assumes that net income will rise in subsequent years and that the property will increase in value. But he makes his decision because he knows enough about the market to conclude that the price and terms are reasonable. Under no circumstances should the average investor attempt to rationalize a high price and terms by using multiyear "guesstimates" about cash flow and value appreciation.

For small investors, measures such as cash-on-cash tend to reflect the world better than does IRR. Almost anything can be justified with IRR if the right assumptions are plugged into the analysis. Furthermore, when it comes time to sell, the next buyer may be using current-year measures instead of IRR.

CONCLUSION

Although IRR is a sophisticated analytical tool, it has many flaws, the most important of which may be that it can give the average real estate investor a false sense of security. The technique treats all of the benefits as equal. It disregards the differences in certainty among benefits arising from cash flow, tax benefits, and value appreciation. If the estimates and assumptions are wrong, so will be the results, and the mathematical sophistication of the technique gives an illusion of exactness that is unwarranted.

Certainly there are real estate deals that call for the use of IRR. Any time that future cash flows and other benefits are known with a high degree of certainty, use of IRR is probably justified. Deals involving bonded net leases or possibly any long-term lease involving an AAA tenant should be analyzed by the IRR technique. But even if the property is subject to a long-term lease, the analyst must consider the difficulty of estimating reversion value.

Nothing in this article suggests that the IRR mathematics are unsound. Once the multiyear benefits are surmised, the IRR mathematics are unquestionably sound. To repeat, the IRR is simply a number that solves an equation. However, a chain is only as strong as its weakest link. The weak link in the IRR process is the usual lack of reliability of the assumptions from which the multiyear benefits are estimated.

Small real estate investors who engage in guessing at multiyear benefits for the IRR analysis at the expense of sound judgment are asking for trouble. The real world for the average investor is centered around the use of simple profitability measures such as capitalization rate and cash-on-cash. In the example, what is the relationship between the market-oriented 5.96 percent cash-on-cash (14.02 percent after-tax) and the 20.62 percent after-tax IRR that is based on a four-year cash-flow "projection" and a sale that presumably will cash out the investor after four years?

The use of the IRR may lead small investors into a trap. It permits them to rationalize paying a high price and accepting a low cash return because the property can be resold four or five years later to another investor ("greater fool") who will accept the same low initial return. It assumes that inflation will continue to push up values.

8 Real Estate Syndication

The Unique Tax Characteristics of Partnerships

Jerry S. Williford

The partnership or joint venture is the most common form for owning and operating real estate. However, the federal income tax treatment of partnerships is often misunderstood not only by investors but also by tax practitioners. The confusion begins with the definition of "partnership" for federal income tax purposes. The tax definition is much broader than the general legal definition. The income tax regulations define a partnership to include a syndicate, group, pool, joint venture, or other unincorporated organization through which any business or venture is carried on. Often the parties, at the advice of the attorney, may use the term "joint venture" in the entity's name and, for state law purposes, the entity may indeed be a joint venture. But for federal income tax purposes the entity is a partnership. For the "privilege" of being a partnership, the partners must prepare a partnership income tax return and the entity is subject to a part of the Internal Revenue Code that deals specifically with partnerships.

WHEN A PARTNERSHIP IS NOT A PARTNERSHIP

However, as is generally the case in dealing with the Internal Revenue Code, there are exceptions to the above. Although a partnership owning and operating an office building, apartment complex, or other structure usually cannot elect out of the partnership provisions, certain partnerships can elect not to be treated as a partnership. In real estate partnerships, this election is usually possible for joint holders of land for investment that carry on no trade or business or that perform no services. Where the partnership elects out, each partner can usually handle his tax reporting in his own manner. For example, one partner may expense interest whereas another may elect to capitalize it.

THE PARTNERSHIP AS BOTH ENTITY AND AGGREGATE

Partnerships are not subject to taxation but serve as conduits through which income, gains, losses, and credits pass through to each partner, based on that partner's pro rata share of these items. Each partner is treated as if he owned an undivided interest in the specific property. The concept of a partnership as the aggregate of each partner's ownership of undivided interests in the property is referred to as the *aggregate* theory.

On the other hand, the partnership is sometimes also treated as a separate entity. In accordance with the *entity* theory, the partnership has its own taxable year, and the partnership may engage in a transaction with a partner who acts in other than his capacity as a partner. Furthermore, the partnership may elect to expense, rather than to depreciate, up to $5,000 (increasing to $10,000 in 1986) of certain property. The $5,000 limitation applies to the partnership. If a partnership composed of five partners owns five pieces of like equipment, it nevertheless may expense only $5,000; $1,000 of which would be allocated to each of the five partners. However, if each partner individually owned one of the pieces of equipment, each could take the full $5,000 deduction.

THE PARTNERSHIP AGREEMENT

Usually there is a written partnership or joint venture agreement, although the income tax regulations do not require a partnership to have a written agreement. In fact, the regulations specifically state that the agreement can be oral. However, the partners of a partnership based on an oral agreement have the burden of proving the terms of the particular partnership. The terms of a limited partnership or one containing special partner allocations must be written.

The income tax regulations concerning amendments to a partnership agreement are liberal. The regulations allow a partnership agreement applying to a particular year to be amended up to the time for filing that year's tax return, not including any extensions (that is, up to the fifteenth day of the fourth month following the partnership's year-end).

GENERAL VERSUS LIMITED PARTNERSHIP

The major difference between a general partnership and a limited partnership is the limited liability of the limited partners in a limited partnership. The laws vary in different states, but generally the limited partner is liable for partnership debts only to the extent of his investment in the limited partnership. A limited partnership must always contain a general partner. That general partner must be a substantial partner. Specifically, the IRS ruling is that the general partner must own at least a 1 percent interest in all items and must meet certain net worth requirements.

Although the major differences between the general and the limited partnership are specified by state law, there are also significant differences from a federal income tax standpoint.

Basis for Deducting Losses

In general, partnerships are subject to the so-called at-risk rules. These rules, first enacted in the Revenue Act of 1969, limit a partner's deduction for losses and investment tax credit to the amount he has "at risk." The amount at risk includes the amount that the partner contributed to the partnership plus the value of loans for which the partner is personally liable. However, in a limited partnership, the limited partner does not share in all liabilities. Consequently, if the general partner is personally liable on a loan, the limited partners cannot include that liability in their basis. Therefore, the limited partner's basis generally equals only his investment (plus profits and less losses).

The rules for real estate partnerships are an exception to the general rule. Although a partner in a real estate partnership can deduct his share of any loss only to the extent of his basis in the partnership, his basis can include liabilities for which he is not personally liable. The income tax regulations state that if no partner has any personal liability on a loan (as would be the situation in the case of a mortgage on real estate), then all the partners, including the limited partners, share in that nonrecourse mortgage and they may add their pro rata share to their basis. This exception generally provides the basis needed to attract limited partners into real estate partnerships.

Because of the creative structures that arise in real estate financing today, it is sometimes difficult to determine if the loan is actually a loan or an equity contribution. The recharacterization of an amount from a loan to equity could be disastrous to most partners because the partners generally depend on the loan for a basis in deducting losses. Is the loan to the partnership from a partner actually a loan or an additional equity contribution? How will the IRS characterize a loan that can be converted to equity in future years? How should it treat a loan that specifies that the lender share in future appreciation? The answers to these questions are not yet clear.

NEGATIVE CAPITAL ACCOUNT

Negative balances are common in real estate partnerships or any tax-shelter type of partnership. Often partners become alarmed when they see that they have a negative capital account balance. A negative balance of this sort is sometimes referred to as a *negative basis*. This designation is incorrect because basis can never be less than zero. If, as mentioned above, the partner's basis includes his share of liabilities, he may have a negative capital account but his basis may be positive.

The negative capital account gives a partner some indication of what his potential gain might be. Generally, if the partner "walked away" from his partnership interest without receiving any consideration, he would have to report a gain equal to his negative capital account.

A negative capital account and the potential gain cannot be eliminated by abandoning the partnership interest or giving it away to a relative or to a charity. There is actually only one way to get rid of it without paying tax, and that is to die. Upon death, the deceased partner's interest is brought up to its fair market value. It has also been suggested that a partner may avoid this potential gain by getting a divorce and letting his or her spouse have that interest.

THE SUBCHAPTER *S* CORPORATION AS AN ALTERNATIVE TO A PARTNERSHIP

The *Subchapter S* corporation, like the partnership, allows the owners to share directly in income or losses. Also, like a limited partnership, it provides its owners with limited liability. However, there is a major difference between a Subchapter S corporation and a partnership in the determination of basis. Furthermore, shareholders in Subchapter S corporations are limited in the amount of losses they can deduct. In a real estate partnership, a partner's basis includes his share of liabilities. In a Subchapter S corporation, however, a shareholder's basis is the amount he contributed to the corporation plus any amounts he loaned to the corporation. Thus a Subchapter S shareholder cannot include in his basis loans made to the corporation by other parties even if the shareholder has guaranteed the loans. In order for the shareholder to include the amount of the corporate loans in his basis, he would have to borrow the funds himself and personally loan them to the corporation.

TREATMENT OF PROPERTY CONTRIBUTIONS TO PARTNERSHIPS

The Internal Revenue Code provides that no gain (or loss) may result to either the partnership or the partner when the partner contributes property, including cash, to the partnership in exchange for a partnership interest. Also, the holding period of the partnership interest includes the holding period of the property contributed.

The partnership's basis in the contributed property is the contributing partner's basis in the property. Thus there is a "carryover" basis. The partner's basis in the partnership interest he receives is generally the same as the basis he had in the property contributed.

If the partner acquired the property prior to January 1, 1981 (the effective date of the accelerated cost recovery system [ACRS] enacted by the Economic Recovery Tax Act of 1981), and contributed the property after the ACRS effective date, the partnership may not depreciate the property using the favorable ACRS lives.

DISTRIBUTIONS FROM PARTNERSHIPS

In general, distributions of property, including cash, by partnerships to partners do not result in either gain or loss to either the partnership or partner. However, if the cash distribution exceeds the partner's basis in the partnership, gain results. Furthermore, the relief of liabilities is treated as a "deemed" distribution of cash. Thus, gain can occur in connection with a reduction of liabilities even though no actual cash is distributed. Consequently, a reduction of a partner's interest in the partnership may result in an unexpected gain. Since a partner generally shares in liabilities based upon his loss-sharing percentage of ownership, a reduction in his loss-sharing percentage results in a reduction in his share of liabilities. This reduction is treated as a deemed distribution of cash. To the extent the deemed distribution exceeds his basis, the partner has a gain.

When a partner receives a distribution of property other than cash, his basis in the property is generally the same as the basis of the property to the partnership (plus any gain recognized) unless the distribution is in liquidation of his interest. This reflects the carryover basis rule of contributions. If the distribution is in liquidation of the partner's interest, the basis of the property is generally the same as the basis of his partnership interest. This is known as the *substituted basis* concept.

As to the holding period, there are two rules. If the property received is not in liquidation of the partner's interest, the holding period includes the time the partnership held the property. However, if the distribution is in liquidation of the partner's interest in the partnership, the holding period becomes the holding period of his partnership interest.

SPECIAL ALLOCATIONS

One of the major advantages of using the partnership form of ownership is the ability of the partnership to allocate income, gains, losses, and credits specially among the partners. Special allocations are not available to corporations, or even to Subchapter S corporations.

For any special allocation to be recognized by the Internal Revenue Service, it must have "substantial economic effect." The meaning of this term is not entirely clear, but it generally means that the special allocation must affect the amount of cash the partners will ultimately receive. Generally, for the special allocation to stand up, the final liquidating partnership distribution must be based in part on the capital account balances of the partners. Thus, he who receives a greater share of losses gets a lesser share of the cash. Looking at it another way, he who deducts the losses must actually bear the losses or pay for the losses by receiving less cash. There is no such thing as sharing in the losses "for tax purposes only."

Any special allocations must also be made for financial or book purposes. Therefore, when a partner receives a special allocation of losses, that partner is trading more *losses* today for less *cash* in the future. Obviously, the shorter the interval between the receipt of the special allocation of losses and the liquidation of the partnership, the less advantageous the special allocation. Assuming, for example, that future after-tax income is discounted at 6 percent and that the tax rate is 50 percent, $1,000 of additional *losses* today equals the present value of $1,000 less *cash* in approximately thirteen years. Thus, for the taxpayer to break even on a special allocation of losses this year, the property would have to be held for at least thirteen years.

Recently, tax advisers have recommended the use of a *gain chargeback* provision in the partnership agreement in order to prevent the trading of losses for cash. This provision specifies that the partner who received the special allocation of losses receive a greater than proportionate share of the gain on sale of the partnership assets. Thus, that partner's capital account is "charged back" so as to increase his capital account balance as if he had never received a special loss allocation.

Although the Internal Revenue Service may ultimately question this provision, the author recommends that any partnership agreement containing a special allocation of losses should also contain the gain chargeback provision.

Although income, gain, and losses are generally easy to allocate specially, credits (such as the investment tax credit) generally cannot be allocated specially. The regulations state that the investment tax credit is to be allocated in accordance with the profit-sharing ratios.

Retroactive Allocations

Often, upon the admission of a partner, the partnership attempts to allocate retroactively to the new partner losses from the beginning of the year. This practice is generally prohibited by the Tax Reform Act of 1976. Generally, a partner may be allocated losses (or income) only from the date he is admitted into the partnership or purchases his interest. However, at least one court has allowed an exception. In that case, the partnership used cash basis accounting, and the partnership paid a large share of previously incurred expenses after the new partner was admitted.

SPECIAL BASIS ELECTION

The partnership provisions of the Internal Revenue Code provide a unique election for certain partners to receive a basis adjustment to their share of the assets of the partnership. This election, generally referred to as a Section 754 election, usually occurs in two situations: when someone purchases a partnership interest and when someone acquires the interest of a partner who has died.

The code allows the partnership to elect to adjust the new partner's share of the partnership assets to his purchase price (or, if the partner has acquired the estate of a deceased partner, to the value for estate tax purposes). This provision appears to be based on the aggregate theory discussed earlier, rather than on the entity theory. The law permits the new partner to increase his basis inside the partnership so as to reflect what he paid for the interest (or the value on which estate taxes were paid). The step-up must be allocated among the assets (such as land, building, and so on). To the extent the step-up is allocated to depreciable property, the new partner is able to obtain higher depreciation. There is some question at this time as to whether the step-up will be subject to the liberalized depreciation lives under the ACRS if the asset was acquired by the partnership prior to the 1981 enactment of ACRS and the step-up transaction occurred after the effective date of ACRS.

It should be noted that the partnership must elect to make this adjustment. Thus, a partnership agreement should contain a provision that requires the general or managing partner to make the election for the partnership when requested by any of the partners. Also, it should be noted that once the partnership makes the election, it is binding on all subsequent transfers. This binding election usually presents no problem, but it could if the value of the partnership assets falls below the partnership's basis in the assets. In that case, the adjustment would result in a decrease rather than an increase in the basis of the partnership assets.

It should also be noted that whether or not the partnership makes the election, the partner's basis in his partnership interest is the amount that he paid for it. The election merely allows the basis of his partnership interest to be spread among the specific assets inside the partnership.

DEALINGS BETWEEN PARTNER AND PARTNERSHIP

The Internal Revenue Code allows a partner to deal with the partnership as if he were any outside party. Payments made to a partner for the use of capital (interest) or for services (such as a management fee) are called *guaranteed payments*. The guaranteed payment is reported on the Schedule K-1 of the partnership return, which supposedly ensures that the partner will include the payment in his income. The partnership is not required to issue a Form 1099 to that partner for the guaranteed payment.

The section of the Internal Revenue Code dealing with transactions between a partner and the partnership also contains a provision that prohibits the partner from deducting a loss on the sale or exchange of property between the partner and partnership if the partner owns more than 50 percent of the partnership, either directly or indirectly. This same section requires that gains from the sale of certain assets between the partnership and a partner owning more than 80 percent of the partnership shall be ordinary income.

SALE AND EXCHANGE OF PARTNERSHIP INTERESTS

A partnership interest is generally a capital asset, so that a sale of an interest results in either a capital gain or loss. However, if partnership property includes property that, if sold at a gain, would produce ordinary income (for example, inventory), all or a portion of any gain on the sale of the partnership interest may be ordinary income. In addition to inventory, other examples of such property are unrealized rent receivables and depreciation recapture. These assets in the partnership that would produce ordinary income are known as "hot assets."

The tax laws permit properties of like kind to be exchanged without the immediate payment of tax. Any gain from the exchange is postponed until the property is disposed of in a taxable transaction, such as a sale. Generally all real estate is like kind; stock and intangible security interests are not. But what about partnership interests in partnerships owning real estate?

The Internal Revenue Service has ruled that partnership interests do not constitute like-kind property. However, the tax courts have consistently held that such interests are like kind where the partnership assets are like kind. Here the IRS seems to be applying the entity theory discussed earlier, whereas the courts are applying the aggregate theory.

What type of partnership interests may be exchanged? The court cases permitting an exchange have involved the exchange of a general partnership interest for another general partnership interest. The courts do not allow an exchange of a general partnership interest for a limited partnership interest. It is not known whether the courts would allow the exchange of a limited partnership interest for a limited partnership interest.

INADVERTENT TERMINATIONS

An often overlooked rule in the partnership tax laws is the provision that causes a partnership to be deemed terminated if there is a sale or exchange of 50 percent or more of the partnership interests within a twelve-month period. If the partnership is deemed terminated, the property is deemed to be distributed to the partners who recontribute it to the new partnership. In some cases, this can result in some added problems for the partners and partnership, and this situation should be avoided if at all possible.

SYNDICATION AND START-UP EXPENSES

Syndication fees are those connected with the issuing and marketing of interests in the partnerships, such as brokerage fees, registration fees, and underwriter fees. The Internal Revenue Code specifically prohibits the partnership from deducting fees paid to syndicate the partnership. On the other hand, organizational costs can be amortized over a period of not less than five years if the partnership so elects. Otherwise, they are not currently deductible. Organizational costs include legal fees for preparing the documents, fees for establishing an accounting system, and so on.

Partnerships and other businesses generally attempt to deduct certain start-up or preopening expenses such as travel, advertising, salaries, and general overhead. The Internal Revenue Service takes the position that these expenses are not deductible until business has actually started. The IRS contends that in the case of real estate, business does not begin until the rental income is received. In other words, during construction of the property, these expenses will be disallowed and capitalized.

Congress, realizing this problem, recently provided that the partnership may elect to amortize these expenses over a period of not less than five years. If the election is not made and the partners' deducted expenses are later disallowed on audit by the IRS, it is doubtful whether the partnership can make a retroactive election.

ACCOUNTING METHOD AND PERIOD

A partnership may adopt any method of accounting permitted by the Internal Revenue Service—cash method, accrual method, or a hybrid method. The one primary requirement, which applies to all entities, is that the method selected must "clearly reflect income." Once a method is adopted, it must be used consistently and cannot be changed without the consent of the IRS.

Often, a partnership agreement for a partnership involving real estate will specifically state that the cash method is to be used. However, a real estate partnership, especially one that is constructing real estate, should not use the cash method. During the construction period, interest on the construction loan is sometimes paid by merely increasing the loan balance. This does not constitute "payment," which is essential for deducting an expense under the cash method. If the partnership adopted the accrual method, such interest expenses may be deductible because they are accruable and payment is not required. However, the Internal Revenue Service recently issued a ruling that required a partnership constructing an apartment project to use the cash method because that method "more clearly reflected income."

Book Versus Tax Accounting

The income or loss from a partnership will most likely be different for its book or financial purposes and for its tax purposes. For instance, under generally accepted accounting principles, interest during construction is required to be capitalized into the cost of the building, whereas for tax purposes the amount is usually amortized over a ten-year period. Similarly, depreciation for the books is usually based on economic lives (say, thirty years), whereas the lives used for tax purposes may be the statutory lives under ACRS (say, fifteen years).

The balance sheet on page 4 of the partnership federal income tax return, known as Schedule L, can be either a book basis or a tax basis balance sheet. The partnership return also contains a reconciliation of the beginning-of-the-year capital account to the end-of-the-year balance in the capital accounts. Generally, if the balance sheet is a book basis balance sheet, thus reflecting the capital accounts on a book basis, then the reconciliation will reflect those items which are deductible for book but not for tax purposes and those items that are treated as income for book but not for tax purposes. If the balance sheet is a tax basis balance sheet, these book-to-tax differences will not be shown.

Year-Ends

Partnerships, unlike corporations, are not permitted to adopt any fiscal year-end. Generally, a partnership must use a calendar year-end. However, in certain cases, a partnership can end its year in September, October, or November. Also, if all of the partners have the same year-end, the partnership may use that year-end.

CONCLUSION

This discussion was intended to serve only as a general overview of partnership taxation as it relates to the real estate industry. Many issues have not been addressed and not all the rules and exceptions have been discussed. However, this article highlighted some of the opportunities available to businesses operated in the partnership form, as well as several of the pitfalls that partners may encounter.

Syndicating Low- and Moderate-Income Housing

John R. Nolan and Michael G. Smith

The field of equity syndication of housing for low- and moderate-income households has been focused upon heavily subsidized, relatively large new construction or substantial rehabilitation projects. The Internal Revenue Code has offered special tax benefits to the owners of such projects and has further favored these projects by approving syndications where it was clear that the investor's exclusive interest was in tax benefits and did not extend to the other potential rewards of ownership, namely cash flow and appreciation.

Today, long-term intensive subsidies for low-income housing have virtually disappeared. In their absence, housing for low- and moderate-income people will not be constructed or substantially rehabilitated, except in rare cases. Instead, the housing needs of households of limited means will be solved primarily through lower-cost solutions that emphasize the improvement and moderate rehabilitation of existing buildings that are less seriously substandard.

The tax law has recently been changed to offer new incentives to those who invest in the rehabilitation of housing for low- and moderate-income persons. These incentives serve to attract investor capital, but only where that investment will yield competitive returns. The use of syndication as a method of structuring investor participation in real estate ownership has been much heralded as a method of enhancing the feasibility of rehabilitation projects for low- and moderate-income housing.

The purpose of this technical discussion is to explore the most relevant issues involved in the syndication of housing rehabilitation projects. What are the risks and rewards of syndication? How much capital can be attracted through syndication? What price must be paid for the investors' money? How can syndications be structured to enhance low-income occupancy and eventual ownership? What roles can neighborhood development organizations play in syndications? What are the benefits and pitfalls of nonprofit syndications? First, several basic aspects of syndication must be discussed.

The Limited Partnership Vehicle

The risks and rewards of ownership are shared in the syndication of a real estate project. Investors join with a developer or syndicator to provide the equity needed to make a project feasible. The vehicle used to syndicate this equity, or ownership interest, is a partnership. In most cases, the investors

---

* John R. Nolan and Michael G. Smith, *Syndicating Low- and Moderate-Income Housing.* Copyright © 1983 Center for Community Development and Preservation, Tarrytown, New York. Reprinted by permission.

want no involvement in the actual management of the project. They rely on the developer or syndicator to conceive and execute the development concept, obtain construction and long-term debt financing, supervise rehabilitation, and manage the housing and the partnership over time. The investors want to be passive partners with limited responsibility and limited liability. To accomplish this, they purchase limited interest in a partnership that is called a *limited partnership*.

Limited Liability of Investors

In a limited partnership, the partnership agreement is drafted to ensure that the investor's role is a limited one. The agreement provides that limited partners will not be involved in the project other than as investors and that their financial liability is limited to the amount that they have invested. On the other hand, the general partner, who is usually the developer or syndicator, is fully responsible for managing the property and for any and all liabilities of the partnership. The general partner owes a fiduciary obligation to the limited partners. The affairs of the partnership must be managed with the best financial interests of the limited partners in mind.

The Rewards of Investment

There are three principal financial interests in a syndicated project. Partners in a limited partnership share the economic benefits of the tax losses, cash flow, and appreciation. The partnership papers spell out how these economic benefits of ownership are to be divided. The right to receive a project's cash flow and the appreciation of its value on sale are the incidents of ownership that partners must have in order to be classified by the IRS as the beneficial owners of the project. If these rights have been bargained away, the partners may not qualify as owners and may not then be entitled to the tax benefits of ownership. The partnership cannot be structured principally as a conduit for tax advantages. If the IRS finds no possibility of cash flow or appreciation for the investors, it may conclude that the partnership was created solely as a vehicle for tax avoidance and thus deny the investors the deductibility of tax losses and the use of tax credits.

The Risks of Investment

Although an investor enjoys limited liability in a limited partnership, there are several notable risks associated with investing in a syndicated project. The first is alluded to above: if the IRS concludes that the partnership was improperly structured, the investor may be denied the tax benefits that are promised. The second is the risk that the project may not evolve as projected. If it is not developed on schedule and on budget, the tax losses projected, the economic benefit promised, and the underlying feasibility of the project may all be jeopardized. Furthermore, if a project fails in midstream and is foreclosed by the lender, investors will recapture, for income tax purposes, any excess depreciation that they have taken. Since excess depreciation is one of the major tax advantages of many housing rehabilitation projects, this prospect is very much on the mind of potential investors. Because this excess depreciation is taxable on foreclosure as if it were ordinary income to the investor, this risk is onerous. In the event of a threatened foreclosure, the investors may be asked to put up additional cash to avoid recapture—perhaps a more favorable, but still costly, result.

These risks figure heavily in the investment decision. The investor must consider many questions, such as: How capable is the developer? What assurance do I have that the project can be developed within the budget? If problems occur, does the developer have sufficient assets to cover cost overruns, or is the developer likely to ask me to put additional money into the project? What track record does the developer have in managing projects over time? What chances are there that this project will run into financial trouble?

THE DEVELOPER'S DECISION: THE RESPONSIBILITIES, RISKS, AND REWARDS OF SYNDICATION

Syndications are typically put together because the developer needs additional equity to make a project feasible. Alternatively, the developer may have the required equity but be interested in syndicating the project in order to share the risks of the investment or to sell to other investors tax benefits that the developer may not need. Thus, syndication makes the project economically attractive to the developer by providing needed equity, mitigating the developer's risk, or maximizing the tax benefits of the project.

The primary benefit of syndication to the developer is the use of the investors' capital over the life of the project. The developer is equally interested in fees that will be paid out of these funds, and out of the project, for the work of developing and managing the project. In addition, the developer typically retains a percentage share of ownership, including the right to receive some proportion of the cash flow, tax benefits, and appreciation.

The price the developer pays for the benefits of syndication can be substantial. If cash flow and appreciation are projected, a healthy portion will be bargained away to win the investors' participation. The fiduciary duty that the developer owes the investors requires that the project be managed for their financial interest, not exclusively for his. The developer may also be liable to the investors, if he fails to assess and disclose the risks of their investment accurately. The developer must weigh this price against the amount of equity that can be obtained from the investors and the other benefits of syndication.

Setting a Price for the Limited Partners' Investment

How much of an investment an investor will be willing to make is fixed by the risk and reward considerations outlined above. The investor will weigh the amount and timing of the investment against the potential economic rewards and the risk that those rewards may be diminished or lost:

1. When is my money needed? Is my investment needed at the outset or is it to be phased over a period of a few years?

2. What is the net present value of my share of the project's future cash flow, after-tax benefits, and net profit at the time of sale?

3. What is the likelihood that the projected economic benefits will materialize? Does the developer's estimate seem reliable?

4. What risk is there that the project will fail? What is the developer's track record? If the project fails, what penalty will I pay?

Historically, the syndication of housing for low- and moderate-income households has occurred because of the favorable tax treatment accorded such activity. Significant legislation has been found in the Internal Revenue Code, providing owners of low- and moderate-income projects accelerated depreciation deductions and allowing them to write off construction-period taxes and interest payments. Compared to other real estate investments, in which owners are allowed to deduct depreciation only on a straight-line or modestly accelerated basis and to amortize construction-period taxes and interest over a period of several years, low- and moderate-income housing projects looked very attractive to high-bracket taxpayers. Their principal concern was to shelter their income from taxes and the principal attraction of low- and moderate-income housing projects was tax benefit. There was typically little hope of a cash-flow return or of significant appreciation on sale.

As a result of this equation, the value of an investment in such housing was often expressed as a ratio between the amount invested and the tax losses produced—the one predictable benefit of the investment. These ratios were developed for projects in which it was expected that the investment would remain in the project for up to twenty years. Typically, the bulk of the available tax losses would occur during the first few years of the project, when the benefit of accelerated depreciation was most pronounced. Often, the investors were asked to invest their funds during the first five years. During this period, the ratio of tax losses to dollars invested in a substantial rehabilitation project might average 2.5:1. Over the longer holding period, the ratio might average 3:1. If an investor's share of the tax losses were estimated to be $100,000 over the life of the project, then the amount invested would be $33,333.

This type of shorthand equation was helpful in setting a value on a Section 8 Substantial Rehabilitation Project. But note the assumptions that were at work in using this method of appraising the investment:

1. Risk would be minimized because the developer was an experienced Section 8 developer of substantial net worth and because cash flow was guaranteed over the life of the investment by the Section 8 Housing Assistance Payments Contract.

2. The investors had little interest in, or expectation of, cash flow and appreciation.

3. The investment was expected to remain in the project for about twenty years to avoid the recapture of accelerated depreciation as ordinary income.

4. The investment was phased over a period of up to five years to equalize the realization of tax losses during those years with the amount invested.

Even given these assumptions, the pricing of equity investment in Section 8 projects varied according to the developer's track record, the location of project, and the condition in the financial markets. But, as these assumptions are changed, the shorthand formula for establishing the amount of the investment becomes less and less useful. If, for example, the developer is a Neighborhood Development Corporation, if a Section 8 Housing Assistance Payments Contract is not involved, or if all the investor's contribution is needed in the first year, the ratio between tax losses generated and the amount of the investment might have to be increased significantly. Conversely, if there is a shorter projected holding period, a realistic expectation of cash flow or appreciation, or the possibility of tax credits in addition to tax losses, that ratio might decrease.

Today, rehabilitating housing for low- and moderate-income households is a much more dynamic process than it was under Section 8 and its predecessor federal subsidy programs. There is greater diversity among developers, with neighborhood development corporations and smaller private firms becoming involved. There is greater variety in the level of rehabilitation, with projects often keyed to tax code requirements rather than federal minimum property standards. The income levels of the occupants, the anticipated holding period, and the inducements offered investors are much more diverse because of the flexibility found in recent changes in the Internal Revenue Code.

In this setting, the risk/reward equation is harder to describe in general terms. Developers may offer investors realistic expectations of tax losses, tax credits, cash flow and appreciation or any combination thereof. The risks may be mitigated by shorter expected holding periods or increased by a variety of factors. Here, the risks must be assessed carefully in deciding on the feasibility of offering investors an opportunity to participate. As will be explained later, the developer/syndicator has a serious legal responsibility to spell out all of the risks associated with a project when marketing it to investors. Here, too, all of the economic benefits produced by a project over time must be assessed in weighing the financial rewards of the project. If, for example, a project is expected to be converted to condominium ownership after a few years, there may be substantial anticipated appreciation that can be expressed in present value terms. The computation of the present values of the cash flow, appreciation, and tax benefits is beyond the scope of this discussion, but must be done to express the value of a particular project to potential investors. Under current practice, each project will have to be evaluated according to its own risks and rewards as investors weigh the wisdom of participation.

The Syndication Process and the Developer's Responsibilities

The developer/syndicator of a residential rehabilitation project must first bring the project to the point of feasibility. This requires that a building be identified and a development concept defined. Where the developer's objective is to market the units to persons of low and moderate income, the development concept must focus on that fact. Normally, the developer has chosen that objective because the market in the neighborhood where the building is located is geared to such occupancy, so that to plan a middle-income project would be at odds with the reality of the market.

In refining the development concept, the developer has many choices. Should the units be rented or sold? What level of rehabilitation is needed, desired, and affordable? Can the rehabilitated property be sold either to a third party or to the occupants within the foreseeable future? Will that sale generate a profit? If so, how much? Are there any public funds available to subsidize project costs or supplement the rents paid by the occupants? How much long-term financing is available and at what cost? How is the project to be managed, by whom, and at what cost? A concept for the development and management of the project must be designed that seems realistic and profitable to the developer. Once such a concept is decided upon, an option to purchase the building may be negotiated if it is not already owned, and detailed project planning begun.

At this stage, the developer's skill in estimating project costs, projecting revenues, and lining up construction and long-term financing is of paramount importance. Countless projects fail to survive this detailed planning process because sufficient debt and equity financing cannot be obtained at a cost that is compatible with projected revenues and operating costs. When this happens, the developer loses the option money, value of the time expended, and cost of professional fees and other predevelopment expenses, but has not risked substantial amounts of capital. This lesser loss is far preferable to acquiring title and proceeding with the development, only to learn that costs were underestimated, financing is not available, or revenues were overestimated. In such a case, the developer's equity, and that of any investors involved, is risked and lost.

It is here that the developer's trade is practiced and here that he earns his living. In a conventional project, the developer includes fees for this work and a satisfactory profit in computing project costs. In a syndication, the developer typically retains a percentage of investors' contributions, perhaps 15 to 20 percent, in return for this function.

Covering Project Costs

The developer's estimated total project costs must be paid. The sources of funds are limited to the debt the seller takes back, if any, the permanent mortgage assumed or taken out, any public subsidies committed to the project, and the equity contributed by the developer and any outside investors. The question that must be asked at this stage is whether the project's economic benefits are sufficient to attract this level of funding.

The function of real estate syndication in this setting is to attract additional capital by pledging a portion of the project's economic benefits. This can be done to reduce the developer's equity commitment, to contain the amount of debt financing needed, or to cover or increase project costs. The bundle of benefits available is fixed and can be divided in only so many ways. Developers, lenders, and investors all compete for these benefits. The cash flow available to the owners is limited by the rate paid the mortgagee. The lender may want to share in cash flow and possibly appreciation, in addition to earning interest on the mortgage loan. The developer may have an interest in receiving cash flow and appreciation that may have to be compromised to attract investors.

The benefits that are available to be divided among developer, investor, and lender are defined by the operations stage of the project, which can be projected only at the time financing is to be committed. Again, the developer's experience in similar projects is of paramount importance. How reliable is the developer's estimate of gross revenue? What vacancy and collection loss will there be? How realistic is the estimate of operating and maintenance costs? After these costs and losses are subtracted from projected gross revenues, what net income is available for debt service and cash-flow distributions? Can this net income be divided between the investors, developer, and lender to compensate them adequately for their investment and the risk they are asked to assume? If not, are the estimated tax benefits and appreciation in value sufficient to bridge the gap? If so, the project is feasible: if not, it should not proceed.

These considerations often lead developers to offer investors shares in excess of 95 percent of a project's ownership and an equally high percentage of available cash flow and tax benefits. The developer is compensated in a variety of ways that may include the remaining percentage of cash flow and tax benefits, a developer's fee, an acquisition fee, a fee for managing the property, a separate fee for managing the affairs of the syndicate, and a residual interest in any gain on the sale of the property.

Marketing the Syndication

Based on an appropriate division of the various benefits among the providers of financing for the project, the developer can begin the process of looking for limited partners. The developer has, by this time, determined the economic value of the tax benefits, cash flow, and appreciation and what percentage of those benefits to offer investors in order to obtain the amount of investor capital needed. In marketing the syndication, the developer will find out whether his perception of the investors' risks and rewards is correct.

The sale of interests in real estate is governed by federal security laws; technically, the sale of an interest in real estate is the sale of a "security." Federal laws provide a series of protections for the purchasers of securities. They require that those who sell securities be licensed, that certain securities be registered, and that investors receive complete information regarding the risks associated with the security they are purchasing. Careful attention must be paid to these requirements: a developer who sells participations in a limited partnership without complying may be liable to repay an aggrieved investor his entire investment plus interest, simply because of this noncompliance. Most smaller syndications fall within one of several exemptions the law allows from the exceedingly expensive registration process. But the license and disclosure requirements apply regardless of the size or manner of the offering. In addition, state Blue Sky laws impose separate disclosure requirements that must be met.

Because of these requirements, developers regularly retain experienced accountants and attorneys to ensure that all federal and state disclosure and registration requirements are met. A principal concern is that the investors be appraised of all the risks associated with the project. Full disclosure means that the possibility of default and foreclosure, denial of tax benefits, difficulties in getting out of the limited partnership, possible changes in the market, and all other risks be described. The developer is called upon to detail the assumptions on which he based the feasibility of the investment and to outline everything that could possibly go wrong with the project. These disclosures are typically contained in a formal offering memorandum that is given to each prospective investor.

A developer cannot engage in the business of selling "security interests" without a license. A one-time sale of interests does not constitute being in the business, although repetitive sales do. When a broker or underwriter is engaged to market investments in a real estate project, a percentage of the capital raised is paid as an underwriting fee. The fee will vary given the size of the offering, the nature of the commitment the underwriter makes to obtain investors, and other factors. For public offerings registered with the Securities Exchange Commission, fees of up to 15 percent may be charged.

These requirements complicate the business of developing a limited partnership for the purpose of raising equity for a relatively simple rehabilitation project. No matter how small a project is, its syndication must comply with these disclosure and license requirements. Even if the offering is exempt from federal registration, a document known as Form D may have to be filed with the SEC to qualify for the exemption. Developers of small projects may proceed to syndicate in ignorance or disregard of these requirements, but only at great risk. Federal laws and securities regulations offer powerful remedies to investors, should they ever become disenchanted with the project. If developers violate registration regulations, limited partners may be able to force the developer to return their investment equity, if the project does not work out—a significant remedy to investors who bought into a syndication that was not correctly structured.

Completing the Project

Once the developer determines that the project is marketable to investors and that the equity needs of the project are going to be met, he typically proceeds to close on the construction loan and attend to the rehabilitation of the property. The developer must syndicate the project prior to the time that the property is placed in service. Usually, this occurs when construction is finished; that is, when the rehabilitation is substantially completed. If construction-period interest and taxes are to be deducted currently, as is allowed for low-income projects, then syndication must occur before those expenses are paid. Investors who buy into a syndicate can deduct their share of the construction-period taxes and interest paid or accrued beginning in the month that they become limited partners. In the case of a building that is being rehabilitated with tenants in place and on which depreciation under Section 167(k) is to be taken, special rules apply as to when the building and the individual units are placed in service. Upon the completion of rehabilitation, a permanent mortgage is secured and the project is occupied and managed over time. As noted, the developer/general partner often retains management responsibility for both the property and for the affairs of the syndicate and receives a fee for both, in addition to his share of the cash flow and tax benefits. When it is economically feasible to do so, the property may be sold and the gain on the sale distributed as agreed.

TAX CREDITS AND TAX LOSSES FOR HOUSING REHABILITATION

The syndication of housing rehabilitation projects can offer investors a combination of economic benefits. In the right neighborhood, substantial cash flow during operations and appreciation on sale might be anticipated. These benefits are often, but not always, minimal in housing rehabilitation projects in marginal areas. As a result, the developers of such projects, whether private firms or neighborhood development corporations, are intensely interested in the tax benefits and losses that housing rehabilitation is accorded under the Internal Revenue Code (IRC).

The Structure of the Tax Law

The Internal Revenue Code, though an inordinately complicated statute, operates in a straightforward manner. It imposes a tax on income, allows deductions from income before figuring the tax imposed, and provides dollar-for-dollar credits against the tax owed in certain instances. The IRC also provides that in certain cases, where credits against income are taken and where depreciation of real estate is deducted from income, some of these tax benefits will be recaptured if the property is sold or transferred.

In drafting the Internal Revenue Code, Congress has infused it with healthy doses of social and economic policy. Today, in the absence of deep federal subsidy programs, some contend that the most significant federal housing legislation is found in various sections and subsections of the IRC. It allows, for example, a tax credit equal to 25 percent of the cost of rehabilitating a qualified historical structure. Similarly, it allows taxpayers who rehabilitate rental housing for low-income occupancy to depreciate, or deduct from their incomes before figuring taxes, one-fifth of the rehabilitation expenditures each year for five years. Here, Congress offers valuable tax incentives for certain real estate activities—historic preservation and the provision of low-income rental housing—that it wants to encourage. These tax credits and a variety of depreciation deductions, combined with recapture rules, constitute the basic elements of a federal housing program contained in the Internal Revenue Code.

The Tax Treatment of Partnerships

A partnership does not pay federal income taxes. At the end of its tax year, the partnership completes a tax return, but the effect of that return is to allocate to each partner his share of any taxable income or loss and any gain or loss on property sold. Thus, the partner's share of the partnership's income, gains, or losses are combined with that partner's other income, gains, and losses and reported separately on his individual tax return, or corporate tax return, if the partner is a corporation.

The IRC generally recognizes the method of sharing income, gains, losses, deductions, and credits that is spelled out in the partnership agreement. If a limited partnership is established to rehabilitate a historic building and a particular partner is entitled to a 20 percent share of the partnership's tax credits, one-fifth of the historic tax credit generated would pass through to that partner's individual tax return. Deductions for the depreciation of real estate are handled similarly. The partnership tax return accounts for all partnership income and then deducts allowable expenses, including depreciation, to arrive at the partnership's taxable income or tax loss. Again, the partner's share of taxable income or loss is passed through and reflected on that partner's personal tax return.

There is a limit to the amount of losses that a partner is allowed to make use of. The IRC requires that partners deduct losses only up to the amount of their basis in the partnership. *Basis* is generally defined as the amount a partner has invested in the partnership, or the extent of that partner's liability, minus any losses previously taken. This basis requirement would normally prevent limited partners in a syndicate from taking advantage of tax losses in excess of the amount invested because their liability is specifically limited to the amount they have invested. However, regulations of the Internal Revenue Service provide that the basis of a limited partner includes his share of the partnership's liability on a nonrecourse loan. A *nonrecourse loan* is one in which no individual partner is personally liable. In the case of a mortgage on real estate, the lender must agree not to require the partnership or any individual partner to assume personal liability for payments on the mortgage. The Internal Revenue Service reasons that if no one partner is personally liable on the mortgage, then that liability may be shared proportionately by all the partners, including the limited partners, for the purpose of establishing their basis in the partnership.

This interpretation of the effect of a nonrecourse loan on the basis of the limited partners makes the syndication of housing projects possible in many instances. Without this excess basis, the limited partners would not be able to take advantage of tax losses beyond the amount of their cash investment. This restriction would prevent them from realizing any return on that investment due to the dollar value to them of the partnership's tax loss. Without this tax loss return on investment, they would have to look solely to their share of cash flow and long-term appreciation. In most housing rehabilitation projects, these would be insufficient to induce investors to invest the equity needed by the developer to make the project feasible.

TAX TREATMENT OF HOUSING REHABILITATION

With this general understanding of the way that real estate syndication and the Internal Revenue Code work, we can examine in more detail the tax treatment of housing rehabilitation projects. The owners, including the limited partners in a syndication, are interested in several key features of the tax code with respect to their investments. Principal among these features are their eligibility for tax credits, their ability to depreciate, or deduct, a relatively large proportion of their investment in the early years of ownership, and their ability to deduct other costs during the project development stage. Investors are also interested in tax code restrictions or penalties assessed on the resale of the project. These four features of the Internal Revenue Code are explained in general terms below and then used to analyze the tax aspects of five separate types of housing rehabilitation.

The following material is based on the Internal Revenue Code as amended through 1984. The numerical examples used are simplified to illustrate the gross effect of the tax treatment of housing rehabilitation. The actual tax treatment may differ depending on the taxpayer's status, the application of minimum tax, tax preference and other tax provisions, and the provisions of state tax law.

Tax Credit Eligibility

Under Section 38 of the Internal Revenue Code, taxpayers are allowed a credit against the federal income tax they owe at the end of the year. The credit is figured as a specified percentage of eligible investments made by the taxpayer during the year. Here again, the tax code is working to provide an incentive to encourage taxpayers to invest in property in ways that Congress deems advantageous. For example, the Code has provided credits figured as a specified percentage of amounts expended by taxpayers for energy conservation, purchasing fuel from nonconventional sources, and for work incentive programs. In 1981, Congress added a provision to the Code that allows taxpayers to take a credit equal to 25 percent of qualified expenditures for the rehabilitation of certain historic structures, whether used for residential or commercial properties, and a credit of 15 to 20 percent for qualified expenditures for the rehabilitation of older commercial properties.

Tax credits are highly beneficial to taxpayers. They amount to a dollar-for-dollar reduction of the tax owed to the federal government. For example, a 25 percent credit on $50,000 spent to rehabilitate a historic structure would reduce an individual's taxes by $12,500. To put this in perspective, a married couple with a taxable income of $60,000 in 1982, filing a joint return, would normally have to pay $17,705 in federal income taxes. Had that couple made this $50,000 investment in rehabilitating a historic structure, their tax would be reduced to $2,205. Normally, a tax of approximately $2,200 would be paid by a married couple with an income of about $17,500. The effect of the tax credit is to reduce the couple's income for tax purposes from $60,000 to $17,000!

Acceleration of Depreciation Deductions

Traditionally, the tax code has allowed taxpayers to deduct from their taxable incomes the amount by which certain tangible property depreciates in the tax year. Depreciation is described as the exhaustion, wear and tear, or obsolescence of property. Actual depreciation need not be shown; instead, allowances are created by the Internal Revenue Service that allow a certain amount of depreciation to be taken each year over the established life of the class of property in question. Only business property—that is, property used in the taxpayer's trade or business or for the production of income—is allowed a depreciation allowance.

Congress encourages investments in certain types of business property by allowing those investments to be depreciated more rapidly than others. Prior to 1981, an elaborate set of rules prevailed that established the useful lives of various classes of business property and allowed taxpayers one or more options for depreciating their property over its lifetime. A variety of accelerated depreciation allowances were provided that allowed taxpayers to speed up the rate at which depreciation was taken on certain types of property. These allowances varied depending on the nature of the property and whether it was new or used.

Under the amendments to the Code contained in the Economic Recovery Tax Act (ERTA) of 1981, the rules governing depreciation were greatly simplified. All real estate was given a fifteen-year useful life, although longer periods can be elected. The Code allows taxpayers to depreciate their investments in real estate under a method that uses a 175 percent declining balance schedule in the early years, and crosses over to straight-line depreciation in later years. Alternatively, straight-line depreciation can be taken over the fifteen-year, or longer, period. This is generally known as the Accelerated Cost Recovery System (ACRS). This system was amended again in 1984 to lengthen the depreciation period from fifteen to eighteen years. The fifteen-year period was retained for low-income housing developments, giving them a relative advantage over other real estate investments, in respect to depreciation.

In this instance, straight-line depreciation means that one-fifteenth of the investment in depreciable property can be taken as a deduction each year for fifteen years. The 175 percent declining balance allows the taxpayer to deduct roughly 175 percent of the straight-line amount in the first year; the amount declines proportionately thereafter. If the taxpayer invested $150,000 in depreciable property, he would be allowed a deduction of $10,000 in the first year and each year thereafter under the straight-line method. Under the 175 percent method the deduction allowance would be $17,500 in the first year.

The actual amounts allowed are computed using a table prepared by the Internal Revenue Service that approximates the 175 percent declining balance method in the first six years and then switches to a modified straight-line method. For real estate placed in service in the first month of the tax year, then, the depreciation allowance on the $150,000 investment discussed above would be as follows:

Year	Depreciation	Percentage Used
1	$18,000	12
2	15,000	10
3	13,500	9
4	12,000	8
5	10,500	7
6	9,000	6
7	9,000	6
8	9,000	6
9	9,000	6
10	7,500	5
11	7,500	5
12	7,500	5
13	7,500	5
14	7,500	5
15	7,500	5
	$150,000	100%

Using this new ACRS schedule, over 30 percent of the depreciable base is deducted during the first three years. During the first three years, an average of 10 percent depreciation is taken each year using this method. If the fifteen-year straight-line method were used, the average annual depreciation rate would be 6⅔ percent. This has the effect of allowing substantially larger incentives during the first three to five years after the investment is made in the depreciable property.

The effect that the depreciation deduction has on a taxpayer's tax bill is notable, but substantially less than the effect of a tax credit. Depreciation is deducted, as is any business expense, from gross income to figure taxable income. For an individual taxpayer in the 40 percent tax bracket, the effect of such a deduction is to reduce taxes by forty cents for each dollar deducted. For such an individual, the dollar value of depreciation is equal to forty cents compared to the dollar value of the tax credit. If our married tax-paying couple had invested the same $50,000 to become a one-third owner of the $150,000 depreciable asset described in the example above, they would have been able to deduct their share, or one-third of the $18,000 depreciation allowance provided for in the first year. Their one-third ($6,000) would reduce their $60,000 taxable income to $54,000; their tax would be reduced from $17,705 to $15,065 for a net tax savings of $2,640. For that same $50,000 investment in the previous example, they obtained a tax credit worth $12,500 in the first year, a benefit nearly $10,000 greater than the first-year value of the 175 percent depreciation allowance.

The IRS is currently preparing a new, eighteen-year ACRS table that will apply to the depreciation of investments in real estate projects that are not qualified low-income housing developments. Most qualified low-income housing projects, however, will not elect to use the IRS table shown above. This is because, under the 1981 law, such projects were allowed to elect a 200 percent declining balance method of computing depreciation, described in example C. The net result of the 1981 and 1984 changes is to give low-income housing projects two distinct advantages over other real estate developments: first, they carry a fifteen- rather than an eighteen-year depreciation period; second, they can be depreciated at a 200 percent declining balance rate, rather than 175 percent.

Recapture of Credits and Excess Depreciation

Looking at the short-term economics of these tax benefits, it is easy to see why an owner would be interested in selling investment tax credit property or depreciable real estate after a few years. The entire tax credit may be realized in the first year, and nearly 30 percent of the depreciation allowed over a fifteen-year period will have been taken in the first three years. Predictably, however, the Code provides a penalty in the event of early disposition of such property. Under Section 47(a)(5) of the Code, added by ERTA in 1981, the tax on an investment tax credit property sold within five years of being placed in service is increased by a percentage of the credit taken. That percentage declines in 20 percent increments each year from 100 percent, if the property is sold in the first year, to 80 percent in the second year, to 20 percent if sold during the fifth year. This means that if the taxpayer who obtained the $17,500 credit discussed in our earlier illustration were to take that credit and then sell the property in the second year, 80 percent of the $17,500 ($14,000) would be added to the tax due to the IRS on the sale of the property. Since the tax credit provided a dollar-for-dollar decrease in taxes due, the recapture of that credit results in a proportionate increase in the dollar value of taxes owed.

The Code also provides for the recapture of depreciation deductions taken in respect to depreciable property sold. It stipulates that if depreciation is taken on a straight-line basis, no recapture will occur. In other words, there is no reason to assess a penalty on the early sale of depreciable property if no accelerated depreciation is taken. If a taxpayer elects to use the 175 percent declining balance method of depreciation for a residential project, however, recapture will result in the case of an early sale. Any gain on the sale of such a project is treated as ordinary income to the extent that prior depreciation taken exceeds the amount that would have been taken had the straight-line depreciation method been used. Gain on the sale of real estate is figured by subtracting from the net sales price the taxpayer's cost of purchasing and improving the property, minus any depreciation taken. This gain is normally taxed at the capital gains tax rates, which is substantially lower than the tax levied on the ordinary income of high-bracket taxpayers. By recapturing excess depreciation as ordinary income, the Code effectively treats an early disposition as though straight-line depreciation had been taken.

Commercial property is treated differently in respect to recapture. The Code assesses a substantial penalty for the early sale of commercial, as opposed to residential, property on which accelerated depreciation was taken. In this case, all of the amounts depreciated are recaptured as ordinary income, not just the amount in excess of straight-line.

Treatment of Construction-Period Taxes and Interest

Prior to the enactment of the Tax Reform Act of 1976, the ability to deduct that year all of the real estate taxes and interest on construction loans incurred prior to the completion of a real estate project was one of its prime tax benefits. In 1976, the Code was amended to require that these interest and tax payments be considered project costs and amortized, or deducted, over a ten-year period. This decreased the attractiveness of the tax benefits and, hence, the syndication of real estate. When this provision was added, it was not to apply to low-income housing projects until 1982, at which time it was to phase in gradually. ERTA repealed this phase-in provision and exempted low-income housing from the ten-year amortization requirement. This means that low-income housing projects are the only type of real estate venture afforded the benefit of deducting construction-period taxes and interest in the years in which they occur.

Summary of Pertinent Tax Code Features

Tax Credits. Investors are allowed a tax credit equal to a specified percentage of their investment in the rehabilitation of certified historic structures and older commercial properties. This credit is used to reduce the tax owed; as such, it shelters a proportionately large amount of the investor's income from tax.

Accelerated Depreciation. The depreciable base of real estate investments can be written off, or deducted, from the owner's gross income at rates that exceed straight-line depreciation. This acceleration of depreciation allows taxpayers to deduct disproportionately large amounts of the value of business property in the first few years of ownership. Depreciation deductions reduce the income on which taxes are paid, rather than the tax itself.

Recapture. The tax code assesses a penalty in certain cases when business property is disposed of soon after investment tax credit or accelerated depreciation has been taken in respect to such property.

Construction-Period Taxes and Interest. These construction costs cannot be deducted in the year in which they occur. Instead, they must be amortized during a ten-year period. The only exception to this rule is low-income housing.

TAX ASPECTS OF FIVE TYPES OF HOUSING REHABILITATION

The tax benefits and features of investments in housing rehabilitation are principally defined by these four tax code features. They apply variously to housing rehabilitation projects, depending on the type of building rehabilitated and its use and occupancy. Based on these tax features and building characteristics, rehabilitation projects can be divided logically into five separate categories.

Historic Properties

Buildings that are listed in the National Register or that are of historic significance to a recognized historic district are eligible for the 25 percent tax credit described above. The credit is figured as a percentage of the capital costs of rehabilitation, not including the costs of acquiring the building or enlarging the structure. All of the rehabilitation must be certified by the Secretary of the Interior as being consistent with the building's historic character. The cost of rehabilitation carried out during a 24-month period must exceed $5,000 or the taxpayer's adjusted basis in the building. *Adjusted basis* is defined as the initial cost of the building (not including the land) plus the cost of any improvements made prior to rehabilitation, minus any depreciation taken. Thus, if the taxpayer were to invest $150,000 in qualified rehabilitation expenditures in a qualified historic structure, the original cost of the building plus the cost of any capital improvements completed prior to rehabilitation, minus any depreciation taken, would have to be less than that $150,000.

If a taxpayer elects to take advantage of the investment tax credit, he must elect to take depreciation on a straight-line basis. Further, half of the credit taken must be subtracted from the taxpayer's basis before the straight-line depreciation schedule is established. The combined tax benefits of historic property rehabilitation include the 25 percent credit and unaccelerated, or straight-line, depreciation.

Example A. Assume that a taxpayer purchases a certified historic property for $100,000 and that of this amount the cost attributable to the land is $30,000. During the first two years, the owner makes $25,000 worth of capital improvements in the building and takes $13,000 worth of depreciation deductions on his tax return. In the third and fourth year, the taxpayer invests $150,000 in rehabilitating the property according to the Secretary's standards. The tax treatment in this situation would be as follows:

Total Costs	$100,000
Less Land Cost	(30,000)
Cost of Building	70,000
Plus Capital Improvements Made	25,000
Less Depreciation Taken	(13,000)
Adjusted Basis	82,000
Rehabilitation Expenditures	150,000
Post-Rehabilitation Basis	$232,000

The taxpayer would be allowed to take the tax credit because the building is eligible, the rehabilitation is certified, and the amount of the rehabilitation ($150,000) exceeds the taxpayer's adjusted basis ($82,000).

In the first year, the taxpayer could take a tax credit of 25 percent of the $150,000 rehabilitation expenses ($37,500) which reduces his tax bill by that amount. During the first year after rehabilitation and every year for 15 years thereafter, the taxpayer can deduct in depreciation $14,217 from his income before paying taxes. If the taxpayer were in the 40 percent tax bracket, that deduction would be worth approximately $5,700. The total first year dollar value of these tax benefits is $43,200. Thereafter, the dollar value of the depreciation is $5,700. The total dollar value of these benefits over the first five years would be as follows:

Year	Dollar Value
1	$43,200
2	5,700
3	5,700
4	5,700
5	5,700
Five-Year Total	$66,000

Low-Income Properties (Section 167(k))

Special tax treatment is afforded to investors in the rehabilitation of low-income housing, under two separate provisions of the Internal Revenue Code. The first of these is Section 167(k), which allows extremely rapid depreciation of the costs of rehabilitating housing held for occupancy for low- or moderate-income households. At least $3,000 per unit must be invested in rehabilitation. Up to $20,000 of rehabilitation costs per dwelling unit may be written off over a five-year period and up to $40,000 per unit may be depreciated over the five years if the rehabilitation is done under an approved program and held for sale to the tenants without profit to the taxpayer.

Only the costs of rehabilitation, not the cost of acquiring the building, are depreciable under Section 167(k). The cost of acquisition can be depreciated using the ACRS method. Low and moderate income is defined as 80 percent of area median income. The income of each household must be certified as being within the income limit; if an ineligible tenant occupies a dwelling unit, rapid depreciation on that unit may not be taken. The benefit of Section 167(k) is limited to housing; it does not cover hotels, motels, inns, or buildings used on a transient basis.

If the property is also a historic structure, the taxpayer can choose to elect the 25 percent tax credit and straight-line depreciation option or this five-year rapid write-off method; the two may not be used together.

Example B. Assume that a taxpayer purchases a ten-unit rental building for $100,000 and that of this amount, $30,000 can be attributed to land. He then invests $150,000 in rehabilitating the property in conformance with the local building code. The tax treatment would be as follows:

Cost of Property	$100,000
Less Land Costs	(30,000)
Cost of Building	70,000
Cost of Rehabilitation	150,000

The annual amount of depreciation allowed on rehabilitation costs equals $30,000 ($150,000 ÷ 5).

The annual amount of depreciation allowed on the $70,000 cost of the building (using the 200 percent declining balance method) would be as follows:

Year	Depreciation
1	$9,100
2	8,400
3	7,000
4	6,300
5	5,600
6–9	4,100
10–15	2,900

To a 40 percent bracket taxpayer, the worth of this depreciation allowance each year during the first five years would be as follows:

Year	Rapid Depreciation	175% Depreciation	Dollar Value
1	$30,000	$9,100 = $39,100 × .40 =	$15,640
2	30,000	8,400 = 38,400 × .40 =	15,360
3	30,000	7,000 = 37,000 × .40 =	14,800
4	30,000	6,300 = 36,300 × .40 =	14,520
5	30,000	5,600 = 35,600 × .40 =	14,240
	Five-Year Total Dollar Value		$74,560

Low-Income Properties (Section 168(b)(2))

The second tax code provision that affords special treatment of housing rehabilitated for low-income occupancy is found in Section 168(b)(2). Section 168 contains the Accelerated Cost Recovery System. Under the ACRS system, most structures are given an eighteen-year life and taxpayers are allowed to use a 175 percent declining balance method of depreciating the value of such structures. The IRS has published a table that is used to compute the annual depreciation allowance on real estate, using the 175 percent method. These IRS percentages use the 175 percent declining balance method in the first five years and then switch to a modified straight-line system during the last ten years. As noted, the IRS is preparing a new table for non–low-income projects, based on the new eighteen-year depreciation period.

Cost of Property	$100,000
Less Land Costs	(30,000)
Cost of Building	70,000
Plus Cost of Rehabilitation	150,000
Depreciable Base	$220,000

Annual amount of depreciation allowed, using the 200 percent declining balance method shown in Table B:

Year 1	$28,600
Year 2	26,400
Year 3	22,000
Year 4	19,800
Year 5	17,600
Five-Year Total	$114,400
Year 6	15,400
Year 7	13,200
Years 8–10	11,000
Years 11–15	8,800

Section 168(b)(2) allows additional accelerated depreciation to be taken in the case of low-income housing. Here, the 200 percent declining balance method is used. The annual percentages allowed are shown in Table B. Again, a switch to a modified straight-line method occurs in the eighth year.

Under Section 168(b)(2), low-income housing is defined as government-assisted housing for low-income households. Housing that is insured under the federal government's Section 221(d)(3) or 236 programs or Title V of the Housing Act of 1949 is eligible for the 200 percent declining balance treatment. Housing that is financed or assisted by direct loan or tax abatement under state or local programs, in which the owner is limited as to the rate of return on his investment as well as to rentals charged to the tenants, is also eligible. Eligibility is further extended to housing in which the dwelling units are held for occupancy by households eligible to receive subsidies under Section 8 or similar levels of subsidy under state or local programs.

The investment tax credit for historic structures and Section 167(k) rapid depreciation for low-income housing limits favorable tax treatment to the amounts invested for rehabilitating a qualified structure. Section 168(b)(2) applies to all of the taxpayer's depreciable base, including the cost of building acquisition. Under this provision, there are no minimum or maximum amounts that must be invested, as long as the relevant federal, state, or local program requirements are met.

Example C. Assume, for example, that a taxpayer purchases a building for $100,000, of which $30,000 is attributable to the cost of the land. The taxpayer then invests $150,000 in rehabilitating the property in conformance with the local building code. The tax treatment would be as follows:

To a 40 percent bracket taxpayer, the worth of this depreciation allowance each year during the first five years would be as follows:

Year	200% Depreciation			Dollar Value
1	$28,600	×	.40	$11,440
2	26,400	×	.40	10,560
3	22,000	×	.40	8,800
4	19,800	×	.40	7,920
5	17,600	×	.40	7,040
	Five-Year Total Dollar Value			$45,760

Conventional Residential Properties

The tax advantage of rehabilitating housing that does not qualify as historic or low-income property is principally the 175 percent accelerated depreciation afforded to real estate under the Section 168 ACRS system. The depreciable base of such property includes the cost of acquisition of the building as well as capital costs of rehabilitation. For purposes of the following example, 175 percent accelerated depreciation over 18 years has been approximated in anticipation of the IRS table.

Example D. Assume that a taxpayer purchased a building for $100,000, of which $30,000 is attributable to the cost of the land. The taxpayer then invests $150,000 in rehabilitating the property in conformance with the local building code. The tax treatment would be as follows:

Cost of Property	$100,000
Less Land Cost	(30,000)
Cost of Building	70,000
Plus Cost of Rehabilitation	150,000
Depreciable Base	$220,000

Annual amount of depreciation allowed using 175 percent declining balance method over 18 years:

Year	Depreciation
1	$21,400
2	20,400
3	17,300
4	15,600
5	14,100
Five-Year Total	$88,800

To a 40 percent bracket taxpayer, the worth of this depreciation allowance each year during the first five years would be as follows:

Year	175% Depreciation			Dollar Value
1	21,400	×	.40	$8,560
2	20,400	×	.40	8,160
3	17,300	×	.40	6,920
4	15,600	×	.40	6,240
5	14,100	×	.40	5,640
	Five-Year Total Dollar Value			$35,520

Mixed Commercial/Residential Property

An older building that contains some space appropriate for commercial use and some for residential may qualify for the separate tax benefits afforded both these types of property. The tax code provides a tax credit of 15 percent of qualified rehabilitation expenses for a thirty-year-old building; the credit is 20 percent for a building forty years old or older. On that portion of the building, depreciation must be taken on a straight-line basis. On the residential portion, depreciation can be figured according to the category of housing involved: 167(k) low income; or 168(b)(2) low-income or conventional residential.

Example E. Assume that a taxpayer purchased a two-story, forty-year-old building for $100,000, of which $30,000 is attributable to the cost of the land. Of the remaining $70,000, $40,000 represents ground-floor retail space and the remaining $30,000 second-story apartments that will be occupied by low-income tenants. The taxpayer invests $150,000 in rehabilitating the property—$100,000 for the commercial space and $50,000 for the residential portion—and uses the residential portion of the building as a qualified low-income project. The tax treatment would be as follows:

COMMERCIAL PORTION

Acquisition Cost of Building	$40,000
Qualified Rehabilitation Expenses	100,000
Tax Credit Percentage	20%
Tax Credit Amount	20,000
Total Depreciable Base	140,000
Less ½ Tax Credit Amount	10,000
Remaining Depreciable Base	130,000
Annual Straight-line Depreciation (÷ 18)	$7,222

RESIDENTIAL PORTION

Acquisition Cost of Building	$30,000
Rehabilitation Costs	50,000
167(k) Depreciation Amount	50,000
Annual 167(k) Depreciation (÷ 5)	10,000
Remaining Depreciable Base	30,000
Depreciation Rate	200%

TABLE B AMOUNTS (200%)

Year	
1	$3,900
2	3,600
3	3,000
4	2,700
5	2,400

Year-by-year depreciation allowance:

Year	Commercial		167(k)		200%		Total
1	$7,222	+	$10,000	+	$3,900	=	$21,122
2	7,222	+	10,000	+	3,600	=	20,822
3	7,222	+	10,000	+	3,000	=	20,222
4	7,222	+	10,000	+	2,700	=	19,922
5	7,222	+	10,000	+	2,400	=	19,622
	Five-Year Total						$101,710

Dollar value of tax benefits to 40-percent-bracket taxpayer:

Year	Tax Credit	Depreciation	Total Dollar Value
1	$20,000	(21,122 × .40 = $8,500)	$28,500
2	—	(20,822 × .40 = 8,300)	8,300
3	—	(20,222 × .40 = 8,100)	8,100
4	—	(19,922 × .40 = 8,000)	8,000
5	—	(19,622 × .40 = 7,800)	7,800
	Five-Year Total Value		$60,700

REAL ESTATE SYNDICATION FOR NONPROFIT SPONSORS

The previous section focused on the structure of real estate syndications and on the particular provisions of the tax code that make certain types of properties particularly attractive to investors. For nonprofit sponsors, however, syndicating a property can offer both benefits and problems. The benefits may include the availability of a new source of capital, the ability to take advantage of tax subsidies that normally are of no use to a nonprofit sponsor, and the availability of sophisticated and experienced assistance with financing, tax structuring, meeting the requirements of the securities laws, and managing the property. Problems may stem from a conflict between the investors' financial goals and the nonprofit sponsor's socially motivated priorities.

ROLES OF THE NONPROFIT SPONSOR
Community Force

Some nonprofit sponsors may not have prior experience or specific credentials with respect to developing and operating housing, but may, nevertheless, represent a powerful political and social force in their neighborhood or community. An influential nonprofit sponsor can be very valuable to a developer/syndicator team that is attempting to construct or acquire low- or moderate-income housing within the nonprofit sponsor's community. The nonprofit sponsor can assist in satisfying community concerns and dispelling any community opposition to the project. The nonprofit sponsor's political influence may facilitate the process of obtaining the local government permit and their approval. Similarly, the continued involvement of the sponsor in project operations may provide a valuable line of communication between project owners and residents.

Whereas a nonprofit community organization may not be able to fit into the ownership structure of the project and the partnership, the sponsor may nevertheless influence project operating decisions in an advisory capacity or through a more formal contractual arrangement. In return for the benefits provided to the project, and, consequently, to its owners and investors, concessions might be made to the nonprofit sponsor with respect to property management issues, tenant selection and eviction policies, social programming for project residents, and commitments to preserve the units as low- and moderate-income housing.

Co-General Partner

Perhaps the most sensible role for a nonprofit sponsor is the position of co-general partner with the syndicator or some other investor representative. Through the use of co-general partners, the diverse interests of the nonprofit sponsor and the investors can be acknowledged expressly and an appropriate framework can be structured for resolving the inherent conflicts between the investors' economic goals and the nonprofit sponsor's social responsibilities.

A broad spectrum of arrangements is possible. A common situation provides for split responsibilities. The nonprofit general partner is free to pursue honestly the goals and objectives of nonprofit housing, while the syndicator exclusively represents the interests of the investors. Each co-partner operates in this state of dynamic tension pursuant to the fairly detailed mandate of the partnership agreement. The agreement delineates the separate responsibilities, defines the outer limits of the authority of the respective general partners, and provides a mechanism for resolving disputes and deadlocks that are detrimental to the project's well-being.

There is a clear benefit to this structure from the perspective of the nonprofit sponsor. Simply stated, the nonprofit sponsor is not faced with the dilemma and potentially troublesome legal risks of wearing two hats. By agreement between the co-general partners, the syndicator co-general partner can be delegated the responsibility and the concomitant liabilities for raising the equity capital, adequately disclosing the respective roles of the co-general partners, and satisfying the securities law requirements of the real estate offering.

The syndicator general partner can also be assigned the responsibility for ongoing partnership management issues, including such duties as communicating with investors, monitoring and processing transfers of partnership interests, preparing tax returns and assisting in investor tax audits, main-

taining investor records, and generally overseeing the status of the syndicated properties. The nonprofit general partner, on the other hand, should
be able to concentrate on day-to-day property management concerns, tenants' issues, neighborhood and community problems, and the general well-
being of the project. The nonprofit sponsor may often benefit, however,
from the assistance of the syndicator general partner in project management, particularly if the nonprofit sponsor is inexperienced or the syndicator
has special expertise.

Even when project and partnership affairs are proceeding smoothly, however, there is potential for conflict between the co-general partners. A common area of dispute concerns priorities for cash expenditures, with the
nonprofit partner typically seeing a need to increase maintenance, security,
or project reserves and the syndicator being interested in distributions to
investors or reimbursement for expenses in handling investor inquiries and
communications. These conflicts are inherent in the relationship and should
be anticipated through provisions in the partnership agreement.

Moreover, when significant issues arise, even greater involvement, inter-
action, and intervention should be expected from each general partner. The
partnership agreement can define the types of issues that are so significant
as to warrant the intervention of one general partner into the delegated
realm of the other. For example, inordinate vacancy or collection loss problems might be expected to trigger a response from the syndicator general
partner. On the other hand, the threat of an action for an accounting by a
limited partner against the general partners would probably stimulate the
involvement of the nonprofit general partner in partnership management
issues.

Sole General Partner

There are obvious benefits for a nonprofit sponsor in being the sole general partner. Clearly, the principal benefit is control. As the sole general
partner, the nonprofit sponsor has considerable latitude in deciding most
major issues relating to project design, construction, operation, and disposition. While limited partnership agreements bestow upon the limited partners
the authority to vote upon certain critical partnership issues, partnership
affairs usually must have deteriorated seriously in order to stimulate the
limited partners into asserting an active role in partnership business.

The clear drawback for a nonprofit sponsor serving as a sole general
partner, even if qualified to do so, relates to the inherent conflict between
nonprofit housing goals and the interests of the investors. If there is no co-
general partner having the responsibility and duty of representing the investors' interest, that obligation falls on the nonprofit sponsor. In an effort to
discharge its legal duties to the investors, the nonprofit sponsor may be
faced with the dilemma of compromising unduly its own housing goals and
jeopardizing its tax-exempt status, if any.

On the other hand, if the nonprofit sponsor is excessive in disregarding
the investors' interests, legal disputes can ensue. Even in the absence of

protections in the partnership agreement, the limited partners nevertheless have statutory rights to: have full access to all partnership books and records; demand a formal legal accounting of partnership affairs; and petition a court for dissolution. In the end, it may simply be more workable for the nonprofit sponsor to interact with a co-general partner representing the investors than to face the conflict of interest every time the nonprofit sponsor's goals compromise the investors' interests.

Master Lessee

Some nonprofit sponsors achieve the control they desire over project operations simply by leasing the low- or moderate-income housing project from the partnership. The nonprofit sponsor then operates the property and subleases the rental units to the residents.

The master lease arrangement provides a fairly clean separation of roles and responsibilities between the investor-limited partnership and the nonprofit sponsor. The nonprofit sponsor achieves the desired authority to operate the property in accordance with its own policies—subject, however, to its specific obligations to the lessor-partnership pursuant to the lease.

Under the lease, the rental schedule between the partnership and the nonprofit sponsor is established at the outset, so that subsequent disputes are less likely to arise with respect to future rent increases and cash flow to the investors. The operating risk for the nonprofit sponsor, however, is that increased operating expenses or unanticipated vacancies and collection losses will undermine the nonprofit sponsor's ability to meet its rental obligations, leading, possibly, to a lease default and termination of the nonprofit sponsor's leasehold interest.

If the nonprofit sponsor should fail to meet its leasehold obligations, the consequences could be more summary and drastic than when the nonprofit sponsor functions as a co-general partner. As a co-general partner, at least, the nonprofit and syndicator co-general partners share the problems and responsibilities of dealing with a troubled project.

Another issue arising out of the master lease arrangement involves the ultimate sale of the project by the partnership after exhaustion of the tax shelter. The nonprofit sponsor's leasehold interest alone does not provide any protection beyond the lease itself. The sale decision resides with the partnership; the nonprofit sponsor has no legal authority to influence that decision.

Clearly, there are ways to address the disposition problem, but they must be anticipated and negotiated at the initiation of the leasehold term, not after the fact. One approach is for the nonprofit sponsor to have a long-term lease or a lease with renewal options, so that the leasehold duration stretches beyond the tax-shelter period (fifteen or so years). The partnership's sale of the property at the end of its holding period is then subject to the nonprofit sponsor's leasehold interest. Of course, the issue of ultimate disposition of the property will arise eventually as the master lease approaches its termination date.

Another possible technique for dealing with the disposition issue involves giving the nonprofit sponsor an option or right of first refusal to acquire the property upon sale by the partnership. The price and terms of such a right have to be realistic from the nonprofit sponsor's perspective, if this technique is to preserve its control over the property.

PRESERVING AFFORDABILITY

If a nonprofit or local government entity decides to enter into a partnership with private investors to acquire and syndicate housing for low- and moderate-income people, it must address, in structuring the partnership, the issue of long-term affordability. Investors look to sale or refinancing to provide gain from appreciation to offset tax liabilities. Investors may also anticipate realizing significant gain by converting a project to uses other than low- or moderate-income housing. A refinancing or sale at a substantially appreciated price will demand significantly higher rents to carry the additional burden of debt. Increased rents may force immediate or eventual displacement of existing low- or moderate-income housing.

Long-term affordability can best be assured if the nonprofit sponsor structures the partnership to ensure eventual return of the property to itself or to a similar entity. The first critical time period is likely to be approximately fifteen years from acquisition of the property: the tax-shelter "burnout" point.

There are two approaches to ensuring long-term nonprofit control. One is for the nonprofit sponsor to have a significant direct economic interest in the property, or a partnership interest. If the nonprofit agent eventually ends up with a significant ownership interest in the project, or in the partnership, the ultimate value of the project at the end of the tax-shelter period is often less significant. Even if the value appreciates substantially as real estate, unfettered by rent or use restrictions, the substantial economic interest of the nonprofit sponsor in the property or partnership means that less is required to buy out the remaining interests of the investors. Essentially, therefore, the substantially increased interest of the nonprofit sponsor often effectively squeezes out much of the equity or appreciation gain from which the investors would otherwise benefit.

The second approach is to impose rent and use restrictions on future sales. These restrictions can be used as an alternative or in combination. The following restrictions deserve consideration: ground lease; accrued indebtedness; option on the property; sinking fund; long-term restrictions; equity participation; and charitable contributions.

Ground Lease

Under this mechanism, the nonprofit or other entity retains the ownership of the land. If an existing building or complex is being syndicated, the land and the buildings must be legally separated. The nonprofit sponsor sells the building to the partnership but retains ownership of the land. The partnership then enters into a ground lease with the nonprofit sponsor, which permits the partnership to use the land.

Upon termination of the lease or default of certain major covenants by the lessee, the land reverts to the nonprofit or other entity, which also becomes owner of all the improvements.

This structure does not provide for the automatic involvement of the nonprofit or other entity in the partnership's development, construction, rehabilitation, or management activities; to the extent such involvement is desired, it must be separately provided for in the partnership agreement.

From the viewpoint of the nonprofit participant, a ground lease offers the greatest assurance of eventual reversion of the property. The potential disadvantage is, of course, the cost to the nonprofit sponsor of acquiring the land. If the nonprofit already owns the land, or can acquire it at a below-market price or at no cost, then the ground lease option should be considered seriously.

To the partnership, the ground lease offers potential additional return. The partners' funds do not have to be used to acquire nondepreciable land, but can be used almost entirely for depreciable buildings. Rental payments for the land are deductible expenses. Thus, the ground lease can enhance the tax-shelter value of the partnership to investors.

Lease Term. Investors are unlikely to agree to a lease term of less than 15 years, since it would not be in their interest to dispose of the property while it still offers them tax shelter. Indeed, it may be in the investors' best interest to seek a longer-term lease; for example, a forty-year lease term would permit sale to a second investor group, which could "re-run" all the tax shelter benefits.

The nonprofit entity might well prefer a shorter term lease so as to be able to assume full control of the property sooner, and so as to reduce the opportunities for investor speculation. The nonprofit could address this problem by inserting rent and use restrictions in the ground lease. These restrictive covenants should be enforceable against the first and subsequent owners.

The interests of the lender must also be considered. The lender needs to be assured that if it has to foreclose on the lessee-borrower, the lender can acquire a building and ground lease interest of sufficient duration to have a market value of at least the amount of the oustanding loan. Most lenders therefore will lend on leasehold only if the lease does not expire for at least ten years beyond loan maturity; thus, a thirty-year loan would require a forty-year lease. Finally, state limitations on lease terms must be considered. For example, there are specific limits for lease terms in California.

Rent. Since the ground rent will often be paid from building or project income, lowering of the ground rent will promote affordability by keeping tenant rents down. If the nonprofit sponsor acquired the land at market interest rates, it has no choice but to pass on those costs to the lessee partnership. If the nonprofit acquired the land at below market cost, or free, from local government or other sources, then it will be able to charge a lower ground rent and thus reduce costs to the tenants. The nonprofit can, however, also "have its cake and eat it too," by deferring payment of the rent altogether, taking a promissory note, with accrued rent plus interest, to be paid out of sales proceeds or upon assignment of the leasehold interest. The advantages of doing this are discussed more fully immediately below.

Accrued Indebtedness

This mechanism is conditioned upon the ability of the nonprofit to contribute valuable assets to the partnership. The assets might consist of land, buildings, grant funds, or something less tangible, but still capable of being assigned a value, such as the packaging of a development or syndication. The contributed assets would be reflected on the partnership's books as a debt owed by the partnership to the nonprofit, bearing interest at the market rate. The nonprofit could then eventually apply this debt and its accrued interest against the proceeds to be derived from the sale by the partnership. Since the appreciation on the property would be reduced by the amount of this debt and its interest, the nonprofit participant might be in a position to purchase the property.

This mechanism offers many advantages both to the nonprofit entity and to the investors. The nonprofit realizes the full value of its contribution to the partnership, but the cost is borne by the investors at time of sale, not by the tenants out of their rents. The partnership may, if it reports on an accrual basis, deduct the accrued, unpaid interest on its debt to the nonprofit, even though it has no current cash outlay. Further, although the accrued interest may be deducted by the partners out of ordinary income, the partners' accrued liability, when paid, is treated as a capital gain. Thus the partners are in the happy position of saving taxes at the 50 percent rate, if they are in the 50 percent tax bracket, while paying tax on the eventual proceeds at the 20 percent capital gains rate.

While the above situation might seem to have few disadvantages for either the nonprofit or the investors, the tax aspects of such an arrangement are extremely complex. Numerous IRS challenges are possible, and extreme care is needed in structuring the deal.

Option on the Property

This alternative requires the nonprofit to negotiate with the investors an option to reacquire the property. The option would generally be exercised either at the end of the tax-shelter holding period or upon notice that the investors wish to dispose of the property.

The exercise price is a subject of negotiation. It could be established at a fixed cash amount or some percentage of the fair market value of the property established by the appraisal as of the exercise date. The advantage of this alternative is that it clearly establishes the respective rights of the parties at the outset. The nonprofit knows the buy-out formula, and the investors know the limits of the appreciation on the property. The problem for the nonprofit is, of course, that it must accumulate sufficient funds to buy out the investors when the option is exercised.

Various approaches might be taken by a nonprofit to assure its ability to exercise its option. If the investors wish to realize appreciation on the property, the nonprofit will have to find significant cash. Possibilities for providing the necessary funds include (1) the establishment of a sinking fund; (2) placing use restrictions on the property that will survive sale, thus reducing the future value of the property; and (3) using some form of indebtedness mechanism. If the investors' needs will be satisfied by something less than the fair market value of the property, such as recovery of their original contributions or of sufficient cash to pay their taxes, the burden on the nonprofit may be less. The tax issues of this alternative also have to be examined carefully; particularly the need to establish that a real transaction has taken place, rather than a maneuver to avoid tax obligations.

Sinking Fund

To establish a sinking fund for acquisition of the property, the nonprofit must set aside and invest funds sufficient to meet the estimated long-term need. The initial investment might come from syndication proceeds; the fund might be increased by any fees received by the nonprofit as managing general partner. It is essential for the nonprofit to be tax-exempt, so that interest received on the fund would not be taxable. The problem with the sinking fund approach, however, is that it may not generate sufficient funds for acquisition of the property.

Rent and Use Restrictions

There are various ways that rent and use restrictions can be imposed on a property. These include:

- deed or other restrictions as used, for example, in inclusionary zoning programs;
- a recorded option on the property exercisable by local government, a public housing authority, a redevelopment agency, or other entity at sale or disposition at a price which limits the future value of the property;
- recorded options, rent and use restrictions in a ground lease;
- rent and use restrictions incorporated in the partnership agreement which perpetuate the affordability of the housing for low- and moderate-income people.

In addition to requiring that the property be used for low income-purposes, the restrictions are advantageous to the nonprofit, in that they limit opportunities for future appreciation of the property, and therefore make it easier for the nonprofit to buy out the investors. The restrictions have obvious disadvantages for an investor interested in significant appreciation.

Legal questions again arise as to whether use restrictions are enforceable against future owners. Also in question is whether recorded options would have priority over the interests of the mortgagees. The law is unclear in many of these areas. The restrictions may, however, cloud the title sufficiently to intimidate potential future investors in the property into either complying with them or avoiding the property.

Enhanced Equity Participation

This approach, often referred to as a "flip-flop," structures the partnership so as to give the nonprofit a substantial interest in the economic gain on disposition of the property, thus putting it in a better position to buy out the partner interests. Generally, the nonprofit general partner has only a 1 percent or 2 percent interest. This approach would give the nonprofit general partner perhaps a 1 percent interest in operations, but a 40 percent interest in the distributions after payment to the investors of their original contribution. The "flip-flop" is a frequently used device and, as such, may be readily acceptable to knowledgeable investors. The disadvantage is that the increased percentage interest becomes effective only *after* recovery by the investors of their original contributions; it may, therefore, produce only limited cash for a buy-out.

The California Corporations Commission has imposed limitations on the percentage interest in distributions after recovery of the capital contribution which would probably result in not more than 25 percent of the residual distributions going to the nonprofit. Further, this is a very uncertain area with respect to tax law, and any arrangement might be subject to challenge.

Charitable Contribution

Under this arrangement, the partnership would make a charitable contribution of the project to a tax-exempt nonprofit at the end of the optimum holding period. The partners would then take their proportionate share of the contribution as a charitable deduction for tax purposes.

In general, this is an ineffective way to assure eventual ownership by the nonprofit. First, there are no assurances for the nonprofit that the contribution will be made, since to meet IRS requirements, the donation must be spontaneous, not compulsory, and must not be motivated by some anticipated benefit. Further, sale of the property is generally found to be much more advantageous to the partners than a charitable contribution. Nevertheless, investors may be found who are charitably motivated and can be relied upon to make the contribution.

Every deal is different, the resources of every nonprofit vary, and syndicators differ with respect to the types of arrangements they find acceptable. Accordingly, the above variety of mechanisms offers a range of models which may be considered in structuring a given transaction. Clearly, the shadow of the IRS looms over most of them. Any deal must be put together with the assistance of an experienced tax attorney who is sensitive to the low-income housing and economic substance issues, current on the constantly changing state of the law, and skilled in legal drafting and negotiations.

Project Syndication: How It Works

Joseph T. Howell

Times are not easy for public housing authorities: deteriorating buildings built years ago, many having outlived their useful lives; increasing operating and maintenance costs; scarce modernization funds and operating subsidies; and the vast array of tenant problems that normally accompany families without access to good jobs, education, or decent incomes. Of course, none of this is new to public housing authorities. What is new is the harsh reality of the 1980s that housing is not a priority under the current administration and that the view held by a majority of Americans is that as a nation we no longer can "afford" many of the past social programs.

In short, don't expect any more public bailouts from Uncle Sam. The federal government has sent the message loud and clear: find new and creative solutions to your problems, involve the private sector, be more efficient and businesslike but, whatever you do, don't call us.

It is no wonder then that public housing authorities increasingly are turning to new solutions, and one solution that keeps surfacing is real estate syndication. More and more public officials are asking the question: why not syndicate public housing projects thus bringing in private capital to help rehabilitate older buildings, build up operating reserves, and increase operating income? Department of Housing and Urban Development Section 236 projects, 221(d)(3) and (d)(4) projects, and Section 8 projects were syndicated and are being resyndicated. Why not public housing? In many ways, the concept of syndication seems especially suited to the times, given the public/private partnership concept and the concept of self-help and business solutions to social problems being espoused in Washington.

Perhaps so. But, as the warning goes, not so fast. Syndication may be an appropriate solution in some cases, but in many others it may not. More important, before getting too far down the road one must have a pretty good idea of what syndication is and the potential problems—both short- and long-term—that you may run into. And before any such syndication takes place you will have to obtain HUD approval.

HOW IT WORKS

The first big area of confusion about syndication is the concept itself. At the mention of the word "syndication," often people's eyes light up and a smile comes across their face as they conjure up images of modern-day alchemy whereby men wearing black hats and calling themselves syndicators magically turn "losses" into gold. In reality, syndication is much more mundane and straightforward. It is simply the process of selling limited partnership interests in income-producing properties. In capsule, the process works like this:

- A limited partnership is formed. The limited partnership must have at least one general partner and one limited partner. The general partner has unlimited liability. The limited partners have their liability limited by the amount of their investment. The limited partnership vehicle (unlike a corporation) enables the direct pass-through of profits and losses to the partners in the partnership.
- The limited partnership takes title to an income-producing property (or in some instances, acquires the partnership interest of the previous limited partnership that owned the property).
- The general partner in the limited partnership then sells the remaining limited partnership interests in the project to investors. These investors sign a limited partnership agreement, which entitles them to shares of ownership based on the amount of money ("capital contributions") they put into the limited partnership. The limited partnership agreement also spells out how the profits and losses are allocated among the partners.
- The payments from limited partners that flow into the limited partnership are combined with the mortgage proceeds, which together comprise the total sources of cash available to the project. When the total sources of cash are greater than the applications of cash (for acquisition, rehab or construction, financing costs, and so on), there is money available to pay the general partner a developer's fee, which becomes, in effect, the profit he or she makes from syndication.
- Because the syndication process must conform with strict (and everchanging) tax laws, Securities and Exchange Commission regulations, and state "blue sky" laws, all syndications require legal assistance and many utilize the services of a middleman or syndication firm whose role is to match investors with general partners and to be sure the process meets all legal requirements, including that of full disclosure required by the SEC.

The key to understanding the business side of a real estate syndication is the fact that investors make capital contributions in order to receive an economic benefit. While this seems apparent, it can easily be overlooked by persons seeking to get involved in a syndication and has significant implications for public housing authorities. In short, there must be something to sell and it must produce economic benefits to the limited partners.

Economic benefits consist of three things: cash return (usually distributed to the partners at the end of the partnership's fiscal year), the opportunity for profits in the future when the project is sold, and so-called tax benefits. Syndications often involve a combination of all three benefits, although in the case of most low-income housing syndications (and this will surely apply to many public housing syndications when and if they occur), the tax benefit has been the main benefit that has been sold to investors.

NEW OR REHABILITATED?

Look briefly at the standard way most low-income housing syndicators have worked in the past. There are two basic types of such syndications, both of which may be applicable to public housing authorities in certain situations. The first involves what is essentially a new project—involving new construction or substantial rehabilitation. The second is the sale of an existing property where not much changes except the project ownership.

Many public housing authorities have been directly or indirectly involved in such projects in the past, the most prevalent examples of which are Section 8 projects. Although the Section 8 program is no longer available, the principles involved are applicable for the syndication of some PHA-owned properties, which may be substantially rehabilitated or torn down and diverted to new use. The process works like this:

1. A developer puts together a viable income-producing multifamily housing project. In developer's parlance this is commonly referred to as "a deal." The developer has an option on a site or building, has hired an architect to prepare plans, has reasonable assurance that upon completion tenants will move in and pay the necessary rents to cover operating and debt service costs (in the past this meant receiving a Section 8 fund reservation), and has a financing commitment for a nonrecourse loan from a lender—typically a firm commitment from HUD or a state housing finance agency.

2. At about the time the project goes to initial closing—when all legal documents are signed permitting the construction lender to advance funds —and construction begins, the developer, who is now the general partner in the limited partnership that owns the project, signs an agreement with a syndication firm to raise equity capital from limited partners.

3. Working with the general partner, the syndication firm prices the equity by projecting the "losses" the project will produce over five years. The formula works like this:

	Gross income from project
Less	vacancy and collection allowance (usually 5%)
Less	all operating costs
Less	Interest on project financing
Less	depreciation (now called accelerated cost recovery system, or ACRS)
Equals	profit or loss for each year over a five-year period

Because of the concept of depreciation, the project will show an accounting loss each year. To this loss, the syndicator will apply a market ratio—usually about 2:1—which means that for every $1 invested, an investor will receive $2 worth of tax losses. This means that an investor in the 50 percent marginal tax bracket comes out even. If the investor was not putting money into the limited partnership, the money would be going to federal income taxes.

Because the pay-in period is usually over five years and because the "losses" usually continue through the eleventh or twelfth year, the ratio of losses to the initial investment is 3.0 or 3.5 to 1 over the projected fifteen-year holding period.

In general, it works like this:

(1) Losses year 1–5 divided by market ratio 2.0 (ranges from 1.8–2.2) equals gross syndication proceeds

(2) Gross syndication proceeds less costs of syndication (15–20 percent of gross proceeds) equals total net equity raised

(3) Total net equity plus mortgage proceeds equals total sources of cash

(4) Total sources of cash less applications to project

—construction or rehabilitation

—acquisition

—soft costs

—all other project costs

equals amount left over for developer's fees and profits

Until 1981, there was very little interest in purchasing and syndicating existing or "second user" properties largely because of the difference in the way the tax code treated such properties (allowing much lower accelerated depreciation for such properties). The Economic Recovery Tax Act of 1981 eliminated any distinction between first and second user properties, and, at the same time, shortened the depreciation or cost recovery period to fifteen years for all real estate. There also was intense interest in syndicating or resyndicating older low-income housing properties—especially those properties that had "used up" their depreciation and whose owners were ready to sell.

The syndication of existing properties is very much like new construction syndication in some ways and very different in others. In terms of pricing the equity that can be raised, the concept is the same. Basic losses are calculated for each year during a five-year pay-in period. The amount of losses each year is divided by a ratio determined by the market (typically $2.10 of losses for every $1 of investment). This number then becomes the gross amount of equity that can be raised from the syndication from which the costs of syndication must be subtracted. The net equity plus the mortgage proceeds are available for use in the project including acquisition, closing costs, project fix up, and so on. What funds do not go directly into the project are available to the general partner for overhead, fees, and profit.

The big difference between existing property syndications and new construction or substantial rehabilitation syndication involves the use of a purchase money note taken back by the seller. Usually the note is not a second trust, but rather a loan secured by limited partnership interests, and the note carries a simple interest rate that accrues until the loan comes due in twelve to fifteen years.

The intent of the purchase money note is to increase the tax basis—defined as what you pay to acquire the property and what therefore can be "written off" for tax purposes—of the property without altering the basic economic relationships of the project. The original loan stays in place. The original tenants stay in place, usually at the same rents. And since no funds, except for a cash payment, actually pass from the buyer to the seller of the building, the basic cash flow stays the same. Because of the higher tax basis (to which is applied the ACRS annual percentage amounts for accelerated depreciation allowed for low-income housing), the project suddenly generates significant losses that are available to shelter income of wealthy individuals—just as is the case with new construction or rehabilitation projects. These losses thus generate the attraction for new equity capital. The formula, which is very similar to the formula shown above, is shown as:

	Gross income from project
Less	vacancy and collection allowance
Less	all operating costs
Less	interest on existing first trust
Less	accrued interest on purchase money note
Less	depreciation or ACRS based on the new acquisition price of the building
Equals	profit or loss for each year

Contributions from limited partners are made each year during a five-year period by dividing the loss each year by the market ratio averaging about 2.1.

Indeed, with the concept of syndication or resyndication of existing properties, the notion of syndication as modern-day alchemy may not be all that farfetched. Herein lies the major problem with such deals. All financing must be nonrecourse, which means that the lender must look only to the property, not to a general partner, for repayment of the loan. It therefore could be argued that if the seller can receive enough cash for a down payment, he or she is not all that concerned about getting the purchase money loan or accrued interest back in the future. Thus, the higher the price the better because the higher price means a higher tax basis which in turn means more depreciation, more losses, and hence more capital contributions.

There are two restrictions that prevent major abuses in this area. The first is the HUD requirement that the combination of the balance of the existing first trust, plus the purchase money note, plus the interest that will be accrued on the purchase money note over the life of the loan cannot exceed 75 percent of current replacement cost of the project. While the rationale for this precise formula is not readily apparent, it does have the practical effect of keeping the amount of the second trust reasonable.

The second restriction is the more troublesome for buyers and sellers of such properties. This is the IRS provision that the tax basis used for the purpose of depreciation or capital recovery cannot exceed the fair market value of the project. Therefore, every syndication of existing properties requires a valid appraisal by a qualified third-party appraiser.

The real key to this type of syndication boils down to the appraisal. Moreover, the appraisal process is further complicated by the fact that the IRS does not permit fair market value to be determined exclusively by tax benefits. In addition, there must be other data to support price such as comparable sales, economic value (based on the net income generated), and the potential for appreciation. Some appraisers have been willing and able to give appraisals that support the acquisition costs of such projects. Others have shied away. The issue is still controversial.

What is clear, however, is that it does make a difference where the project is located, its condition, appearance, and operating history. Projects that clearly do not have any basis for value other than the tax benefits will have difficulty justifying the losses in an IRS audit, which could mean that the investors would have to pay the taxes that were avoided and deep trouble for promoters of such shelters.

With the passage of the 1984 tax act, the interest that is accrued on a purchase money note must show up on the seller's tax return as income for the year it is due, even though it may not be earned. While this provision is expected to have the result of stopping most sellers, some second user resyndications will continue—especially those that generate real economic values.

The same principles that apply to syndication apply to properties owned by public housing authorities. In other words, if housing authorities are going to syndicate deals, economic benefits must be generated that are based on legitimate values and economic relationships. This means, in short, that projects must meet at least one of these three criteria: (a) they make money, that is, show a positive cash flow after paying all bills and debt service on project financing; (b) they are likely to appreciate in value; and (c) they produce a tax shelter that is based on bona fide acquisition prices supported by an independent appraisal of "fair market value."

PHA IMPLICATIONS

Herein lies the major stumbling block affecting the syndication of public housing. Projects that do not make money, that do not have appreciation potential, and that cannot justify a "fair market" price sufficiently high to generate a tax basis high enough to produce large deductions do not offer the necessary economic benefits to attract investors. For such projects, syndication is not the answer.

On the other hand, there are clearly some projects owned by housing authorities that do meet one of these three tests. For deals where one of these conditions is present, it may well be possible to use syndication to raise funds to support the overall operations and objectives of the agency. The major problem is that the deals that make economic sense may not necessarily be in line with some of the social and policy objectives of the agency. For example, older properties on valuable downtown land may have substantial potential for both cash flow and appreciation—but not necessarily if they continue to house lower-income tenants.

Local housing officials may be faced with the painful decision of having to syndicate or sell some assets in order to generate funds to provide the necessary money to assist other units or simply to keep the operation afloat.

But in selling or syndicating these properties, a PHA may not be able to maintain them for housing the poor.

In the context of an overall housing strategy this might make sense—but only as part of an overall strategy. Simply selling off or syndicating a project will be difficult to justify unless it clearly produces overall benefits to the authority.

Apparently some syndicators have made offers that suggest that after a 15-year holding period, the project will automatically revert back to the local authority once the tax shelter has been "used up." Since many deals with the housing authority also usually would provide that the tenants remain in place and that the housing authority continues to manage the property, such an offer is especially tempting.

Be very careful before entering into such deals. Because there can be no fixed agreement to buy back a project at a fixed price (to do so would negate the "economic motive" of the investment—in contrast to the "tax avoidance motive"—and would thus invalidate the tax write-offs for the investors), the fine print usually states, "the right of first refusal for the housing authority to buy back the project in the future at fair market value." If the assumption is that the project will have a very low fair market value at that time, perhaps it may be affordable by the authority. But the housing authority and the promoter/syndicators also must ask the question—if they don't, surely the IRS will—if the project does not have a high value at that time, then how can the relatively high values used for the purposes of equity syndication be justified now? This is not to say that all such deals will not work. It is to say a PHA should be very careful.

OPPORTUNITIES

There are essentially two types of syndication deals in which PHAs might participate. The first are the PHA-owned Section 8 deals. These are typically Section 8 projects owned directly by local housing authorities or their instrumentalities that were completed in the mid- to late 1970s during the early years of the program. Such projects are generally in pretty good shape. Some even generate positive cash flow and have substantial reserves.

The syndication of the deals would follow the existing property approach already described, and there is no economic or legal reason why many of these projects could not be syndicated. That is provided, of course, they meet the legal tests. There are policy reasons, however, and here is the rub.

HUD's permission is required in order for the HAP contracts to be transferred from one owner to another, and according to HUD officials, it is unlikely that permission will be granted. While there are a number of difficult practical concerns—like what happens with regard to paying real estate taxes when the project's real estate taxes are based on a payment-in-lieu-of-taxes, or a PILOT, instead of the real estate standard assessment—the major concern is a policy one.

Why allow more tax dollars to be diverted from the federal government when no further social objectives are being achieved? Most of these projects need no money for repairs. Most have been well managed. (Thus far HUD does not see raising private capital to subsidize PHA operations on "public purpose.") Rather by allowing such syndications, what is happening, according to HUD officials, is an indirect "augmenting of appropriations." Accordingly, HUD's original position was to allow for syndication of PHA-owned Section 8 deals in certain situations, provided modernization funds and operating subsidies were reduced from HUD to the PHA on a dollar-for-dollar basis for each syndication dollar earned. However, upon receiving notification from the Office of Management and Budget in February [1984] that no such syndications would be permitted, HUD's current position is not to allow syndications of PHA-owned Section 8 projects under any circumstances. It is doubtful that this position will change soon.

The other type of potential syndication deal is the syndication of conventional public housing projects financed through housing authority bonds retired through annual contribution contracts. Here the situation is very different and potentially much more promising.

The Housing and Urban and Rural Recovery Act of 1983 amended the 1937 Housing Act by adding Section 18 dealing with the disposition and demolition of PHA-owned conventional public housing. In general, this section of the housing act provides wide latitude for public housing authorities to dispose of and/or demolish public housing projects that may be in areas unfit for housing or that are not in the "best interests of the tenants or the public housing agency."

In other words, the way has now been paved for PHAs to sell property to generate funds for supporting the social and policy objectives of the agency. The major conditions in undertaking disposition or demolition are that any net proceeds must be used first for the "retirement of outstanding obligations used to finance original development or modernization of the project"; that all other profits must be used for the general purpose of providing low-income housing; that the agency must consult with tenants and tenant councils in the preparation of a disposition plan; and that any existing tenants in the projects being sold must be relocated to decent, safe, sanitary, and affordable housing. Draft regulations have been written and will be issued for public comment this summer.

While it is clear that if such properties are sold, they must be sold for the highest value—and probably only on a legitimate competitive basis unless the sale is to a public body—in some situations the PHA might stand to gain the most by participating in some form of joint venture or syndication with a co-developer. While the disposition or developer selection process must be competitive and fair, there is no reason why the PHA might not become a partner in the development entity that purchases or leases the property on a long-term basis from the PHA. The regulations due this summer should clarify what is permitted.

In these types of potential deals, the kind of syndication that will most likely be involved will follow the method already described under the new construction or substantial rehabilitation method. Basically all things are possible. One example is the redevelopment of older public housing projects that are now obsolete and yet situated on extremely valuable downtown land. Clearly some PHAs will have the opportunity to convert some of these properties to a "higher and better" use using the profits from the sale or development of the properties to serve the needs of lower-income tenants more efficiently and in different locations.

In getting involved in these deals, the same warnings apply regarding the fundamental financial soundness, marketability, and legality of the undertaking. Section 18 of the housing act may usher in a new age of public housing entrepreneurism whereby older obsolete properties are sold or converted to new uses with the profits and proceeds of the deals used to benefit low-income tenants in other project locations in the city, to build new low-income housing, or to subsidize low-income tenants directly.

CONCLUSION

Syndication should not be viewed as a substitute for ongoing federal assistance to PHAs in the form of modernization funds and operating subsidies. The large majority of public housing projects are not suited for syndication because they do not generate the basic economic benefits necessary to attract investors. For this reason, PHAs that view syndication as a possible panacea for their problems are likely to be sadly disappointed.

At the same time, syndication does offer a tool that may work in some situations and if used as part of an overall housing strategy may serve a very useful purpose. The most promising place to look for potential deals is not the PHA-owned Section 8 projects, because HUD is unlikely to permit such syndications, but rather in the creative reuse and recycling of older conventional public housing projects, especially those located in marketable locations. Section 18 of the housing act grants wide latitude for public housing authorities in terms of maximizing their economic resources, and it appears that opportunities will be available for the reuse and redevelopment of many older public housing properties, both with regard to selling the properties to competitive bidders and to joint venturing with co-developers. Whichever approach is taken, syndication is likely to play a key role in the process.

Qualifying a Property for Syndication
Robert A. Stanger

The investor who holds real property in his personal portfolio and the syndicator who acquires it on behalf of a group of prospective partners have ultimately the same goals in mind: to maximize cash flow, appreciation, and tax benefits. But the two go about it in quite different ways. In simplest terms, the private investor makes his own decision about the balance to be struck among the three objectives, invests his own money, and incurs no "marketing and organizational costs." The syndicator, on the other hand, is faced with two specific problems:

1. He must incur substantial costs in organizing the syndicate and marketing the interests, including compensation to himself; and

2. He must create a balance among the three goals of cash flow, appreciation, and tax benefits that will appeal to the particular market to which he is seeking to sell.

Inevitably, a syndicator who acquires property from a nonsyndicate owner must "restructure" the transaction so that a satisfactory return remains for the investors despite the substantial costs the syndicator incurs.

The lengthy example that follows is intended to demonstrate this restructuring process.

THE PROPERTY

Adams, a well-known real estate developer, is offering for sale his Pidgeon Run project in North Carolina. Knowing that in the current market the highest prices were being paid by real estate syndicators, he contacts three syndicator friends: Baker, Charles, and Dawson. He sends them a brochure on Pidgeon Run with the demographics of the area, conditions of the local economy, a listing of tenants and lease terms, pictures of the property, and a pro forma financial projection of rents, expenses and cash flow. (Adams' pro forma appears as table 15-1.)

Pidgeon Run has operated successfully since opening five years ago and has produced steadily increasing rental income. Operating expenses are under control and cash flow increases steadily. The project is worth $10,000, according to Adams. The mortgage loan, while at an attractive rate of 11 percent, is only in the amount of $6,000. Adams realizes the buyer will have to come up with a large amount of cash ($4,000) relative to property value, so he offers the property at an attractive free and clear capitalization rate of 10 percent (net operating income of $1,000 divided by the offering price of $10,000). On the ten-year pro forma in table 15-1, the buyer's internal rate of return is 19 percent if an 8 percent inflation rate is assumed.

Table 15-1. Pidgeon Run

	1	2	3	4	5	6	7	8	9	10
Rents	$1,700	$1,836	$1,983	$2,142	$2,313	$2,498	$2,698	$2,914	$3,147	$3,398
Less: Operating expenses	−700	−756	−816	−882	−952	−1,029	−1,111	−1,200	−1,296	−1,398
Net operating income	$1,000	$1,080	$1,167	$1,260	$1,361	$1,469	$1,587	$1,714	$1,851	$2,000
Less: Debt service (interest and principal)	−720	−720	−720	−720	−720	−720	−720	−720	−720	−720
Net cash flow	280	360	447	540	641	749	867	994	1,131	1,280
Adjustment for noncash items:										
Depreciation	−600	−600	−600	−600	−600	−600	−600	−600	−600	−600
Principal amortization	+60	+66	+73	+81	+89	+98	+108	+119	+131	+144
Taxable income (Loss)	($ 260)	($ 174)	($ 80)	$ 21	$ 130	$ 247	$ 375	$ 513	$ 662	$ 824

Note: Purchase price of $10,000 was allocated 10% to land and 90% to buildings. Cash investment was $4,000, subject to a $6,000, 11% fully amortizing mortgage at 12% constant. Rents and expenses increase 8% per annum. Operating expense ratio starts at 41%. Depreciation was calculated over 15 years on a straight-line method. Sale price was ten times net operating income in the tenth year less remaining debt balance (original debt less principal amortization, sometimes called equity buildup).

Public Offering

Several days after sending out his brochure, Adams receives a visit from the first syndicator, Baker. Baker has already looked at the property with his engineering consultant and talked to a local appraiser about comparable property values. He offers on the spot to buy Pidgeon Run from Adams at the offering price.

To see if Pidgeon Run would fit the requirements of a public offering, Baker had "restructured" the transaction (table 15-2). He adjusted the pro forma to "gross up" the property to reflect the fees and costs of a public offering. He also changed the method of depreciation (breaking out personal property from the building), and he assumed that certain fees could be deducted for tax purposes. The adjusted cash price of the property to the public was $5,542 (up from the $4,000 that the syndicator would pay Adams). Pidgeon Run's first-year cash flow remains at $280, but first-year tax savings of $312 (50 percent of the $624 tax loss) raise the first-year free and clear return in excess of 10 percent. Investors' returns rise nicely to 13 to 14 percent in five years. Sale of the property ten years out (assuming that net income increases at 8 percent per annum) would provide the investor in the 50 percent tax bracket with a 14 percent internal rate of return.

Private Placement

The next person to call on Adams was Charles, a syndicator who specializes in private placements. He proposed that if Adams is willing to accept payment of the purchase price over a period of years, Charles will pay a somewhat higher price for Pidgeon Run. Justification for the higher price is that the property is expected to produce more cash flow several years from now when the purchase will be completed. Of course, Adams would want to keep his hand in management of the property during the pay-in period in order to protect the security for the unpaid purchase price.

Adams' original projections (see table 15-1) indicate that the property is expected to produce $1,200 to $1,300 of net operating income in years 3 and 4 and would then be worth $12,000 to $13,000 (assuming a sale price of ten times net operating income). This price compares with the $10,000 Adams is asking for an immediate sale. Charles is willing to pay the extra money, but he wants Adams to take back a note for some of the increase. Because Charles specializes in "risk-free transactions," he offers Adams all the cash flow from the property for the three-to-four-year pay-in period in return for Adams' ironclad guarantee against negative cash flow. This would mean that the investors would receive no cash flow during this period, but if the deal could be structured so that tax losses about equaled the limited partner capital contribution for the first four years, then raising the equity in a private placement should be assured.

In table 15-1, Adams' first-year taxable loss was $260. In table 15-2, Baker produced a first-year loss of $624. Table 15-3 indicates how Charles was able to increase tax losses. First-year loss was $1,798, produced by higher

Table 15-2. Public Offering

	1	2	3	4	5	6	7	8	9	10
Net operating income (from table 15-1)	$1,000	$1,080	$1,167	$1,260	$1,361	$1,469	$1,587	$1,714	$1,851	$2,000
Less: Debt service	−720	−720	−720	−720	−720	−720	−720	−720	−720	−720
Property cash flow[a]	$ 280	$ 360	$ 447	$ 540	$ 641	$ 749	$ 867	$ 994	$1,131	$1,280
Adjustment for noncash items:										
Depreciation	−800	−800	−800	−800	−800	−500	−500	−500	−500	−500
Amortized fees	−164	−164	−164	−165	−165	—	—	—	—	—
Principal amortization	+60	+66	+73	+81	+89	+98	+108	+119	+131	+144
Taxable income (Loss)	($ 624)	($ 538)	($ 444)	($ 344)	($ 235)	$ 347	$ 475	$ 613	$ 762	$ 924

a. Before allocations to general partner.

Note: Equity contribution was recalculated for front-end load as follows: An acquisition fee equal to 6% of $10,000 original purchase price was added to $4,000 of cash investment. $4,600 was divided by .83 (5% working capital, 4% offering and organization costs and an 8% sales commission) to determine offering amount of $5,542. GP receives 10% of cash flow, 1% of taxable income or loss. From the base model, depreciation was increased in early years by allocating 10% of purchase price to land. 75% to building and 15% to personal property. Depreciation of real and personal property was calculated over 15 and 5 years respectively on a straight-line method. An amount equal to acquisition fees and offering and organization costs was amortized over five years on the theory the GP could convert some hard costs to deductible items.

Table 15-3. Private Placement

	1	2	3	4	5	6	7	8	9	10
Net operating income (from table 15-1)	$1,000	$1,080	$1,167	$1,260	$1,361	$1,469	$1,587	$1,714	$1,851	$2,000
Less Debt service	-900	-900	-900	-900	-900	-900	-900	-900	-900	-900
Property cash flow[a]	100	180	267	360	461	569	687	814	951	1,100
Cost of seller's cash flow guarantee	-100	-180	-267	-360	—	—	—	—	—	—
Cash flow before noncash items[a]	—	—	—	—	461[a]	569	687	814	951	1,100
Management fee to seller[b]	-115	-115	-115	-116	—	—	—	—	—	—
Depreciation	-1,484	-1,298	-1,206	-1,113	-1,020	-556	-556	-556	-556	-464
Amortized fees	-199	-199	-199	-200	-200	—	—	—	—	—
Taxable income (Loss)[a]	($1,798)	($1,612)	($1,520)	($1,429)	($ 759)	$ 13	$ 131	$ 258	$ 395	$ 636

a. Before allocations to general partner. Fifth-year cash flow paid to seller for accrued management fee and not available for distribution.

b. Accrued and paid in fifth year.

Note: Original transaction was assumed renegotiated to allow pay-in of equity contribution over four years. In the fourth year the net operating income is projected at $1,260 indicating a property value of $12,600 vs. $10,000 based on the first year. The GP agreed to pay $4,864 in cash ($4,000 purchase price plus $864 interest on deferred payments) and give a note to seller for $1,500 in the form of a 12% interest only wraparound for $7,500 (includes first mortgage of $6,000). Interest on deferred capital contributions was calculated at 13.3% interest. The purchase price of $12,364 ($7,500 mortgage loan plus $4,864 in cash) was increased by a 6% acquisition fee which increased the required equity contribution. This figure was divided by .88 to calculate the total equity contribution of $6,370. No provision was made for working capital (compared with public offering model) because of the seller's no negative cash flow guarantee. The seller manages the property during pay-in for an annual fee (accrued if not earned). In addition, the seller guarantees the partnership against operating losses for the first four years in return for the first four years' cash flow. Depreciation was recalculated on the higher purchase price (with the same percentage allocation to land, buildings and personal property as the public offering model) on an accelerated method over fifteen years (five for personal property). The GP fees and syndication costs are calculated by the same method as the public offering model including the assumed five-year deductible items. The only exception is that in this model the GP receives 1% of cash flow.

debt service, the cost of the cash flow guarantee, and above all the use of accelerated depreciation on the higher purchase price.

As shown in table 15-3, losses during the four-year pay-in period amount to $6,359, virtually equal to the cash investment of $6,370. The cash-on-cash return on the second year after pay-in is completed is 8.9 percent ($569 return on $6,370 equity). The slight increase in the mortgage from $6,000 to $7,500 (the extra $1,500 representing the increase in purchase price paid to Adams for his willingness to stretch out payments) will not hurt the economics very much if the property appreciates. The tax lines (cash flow versus taxable income) do not cross for more than twelve years. And at an assumed 8 percent appreciation rate, Charles stands to put about half of the limited partners' capital contributions into his own pocket over the life of the deal.

Tax Loss Offering

The last of the three professional syndicators to respond, Dawson, has a more difficult task than his competitors, for his objective is to produce the magic 2-to-1 formula—$2 of tax loss for every $1 of investment. In this way, investors can be promised "no net investment."

Dawson's starting point for his pro forma is the same transaction made between Charles and Adams. But he must add to this both increased leverage and stretched-out capital contributions (to five years or more) in order to yield the hoped-for tax result.

The stretched-out capital contributions are financed by a second mortgage lender (secured by investor notes) who provides the cash to pay Adams. Dawson takes most of his compensation in the form of a mortgage on the property so that no additional cash is needed up front. Both the second and third mortgage increase the purchase price and also the basis for depreciation so that higher tax write-offs will be available. In addition, both mortgages accrue interest, with payment to come from sale and refinancing proceeds rather than from investor cash contributions or from the property's cash flow. At the same time, the accrued interest is deductible and so increases tax write-offs (table 15-4).

BEHIND THE SCENES

To quote the old saw, "There's only so much juice in the orange." You have just been party to the process of syndicating a real estate property. Start with a pro forma on a property. Adjust for the impact of investor costs in a typical public offering. Take the deal private by deferring limited partner pay-in over a period of years. Carry the process of structuring for tax loss to its logical extreme. Through each step along the way, cash investment (or the price of the property) increases. The dollar amount of return decreases. Appreciation necessary to break even on sale goes up. The internal rate of return heads down. Syndicator benefits go up and cash-on-cash return goes down.

Table 15-5 shows a comparison of economic benefits of each of the four

Table 15-4. Tax Loss Structure

	1	2	3	4	5	6	7	8	9	10
Cash flow before noncash items[a] (from table 15-3)	$ -115	$ -115	-115	$ -116	$ 461[a]	$ 569	$ 687	$ 814	$ 951	$1,100
Management fee to seller	—	—	—	—	—	—	—	—	—	—
Depreciation	-1,643	-1,429	-1,327	-1,225	-1,123	-612	-612	-612	-612	-510
Amortized fees	-199	-199	-199	-200	-200	—	—	—	—	—
Syndicator asset management fee	-45	-45	-45	-45	-46	—	—	—	—	—
Additional interest accrued[b]	-471	-535	-608	-691	-784	-727	-749	-743	-733	-703
Taxable income (Loss)[a]	($2,473)	($2,323)	($2,294)	($2,277)	($1,692)	($770)	($674)	($541)	($394)	($113)

a. Before allocations to GP. Cash flow of year 5 is applied to unpaid accrued seller management fee. Cash flow of years 6 through 10 is applied to unpaid accrued interest obligations and is not available for distribution to LPs.

b. Increment compared to private placement model (table 15-3).

Note: Two additional financings were arranged which increased the total purchase price and hence depreciation and interest cost. A second mortgage from a savings and loan was arranged on a 13% interest only basis (accrues and adds to the balance owed if unpaid) for $1,500. $1,274 was used to allow the investor to stretch pay-in to five years, with the balance paid to the GP over five years as a syndicator asset management fee. The second mortgage is secured by investor notes representing pay-in obligations. The GP reduced his cash acquisition fee from 6% to 3% of the purchase price for a two-times-larger fee (equity in his wraparound mortgage) which he will benefit from when the property is sold. The arrangement resulted in a new interest only wraparound mortgage note of $8,400 (including the $7,500 seller wraparound) accruing at 14% per annum (unpaid interest added to the balance). Other offering and organization costs and commissions calculated as for the private placement model except the GP is entitled to 25% of sale proceeds after return of cash investment in liquidation.

Table 15-5. Economic Benefits Net to Investor, After Tax

Year	Pidgeon Run Cash Flow	Tax (Cost) Savings	Total	Public Offering Cash Flow	Tax (Cost) Savings	Total	Private Placement Cash Flow	Tax (Cost) Savings	Total	Tax Loss Structure Cash Flow	Tax (Cost) Savings	Total
1	$ 280	$ 130	410	$ 252	$ 309	561	$ —	$ 890	890	—	$1,224	$ 1,224
2	360	87	447	324	266	590	—	798	798	—	1,150	1,150
3	447	40	487	402	220	622	—	752	752	—	1,136	1,136
4	540	(10)	530	486	170	656	—	708	708	—	1,127	1,127
5	641	(65)	576	577	116	693	—	376	376	—	838	838
6	749	(123)	626	674	(172)	502	563	(7)	556	—	381	381
7	867	(188)	679	780	(235)	545	680	(57)	623	—	333	333
8	994	(256)	738	895	(303)	592	806	(128)	678	—	268	268
9	1,131	(331)	800	1,018	(378)	640	941	(195)	746	—	195	195
10	1,280	(412)	868	1,152	(457)	695	1,089	(315)	774	—	56	56
Totals	$7,289	($1,128)	$ 6,161	$6,560	($464)	$ 6,096	$4,079	$2,822	$ 6,901	—	$6,708	$ 6,708
Net proceeds of sale			+10,968			+10,353			+4,757			+2,790
Total return			$ 17,129			$ 16,449			$ 11,658			$ 9,498
Original cash investment			$ 4,000			$ 5,542			$ 6,370			$ 6,503
Ratio of return to original investment			4.3:1			3.0:1			1.8:1			1.5:1
Internal rate of return			19.0%			14.2%			11.5%*			11.3%*

* To calculate internal rate of return, the present value investment amount of $5,507 was used.

Note: Assumes 50% tax rate for tax savings and ordinary income recapture and 20% capital gains tax. Pidgeon Run (table 15-1)—100% ownership. Public Offering (table 15-2)—G.P. receives 10% of cash flow. 1% of tax loss and upon sale 3% of sale proceeds plus 15% incentive fee after return of capital plus 6% per annum. Private Placement (table 15-3)—G.P. receives 1% of cash flow and tax loss plus 50% of sale proceeds after return of cash investment from sale proceeds. Tax Loss Structure (table 15-4)—G.P. receives 1% of cash flow and tax loss plus 25% of sale proceeds after return of cash investment from sale proceeds.

ways of looking at this transaction. Notice changes in the level of cash flow, tax savings, and net proceeds of sale for each one. Obviously, there is only so much juice in the orange. You cannot maximize cash, tax, and appreciation benefits simultaneously in a single real estate transaction.

In Adams' hands, Pidgeon Run shows almost $7,300 of cash flow over ten years and approximately $11,000 of sale proceeds based on an inflation rate of 8 percent. The cumulative tax is about $1,100 of net taxable income during the period. The total return is $17,000 compared to $4,000 of original cash investment. The internal rate of return is 19.0 percent.

Baker's public offering alternative shows $6,500 of cash flow and $10,000 of sale proceeds with a modest net tax cost during the ten-year period. The total return after tax is almost $16,500 compared to a $5,542 investment. The return to original investment ratio is 3 to 1 and the internal rate of return is 14.2 percent.

Charles' economic private placement model shows $4,000 of cash flow, $2,800 of tax savings and about $4,800 of proceeds of sale after tax. The total return is $11,600 or 1.8 times the $6,370 cash investment. The internal rate of return is 11.5 percent.

Dawson's tax loss structure shows no cash flow, $6,700 of tax savings and about $2,800 of sale proceeds after tax. The $9,500 total return is 1.5 times the $6,503 cash investment. The internal rate of return is 11.3 percent.

Table 15-6 shows fourteen different methods of comparison of the four transactions. Notice the increasing amount of debt to which the property is subject and the increasing equity investment necessary to purchase the property. The public offering model offers the best investment economics principally because the markups (in whatever form they take) are not as great as with the private placement alternatives. The difference between the transactions in total benefits measured in dollars is much greater than the difference between the internal rates of return. Pick the benefit you are aiming for and do not fool yourself.

Table 15-6. Comparison of Results

	Pidgeon Run	Public Offering	Private Placement	Tax Loss Structure
1. Equity	$ 4,000	$ 5,542	$ 6,370	$ 6,503
2. Debt balance 10 years out	$ 5,031	$ 5,031	$ 7,500	$11,538
3. Purchase price	$10,000	$11,542	$13,870	$16,403
4. Gross rent multiplier	5.9	6.8	8.2	9.6
5. Capitalization rate on NOI	10%	8.7%	7.2%	6.1%
6. Cash-on-cash return	7%	4.5%	None	None
7. Years to payback—cash	7.2	9.1	Sale	Sale
8. Years to payback—after-tax	7.3	9.2	9.3	8.2
9. IRR on sale	19.0%	14.2%	11.5%	11.3%
10. Price to cash break-even	$ 9,031	$11,483	$13,871	$17,662
11. Break-even to Pidgeon Run purchase price	−9.7%	+14.8%	+38.7%	+76.6%
12. Net after-tax cash in deal after five years	$ 1,550	$ 2,420	$ 2,846	$ 1,028
13. Total investor benefits (after-tax)	$17,129	$16,449	$11,658	$ 9,498
14. Total syndicator benefits (pretax)	0	$ 3,261	$ 3,887	$ 4,952

1. Limited partner capital contribution.
2. Principal balance unpaid on mortgages at end of tenth year.
3. Equity plus debt on property at commencement date.
4. Purchase price divided by gross rents.
5. First year net operating income divided by purchase price.
6. First year cash flow after debt service divided by equity.
7. Point in years when cumulative cash distributions equal equity.
8. Point in years when cumulative economic benefits after-tax equal equity.
9. Internal Rate of Return—the discount rate which equates equity in period zero (future pay-ins discounted to present value at 13.3%) to periodic benefits after-tax annually, and sale proceeds after-tax in period 11.
10. Price on sale necessary to return 100% of equity in cash (pretax) after syndicator compensation.
11. Percentage difference between #10 and Pidgeon Run purchase price ($10,000).
12. Equity less 5-year cumulative economic benefits after-tax.

The Resyndication Opportunity for Subsidized Housing Partnerships

David A. Smith

Since August 1981, when the Economic Recovery Tax Act of 1981 (ERTA) was signed, developers, owners and syndicators of subsidized housing have been thinking about ways to *resyndicate* existing subsidized housing properties. Declining federal subsidies and high interest rates have slowed the rate of new residential construction to a trickle. As long as new construction activity remains sluggish, resyndication will be the best real estate opportunity available.

A new game, resyndication has new rules, presents new problems, and offers new opportunities. Before we get into details, we must begin with a proper definition of the topic. Resyndication is a change of more than 90 percent of the beneficial interest of a real estate property and the packaging and sale of the new limited partnership interests thus created.

This definition is important both for what it says and for what it does not say. In a resyndication, you do not have to terminate the selling partnership. You do not have to change controlling general partners. You do not have to have a property which was originally syndicated; unsyndicated existing properties or nonprofits converted to limited dividend both qualify. You do, however, have to transfer 90 percent of the assets to an unrelated entity—a mere 50 percent transfer will be insufficient.

ELEMENTS OF RESYNDICATION

Resyndication is likely to be the best solution for the problems of owners of virtually all troubled or marginal properties. For healthy properties, re-syndication represents an opportunity to restructure the transaction, cash out a favorable residual, and if necessary inject more cash into the property.

The resyndication approach has many different variations. All of the following structural variables are likely possibilities:

· The controlling general partners may stay the same, or they may change completely. The property's management agent may also change.
· Often, more money will be raised on a resyndication than was raised on the original syndication. These funds will be divided among the seller investors, the general partners (old and new), the property, and the lender. Each party has a say in the final structure of the transaction; each party will review any proposal meticulously; each party has a veto.
· Secondary financing, a financing tool unavailable in new construction syndications, is often the crucial element in a resyndication. Without it, the equity that buyers are willing to commit would be inadequate to make the old investors willing to sell. But secondary financing *increases* the proceeds of equity investment. It makes possible a higher depreciable basis

than would otherwise be available. It also usually creates extra tax deductions for interest which will be accrued but unpaid.
· The resyndication may be accomplished either by selling the project from one partnership to another or by selling the partnership interests of the original partnership to a group of new owners. Buying the property directly is analogous to buying a piece of conventional real estate. Buying the partnership interests is more like buying a business. It has financial advantages, but it is more complex and requires much more extensive negotiation.

Each of these structuring variations involves trade-offs. Each resyndication must be individually negotiated between buyer and seller. The crucial issues change from deal to deal.

Like any other complex financial transaction, a resyndication consists of three major elements: economics, structure, and mechanics. We shall consider each of these separately.

RESYNDICATION ECONOMICS

Three components create the new value in a resyndication: better depreciation, higher basis, and secondary financing.

Better Depreciation

Before ERTA, depreciation had to be calculated on individual building components with individual useful lives. These lives were factual questions subject to challenge by the IRS. Most reasonable subsidized housing syndications used a thirty-three-year life for the main building component. But there was no industry norm, only a spectrum of lives.

Auditing or litigating depreciation issues were cumbersome and unproductive. So ERTA eliminated component depreciation and replaced it with the accelerated cost recovery system (ACRS). ACRS allows an owner of real residential property to use the same accelerated methods that were previously available, but with an audit-proof *fifteen-year* life.

The substantial reduction in the effective useful life boosted depreciation deductions that owners can receive over the expected holding period, and it concentrated more of them in the first five years. Even though ERTA also cut the top tax bracket from 70 percent to 50 percent, the extra depreciation more than counter-balanced this change.

Higher Basis

A taxpayer's basis in depreciable property is initially the fair market value of that property. Depreciation deductions taken by a partnership reduce its adjusted basis in that property, so that the basis from which future depreciation is generated declines. Many years of accelerated depreciation have, therefore, reduced the depreciable basis of existing subsidized housing properties greatly. The tax deductions for these properties are running out.

Within two to eight years, many properties are likely to begin producing taxable income but will have no cash flow to cover the associated federal income taxes.

A second user of a piece of property may step up the property's basis back to its current fair market value—as determined by its new purchase price. In effect, the new investors may redepreciate at the new rates the old losses taken by the former investors. Conversely, the former investors must report taxable gain essentially equal to the excess of the losses they have taken over the equity they have contributed. One group of investors receives new losses; the other pays termination taxes.

Before ERTA, second-user property could be depreciated no faster than by the 125 percent declining balance method. Thus, the second user had lower deductions than the 200 percent declining balance method produced for the first user. But ERTA eliminated the distinction between first- and second-user depreciation. Coupled with the reduction in allowable depreciable lives, ERTA has made most subsidized housing more valuable to new owners than it is to the current owners.

Secondary Financing

Long an investment tool for conventional apartments, secondary financing only recently became available for subsidized housing. In a resyndication, the secondary financing is usually some form of purchase money note representing a portion of the overall purchase price agreed upon between buyer and seller.

Secondary financing serves several useful purposes for both buyer and seller:

· It allows the buyer to take more depreciation deductions. Even if the secondary financing carries a reasonable below-market interest rate, the buyer is allowed to include the full face amount in its depreciable basis, provided that the total purchase price does not exceed the fair market value of the property.
· Accrued but unpaid interest on valid secondary financing is currently deductible for tax purposes each year by an accrual-basis taxpayer. Thus in effect secondary financing may create twice the deductions of ordinary financing—both depreciation deductions and interest accruals.
· Secondary financing permits the seller to quantify residual value. Some day the secondary financing will balloon (become due and payable in full). At that time the seller will have the right to receive full payment on the secondary financing—including any accrued but unpaid interest.

Secondary financing is, therefore, a valuable tool for both buyers and sellers. It has long been a component in the purchase and sale of conventional real estate. Secondary financing had been prohibited on HUD properties, but in March 1981 HUD reversed its position. HUD now permits secondary financing as long as: (1) it is clearly subordinate to the primary financing; (2) it is paid solely from surplus cash flow and is not included in the rent formula; and (3) it creates no lien that might permit the first mortgagee to assign the loan.

HUD has, however, provided an administrative guideline for secondary financing commonly known as the "HUD 75 percent test." To receive field office approval of a resyndication, the total of the HUD mortgage assumed, plus the face amount of any secondary financing, plus the interest on the secondary financing projected to be accrued but unpaid before the note's maturity date, cannot exceed 75 percent of the property's current replacement cost (90 percent for properties less than five years old).

Subject to HUD review, HUD imposes on the mortgagor the obligation to demonstrate compliance with the HUD 75 percent test. This is a blessing in disguise: HUD will probably accept a credible analysis presented by a qualified syndicator. And who is to say how much interest is likely to be unpaid? Or what current replacement cost is?

The HUD 75 percent test provides a uniform standard which permits secondary financing in reasonable proportion to the original cost and current value of the property. Of course, if individual circumstances warrant, HUD Washington has reserved the right administratively to adjust the HUD 75 percent test, or to waive it entirely. And as its knowledge and experience in resyndication grows, HUD can reasonably be expected to review, and possibly refine, the test.

Secondary financing may take a number of forms. For example, it may be secured by the property or by a pledge of the buying partnership's interests. Creating a junior lien may violate lender or regulatory agent restrictions. (Under HUD documents, it requires the consent of the first mortgagee, a consent unlikely to be given.) But a pledge of all the partnership interests of the buyer will likely require no lender consent. If proper covenants are attached to this pledge, its business impact can be almost indistinguishable from a true second mortgage.

Fair Market Value

Of the three benefit components, two are fixed: the ACRS depreciation and the step-up in basis that arises from the redepreciation of losses taken by the previous owners. The benefits of secondary financing can vary, however, and creative structuring can add value.

The larger the secondary financing, the better for both seller and buyer; depreciation and interest accruals will both be increased. Tax deductions available to the buyer will be greater, so the buyer will pay more cash with secondary financing than without it.

Only two constraints limit the amount of secondary financing that can be placed on a property: lender or regulatory agency restrictions and fair market value. Except for the HUD 75 percent test, no regulatory agent will be likely to insist that a given amount of secondary financing is too high. However, the HUD 75 percent test does not bind the IRS and is unlikely to carry much weight with an IRS agent. Valuation is therefore the real constraint. The IRS will deny deductions based on overvaluation. A property is overvalued if the total purchase price paid exceeds the fair market value of the property. If the property is deemed to be overvalued, the secondary financing could be recharacterized from debt to equity. If so, the buyers would not own their property; instead, they would be deemed to own, essentially, an option to purchase it. This means that if the IRS or a court determines that the secondary financing has inflated the selling price beyond a property's true value, all of the deductions could be attacked. Buyers can afford neither to lose this issue nor even to compromise on it.

The recently passed Tax Equity and Fiscal Responsibility Act of 1982 (TEFRA) imposes tough new penalties on sponsors or promoters of tax shelters which substantially overvalue property. ABA Ethical Advisory Memorandum No. 346 and proposed Treasury Circular No. 230 also take a hard line against overvaluation and impose stiff penalties of their own. The AICPA is now considering similar guidelines for certified public accountants.

Secondary financing in resyndications is like TNT. Used properly, it creates enormous tax-shelter bang. Handled improperly, it can blow up in the user's face. Syndicators must protect a resyndication with a sound tax opinion and a sound appraisal.

It is ironic that ERTA, which sought to eliminate factual arguments about depreciation, instead created larger, more difficult factual issues about fair market value. And appraising subsidized housing is hideously complex. The potential for inflated values, and the difficulty of litigating each case on its factual merits, may lead the IRS to attack the secondary financing on other grounds; for instance, that the deduction of accrued but unpaid interest constitutes a distortion of income. Since that argument runs counter to existing case law and even to other positions previously taken by the IRS, it will probably fall short of the mark. But the IRS is likely to continue to shine its spotlights (audits, rulings, regulations, or even legislative requests) on secondary financing.

Virtually all subsidized properties have a lock-in period (usually twenty years from final endorsement) during which the property must be operated as low- or moderate-income housing. These lock-in provisions suppress value. Sometimes they are extended to forty years—through disposition agreements required by some agencies or by HUD flexible subsidy. This makes it virtually impossible for an appraiser to find meaningful residual value and virtually eliminates secondary financing as an element in resyndications.

RESYNDICATION STRUCTURE

Three types of technical issues arise in resyndications: real estate, tax and accounting, and securities.

Real Estate Issues

Unlike a new construction syndication, which is based solely on projections of a property to be built, a resyndication involves the transfer of ownership of an operating property with an operating history. Most resyndications will be structured to resemble a conventional real estate sale. There will be a purchase and sale agreement, with representations, escrows, and contingencies. Many items will be prorated based on closing date. The parties will have to agree on division of closing costs.

The sellers will be required to disclose to the buyers all material facts about the property, not only its physical but also its financial condition. Books and records will be turned over and certified complete. Indemnities against undisclosed liabilities will usually be involved. The sellers will make various representations about authority and consent, and the buyer will have to satisfy HUD previous participation clearance. Lender or regulatory agency approval of the resyndication will likely be required.

Tax and Accounting Issues

ERTA's depreciation benefits came with strings attached. Congress wanted to prevent sham transactions where property was transferred solely for the purpose of obtaining ACRS depreciation but had no business substance. To do this, Congress introduced the so-called anti-churning rules. Sales to "related parties" are denied the benefits of ACRS depreciation. A sale to "related parties" was sloppily defined to mean, essentially, any sale in which the seller's interest in the buyer exceeded 10 percent.

Churning. The 90 percent threshold in the antichurning provisions appears to be overkill. After all, if the sellers pay their termination taxes, should not the buyers be permitted ACRS? Nevertheless, no responsible tax attorney is willing to issue a tax opinion unless at least 90 percent of each element—capital, profits, losses, cash flow, *and residuals*—is transferred.

A general partner who controls a property before a resyndication may still do so afterwards; nothing prevents that entity from becoming a managing general partner of the buyer as well as of the seller. Management may remain in that general partner's hands. But the reduced residual potential mandated by the current anti-churning provisions are a major negotiating issue for any continuing general partner. To satisfy anti-churning rules, yet retain meaningful upside, general partners often seek to hold a portion of the secondary financing being created. This is reasonable (the entity that controls the property should be given a large incentive to do a good job), but it places continuing general partners squarely in the middle of some highly complicated conflicts of interests.

Payment methods. The method of characterizing payments is also a structuring question. Installments of sale proceeds generally qualify for capital gains treatment. The buyer will include the payments in its depreciable basis. Characterizing a portion of the equity as fees or interest will convert them to ordinary income or expense. This is good for the buyers (faster deductions), but bad for the sellers (higher taxes). Because of the IRS' rules for imputing interest, chances are that all deferred payments will carry interest at a rate of at least 10 percent simple.

Financing terms. Secondary financing must be structured to be valid indebtedness. If not, the IRS could recharacterize it as some sort of disguised equity position. For the secondary financing to qualify as true debt, it must have:

- A term (usually the earlier of a fixed maturity (ten to twenty years) or the sale or refinancing of the property);
- A stated interest rate (usually constant, usually simple rather than compound);
- A method of payment (usually solely from some portion of cash flow and first available residuals);
- Some form of security (usually assignment of all the limited partnership interests of the buyer); and
- Priority of payment (usually behind the first mortgage but ahead of anyone else).

The more the secondary financing is structured to be true debt, the lower the tax risk but the higher the business risk that it will be a threat to the property. Sellers will seek tough provisions, buyers more liberal ones. Lenders will be concerned that the property not come under the control of an unapproved sponsor. To avoid ambiguity, the initial lender's previous participation clearance rights must be dovetailed with the secondary financing enforcement provisions.

Securities Issues

The federal private placement rules were amended early in 1982. Rule 146 was supplanted by Rule 506 under Regulation D. Rule 506 imposes generally broader disclosure requirements, but eases the suitability standards and streamlines offering procedures. As a result, an issuer must give out more information than before, but can do so more freely to a greater number of less sophisticated people.

As mentioned above, TEFRA incorporated tough new penalties for sponsors and promoters of overvalued property. While there is substantial room for creative structuring of resyndications, it carries higher risk for the syndicator than a new construction transaction. Most reputable resyndicators are moving cautiously.

MECHANICS OF RESYNDICATION

Resyndication is complicated. But to meet the price and terms originally quoted by the buyer, an optimistic timetable must be met. A slew of documents must be produced and approved. Thus the transaction will carry time pressure throughout.

Key Documents

Three types of key documents must be developed:

Purchase and sale agreement. In resyndications in which general partners change, the purchase and sale agreement is the crucial controlling document. Thus it is likely to be heavily negotiated. Lender and regulatory agency and selling investor approval of the transaction and an appraisal at a certain minimum figure will almost certainly be contingencies to closing. What happens to the earnest money if the transaction is not consummated is one of the highly negotiable items.

Loan and regulatory agreements. Although it is theoretically possible to preserve the old loan and regulatory documents, usually they are redrawn to bring them up to the state of the art—the lender's or the syndicator's. Although HUD documents are well standardized, most state agencies have revised their documents many times. The new buyer will generally want to use the old documents, or at least to defang the new documents so that no new restrictive undertakings creep into the resyndication.

Often the document negotiations will involve substantive business points, of which the most significant may be the regulatory agency's attempt to extend the lock-in period (the period during which the property must be operated as low- or moderate-income housing). If agreed to, this would have the direct effect of reducing the fair market value which an appraiser will be able to justify. It could even abort the transaction.

Offering documents. The offering memorandum must state every material fact that an investor should know. Nor can it fail to state a fact that might be material. As such, it should always contain the following useful information:

· *Benefit projections and assumptions.* These enable any prospective investor (and any other interested party) to review exactly what benefits investors expect and the assumptions necessary to produce those benefits.
· *Accountant's letter.* The accountant's review letter says merely that the accounting firm has satisfied itself concerning the mathematical accuracy of the compilations in the schedules. But it usually implies that the accounting firm has also reviewed the reasonableness of the tax positions presented in the memorandum, and that it believes them reasonable and proper.
· *Appraisal.* Appraisals are usually not included in the offering documents, but they must be available to any investor upon request.
· *Marketability study.* Marketability studies are often incorporated into the appraisal. They survey the existing rental market and relate the property's projected operations to that market. In a resyndication, the study can also compare projected and historical operations. Any property projected to improve its operations should be buttressed by a sensible marketability study that shows why that improvement is believable.
· *Tax opinion.* Like the accountant's letter, a tax opinion implies more than it says. Under ABA No. 346, an opinion from a law firm that discusses

federal income tax matters must review each material tax issue and must judge whether or not the taxpayer is "more likely than not" to prevail on the issue if challenged in court by the IRS. Further, the lawyer must also state whether in his opinion "the bulk of the benefits" available from the transaction are likely to be received. Lawyers who give ABA No. 346 opinions are enjoined from closing their eyes to material facts; they must make a reasonable investigation and satisfy themselves that the presentation in the offering material is consistent with those facts. Moreover, under ABA No. 346, the offering memorandum section "Federal Income Tax Considerations" is deemed incorporated by reference in the opinion. As a result, that formerly dry section now merits detailed study.

· *Partnership opinion.* A partnership opinion generally attests to the due formation and valid authority of the buyer. It is necessary but routine.

Timing of the Resyndication Process

A resyndication is a six-step process; each step should be substantially complete before the next begins. Time pressure often forces the parties to try to run the steps "in parallel," but this is dangerous. If a crucial element of an earlier step changes, much work in later steps will have to be redone under great time pressure.

Step 1: Initial proposal. The buyer or syndicator solicits a developer/owner (or vice versa). Initial conversations take place. The competing buyers submit short-form proposals; the seller chooses the best among them. The losing offers will probably have no further involvement after that choice is made.

Step 2: Purchase and sale. The purchase and sale agreement is drafted, negotiated and renegotiated, and signed. Key contingencies, adjusters, and all other terms between buyer and seller are negotiated.

Step 3: Approvals. Three key approvals must be obtained:

· *Appraisal.* The appraisal must be secured. It must support the proposed purchase price and must be sound enough to satisfy the syndicator and tax attorney who will be giving the tax opinion.
· *Loan and regulatory approval.* Under most regulatory agreements, sale of the property before the expiration of the lock-in period requires lender or regulatory agency consent. But whether approvals are required for the mass sale of partnership interests is less clear. HUD and most state agencies have taken the position that consent is required.

Inevitably, there will be some resyndications that challenge or shortcut this regulatory consent process—but prudence dictates complying with the guidelines. After all, HUD has publicly stated that it encourages resyndication. The government has volunteered to be the owner's ally; it makes sense to make use of that support.

HUD calls a resyndication a "transfer of physical assets" (TPA). HUD Central has now put out detailed administrative guidelines for TPA approval processing. These guidelines govern what must be submitted and what the field office will review. The buyer probably can take no tax benefits from the investment until the final TPA approval has been received and all documents recorded. Resyndications that meet the HUD 75 percent test and the physical and financial needs of the property should receive HUD local office approval within sixty days of submission. No higher review is required.

Owners contemplating a resyndication would do well to obtain copies of HUD's TPA instruction sheet (HUD 92266), and to alert the local HUD office to the prospect of a resyndication as early as possible.

· *Seller investor approval.* The selling entity is usually a syndicated partnership with general and limited partners. The general and limited partners must agree among themselves how the proceeds will be split up.

The residuals sections of most old partnership agreements are primitive. They make no provision for allocating staged payments or for trading off between cash and secondary financing. Applying the letter of those residual sections may produce ambiguous or anomalous results. In most cases, an intrapartner negotiation will be required. This can be tricky. Some otherwise attractive resyndications will prove infeasible because the partners can find no reasonable compromise. Other resyndications (especially those in which partnership interests are transferred) require *unanimous* investor consent. That is difficult and may defeat many proposed transactions.

Step 4: Offering documents. Some sponsors try to produce offering documents before the approvals are in hand, but this is generally unwise. Few resyndications will receive unanimous blanket approval. More often, one or more of the parties will request changes. Material changes in the business arrangements will compel the syndicator to supplement the offering memorandum. Each potential investor will then be acutely aware of whatever erosion has been conceded. Some investors who originally subscribed will change their minds. Others, previously undecided, will be deterred from buying. It is wiser to postpone drafting the offering memorandum until the purchase and sale has been signed and the new loan documents agreed to.

Step 5: Marketing. Once the offering memorandum is available, the syndicator and broker/dealer may begin to obtain securities clearance and then make offers and sales. Some marketing activity may commence before the offering memorandum is fully ready, but usually the selling effort really begins only after the offering memorandum is printed.

Step 6: Closing. Once all approvals have been received and all investor interests sold, the parties must execute all necessary documents, close the transaction, and move the money. Because a whole property is changing hands, partial closings will be difficult, only marginally beneficial, and rare.

A typical timetable for a resyndication, assuming that everything proceeds smoothly, would look like table 16-1.

A few lucky transactions will proceed more quickly. Many unlucky or

Table 16.1. Typical Timetable for a Resyndication

Step	Normal Time Frame	Reasonable Expectation
1	15–60 days	40 days
2	5–25	15
3	30–90	45
4	10–45	30
5	30–90	60
6	0–15	5
Total	90–325 days	195 days (6½ months)

poorly planned transactions will take even longer. Processing delays by themselves have killed many resyndications.

THE PARTIES TO THE RESYNDICATION TRANSACTION

Although the general and limited partners of the seller may have many different objectives, they are united on one group of issues. Both want to maximize proceeds to themselves, minimize funds injected into the property, accelerate payments, and minimize or eliminate contingencies. They both also want releases from liability to all other parties—including the buyer, lender and each other.

The Selling Investors

The selling limited partners will first net the sale offer against their contingent tax liability. Under the revised installment sale guidelines, any transaction with payments in more than one taxable year constitutes an installment sale (for federal income tax purposes; some states still use the old rules). Taxes payable upon an installment sale consist of two components: a locked-in tax associated with relief from indebtedness and incremental capital gains and ordinary income resulting from the receipt of the cash proceeds. The locked-in tax is incurred in the year that ownership transfers, while tax on the cash proceeds is incurred only as the money comes in.

Some of the lock-in tax consists of recapture of accelerated depreciation, taxable at ordinary income rates—but not much. Depreciation taken before 1976 will be subject to the older, more favorable recapture phaseout rules. Depreciation taken in 1976 and later years will have produced little tax preference. Of the total gain, we would expect that less than 10 percent will be ordinary income.

If you want a quick estimate of how much equity the seller will need to cover its taxes, ignore recapture. Just multiply the negative capital account by 0.2 to estimate the lock-in tax, then divide this result by 0.8 (the value of an incremental dollar of capital gain cash).

Once the investors have calculated the after-tax flow of funds resulting from the resyndication, they will compare this stream with the alternative of holding the property. In either case we recommend that investors ignore future residuals: they are hard to quantify. Also, who can confidently say which is superior: holding an interest-bearing note for a fixed quantity or having a priority right to a non-interest-bearing return of capital plus some (usually 50 percent) of the proceeds beyond that?

Eliminating residuals from the calculation is also convenient because all other benefit components in both alternatives are relatively predictable. The sale is, of course, a known quantity. The value of holding, on the other hand, depends heavily on remaining depreciation; it too can be accurately predicted.

Eventually investors should be able to reduce each alternative to a single number: its expected cumulative discounted after-tax present value using a reasonable alternative investment rate (we use 8 percent). In the absence of unusual circumstances which make one alternative significantly riskier than the other, we recommend picking whichever alternative yields the higher present value. Holding and controlling a healthy property is probably as safe as selling it, giving up control and taking back a large nonrecourse note. So, why not take the higher offer?

On the other hand, if there is a current or potential problem, accepting the sale, even at a lower present value, may be wise (the "bird in the hand" theory). Investors should probably accept resyndication offers when any of these five criteria are true:

- The property is troubled or becoming troubled;
- The property is ten or more years old and has insignificant funded replacement reserves;
- The investment has reached crossover and is now producing taxable income;
- The resyndication proceeds equal more than twice the lock-in tax; or
- Many of the partners have reduced termination taxes which result from changed financial circumstances (estates, interests acquired through isolated resales, retirees).

The General Partners

For general partners, the key question is whether they wish to keep control of the property. Most potential buyers regard the controlling general partner position as a valuable asset. The seller general partner who wishes to retire should be able to command a premium.

General partners who wish to remain must contend with the anti-churning rules and with the extensive conflicts of interest to which they will be subject. For instance, a general partner who wishes to retain a substantial portion of the future appreciation of the property may be allocated a large chunk of the bona fide secondary financing. Any such allocation will have to be negotiated with the seller's limited partners.

A developer who is a general partner of two partnerships, one of which has sold a property to the other, will face fiduciary obligations to both groups. Some of these conflicts will be irreconcilable. Perhaps the worst conflict would occur if the secondary financing could not be paid when it balloons. If the general partner forecloses on the note, the buying limited partners will be unhappy. Conversely, if the general partner refrains from foreclosing, the limited partners of the sellers will be the ones who sue. This already complicated situation will be exacerbated if the general partner also holds a piece of the note directly. Will it foreclose on itself?

These conflicts of interest are inherent in the juxtaposition of roles: They cannot be totally eliminated. But they can be mitigated by defining, up front, precisely what will happen in as many situations as the parties can think of. Also, the parties should structure into the agreement at least one entity each for the buyer and the seller who does *not* participate on the other side of the transaction, and vest in that party some rights to enforce, renegotiate, or waive provisions in the secondary financing.

Holders of the Secondary Financing

The secondary financing should be held by a cash-basis entity which need not report accrued but unpaid interest as current income. To preserve the cash basis of the noteholders, either the note will be distributed directly to the seller's partners or it will be held by a central entity. If the former, the partners must arrange for a collection or monitoring agent. If the latter, the central entity must be structured with care. Converting the selling partnership from the accrual to the cash basis raises tax questions. More often a trust should be designated or created.

The New Syndicator or General Partner

Members of the purchasing groups will also have issues to negotiate among themselves, but they will be generally united on one key issue— protecting the property. They want the property to be sound, free from danger, and financially viable. They also will try to package a transaction that will sell quickly.

These interests generally run counter to those of the sellers. The new buyer and syndicator want to minimize the cash portion of the purchase price to stretch out payment as long as possible, provide the largest feasible property escrows, put funds into the property, and put contingencies on deferred equity payments.

The only element on which seller and buyer agree is the appraisal; they both want it as high as possible. The buyer, however, will be less willing to push up the price, both because of the associated tax risk and because too high a purchase price will eliminate the buyer's residual expectation.

If the buyer's general partner is also the seller's general partner, it will have conflicts of interests with respect to the appraisal and with respect to the amount of its compensation and benefit package. What amounts should properly be paid as fees (and hence come off the top, ahead of distributions to the other selling partners)? This may appear on the surface to be an issue between buyer and seller, but it is really a question to be decided among the seller's partners.

The seller's limited partners are often suspicious of their general partner if it is also the agent for the buyer. If the general partner early on decides to lay all his cards on the table, the transaction will proceed more smoothly. Likewise, a buyer who offers to let the appraisal determine the purchase price will often have a smoother road to seller approval. It may not necessarily obtain a better deal, or a more lucrative deal, but it will usually end up with an easier and quicker deal.

The Role of Lender and Regulatory Agency

In a resyndication, a lender or regulatory agent is primarily interested in protecting the housing in its portfolio. It is concerned with the physical, financial and operational needs of the property, especially the following areas:

Capital improvements. Some may be needed now; others may be upcoming. The syndicator will likely commission an engineering report. Done properly, it will state what is needed and how much it will cost.

Normal replacements. Most properties have underfunded replacement reserves. Properties that are resyndication candidates are probably five to eight years old—roughly at the end of the useful lives of the initial carpeting, appliances, and cabinetry. Wholesale replacement of these items may be necessary. Increasing the annual replacement reserve deposit will probably be desirable.

Ongoing operations. If the property is below break-even, capital improvements and a change in management may bring it back. But the deficits between then and now must be funded. One good way is to put some of the resyndication proceeds into an escrow to cover deficits, with any balance remaining at break-even being paid over to the sellers.

THE MAJOR ISSUES IN THE RESYNDICATION NEGOTIATION

The issues in a resyndication negotiation usually revolve about the following topics:

· Should the general partners be changed?
· Who contributes equity?
· Who contributes secondary financing?
· Should the project itself or the partnership interest be sold?

Should the General Partner Be Changed?

If the general partner does not participate in the new syndication, negotiations on behalf of the seller are more likely to be at arm's length. The general partner position is a valuable asset for which sellers can realize extra consideration. The buyers may benefit because the change may upgrade management.

The above points argue for changing the general partner. But if the general partner stays the same, continuity of management can be preserved. The current general partner knows the property better than anyone else; thus, there is less risk for the buyer of undiscovered problems. The fact that a general partner remains with a property implies that he has confidence in the property. It also usually implies the existence of a strong development organization and commitment to the business. There are fewer players negotiating the transaction, so some economies of scale result. It may be easier to secure lender approval.

We believe that when in doubt, it is wise to change. However, most resyndications involve strong, sophisticated developers who justifiably insist on remaining in control. The key issue is quality. Does the developer's track record create confidence?

Equity: How Much, and to Whom

Each party in a resyndication has its own different view of how much equity the new partnership should raise and the uses to which the equity should be put.

The property. The property probably needs money to fund deferred maintenance or to build up a depleted replacement reserve. Funds probably can be used for capital improvements which may add value for both sides. Funds may be needed to cover projected deficits.

The sellers. The sellers will usually argue that the property is healthy and, if there is a change in controlling general partners, that the buyers have control over their own destiny. The sellers also need proceeds to pay their taxes. Since they are earning fees or gaining ownership positions, the buyers should be willing to make commitments to the property and the sellers.

The buyers. The buyers usually point out that the price has been negotiated to a maximum figure because the sellers assert that the property will encounter no difficulties. Contingencies add value for the sellers, because if funds are contingent the buyers will put more money on the table. Conversely, demanding noncontingent payments must result in a lower price. If the general partners are staying the same, the sellers have some control over their own destiny. To sell quickly and meet the resyndication timetable, the transaction must be priced competitively.

The lender. The lender will usually insist that delinquencies be cured or renegotiated to provide for future repayment. Previous subsidies such as flexible subsidy may be recaptured.

Equity summary. The better the property, the stronger is the position of the sellers. They will receive more money faster. Less of the purchase price will be contingent. If the buyers think they are acquiring an attractive property, their fees will be lower. Therefore, heavily hedged equity payments imply a troubled property. Noncontingent or rapid payments could imply a healthy property, or they could simply mean that the buying syndicator is too easygoing.

Secondary Financing

If property carries a high appraised value (measured as a percentage of its replacement cost), the HUD 75 percent test is the constraint upon secondary financing. If so, a low-rate, high-face-amount note will probably produce better tax savings. However, because of the IRS' imputed interest requirements set forth in Section 483 of the Internal Revenue Code, the interest rate on the note probably should be set no lower than 9 or 10 percent simple.

From the buyer's point of view, simple interest is better than compound. If both produce an equal amount of interest accruals, simple interest produces them more quickly, so it creates a better tax shelter. If for some reason the property cannot be sold when the note balloons, the unexpected additional interest accruals will be lower.

Buying partnerships prefer to pay out all the cash flow to the member partners and to have the entire interest on secondary financing accrue. This structure creates better investor benefits and permits more equity to be raised. Sellers must consider a trade-off: receive extra equity now, with interest paid only upon residuals, or receive a first priority on future cash flows.

Whatever the agreement, the note must be a bona fide indebtedness. And the more interest is unpaid, the harder it is to meet HUD's 75 percent test.

In practice, most transactions will gravitate toward accrual, at least as far as the tax attorneys permit. But the attorneys will likely insist that the majority of the cash flow be used to service the note.

Should the Project or the Partnership Interests Be Sold?

Selling the project is simpler and cleaner. Buyers will not acquire undisclosed liabilities. A straight real estate sale is more widely recognized and easily understood. Standard documents and provisions exist. Selling the property usually requires the approval of only a majority of the selling investors, whereas selling partnership interests usually requires unanimous approval. The buyer can completely redraw the partnership documents; if partnership interests are sold, the buyer may be stuck with an antiquated partnership agreement.

But there are also arguments for selling the partnership interests. Because the sale of payment interests does not require a new deed, it may avoid an annoying real estate tax reassessment; it certainly avoids transfer taxes. Land lease, tax abatement or other incentive kickers which would be triggered by the sale of the property may remain dormant if partnership interests are sold. Selling partnership interests may be administratively feasible when selling the project is not.

THE DIFFERENT ISSUES OF HEALTHY
AND TROUBLED PROPERTIES

For a healthy property, strong developers are usually the prime movers of resyndications. They may keep one eye out for opportunities to resyndicate their own properties. With the other they search for properties ripe for acquisition: properties that are undermanaged, unsyndicated, or owned by a seller who wants out.

The ideal resyndication candidate is a healthy property which has reached crossover and is now producing taxable income. By this standard, for many properties resyndication has come about five years too soon. Crossover occurs somewhere between years ten and twenty. Most subsidized housing is only five to twelve years old—not quite ripe.

In healthy properties, secondary financing is the crucial variable and value, as determined by appraisal, is the crucial constraint.

For the last few years, troubled subsidized housing properties have desperately needed a mechanism to raise capital for repairs and improvements. For these properties, resyndication could have come at no better time. In a troubled property, curing delinquencies and correcting problems, rather than making a large profit, are the primary objectives. In those efforts, the buyer is joined by the lender and regulatory agent. Fortunately, the expectations of the selling partners usually have been greatly reduced, so more funds are available to go into the property.

For HUD-insured properties, assignment is a two-edged sword. HUD wants to avoid calls on the insurance fund, so HUD will give top priority— and the most favorable concessions—to resyndications of marginal properties whose mortgages are unassigned. Conversely, a mortgagor who permits assignment and only later investigates resyndication will find the federal government ill-disposed to the sellers. And once the mortgage has been assigned, HUD gains the privilege of rewriting its terms. Such changes— for instance, increasing the rate or requiring a balloon in ten years—are consistent with current HUD workout policy. Assignment, therefore, is a step not to be taken lightly.

Troubled subsidized housing is, of course, vulnerable to foreclosure. A lender that forecloses on a sound property should be able to resyndicate it, without having to pay the sellers anything. But foreclosure is expensive, time-consuming, and difficult. It stigmatizes the property in a way that hurts its remarketing and probably eliminates the prospects of secondary financing. Although it is a lender's last resort, foreclosure is a threat that should force most mortgagors of troubled properties to consider resyndication.

Resyndication of a troubled property almost always proves superior to a workout with the existing partners. It usually puts more money into the property; it offers greater flexibility with more options, and it is, paradoxically, easier to accomplish.

Acquisition of troubled properties could prove to be a major source of new business for strong developers.

Index